Access to civil procedure abroad

Access to civil procedure abroad

by Henk J. Snijders (editor),
Margreet B. de Boer, J. Henriëtte van Dam-Lely, Marielle E. Koppenol-Laforce, Rob J.P. Kottenhagen, Gerard J. Meijer, Renée Y. Nauta, Peter Smits and Marc Ynzonides (authors)

Translated by Benjamin Ruijsenaars

C.H. Beck Verlag, München
Kluwer Law International, The Hague, London, Boston
Attn. N. Sakkoulas Publishers, Athens
Verlag Stämpfli & Cie AG, Bern
Sweet & Maxwell Ltd., London

Library of Congress Cataloguing-in-Publication Data

Access to civil procedure abroad / edited by Henk J. Snijders.
p. cm.
Includes index.
ISBN 9041102124 (pb)
1. Civil procedure--European Union countries. 2. Civil procedure (International law) I. Snijders, Henricus Joseph, 1951-
KJE3802.A93 1996
347.4'05--dc20
[344.075] 96-2585

Printed on acid-free paper

Exclusive salesrights for Germany:
C.H. Beck Verlag, Wilhelmstrasse 9, 80801 München, Germany, tel 49 89 381890
ISBN 3406405436

Exclusive salesrights for the Netherlands:
Kluwer Law International, P.O. Box 85889, 2508 CN The Hague, The Netherlands, tel 31 70 3081560.
Sold and distributed in the USA and Canada:
101 Philip Drive, Norwell, MA 02061, USA
ISBN 9041102124

Exclusive salesrights for Greece:
Ant. N. Sakkoulas Publishers, 69 Solonos Street, 10679 Athens, Greece, tel 30 (1) 3615440
ISBN 9602324139

Exclusive salesrights for Switzerland:
Verlag Stämpfli & Cie AG, Hallerstrasse 7, CH-3012 Bern, Switzerland, tel 41 31 3006311
ISBN 3727296364

Exclusive salesrights for United Kingdom:
Sweet & Maxwell Ltd., South Quay Plaza, 183 Marsh Wall, London E14 9FT, United Kingdom, tel 44 171 5388686
ISBN 0421569409

Kluwer Law International incorporates the publishing programmes of Martinus Nijhoff Publishers, Graham & Trotman Ltd. and Kluwer Law and Taxation.

Preface

Since the academic year 1990-1991 students at the Erasmus University of Rotterdam have been able to deepen their insight into civil procedure by studying the rules of procedure applicable in our neighbouring states. This optional subject was introduced after consultation with the Netherlands Bar Association. The original, Dutch, edition of this book can be classified as an edited and elaborated version of the syllabus developed for this subject. The English edition before you differs from the first Dutch one (2nd edition now) in that it now also contains a contribution on Netherlands civil procedure. We have also used the opportunity to update the text. Furthermore, contributions on Italian and Luxembourg civil procedure have been added.

Why such a subject? Why this book? The answers to these questions are obvious.

Knowledge of systems of civil procedure abroad deepens the insight into domestic civil procedure and provokes thoughts for its further development. Furthermore, practising law in any European country in this day and age requires some understanding of the structure and contents of other systems of civil procedure with which lawyers are frequently confronted. In this respect legal systems of important trading partners spring to mind, with whom there are also close relationships outside trade. It may be true that lawyers in private practice or corporate lawyers do not often independently conduct litigation abroad, not even if they have a foreign office or branch. Nevertheless, in order to assess procedural developments abroad and to communicate with foreign lawyers instructed by them, lawyers will need to possess some knowledge of the relevant foreign legal system. In that connection one must think of knowledge regarding subjects dealt with in this book such as the organisation of the judiciary, legal assistance, duration and costs of procedures in general, the broad outlines of everyday procedures including the methods of producing evidence and the nature and essence of protective and enforcement measures, and alternative procedures (for instance, summary proceedings in the national courts but also proceedings outside the courts such as arbitration). These essential aspects are also eminently suited for a comparative study of procedural law. This explains the need for a subject of study which explores certain foreign legal systems of civil procedure and it also justifies the publication of a book as this. A similar book does not yet exist in this form. A recent book which is slightly comparable is *Civil Procedures in EC Countries* by David McIntosh and Marjorie Holmes (London 1991). In its discussion of certain aspects (such as costs) that work is more detailed, while other aspects are less so, and there are few references to sources. Another book which is slightly comparable is *European Civil Practice* by Stephen O'Malley and Alexander Layton (London 1989). This thick book pays attention in the first place to civil proceedings in England and Wales respectively the 1968 Convention on Jurisdiction and Judgments and the Civil Jurisdiction and Judgments Act 1982. It also deals with civil procedure in other EC countries. As the title of the book indicates, it has been written primarily for practitioners.

Extinctive prescription periods and other limitation periods for civil claims are not dealt with in this book. See for these subjects E.H. Hondius, (ed.) *Extinctive Prescription: On the Limitation of Actions*, The Hague/London/Boston 1995.

This book focuses on civil procedure in the original EC Member States and England and Wales. Future additions to this book in the form of a consideration of civil procedure in other countries are under review.

The reader who wishes to study a specific legal system or part thereof in greater detail, may benefit from the many entries into literature to which each chapter refers, in particular in section 1.

The structure of the book is quite convenient.

The usual preliminaries are followed by a questionnaire which was used by the authors for their study and description of the different legal systems. As any questionnaire should, this one provides an insight into the approach of the subject matter. Since that approach is identical for each different country, optimal accessibility and comparability of each national contribution is achieved.

The main part of this book constitutes an exploratory and comparative introduction of the subject, followed by a chapter on private international rules of civil procedure, in which international jurisdiction plays an important part (attention to private international procedural law appears to be self-evident in this book, since it will point the way towards the competent court which will determine the law applicable). This chapter on private international procedural law is followed by contributions on English, French, Luxembourg, Belgian, Netherlands, German and Italian rules of civil procedure. Current texts of relevant laws will possibly be published separately in an *'Appendix to Access to Civil Procedure Abroad'*. In their selection the authors have considered which sections were required for the education of students in the relevant subject. For the legal practice and detailed academic study of law this selection may often prove insufficient. For the sake of consistency of the book, the authors have been selected from only two universities. Most authors are associated with the department of private law of the Faculty of Law of the Erasmus University, with the exception of myself, former professor of private law at the Erasmus University, now professor of civil law at Leiden University, M.E. Koppenol-Laforce (who is associated with the department of business law), and Ms. M.B. de Boer (lecturer of civil procedural law, Leiden University). I am grateful for the opportunity to work with such enthusiastic, pleasant and talented colleagues. The authors count themselves fortunate with the remarks made by expert legal practitioners in respect of the Dutch version of this book: for private international law Prof. Dr. P. Vlas (professor of private international law and comparative law at the Free University of Amsterdam); for English law Ms. H.A. Zebregs LL.M. (solicitor, London); for French law R.F.M. Bijloos (avocat à la Cour de Paris, Lefèvre et Associés in Paris); for Luxembourg law Mrs. L. Molenkamp LL.M. (avocat at the lawyers' office Wagener & Rukavina in Luxembourg); for Belgian law Prof. Dr. P. Lemmens and S. Raes (professor respectively assistant lecturer at the Faculty of Law of Leuven University, both lawyers in Brussels); for German law Ms. Hildegard Weidinger (Rechtsanwältin at Boekel de Nerée in Amsterdam) and Dr. Paul Gotzen (Rechtsanwalt in Düsseldorf); for Italian law Prof. Avv. Giuseppe Tarzia (lawyer and Professor of civil procedural law at the State University of Milan) and Prof. T.A.W. Sterk (professor of civil procedural law at Leiden University). Their valuable suggestions have been gratefully used. On behalf of the other authors I wish to express my gratitude to them for their assistance. I further owe many thanks, also on behalf of the other authors, to Ms. H.A. Zebregs LL.M. (Groningen and Pennsylvania) (solicitor, London) and M.R. Smith M.A. (Cantab.), LL.M. (Pennsylvania) (solicitor Simmons & Simmons, London), who were prepared to proofread the English translation and have contributed a wealth of invaluable suggestions; to the Faculty of Law of the Erasmus University of Rotterdam for awarding a research grant which made it possible to publish this English edition; to the Stichting ter bevordering van internationaal privaatrechtelijk onderzoek (Foundation for the promotion of the study of private international law) which granted a subsidy for the translation of the chapter on international procedural law to the students Ms. E.M. Hoogervorst and Mr. B.T.M. van der Wiel for editor's assistance.

A final word. Considering its size, the result of our work could simply be called a book. Yet it is a unique project. The authors of the chapters of the various countries have made out a case for a first but also proper introduction to the relevant foreign legal systems, which has, through the close co-operation of kindred spirits, resulted in a sound, systematically consistent product.

Although the authors as well as many other persons have spent a great amount of time on the checking and adjusting of the original findings, yet when foreign law is concerned a work as this always remains hazardous from a purely scientific viewpoint. That is precisely why imperfections cannot be excluded. There is therefore every reason to emphatically invite readers and users of this book to inform the undersigned or any of the other authors of any criticism they may have.

Henk Snijders (editor)

Rotterdam/Leiden/Warmond,
September 1995

Abbreviations

A

AA	Arbitration Act
ACPC	Ancien Code de procédure civile (Old Code of Civil Procedure, France)
Adv. bl.	*Advocatenblad* (lawyers' review)
Adv. wet	Advocatenwet (Attorneys Act, the Netherlands)
All E.R.	*The All England Law Reports*
art.	article

B

BGB	Bürgerliches Gesetzbuch (Civil Code, Germany)
Brussels Convention	European Convention on Jurisdiction and the Enforcement of Judgments in Civil and Commercial Matters
BS	*Belgisch Staatsblad/Moniteur belge* (Official Gazette, Belgium)
Bull. civ.	*Bulletins des Arrêts de la Cour de Cassation en matière civile* (bulletins of cassation judgments in civil matters)
BW	Burgerlijk Wetboek (Civil Code, Belgium/the Netherlands)

C

Cass.	Corte di cassazione
Cc	Codice civile (Civil Code, Italy)
CC	Code civil (Civil Code, France, Luxembourg)
CCA	County Courts Act 1984
C. Com.	Code de Commerce (Commercial Code, France)
CCPR	International Covenant on Civil and Political Rights
CCR	County Court Rules 1981
Cdc	Code de Commerce (Commercial Code, Luxembourg)
CJ	Code Judiciaire (Judicial Code, Belgium; *see also* Ger. W.)
CJJA	Civil Jurisdiction and Judgments Act 1982 and 1991
CLSA	Courts and Legal Services Act 1990
COJ	Code de l'organisation judiciaire (Judicial Organisation Act, France)

Cost.	Costituzione della Repubblica Italiana (Constitution, Italy)
CPC	Code de procédure civile (Luxembourg)
Cpc	Codice di procedura civile (Italy)
C. trav.	Code du travail (Labour Act, France)

D

D.	*Recueil Dalloz Sirey*
Disp. att. Cpc	Disposizioni per l'attuazione del codice di procedura civile e disposizioni transitorie

E

EC	European Community
ECHR	European Court of Human Rights
ECHRFF	European Convention for the Protection of Human Rights and Fundamental Freedoms
ECJ	Court of Justice of the European Communities
ECR	*European Community Reports*
EFTA	European Free Trade Association
EU	European Union

F

FGG	Gesetz über die Angelegenheiten der freiwilligen Gerichtsbarkeit (Act on cases of voluntary jurisdiction, Germany)

G

Gaz. Pal.	*Gazette du Palais* (Palace Journal, France)
Ger. W.	Gerechtelijk Wetboek (Judicial Code, Belgium; *see also* CJ)
GG	Grundgesetz (German Constitution)
GVG	Gerichtsverfassungsgesetz (Judicial Organisation Act, Germany)
Gr.w	Grondwet (Constitution, Belgium)

I

IPRax	*Praxis des internationalen Privat- und Verfahrensrecht* (German private and procedural law review)

J

J.-Cl. Proc. civ.	*Juris-Classeur Procédure civile*
J.C.P.	*Juris-Classeur Périodique* (Semaine Juridique) (law weekly review)

JZ	*Juristenzeitung* (German jurists' review)

K

K	Wetboek van Koophandel (Commercial Code, Belgium)
KB	Koninklijk Besluit (Royal Decree)

L

LAA	Legal Aid Act 1988
Lugano Convention	EFTA-EC Convention on Jurisdiction and the Enforcement of Judgments in Civil and Commercial Matters

M

MDR	*Monatschrift für Deutsches Recht* (German law monthly review)
MvT	Memorie van toelichting (explanatory memorandum)

N

NCPC	Nouveau Code de procédure civile (New Code of Civil Procedure, France)
NILR	*Netherlands International Law Review*
NIPR	*Nederlands Internationaal Privaatrecht* (Netherlands repertory on conventions, legislation, decisions and literature)
NJ	*Nederlandse Jurisprudentie* (Netherlands court decisions reports)
NJW	*Neue Juristische Wochenschrift* (German law weekly review)

O

OJ	*Official Journal of the European Communities*
Ord.	Order
Ord. giud.	Ordinamento giudiziario (Rules of Judicial Organisation, Italy)

P

Publ. ECHR	Publications of the European Court of Human Rights. Series A. Judgments and Decisions

Q

QC	Queen's Counsel

R

r.	rule
Rev. crit.	*Revue critique de droit international privé* (French review on private international law)
RO	Wet op de rechterlijke organisatie (Judicial Organisation Act, the Netherlands)
Rpfleger	*Der Deutsche Rechtspfleger* (German law review)
Rv	Wetboek van Burgerlijke Rechtsvordering (Code of Civil Procedure, the Netherlands)
RvdW	*Rechtspraak van de Week* (Netherlands Supreme Court decisions weekly review)
RSC	Rules of Supreme Court 1995
RW	*Rechtskundig Weekblad* (Belgian judicial weekly review)

S

s.	section
SCA	Supreme Court Act 1981
sch.	schedule
Stb.	*Staatsblad* (Official Gazette, the Netherlands)

T

Trb.	*Tractatenblad* (Netherlands treaty series)
TvA	*Tijdschrift voor Arbitrage* (Netherlands arbitration review)
TPR	*Tijdschrift voor Privaatrecht* (Belgian private law review)
TVVS	*Maandblad voor Ondernemingsrecht en Rechtspersonen* (Netherlands monthly review for company law and legal persons)

U

Uitv. wet	Uitvoeringswet (Act on Enforcement)

Z

ZPO	Zivilprozeßordnung (Code of Civil Procedure, Germany)
ZZP	*Zeitschrift für Zivilprozeß* (German civil procedure review)

Literature Quoted in Summary Form

Baumbach, Zivilprozeßordnung: Baumbach/Lauterbach/Albers/Hartmann, Zivilprozeßordnung, 52. Auflage, C.H. Beck'sche Verlagsbuchhandlung, München 1994.
Boele-Woelki, Tekstuitgave IPR: K. Boele-Woelki, Tekstuitgave IPR, verdragen en wetten internationaal privaatrecht en aanverwante rechtsgebieden, T.M.C. Asser Insituut, Kluwer, Deventer 1991.
Burg. Rv. (name of author): Burgerlijke Rechtsvordering, loose-leaf edition, Kluwer, Deventer.
Cadiet: L. Cadiet, Droit judiciaire privé, Paris 1992 (Sirey)
Couchez, Procédure Civile: G. Couchez, Procédure Civile, 7th edition, Sirey, Paris 1992.
European Civil Practice: Stephen O'Malley and Alexander Layton, European Civil Practice, Sweet & Maxwell, London 1989.
Fettweis, Manuel de Procédure Civile: A. Fettweis, Manuel de Procédure Civile, 2nd edition, Juridical faculty Liège, Liège 1987.
Het vernieuwd gerechtelijk recht: Het vernieuwd gerechtelijk recht, eerste commentaar bij de Wet van 3 Augustus 1992 tot wijziging van het Gerechtelijk Wetboek (series Bibliotheek van Gerechtelijk Recht van het Interuniversitair Centrum voor Gerechtelijk Recht), Antwerp 1992.
Hugenholtz/Heemskerk: W. Hugenholtz, Hoofdlijnen van Nederlands Burgerlijk Procesrecht, 17th edition revised by W.H. Heemskerk, Lemma, Utrecht 1994.
Kohl, Romanist Legal Systems: A. Kohl, Romanist Legal Systems in: Civil Procedure, M. Cappelletti, Martinus Nijhoff Publishers, The Hague 1984.
Lemmens, Gerechtelijk Privaatrecht: P. Lemmens, Gerechtelijk Privaatrecht, Acco Louvain 1994.
Mandrioli, Corso di diritto processuale civile: C. Mandrioli, Corso di diritto processuale civile I-III, 10th edition (G. Giappichelli Editore), Turin 1995.
McIntosh and Holmes, Civil Procedures in EC Countries: D. McIntosh, M. Holmes, Civil Procedures in EC Countries, An Industry Report, Lloyd's of London Press Ltd. Davies Arnold Cooper, London 1991.
Netherlands Arbitration Law: A.J. van den Berg/R. van Delden/H.J. Snijders, Netherlands Arbitration Law, Kluwer Law & Taxation Publishers, Deventer/ Boston 1993.
O'Hare and Hill, Civil Litigation: J. O'Hare and R.N. Hill, Civil Litigation, Longman Practitioner Series, London 1993.
Perrot, Institutions judiciaires: R. Perrot, Institutions judiciaires, 4th edition, Domat, Paris 1992.

Rosenberg/Schwab, Zivilprozeßrecht: Rosenberg/Schwab, Zivilprozeßrecht, 15. Auflage, C.H. Beck'sche Verlagsbuchhandlung München 1993.
Snijders, Ynzonides en Meijer: H.J. Snijders, M. Ynzonides, G.J. Meijer, Nederlands burgerlijk procesrecht, Tjeenk Willink, Zwolle 1993.
Solus and Perrot: H. Solus and R. Perrot, Droit judiciaire privé, Tome I (Introduction, notions fondamentales et organisation judiciaire), 1961; Tome II (Compétence), 1973; Tome III (Procédure de première instance), 1991 (Sirey) Paris.

Table of Contents

---

* On the usage of the term 'jurisdiction' *see* the footnote on p. 2 of the Questionnaire.

1. Questionnaire

H.J. Snijders

NOTE:

In respect of the legal system of each country considered in this book the authors have used the following questionnaire in order to determine the structure and substance of their contributions. Where there is no equivalent legal concept in a particular country, the authors have tried as much as possible to consider a legal concept which is comparable in respect of its nature and function. *See also* the preface to this book.

1.1. OVERVIEW/SOURCES

1.1.1. Introduction
- name used in the particular country for civil procedural law (e.g. *droit judiciaire privé*)
- sources of law including their relationship to each other (e.g. status of case law versus statute law)
- relevant historical background (e.g. civil/common law)

1.1.2. Act and convention as sources of law

1.1.3. Literature and case law as sources of law

1.1.4. Data bases

1.2. FUNDAMENTAL PRINCIPLES

1.2.1. Introduction

relationship between national and supranational law in particular ECHRFF/CCPR; fundamental principles, doctrines such as fair play

1.2.2. *et seq.*

discussion per subdivision of a fundamental principle:
- brief explanation of the principle
- rationale behind the principle
- sources
- discussion of the principle (if appropriate)

1.3. PRINCIPAL CHARACTERS

1.3.1. Introduction
brief summary of the principal characters

1.3.2. The judge
- various courts and instances
- international jurisdiction outside the Brussels and Lugano Conventions
- constitutional jurisdiction
- sectoral jurisdiction in comparison with administrative and criminal courts and within civil procedure (e.g. *tribunal de commerce*)
- absolute and relative jurisdiction*, number of judges per case, diagram of outlines judicial organisation in civil cases

1.3.3. The lawyers
names and duties, voluntary or mandatory legal representation/ legal assistance

1.3.4. The parties
authority to commence proceedings in general, representative actions in particular;
joinder of parties

1.4. BASIC PROCEDURE FOR CONTENTIOUS JURISDICTION AT FIRST INSTANCE

1.4.1. Introduction
- summary of the basic procedures for contentious jurisdiction
- indication of types of procedure for which contentious jurisdiction is mainly used (reference to chapter 5)

1.4.2. *et seq.*
short consideration of basic procedures: one type of procedure in each subdivision, as follows:

---

* Translator's note: due consideration has been given to the usage of the terms 'jurisdiction' and 'competence'. Since the point of departure of this translation is English, a choice has been made following the usage of the Rules of the Supreme Court (RSC 1995, Ord. 11). Thus, jurisdiction has been preferred as the general term. When referred to in meanings which correspond with the continental usage of 'competence' (compétence/competentie/ Zuständigkeit/Gerichtsbarkeit/competenza), the term jurisdiction has been further modified (sectoral/absolute/relative).

a. introduction
   including names by which the parties are known
b. commencement of proceedings
c. proceedings
   indication of various stages in chronological order and available alternatives; classification of the usual proceedings: formal/informal, oral/written, centralised/decentralised
d. judgment
e. special aspects of procedure
   non-appearance, third parties in the dispute, amendment of claim, counterclaim, production of evidence, settlement

1.5. BASIC PROCEDURE FOR VOLUNTARY JURISDICTION AT FIRST INSTANCE

1.5.1. Introduction
including a summary of the basic types of procedure (if appropriate)

1.5.2. Short description of proceedings
including names by which the parties are known

1.6. MEANS OF RECOURSE

1.6.1. Introduction
summary, rough indication of the availability in case of contentious and voluntary jurisdiction

1.6.2. *et seq.*
description of a legal means of recourse in each subdivision:
- possible means against default judgment
- appeal in the sense of a second instance (whether or not restricted)
- appeal in the sense of a (limited) third instance
- any other means of recourse;
  wherever appropriate, specifying thresholds such as rules for leave to appeal or financial limits, possible effects and a very brief description of the procedure with the names by which the parties are known (using the general approach of referring to the proceedings set out in chapters 4-5 where appropriate)

1.7. SPECIAL PROCEDURES

1.7.1. Introduction
summary and very brief description of special proceedings which are not considered further

1.7.2. Summary procedures
procedures aimed at obtaining a summary judgment whether provisional or final

1.7.3. Small claims procedures
procedures specially intended for the decision of small claims

1.7.4. Sector procedures
procedures exclusively intended for a certain area of law, e.g. divorce proceedings; very brief reference to special rules of procedure for frequently applied sector procedures

1.8. PROTECTIVE MEASURES AND ENFORCEMENT MEASURES

1.8.1. Introduction
summary and brief description

1.8.2. Protective measures other than attachment

1.8.3. Protective measures by attachment

1.8.4. Enforcement measures by attachment

1.8.5. Enforcement measures other than attachment

1.9. DURATION AND COSTS

1.9.1. Introduction

1.9.2. Duration
where appropriate, the difference in duration of proceedings in the various courts and a brief reference to the pressures on the courts and overload

1.9.3. Costs
costs for the parties: court fees and lawyers' fees and other costs; legal aid; order against the losing party to pay the costs

1.10. PROCEEDINGS OUTSIDE THE COURTS

1.10.1. Introduction

brief summary
1.10.2. Arbitration
1.10.3. Binding advice (where appropriate)

2. General Introduction and Comparison

Henk J. Snijders

2.1. Unification, Harmonisation, Differentiation and Evolution

There would have been no need for this book if uniform rules of civil procedure applied in countries with an international outlook. However, such uniformity remains a utopia for the time being.

Insurmountable objections are already encountered in respect of unification of civil procedure in the EC countries alone, notwithstanding heartwarming pleas for European codification of rules of civil procedure. Even a great champion of European codification in our times, the Ghent professor and *advocaat* M. Storme, has had to face this fact: 'his' large-scale harmonisation project, which was started under the auspices of the European Communities, has (however important it may be) so far only resulted in the production of (first) drafts relating to certain specific areas of civil procedure. The final report of this study of possibilities of harmonisation has been published in *Rapprochement du Droit Judiciaire de l'Union européenne* by Marcel Storme, Dordrecht/Boston/London 1994, on which an article by Marcel Storme, 'Procedural Consequences of a Common Private Law for Europe' appeared in *Towards a European Civil Code* (ed. by A.S. Hartkamp *et al.*), Nijmegen/Dordrecht/Boston/London 1994.

The fact that attempts to create uniform rules of civil procedure have so far proved unsuccessful does not come as a surprise. A brief look at the legal systems discussed in this book will lead to the inevitable conclusion that there are enormous differences between the various nations. The differences are particularly remarkable between the rules of procedure applying in England and Wales on the one hand and those applying in continental Europe on the other hand. If you would want to transport the *huissier de justice* or *gerechtsdeurwaarder* (process-server) with his writ across the North Sea, you would receive as warm a welcome as the Armada, let alone if you want to transport the Netherlands court system.

Whoever fervently defends EC-directives for the unification of civil procedure in EU-countries must consider that even those directives do not form a panacea for the problem of procedural differentiation within Europe. Apparently it is difficult even within a small country such as the Netherlands not to create regional rules of procedure (for example, the differences between the rules applying to summary proceedings on appeal in the various Courts of Appeal, as discussed in H.J. Snijders and A. Wendels, in conjunction with A.M.C.D. de Mare-Fröberg, *Civiel appel*, Tjeenk Willink, Zwolle 1992, no. 8.3). *A fortiori* uniform rules of procedure in Europe will only be feasible if substantial national differences are retained. Differentiation remains therefore unavoidable.

In addition, practising lawyers will also point out the drawbacks of the directives for uniform rules of procedure: in numerous civil procedures the national court will be allowed or - at the highest actual instance - obliged to ask the European Court of Justice for a preliminary ruling on a procedural matter (pursuant to art. 177 EC Treaty). It goes without saying that the application for a preliminary ruling considerably delays the proceedings. In respect of a question of procedure, such delay may seem even more acute than in respect of a question of substantive law. What must a party think of a procedure in three instances followed by a referral to the European Court for a preliminary ruling if after that ruling all he knows is that he is free to serve a third-party notice on someone?

All this implies that at least until well beyond the turn of this century we shall have to go on living with legal systems which differ greatly from country to country. Meanwhile it is, however, obvious that a thorough analysis of the foreign legal systems is required for the further development of our own legal systems. It is also only to be welcomed that efforts of unification continue within and outside national legislative bodies. This supranationally oriented pursuit of uniformity of the rules of procedure should in the writer's opinion receive greater priority and could be of greater actual value than the endeavour to achieve national uniformity of civil and administrative rules of procedure. One could say, the closer the legal family ties, the better the chance of fertile unification, and geographical distance seems to bear less weight than differences in the nature of the various areas of law.

It would be realistic primarily to attempt uniformity in model laws. In this connection the extremely fertile work done by the United Nations Commission on International Trade Law comes to mind, which Commission has *inter alia* drafted the UNCITRAL Model Law on International Commercial Arbitration. This model law has been adopted (with some amendments) by e.g. Australia, Canada, Cyprus, Hong Kong and Scotland as their national arbitration law, whilst it has strongly influenced the rules of arbitration in various other countries such as the Netherlands (*see also* the *International Handbook on Commercial Arbitration*, edited by A.J. van den Berg). Unlike the EC-directives, model laws do not require preliminary rulings, which appears to be an advantage particularly in the initial stages.

The advantage of the current situation is undeniably the possibility to study and compare the different solutions adopted by individual countries to solve the same, often global, problem.

Before further considering these national systems of law, the reader must be warned that we are dealing with law which is in a state of flux, which may be an evil, but is definitely also one of the charms of present times. Thus, in Belgium the relatively new *Gerechtelijk Wetboek/Code Judiciaire* was thoroughly amended by the Act of 3 August 1992, the aim of which is to accelerate, and in some cases to simplify, judicial procedures in a number of ways. *See inter alia* Michel Looijens in *Jura Falconis* 1991/1992, no. 1, p. 42 ff.; *see also* section 7.1.2 ff. below. Another telling example: on 1 August 1992 France introduced drastical amendments of the rules relating to enforcement and the protection of rights; *see further* section 5.8 below. In England and Wales a Uniform Code of procedure in the High Court and the county courts is being prepared. *See* McIntosh and Holmes, *Civil Procedures in EC Countries*, p. 77; *see also* section 4.1.2 below. The state of unrest which can at present be observed in relation to the rules of procedure in the Netherlands (both regarding the judicial organisation and the proceedings themselves) is unique (*see also* section 8.1.2).

The 'national' contributions in this book always begin with a summary of the sources, in order to simplify further study of the legal systems under discussion. For legal databases in the relevant countries *see also* A.H. de Wild, *Preadvies Nederlandse Vereniging voor Rechtsvergelijking* 1991, no. 44, p. 19 ff. and Christiane Serkis Bischof, *International Journal of Legal Information* 1993, Vol. 21, no. 1, p. 7 ff.

2.2. Fundamental Principles

It is precisely in respect of the main principles of civil procedure that unification has already progressed far. Article 6 ECHRFF in particular, which applies in all the countries considered in this book, guarantees uniform fundamental principles. Those fundamental principles had already been largely accepted in the national legal systems (usually implicitly). Therefore the contribution of art. 6 to the unification must not be overestimated. By virtue of art. 6 ECHRFF, in (*inter alia*) civil cases everybody is entitled to 'a fair and public hearing within a reasonable time by an independent and impartial tribunal established by law' and 'a judgement (...) pronounced publicly'. In French the wording is that a case 'soit entendue équitablement, publiquement, et dans un délai raisonnable, par un tribunal indépendant et impartial, établi par la loi' and a party is entitled to a 'jugement (...) rendu publiquement'. Both the English and the French text of the Convention are authentic. The essential principles of civil procedure are therefore identical in the countries involved. Article 6 includes a citizen's right to 'effective access to the courts' (as determined by the European Court, for example in ECHR 9 October 1979, NJ 1980, 376 (EAA) in the case *Airey* v. *Ireland*), 'fair play' (including the hearing of both sides and the motivation of the decision), public consideration of the case and judgment pronounced publicly, independence and impartiality of the court and a decision of the case within a reasonable time.

In each country the way in which these fundamental principles are put into practice differ (for instance in Belgium, in spite of the principle of independence and impartiality of the court, 'political' appointments of judges are still made and it is alleged that these judges are only seemingly dependent on their supporters). It must also be considered that art. 6 has no internal (direct) effect in countries with a dualistic system (recognition of an international legal order in addition to, instead of incorporated in, a national legal order) such as England and Wales. The consequence thereof is that art. 6 - even if it is in itself suitable to be used as such - cannot be directly invoked by a citizen before a local court. On the other hand, the European Commission and the European Court of Human Rights do test British judgments against art. 6. Thus, a complaint by the British prisoner Golder (who claimed that effectively he had been prohibited from instituting civil proceedings against his prison guard because he had been denied access to a lawyer) was found to be valid by the European Court of Human Rights, on the basis of a violation of art. 6, which, as stated above, demands effective 'access to the courts' (ECHR 21 February 1975 (*Golder* v. *Great Britain*), Series A, Vol. 18).

However important article 6 ECHRFF may be, it is not a completely new concept in legal thinking or at a supranational level, but rather a natural codification of legal thinking, also as a reaction to the horrifying 'Nazi-rules of procedure' just before and during World War II.

It is remarkable that art. 6 ECHRFF does not play a role of any importance in the internationally well-known report *Les principes fondamentaux du droit judiciaire privé* by W.J. Habscheid (in *Towards Justice with a Human Face*, a collection of articles written for the first international conference on civil procedure, Antwerp/Deventer 1978, p. 29 ff.). Article 6 is not dealt with in *European Civil Practice* either. Possibly art. 6 is regarded as a self-evident 'meta-norm'. There are no other works displaying an equally profound, similar comparative legal consideration of the fundamental principles of civil procedure. However, a great deal of literature about art. 6 and its application by the European Court of Human Rights has been published, including the *Internationaler Kommentar zur EMRK* by Golsong *et al.*

In the meantime numerous fundamental principles of civil procedure remain which are purely national and may differ from country to country for the very reason that they are of less fundamental value. It would not be wise to brush those differences aside as folklore. Their influence on the legal systems to which they relate is far too strong to do that, for instance the *Konzentrationsgrundsatz* in Germany (section 9.2.6). That is why this book also considers these principles, whereby the authors are aware that their choice and classification of purely national principles may to a certain extent be arbitrary.

As we shall discuss now, even in those national principles not incorporated in the ECHRFF more similarities may be found than one might think at first sight.

A national principle which the countries involved largely have in common is party autonomy: the adversarial system in England and Wales (section 4.2.2), the *principe dispositif* in France and Belgium (sections 5.2.2 and 7.2.5), the *partij-autonomie beginsel* in the Netherlands (section 8.2.2), and the *Dispositions- oder Parteiherrschaftsgrundsatz* in Germany (section 9.2.2). It is the parties who decide whether, against whom and about what they proceed, whether they wish to settle or use the legal means available to them. One must, of course, remain aware of the exceptions which apply to this principle everywhere, but that does not detract from the basic assumption. This principle of party autonomy strongly determines the systems of civil procedure involved. It cannot be said that the courts in common law countries such as England and Wales are much more passive than in civil law countries like France, Luxembourg, Belgium, the Netherlands, Germany and Italy. Leaving aside the fact that there is only a gradual distinction which weighs differently from one country to another, the principle of party autonomy does not naturally require a court which is passive. On the continent the court often plays a very active role, without substantially affecting party autonomy. When, for example, a court assumes an active role in gathering facts (in a hearing, expert's report, site inspection etc.), this usually can only be done within the boundaries of the legal dispute as determined by the parties. In general, a court cannot grant more than the plaintiff has claimed, nor reject a claim on the basis of a defence which has not been submitted.

The countries involved also share a principle - subject to many exceptions - which could be summarised for the Netherlands as the fundamental principle of control, unity and development of law (section 8.2.3).

France, Luxembourg, Belgium, the Netherlands, Germany and Italy in principle allow some form of appeal against judicial decisions. It is true that in German literature the availability of an appeal is usually not regarded as a principle of civil procedure, but nonetheless it is recognised that final judgments are '*grundsätzlich mit Berufung oder Revision anfechtbar'* (Rosenberg/Schwab, *Zivilprozeßrecht* p. 804; *see also* section 9.2.1). In England and Wales leave to appeal is required (section 4.6.4) which means that the right of appeal exists only in exceptional cases (leaving aside appeal against default judgments). On the other hand, in England and Wales other correction mechanisms are available, such as the slip rule and rehearing. The slip rule provides an opportunity to correct obvious judicial errors: 'Clerical mistakes in judgments or orders, or errors arising therein from any accidental slip or omission, may at any time be corrected by the Court on motion or summons without an appeal' (RSC Ord. 20, r. 11). Parties may ask the Court of Appeal for a rehearing at first instance, in particular to correct their own mistakes (RSC Ord. 59, r. 3). So everywhere there is a procedure to check judicial decisions for the sake of correction of errors of the parties and the courts (section 4.6.1). 'Only' the extent to which this is possible and the manner in which this is done differ considerably. The special position of England and Wales can hardly be explained by the principle of finality (section 4.2.6) which applies there, implying that proceedings must be finished at some point. Also on the continent lawyers adhere to this principle, expressing it even in Latin ('*lites finiri oportet*'). It could, however, be argued that continental lawyers attach more weight than their neighbours on the other side of the Channel to the need to correct judicial imperfections and omissions by the parties and their lawyers when the case is considered at first instance.

The development of law on the continent shows some more flexibility than in England and Wales, now that the English doctrine of binding precedent particularly in conjunction with the absence of rights of appeal undeniably carries a danger of ossification.

In all countries except the Netherlands a principle applies which could be summarised as the requirement of an (additional) oral consideration of the case. *See* for Belgian law section 7.2.8 on the principle of the written and oral consideration of the case and section 6.2 for Luxembourg law. In French law this is not laid down in a *principe directeur* (section 5.2.1), but nonetheless *le principe d'oralité* is also known as a *principe gouvernant le déroulement des débats* (*see* for instance Couchez, *Procédure Civile*, no. 269). In England and Wales it is called the principle of orality (section 4.2.4), in Germany the principle of *Mündlichkeit* (section 9.2.4) and in Italy the *principio dell'oralità* (section 10.2.7).

Why is there no such principle in the Netherlands? Apparently the Netherlands legal culture offers (some) resistance. The cantonal court rules which were in force until 30 December 1991 aimed to provide a largely oral procedure, but in practice a more or less extensive exchange of written pleadings took place (the new rules, which have been in force since 30 December 1991, are less strongly focused on oral consideration of the case; the scope which the law provides for written consideration is used intensively even today). Another example: proper oral pleadings in civil cassation cases are exceptional; instead there are normally only written explanations followed (at the same time) by written 'reply and rejoinder'. On the other hand, Netherlands courts nowadays on a large scale order the personal appearance of the parties in court pursuant to art. 141a Rv after the defence has been issued (section 8.4.2). This is a *novum* which has also attracted international attention in view of the number of settlements reached after such appearances in court. Furthermore, petition proceedings in the Netherlands normally include an oral consideration of the case (section 8.5.2). For all these reasons, oral communication between courts and parties is also considered to be important in the Netherlands. One may, but need not, use comparative legal arguments to characterise this development as positive and to applaud its further evolution. Imagine the position of a Netherlands cassation court which during the first three instances has been considered only by looking at written documents. The court might easily think that the case has never actually fully materialised. The ECHR clearly tends towards offering litigating parties an oral consideration. *See*, for instance, ECHR 26 April 1995 (*Fischer* v. *Austria*). Publ. CEDH Series A, Vol. 312. Little by little, perhaps, one can speak of a European principle of orality.

It is remarkable that most countries do recognise a duty to motivate legal decisions, but that only the authors on Belgian and Netherlands law name the motivation principle as such (sections 7.2.4 and 8.2.2 respectively). However, one cannot deduct from this that Belgian and Netherlands law differ in principle from the law in the other countries in this book. In France, for instance, the requirement of motivation is also called 'une garantie de bonne justice' (Couchez, *Procédure Civile*, no. 400; *see also* section 5.2.1). However this may be, in 1994 the European Court of Human Rights held that art. 6 ECHRFF includes a duty for the national judges to motivate their decisions. Since that ECHR-decision, we have been allowed to say that the motivation principle is one of the fundamentals of all ECHRFF Member States (ECHR 19 April 1994 (*Van de Hurk* v. *Nederland*), CEDH, Series A, Vol. 288, also referred to in *Ruiz Tonija* v. *Spain* and *Hiro Balani* v. *Spain*, both decided by ECHR 9 December 1994 (Series A, Vols. 303A resp. 303 B)).

2.3. Principal Characters

2.3.1. INTRODUCTION

An analysis of the principal characters reveals certain fundamental differences.

First, the position of the bailiff differs strongly from country to country (*see* especially sections 3.1 of the various chapters). In England and Wales there is no bailiff's monopoly as regards the service of writs. In the Netherlands that monopoly has now also partly been broken by the introduction in cantonal court cases of a special writ which may be sent by registered mail without the bailiff's intervention (section 8.4.3).

Secondly, in some countries there may be a principal character who is not known in the other countries. Germany has the *Rechtspfleger*. Originally this figure was a kind of auxiliary judge dealing with routine cases. Meanwhile the scope of his work has been considerably extended (*see* section 9.3.1). In England there is the master, who in the High Court leads the pretrial stage. The master plays an important role especially in the light of the fact that a considerable number of cases do not proceed further than the pretrial stage (*see* section 4.3.2).

2.3.2. THE JUDGE

A comparison of the judicial organisations in the countries involved shows that most countries have courts of first instance at two levels (the rules of appeal vary widely from one country to another):

– the lower level mainly for less important cases: in England and Wales the county court with appeal to the Court of Appeal (sections 4.3.2 and 4.6.4); in France the *tribunal d'instance* with appeal to the *cour d'appel* (section 5.3.2); the *justice de paix* with appeal to the *tribunal d'arrondissement* or the *tribunal de commerce* in Luxembourg (sections 6.3.2 and 6.6.3); in Belgium the *vrederechter/justice de paix* with appeal to the *rechtbank van eerste aanleg/tribunal de première instance* or the *rechtbank van koophandel/tribunal de commerce* (sections 7.3.2 and 7.6.3); in the Netherlands the *kantongerecht* (cantonal court) with appeal to the *arrondissementsrechtbank* (district court) (section 8.3.2); in Germany the *Amtsgericht* with appeal to the *Landgericht* or *Oberlandesgericht* (section 9.3.2).

– the higher level for the remaining, usually more important, cases: in England and Wales the High Court with appeal to the Court of Appeal (sections 4.3.2 and 4.6.4); in France the *tribunal de grande instance*, the *tribunal de commerce*, the *conseil de prud'hommes* and the *tribunal paritaire des baux ruraux*, all with appeal to the *cour d'appel* (section 5.3.2); in Luxembourg the *tribunal d'arrondissement/tribunal de commerce* and the *tribunal du travail* with appeal to the *cour d'appel* (section 6.3.2); in Belgium the *rechtbank van eerste aanleg/tribunal de première instance*, the *rechtbank van koophandel/tribunal de commerce* and the *arbeidsrechtbank/tribunal du travail* with appeal to the *hof van appel/cour d'appel* or the *arbeidshof/cour du travail* (section 7.3.2); in the Netherlands the *arrondissementsrechtbank* with appeal to the *Gerechtshof* (Court of Appeal) (section 8.3.2); in Germany the *Landgericht* with appeal to the *Oberlandesgericht* (section 9.3.2).

Only in Italy are there three levels for courts of first instance: the *giudice di pace* for minor cases mainly, the *pretore* for less minor cases, both with appeal to the *tribunale*, and the *tribunale* for major cases mainly, with appeal to the *corte d'appello* (section 10.3.2).

This summary not only demonstrates two levels of jurisdiction at first instance, but also shows the division of sectoral jurisdiction in several countries. For instance, the *tribunal du travail* and the *tribunal de commerce/ rechtbank van koophandel* in France, Luxembourg and Belgium are unusual.

It is also noteworthy that in the near future the Netherlands may be in the unique position (compared to the other countries in this book) that it will have only one court of first instance, which is formed by the merger of the *kantongerechten* with the *arrondissementsrechtbanken* of first instance (section 8.3.2).

It is less of an international novelty that in future the Netherlands may in principle also have one appellate court, the *Gerechtshof* (section 8.3.2). As stated above, England and Wales and France have already preceded the Netherlands, while Belgium is also moving in that direction.

As regards appeal, it must be noted that most countries use financial limits for appeal: FF 13,000 (section 5.3.2), LUF 25,000 (section 6.6.3), BF 50,000 or 75,000 (section 7.6.3), Hfl. 2,500 (section 8.6.3), DM 1,200 (section 9.6.3) and Lit. 2 million (section 10.3.2). In England and Wales a system of leave to appeal applies (section 4.6.3).

It is obvious that each country has one supreme court, which mainly deals with appeal 'to the second degree': appeal to the House of Lords, cassation to the *Cour de cassation/Hof van Cassatie* in France, Luxembourg and Belgium, to the *Hoge Raad* in the Netherlands or the *Corte di cassazione* in

Italy and *Revision* to the *Bundesgerichtshof.* With the exception of England and Wales, grounds for appeal are restricted. As stated above, England and Wales have a system of leave to appeal, which restricts access to the supreme court to a few dozen cases per year. The German system could be qualified as a system of partial leave (section 9.6.4). So far the Netherlands has rejected any system requiring leave to appeal to the *Hoge Raad.* Other measures to reduce the overload of the *Hoge Raad* have, however, been taken (*see* section 8.6.4).

It may also be obvious that in most countries the courts are geographically decentralised. Even England and Wales, where the High Court in London deals with the more important cases, are more decentralised than they may seem at first glance: many High Court cases may be dealt with by District Registries and provincial trial centres (section 4.3.2).

Finally a word of warning: beware of pseudo-similarities! For instance, the only task of the Belgian *Arrondissementsrechtbank/Tribunal d'Arrondissement* is to decide jurisdiction incidents (section 7.3.2), and the English Supreme Court consists of the High Court (of first instance) and the Court of Appeal (section 4.3.2).

2.3.3. THE LAWYERS

All countries involved have professionals providing legal assistance, such as the solicitor and the barrister in England and Wales (section 4.3.3), the *avocat* and the *avoué* in France (section 5.3.3) and Luxembourg (section 6.3.3), the *avocat* in Belgium (section 7.3.3), the *advocaat* and the *procureur* in the Netherlands (section 8.3.3), the *Rechtsanwalt* in Germany (section 9.3.3) and the *difensore* (*procuratore* and/or *avvocato*) in Italy (section 10.3.3). District-bound lawyers operating as the parties' representatives in the courts are now only known in France and Luxembourg (the *avoué*), the Netherlands (the *procureur*) and Italy (the *procuratore*) and even so on a limited scale (sections 5.3.3, 8.3.3 and 10.3.3 respectively). Mandatory legal representation does exist, subject to certain exceptions, in France, Luxembourg, the Netherlands, Germany and Italy, but not in Belgium, England and Wales.

The reader who is interested in a detailed consideration of legal assistance in the countries involved and in other countries could consult e.g. *Lawyers in Society*, ed. by Richard L. Abel and Philip S.C. Lewis, University of California Press, Berkeley-Los Angeles-London 1988.

2.3.4. THE PARTIES

In all the countries considered in this book only natural persons as such and legal persons are in principle qualified to act as parties in proceedings. There are differences in particular with respect to the admissibility of representative actions (group actions, general interest actions and such). *See* section 3.4 in each chapter. In this respect the Netherlands takes up a leading position: since 1 July 1994, arts. 3:305a-b BW provide for a general representative action for legal persons which act on behalf of the general interest or of a group interest.

2.4. Basic Procedure for Contentious Jurisdiction at First Instance

The procedure in countries involved varies greatly in important and less important details. If we look at the main features of the procedure, the picture becomes clearer.

On the continent there is one basic procedure for contentious jurisdiction which may vary according to the court before which proceedings are brought. In Luxembourg, Belgium and the Netherlands this is the procedure commenced by writ (sections 6.4.2, 7.4.2 and 8.4.2 respectively), in France also (albeit that there are alternatives available in different courts (section 5.4.2)). In Germany there is a basic procedure, called *Entscheidungs-* or *Erkenntnisverfahren*, or *Urteils-* or *Klageverfahren* (section 9.4.1). In Italy the basic procedure is called *processo di cognizione* (section 10.4.1-3). The situation is more complex in England, in particular due to the large difference between the county courts and the High Court (*see* sections 4.4.2-3).

France, Luxembourg, Belgium and the Netherlands are familiar with the phenomenon that certain contentious matters are exceptionally commenced by petition. *See* for France section 5.4.3 *et seq.*, for Belgium section 7.4.3 and for the Netherlands section 8.5.1.

In all the countries involved the basic procedure for contentious cases is of a more formal nature than the procedure for voluntary cases, which appears most clearly when comparing section 4 with section 5 of each 'national' contribution.

With respect to another criterion to characterise the basic procedure, i.e. the relationship between written and oral consideration of the case, the reader is referred to section 2.2 above.

As regards the rules of evidence, it is striking that England and Wales still use a very formal system with affidavits and witnesses' statements (*see* section 4.4.2c). England and Wales also occupy a special position in the sense that foreign law is regarded as a fact which therefore must be proven. The courts only apply foreign law if parties invoke it and prove its alleged content in case of dispute.

When comparing the procedures in the various countries according to the extent to which consideration of the case is concentrated, first place must be awarded to Germany (sections 9.4.1-2), due to the so-called *Vereinfachungsnovelle* of 3 December 1976, which entered into force in 1977. On the other end of the scale we find the English model with its pretrial phase and discovery (section 4.4.2), which often guarantees a long lingering and possibly exhausting procedure. France, Luxembourg and Belgium take up intermediate positions, like the Netherlands. The advantage of the pretrial options available in the Netherlands - preliminary examination of witnesses and of experts and site inspection (section 8.4.2) - is that the main proceedings do not have to be delayed until the results of the 'preliminary' production of evidence are known. The preliminary production of evidence may in fact eventually be used as definitive evidence in the main proceedings.

Everywhere one sees more or less successful attempts to develop variations within the basic procedure for contentious matters in order to accelerate the procedure. Thus England and Wales have summary proceedings and other procedural methods which may lead to the procedure being terminated in the pretrial stage or being restricted in the trial stage (section 4.7.2), France has the *circuit court* and the *circuit moyen* (section 5.4.2), Belgium has the procedure with *korte debatten/débats succincts* (short proceedings) (section 7.4.2), the Netherlands has the accelerated final procedure (section 8.4.2) and Germany has the settlement with a *frühe erste Termin* (section 9.4.2).

2.5. Basic Procedure for Voluntary Jurisdiction at First Instance

All countries have special rules of procedure in voluntary cases, which is fairly obvious in view of the predominantly formal nature of procedures in contentious cases.

Thus England and Wales have the proceedings commenced by originating summons and by petition (section 4.5), France, Luxembourg, Belgium, the Netherlands and Italy have the procedure commenced by petition (sections 5.5, 6.5, 7.5, 8.5 and 10.5.2 respectively) and Germany has the *freiwillige Gerichtsbarkeit* (section 9.5). For each of these countries the procedure in voluntary cases appears to be more informal, more concentrated and (hence) faster than the basic procedure in contentious cases.

It is remarkable that in all the countries involved the procedure often does not take place in public. Many of these cases will concern matters of a private nature which justify an exception to the principle of publicity. Whether the exception is also justified for the actual decision remains to be seen. Thus art. 451 NCPC, which determines that in principle the pronouncing of 'décisions gracieuses' take place 'hors la présence du public', is at odds with art. 6 ECHRFF. Indeed, art. 6 does not contain any exceptions with respect to the publicity of judgments. Yet the French provision may be saved, for the requirement of publicity stated in art. 6 is interpreted in such a way by the European Court of Human Rights that it is not required to admit the public when the judgment is pronounced, but that there is only a duty of publication which is subject to further rules. *See*, for instance, ECHR 8 December 1983 (*Pretto* resp. *Axen*), Series A, Vol. 71 resp. 72 and ECHR 22 February 1984 (*Sutter*), Series A, Vol. 74.

2.6. Means of Recourse

See sections 2.2 and 2.3.2 above for comparative remarks regarding the appeal in the sense of a second and third instance. It must be noted that cassation is an extraordinary means of recourse in France, Luxembourg and Belgium (sections 5.6.1, 6.6.1 and 7.6.1 respectively) and therefore has no suspensive effect, unlike cassation in the Netherlands (section 8.6.4) and *Revision* in Germany (section 9.6.1). The Italian *ricorso per cassazione* takes up a special position (section 10.6.3). Unlike Belgium (section 7.6.4), the Netherlands (section 8.6.4) and Italy (section 10.6.3), France also has cassation of the court's own motion, i.e. *ex officio* (section 5.4.6).

Leaving aside these forms of appeal, in each country except Italy there is a way whereby a case in which a default judgment has been given, can still be considered in adversarial proceedings: the application to set aside in England (section 4.6.2), the *opposition* in France and Luxembourg (sections 5.6.2 and 6.6.2), the *opposition* (the *verzet*) in Belgium and the *verzet* (also called 'oppositie') in the Netherlands (sections 7.6.2 and 8.6.2 respectively) and the *Einspruch* in Germany (section 9.6.2). It appears to be of secondary importance that Germany does not qualify the *Einspruch* as a means of recourse. Decisive is the similarity of the procedure in all the countries, which is unmistakably due to the central place which the principle of hearing both sides takes in all the countries involved.

Apart from the most obvious means of recourse such as setting aside default judgments, appeal and cassation or their equivalent, many countries have other means of recourse, such as the English application to vary orders (section 4.6.2), the French *recours en révision* and the *contredit* (sections 5.6.1 and 5.6.5), the Belgian *herroeping* (section 7.6.5), Luxembourg and the Netherlands *request civiel* (sections 6.6.1 and 8.6.1), the German *Beschwerde* (section 9.6.5) and the Italian *revocazione* ('ordinaria' and 'straordinaria', section 10.6.1).

Many countries also have a type of rectification procedure, which, admittedly, cannot be classified as a means of recourse, but may nevertheless produce the same effect, because it may lead to a fresh judgment in which errors of a previous judgment are remedied: the *slip rule* and *rehearing* in England and Wales, mentioned above under 2.2, the rectification procedure in France (art. 462 NCPC), the *procédure de rectification du jugement* ('*verbeterings-procedure*') in Belgium (art. 794 *et seq.* Ger.W./C.J.), the *Berichtigung* in Germany (§§ 319-320 ZPO) and the *correzione delle sentenze e delle ordinanze* in Italy (art. 287 *et seq.* CPC). With the exception of article 1060 Rv in respect of arbitration, there are no legal provisions in the Netherlands – or in Luxembourg – allowing rectification, but in practice rectification has been allowed on a limited basis.

It may be that in practice a dispute on enforcement will also deal with errors in the underlying judgment, but obviously a dispute on enforcement only concerns enforcement and not the actual contents of the judgment itself.

2.7. Special Procedures

At least four types of special procedure may be distinguished: (1) accelerated proceedings such as the French *référé*; (2) small claims procedures such as the German *Verfahren nach billigem Ermessen*; (3) special procedures for substantive areas of law such as the divorce proceedings; and (4) special procedures for issues of civil procedure, e.g. the Netherlands procedure for the rescission of penalties. Only the first three types of procedures will be considered in this book. This is an obvious choice in a book which emphasises the broad lines of civil procedure.

In this section a short comment on the accelerated procedure and the small claims procedure must suffice.

Variations within the basic procedure for contentious matters in order to accelerate the procedure were already mentioned above in 2.4. There are also separate accelerated proceedings. Belgium and the Netherlands have the *kort geding* (sections 7.7.2 and 8.7.2); France and Luxembourg have the *référé* (sections 5.7.2 and 6.7.2). Germany has the *einstweilige Verfügung* which is more or less comparable (section 9.7.2), England and Wales have summary proceedings which result in a final decision (section 4.7.2). Italy has the same for specific proceedings. They are called *procedimenti sommari* (section 10.7.2). England and Wales also have interlocutory injunctions, which result in provisional judgments (sections 4.7.2 and 4.8.1-2). *See also* (but not on England and Wales) P. Meijknecht and R. Ch. Verschuur in a conference bundle *Justice and Efficiency*, ed. W. Wedekind, Deventer-Antwerp-Boston 1988, p. 367 ff.

Belgium has a 'summary procedure to obtain an order for payment' of claims not exceeding BF 75,000 (section 7.7.3). France also has the court order to pay (*injonction de payer*), but this is not restricted to small claims; a similar decision there is the *injonction de faire* (section 5.7.3). In Luxembourg the court can give a conditional order to pay for claims nor exceeding LUF 200,000 (section 6.7.3). Germany also has accelerated proceedings for the collection of claims, the *Mahnverfahren*; here, too, there is no financial limit (section 9.7.3). The same applies to Italy, which has a *procedimento d'ingunzione* to be initiated with a *ricorso* (section 10.7.2). In England and Wales there is a simple procedure for small claims in the county courts - especially claims not exceeding £ 500 (section 4.7.3).

In the light of the above, one may wonder whether the Netherlands was right in doing away with the procedure to obtain an order for payment when the new *kantongerecht* procedure was introduced. In particular for small claims there remains a need for accelerated final proceedings if cost-benefit analysis is applied, though the *kantonrechters* and the presidents of the *arrondissementsrechtbanken* actually fill this gap for the main part by issuing provisional payment orders which are often considered by the parties to be final. *See also* section 8.7.3.

2.8. Protective Measures and Enforcement Measures

A distinction may be made between (1) protective versus enforcement measures; and (2) attachment versus other protective or enforcement measures. The chapters on each country show that sometimes it is rather difficult to make those distinctions, but they nevertheless appear to be useful from a comparative law perspective. In those chapters the following subdivision is therefore used: (a) protective measures other than attachment; (b) protective measures by attachment; (c) enforcement measures by attachment; and (d) enforcement measures other than attachment. It is possible to regroup those four subdivisions by referring to them as three separate areas of law: *a* and *b* together form the protective law (law concerning protective measures); *b* and *c* together form the law on attachment; *c* and *d* together form the law on enforcement (law concerning enforcement measures).

This subdivision into four areas does not pose any problem for France, Luxembourg, Belgium, the Netherlands and Italy (sections 5.8, 6.8, 7.8, 8.8 and 10.8 respectively). For England and Wales and Germany it is more difficult to make such a division. Those countries do, however, have comparable legal concepts (sections 4.8 and 9.8 respectively).

In France the new *juge de l'exécution* draws our attention: he plays a central role in the new French law on protective and enforcement measures (section 5.8.1). It is also remarkable that the legislator in France has applied a certain order in the admissibility of the various measures of enforcement (section 5.8.1).

Apart from attachment all countries involved (except Italy) also have indirect means of enforcement. In Belgium, the Netherlands and Luxembourg there is the penalty (which is governed by a Benelux law) (sections 6.8.5, 7.8.5 and 8.8.5), which also applies in France (section 5.8.5). Germany has the *Ordnungsgeld* (section 9.8.5) as a comparable indirect means of enforcement. Civil imprisonment, which is applied in the Netherlands in exceptional cases (section 8.8.5), was abolished in Belgium when the *Gerechtelijk Wetboek/Code Judiciaire* was introduced (section 7.8.5) and in France as early as 1867. In Luxembourg, too, this means does not exist anymore. In Italy, it never applied (section 10.8.5). Germany still has a kind of civil imprisonment, the *Ordnungshaft* (section 9.8.5). In England and Wales there is the possibility of criminal action i.e. committal proceedings for contempt of court in case of non-compliance with decisions (section 3.8.5). *See further* R.M. Blaauw, *Preliminary advice for the Nederlandse Vereniging voor Rechtsvergelijking 1981* (Netherlands Association for Comparative Law), No. 31.

2.9. Duration and Costs

Putting Italy aside, no doubt the English High Court wins the prize for the longest proceedings: on average, proceedings at first instance before this court take about three years (it is therefore only in a fraction of all cases that litigants have the courage to continue proceedings up to and including trial). Germany appears to have the shortest proceedings due to the aforementioned *Vereinfachungsnovelle*. Approximately 90 per cent of cases at first instance are decided within 12 months. 75 per cent of the cases before the *Amtsgericht* and 52 per cent of the cases before the *Landgericht* are 'even' decided within 6 months. France, Belgium and the Netherlands are in the middle bracket. On appeal Belgium has so far made a particularly poor impression with an average duration of 2 to 3 years; more in general, the delays were also one of the reasons for the introduction of amendments of the *Gerechtelijk Wetboek/Code Judiciaire* as referred to in section 2.1 above (statistics concerning the duration of proceedings since the new law entered into force are not yet available). The duration of proceedings before the *tribunal d'arrondissement* in Luxembourg seems remarkably long for such a small country, which should easily be capable of dealing with cases expeditiously. The situation in Italy was most alarming before the reform per 1 May 1995. The average duration of a procedure at first instance was about six years. There is some pessimism about the success of the recent reform. *See* sections 9.2 of the national contributions and also sections 9.2, 9.3 and 10.1 of McIntosh and Holmes, *Civil Procedures in EC Countries*.

The quantitative data on which the above conclusions are based are necessarily rather superficial and any conclusions can therefore only be made with some reservation.

One wishes it were possible to compare figures of the average costs of legal assistance in the countries involved, but there are no such figures available. Yet it is evident, taking into consideration the important part the lawyer plays, that everywhere the costs of civil procedures are high for the parties. This does not apply to cases where legal aid is available, but the relevant criteria to qualify for legal aid appear to be rather strict. *See* sections 9.3 of the national contributions. When proceeding before the High Court, it must be remembered that the assistance of a solicitor *and* a barrister is required and that the loser of the case has to pay the bills of the winning party's solicitor and barrister.

2.10. Proceedings Outside the Courts

In the countries in this book arbitration is the main form of conflicts being decided by others than the parties or the national courts; in all these countries there are only superficial rules for binding advice or similar concepts. Proceedings outside the courts without decision-making by one or more other persons than the parties, such as mediation and minitrial, are not dealt with in this book.

Article 1717 *sub* 4 Ger.W./CJ (dating from 1985) is quite remarkable in that it excludes an application to set aside an arbitral award before the Belgian court unless at least one of the parties is a Belgian national, is domiciled in Belgium or (as a legal person) has been established or has its seat in Belgium. Unless that connection with the Belgian jurisdiction exists, parties in arbitral proceedings are well-advised to realise beforehand that any arbitral award cannot be attacked before the Belgian court, notwithstanding the existence of obvious grounds for the setting aside of the award, but there is a proposal for changing Belgian arbitration law now (section 7.10.1).

All countries involved have signed and ratified the New York Convention of 1958 on the Recognition and Enforcement of Foreign Arbitral Awards (at present, more than a hundred countries have acceded). An exequatur for a foreign arbitral award will therefore not be difficult to obtain in these countries.

Whoever should wish for a further discussion of arbitration abroad, in addition to the summaries in the national contributions on arbitration, is referred to the loose-leaf *International Handbook on Commercial Arbitration* and the *Yearbooks on Commercial Arbitration*, gen. ed. A.J. van den Berg, Kluwer Law & Taxation Publishers, Deventer.

3. International Procedural Law

Marielle E. Koppenol-Laforce*

3.1. Introduction

3.1.1. OVERVIEW

It is vital to gain an insight into the internal procedural requirements of the EU Member States, to which all the countries discussed in this book belong. Lawyers can no longer advise their clients without having at least some notion of foreign procedural law. The term 'forumshopping' is cherished and dreaded. It is only useful to those who know which conditions internal procedural law has to offer regarding, for instance, evidence of witnesses, terms of writs of summons.

It is, however, not only national procedural law which plays a part. There is also international procedural law, i.e. national procedural rules applying to international cases. Each country's laws contain procedural rules which deal with the demarcation of jurisdiction in international cases. In the areas of recognition and enforcement of foreign judgments, too, each legal system has its own rules. International procedural law may appear in a separate part of the procedural law or throughout the entire body of legislation and/or may form part of unwritten rules of law. The purpose of treaties dealing with international procedural law is to unify the rules regarding jurisdiction and/or recognition and enforcement and to simplify procedures. In a number of areas the EU has provided rules for the jurisdiction of EU Member States in respect of EU citizens, whereby the protection of the defendant is very important. Some conventions of The Hague Conference also provide for uniform international procedural law in the EC. Between some of the Member States there are bilateral conventions as well.

Despite the harmonisation of international procedural law achieved so far (*inter alia* the European Convention on Jurisdiction and the Enforcement of Judgments in Civil and Commercial Matters 1968; the Hague Convention of 15 November 1965 on the Service Abroad of Judicial and Extrajudicial Documents in Civil or Commercial Matters; the Hague Convention of 18 March 1970 on the Taking of Evidence Abroad in Civil or Commercial Matters; the

* Thanks are due to Prof. dr. P. Vlas (Professor of private international law and comparative law at Amsterdam Free University).

Hague Convention of 1973 on the Recognition and Enforcement of Decisions relating to Maintenance Obligations), national procedural law still plays an important part in international cases. The court applies the law of the forum, the *lex fori*, to most procedural matters. There is always an interaction between the demands of the conventions and the demands made by national procedural law. Studying foreign procedural law is therefore advisable, but in doing this attention must be paid to co-ordinating international procedural law.

When speaking of access to procedure abroad, the first question to be asked is whether the court addressed has jurisdiction. The court must first consult international procedural laws (this may have been embodied in national legislation, e.g. in the United Kingdom, where the Convention on Jurisdiction and the Enforcement of Judgments in Civil and Commercial Matters has been incorporated into the Civil Jurisdiction and Judgments Act 1982, last amended in 1991). The international attribution of jurisdiction will sometimes determine both the international jurisdiction and the national internal division of competence, but there are also examples of national internal competence being left to the Member State's domestic law. International procedural law may also lead to domestic rules of procedure which would be compulsory in domestic cases being overruled in international cases.

When the court, on good grounds, decides that it has jurisdiction but a court from another State has also assumed jurisdiction, international procedural law may provide a solution. Conventions often contain *lis pendens* and connexity arrangements. In this context national procedural rules of law often play an important role, for the exact time of the commencement of proceedings before the national court is essential. Without a uniform criterion imposed by a Convention or an Act, international procedural law cannot provide a solution for this problem, because national procedural rules differ too much.

In the last stage of the dispute one of the parties obtains a court judgment which needs to be enforced against the other party. In national cases this is not really a problem. Once national cases become international, which can happen quite easily (e.g. a maintenance debtor who takes a job in another country), recognition and/or enforcement is more complicated. In this respect, too, international procedural rules of law within the EU have harmonised large parts of legislation, so that recognition and/or enforcement of a judgment in an EU Member State can be realised without too many formalities. Even here, though, unification does not mean that national procedural rules of law no longer apply. The decision whether a judgment has already become *res iudicata*, or is still appealable or immediately enforceable will remain a national affair, although the outcome of this decision is essential for the recognition and/or enforcement abroad.

International procedural rules of law do not solve everything. Sometimes international rules explicitly refer to national procedure and sometimes there are no international rules. In such cases EU Member States are thrown back upon their traditional (i.e. non-convention) international procedural rules of law.

3.1.2. INTERNATIONAL JURISDICTION, RECOGNITION AND ENFORCEMENT

The most comprehensive set of rules providing for the reciprocal jurisdiction, recognition and enforcement of EU States exists for civil and commercial matters (*see* section 3.2.1 *et seq.*).

In this area the European Convention on Jurisdiction and the Enforcement of Judgments in Civil and Commercial Matters (hereinafter called Brussels Convention) was concluded in Brussels on 27 September 1968. The Brussels Convention is not intended to unify procedural law, but provides for a division of the jurisdiction of the courts for the purpose of settlement of civil and commercial disputes within the EU and a facilitation of the enforcement of judgments of the courts.

This Convention came into force on 1 February 1973 for the Kingdom of the Netherlands (for the Netherlands and on 30 June 1986 for Aruba (not for the Netherlands Antilles)), Belgium, Luxembourg, the Federal Republic of Germany, France and Italy.

The accession of the United Kingdom of Great Britain and Northern Ireland, Denmark and the Republic of Ireland to the EC has led to the accession of these states to the Brussels Convention. A Convention on Accession was therefore concluded on 9 October 1978 in Luxembourg. Pursuant to this (first) Convention on Accession, Denmark acceded to the Brussels Convention on 1 November 1986, the United Kingdom on 1 January 1987 and the Republic of Ireland on 1 June 1988.

In respect of the Kingdom of the Netherlands, this first Convention on Accession came into force for the Netherlands only (and not for the Netherlands Antilles and Aruba). It was stipulated that once the original six States plus one new Member State had ratified this Convention, it would come into force as between the original six and that one new State. This took place on 1 November 1986.

The accession of Greece to the EC led to a second Convention on Accession to the Brussels Convention, concluded on 25 October 1982 in Luxembourg. This second Convention came into force on 1 April 1989 between Belgium, the Federal Republic of Germany, Denmark, France, Greece, the Republic of Ireland, the Kingdom of the Netherlands (for the Netherlands) and Luxembourg. On 1 October 1989 the second Convention also came into force for the United Kingdom. This convention only required ratification of a number of the original States and naturally of Greece. Hence, entry into force for the United Kingdom could be effected at a later stage, which, however, could not give rise to any complicated situations, in view of the fact that this second Convention on Accession merely contained formal adjustments.

A third Convention on Accession, concluded on 26 May 1989 in San Sebastian, provides for the accession of Spain and Portugal to the Brussels Convention. This Convention came into force on 1 February 1991 between the Kingdom of the Netherlands (for the Netherlands), France and Spain; on 1 December 1991 for the United Kingdom, on 1 February 1992 for Luxembourg, on 1 May 1992 for Italy, on 1 July 1992 for Greece and Portugal, on 1 December 1993 for the Republic of Ireland and on 1 December 1994 for Germany (as per 1 September 1995). In this case, too, the ratification by a number of the original States was sufficient. Consequently, two versions of the Brussels Convention apply to these signatory States which have already ratified this third Convention on Accession. This may cause problems, because the third convention does contain drastic substantive adjustments. The authors of the third Convention on Accession did not anticipate the extent of these difficulties, and the Convention therefore does not provide a solution for these problems.

The Brussels Convention applies in the version as amended by the Conventions of 1978, 1982 and 1989 in the relation between the Netherlands, Germany, France, Spain, the United Kingdom, Luxembourg, Italy, Greece, Portugal and the Republic of Ireland (as per 1 September 1995).

As of 1 January 1995, Finland, Austria and Sweden have acceded to the EU. This means that for these countries, too, an Accession Convention for their accession to the Brussels Convention will be drawn up in due course. It must be pointed out that even now, between the EU States which have ratified the Lugano Convention and Finland and Sweden, a system of international rules of procedural law applies which is virtually identical to the system of the Brussels Convention. The Accession Convention will probably only contain formal amendments and will not cause any substantial changes.

3.1.3. LITERATURE

General: the explanatory reports on the different versions of the Brussels Convention, namely

- Jenard report (Brussels Convention 1968), OJ 1979 59/1-70 of 5 March 1979;
- Schlosser report (Brussels Convention 1978), OJ 1979 59/71-151 of 5 March 1979;
- Evrigenis report (Brussels Convention 1982), OJ 1986 298/1-28 of 24 November 1986; and
- Almeida Cruz report (Brussels Convention 1989), OJ 1990 189/35-56 of 8 July 1990.

The holdings of the judgments of the European Court of Justice are published in the Official Journal of the European Communities (OJ); the full texts are published in the Court Reports (ECR).

The Netherlands: P. Vlas, loose-leaf edition Burg. Rv., volume Verdragen, EEX. For the administration of justice in respect of international procedural rules of law based on either conventions or traditional rules the NIPR is an important source. Commentaries on all judgments by the European Court of Justice regarding the Brussels Convention appear at regular intervals in TVVS and NILR.

France: G.A.L. Droz, *Compétence judiciaire et effets des jugements dans le marché commun* (Étude de la Convention de Bruxelles du 27 septembre 1986), Bibliothèque de droit international privé, Volume XIII, Librairie Dalloz, Paris 1972. H. Gaudemet-Tallon, *Les Conventions de Bruxelles et de Lugano; compétence internationale, reconnaissance et exécution des jugements en Europe*, LGDJ (droit des affaires), Paris, 1993. In the *Revue critique de droit international privé* (Rev. crit.) all judgments by the European Court of Justice concerning the Brussels Convention are published in French and commented on.

Germany: J. Kropholler, *Europäisches Zivilprozessrecht: Kommentar zu EuGVÜ und Lugano-Übereinkommen*, schriftenreihe Recht der Internationale Wirtschaft, Band 22, 4., neubearbeitete Auflage, Verlag Recht und Wirtschaft GmbH, Heidelberg 1993. Wieczorek/Schütze, *Großkommentar zur ZPO*, 3. Aufl. Berlin 1994, Band I, Teilband 1, Anhang II zu § 40 ZPO: Hausmann, Kommentierung der Artt. 1*bis* 20 EuGVÜ and Artt. 1*bis* 20 Lugano-Übereinkommen. In the *IPRax* all judgments by the European Court of Justice concerning the Brussels Convention are published in German and commented on.

Belgium: M. Weser, *Convention communautaire sur la compétence judiciaire et l'exécution des décisions. Complété par l'étude des droits internes et des traités bilatéraux des États contractants*, Interuniversitair Centrum voor Rechtsvergelijking, Brussels 1975. The judgments of the European Court are published and commented on in the *Rechtskundig Weekblad*, the *Journal de Tribunaux* and the *Tijdschrift voor Belgisch Handelsrecht.*

United Kingdom: P. Kaye, *Civil Jurisdiction and Enforcement of Foreign Judgments*, Professional Books Limited, Abingdon 1987. Dicey and Morris, *The Conflicts of Laws*, 12th ed. gen. ed. L. Collins, London, Sweet and Maxwell, 1993 and the supplement 1995. Cheshire and North, *Private International Law*, 12th ed. by North, P.M. and J.J. Fawcett, Butterworths, London, 1992.

The judgments of the European Court of Justice are published in the All E.R. and in the Common Market Law Reports.

Italy: F. Pocar, *La convenzione di Bruxelles sulla giurisdizione e l'esecuzione delle sentenze*, (Giuffrè) Milano 1995^3. F. Carpi - M. Taruffo, *Commentario breve al Codice di procedura civile*, Appendici I-II (*Convenzioni di Bruxelles e di Lugano*), a cura di Michele Angelo Lupoi, (Cedam) Padova 1994^3 (*Breviaria Iuris*, a cura di G. Gian e A. Trabucchi).

The judgments of the European Court are published and commented on in *Il Foro Italiano.*

3.1.4. UNIFORM INTERPRETATION OF THE BRUSSELS CONVENTION

In order to guarantee the uniform interpretation of the Brussels Convention, the Convention is accompanied by a Protocol on its interpretation. This Protocol states that the European Court of Justice shall have jurisdiction to interpret the provisions of the Brussels Convention. The system used in the Protocol deviates in some aspects from the procedure provided in art. 177 of the Treaty of Rome. The highest judicial courts in the Member States are under an obligation to request the European Court of Justice to provide an interpretation of the Convention should this be necessary for the settlement of a dispute (art. 2(1) Protocol) and the lower courts may do this if they adjudicate on appeal (art. 2(2) Protocol). The court mentioned in art. 37 Brussels Convention may also ask the European Court of Justice for a preliminary ruling (art. 2(3) Protocol).

The Protocol on interpretation was concluded in Luxembourg on 3 June 1971 and came into force on 1 September 1975 between the original six Member States of the European Community. Later the Protocol also came into force for the Member States newly acceded to the Brussels Convention (the latest ones being Spain on 1 February 1991 and Portugal on 1 June 1992). The European Court of Justice has jurisdiction for preliminary rulings with respect to the Brussels Convention and all Conventions on Accession (1978, 1982, 1989).

The decisions of the Court are of an imperative nature, not merely advisory. The Court has no jurisdiction if the Brussels Convention provisions are used in a national matter to demarcate the jurisdiction between the different parts of the United Kingdom (ECJ 28 March 1995, Case 346/93 (*Kleinwort Benson Ltd* v. *City of Glasgow District Council*), not yet published)).

3.1.5. THE LUGANO CONVENTION

International jurisdiction, recognition and enforcement in civil and commercial matters is developing strongly in the sphere of harmonisation, which movement also takes it outside the EU territory. On 16 September 1988 the Convention on Jurisdiction and the Enforcement of Judgments in Civil and Commercial Matters was concluded in Lugano between the Member States of the EC and of the EFTA (European Free Trade Association).

In 1988 the EFTA Member States were: Finland, Norway, Austria, Iceland, Sweden, Switzerland (and Liechtenstein, but this country has not signed the Lugano Convention). Finland, Austria and Sweden acceded to the EU as per 1 January 1995 and are therefore no longer EFTA Member States. The text of the Lugano Convention is practically identical to the text of the Brussels Convention, which is why the Lugano Convention is also called the 'parallel convention'. In contrast to the Brussels Convention the Lugano Convention is also open to accession by states which are not EU or EFTA Member States.

The Lugano Convention came into force on 1 January 1992 for Switzerland, the Kingdom of the Netherlands (for the Netherlands) and France. Subsequently on 1 February 1992 for Luxembourg, on 1 May 1992 for the United Kingdom, on 1 July 1992 for Portugal, on 1 December 1992 for Italy, on 1 January 1993 for Sweden, on 1 May 1993 for Norway, on 1 July 1993 for Finland, on 1 December 1993 for the Republic of Ireland, on 1 November 1994 for Spain and on 1 March 1995 for Germany. From the EFTA group Austria and Iceland have not joined yet and the same goes for Belgium, Denmark and Greece from the EU group (as per 1 September 1995).

The Lugano Convention needs to be discussed in this book, because for the EU Member States the Lugano Convention, too, must be regarded as an important international procedural instrument within the framework of jurisdiction and recognition of judgments. The Lugano and the Brussels Convention have been drawn up in the same spirit and judicial decisions on both conventions will certainly influence each other. The authors of the Lugano

Convention acknowledged the rivalry between the Lugano and the Brussels Convention in case the Brussels Convention Contracting States should also accede to the Lugano Convention. In art. 54B Lugano Convention rules have been provided for an adjustment between both conventions. In principle, the relationship amongst the Brussels Convention States will remain unaffected, but the Lugano Convention will impose itself when, for example, disputed immovable property is located in a Lugano Convention State. These rules could be applied analogously to cases in which a Brussels Convention court is confronted with two versions of the Convention.

The uniform interpretation of the Lugano Convention cannot be ensured by a preliminary ruling from the European Court of Justice, since no members from EFTA countries have been allowed to take a place on the Court. However, the EFTA countries have indicated in a declaration included in the Lugano Convention that their courts will take into account case law of the European Court of Justice concerning the Brussels Convention. The EU Member States in turn have declared that the European Court of Justice will take into account case law in Lugano Convention countries concerning the Lugano Convention. In art. 1 of the Second Protocol the Lugano Convention Contracting States are obliged to take into account the principles which have been enunciated in relevant decisions concerning the Convention which have been given in different Contracting States.

3.1.6. LITERATURE

The explanatory report on the Lugano Convention is the Jenard/Möller report, OJ 1990 189/57-121 of 28 July 1990. The literature mentioned in section 3.1.3 also provides information on the Lugano Convention. For the Netherlands we may add P. Vlas, loose-leaf edition Burg. Rv., volume Verdragen, EVEX. For the English-speaking regions the 1989 Brussels Convention and the Lugano Convention are discussed in the book *The Lugano and San Sebastian Conventions*, M. Carpenter, M. Haymann, T. Hunter-Tilney, P. Volken, Butterworths, London, 1990.

3.1.7. FREE MOVEMENT OF JUDGMENTS: AN ASSET!

The idea behind these conventions is that within the entire territory of the EU and the EFTA there will be a simple way to recognise and enforce judgments of the national courts. Conditions for such a procedure may be created in several ways. The authors of the Brussels Convention (and those of the Lugano

Convention) have chosen a system whereby there is minimal examination, only allowed in specific situations, of the jurisdiction of the court which has given the judgment whose recognition or enforcement is sought (art. 28 Brussels Convention). Any formal examination, too, (e.g. whether the defendant was summoned in time, whether the decision is irreconcilable with a previous judgment given in the State in which recognition is sought) is limited to a minimum (art. 27 Brussels Convention). To warrant this confidence in each other's judicial systems, a procedure had to be found which guaranteed an identical approach by the national courts to an international case. For that purpose direct attribution of jurisdiction has been included in Title II of the Brussels Convention. The most important change with respect to international procedural rules of law, as existing in national systems, is the exclusion of exorbitant forums (an enumeration may be found in art. 3 Brussels Convention). This means that the Dutch art. 126(3) Rv. (*forum actoris*) is not a valid ground for jurisdiction when the defendant is domiciled within the EU. Invalidity is also the fate of French (and Luxembourg) arts. 14 and 15 CC, which provide that a Frenchman (regardless of his domicile) can summon anyone to appear before a French court or can be summoned by anyone to appear before a French court, and of German §23 ZPO, which gives the German court jurisdiction if there are properties located within its jurisdiction.

In Belgium art. 15 BW and art. 638 Ger.W./CJ no longer apply. In Italy art. 2 CPC (restrictions on the choice of forum for a non-Italian court) and art. 4, paras. 1 and 2 CPC apply. In England all jurisdiction provisions are ineffective which are based on attribution of jurisdiction on the grounds of (a) the circumstance that the writ commencing the action is served upon or notified to the defendant temporarily residing in England; (b) the presence of property belonging to the defendant in England; or (c) attachment by the plaintiff of property located in England.

3.1.8. RULES OF JURISDICTION IN OTHER CONVENTIONS THAN THE BRUSSELS CONVENTION

The Brussels Convention does not regulate jurisdiction, recognition and enforcement in the entire area of civil and commercial law. Subjects falling outside it (*see* section 3.2.1) have sometimes been provided for in bilateral conventions (always older than the Brussels Convention; for the scope of the Convention, however, they are rendered inoperative under arts. 55 and 56 Brussels Convention) and sometimes in conventions also accessible to non-EU Members. In this connection one may think of conventions in the area of transport law and family law. The Brussels Convention provides in art. 57 that it shall not affect the application of any special conventions governing jurisdiction and/or recognition and enforcement which (also) relate to the scope of the Brussels Convention. In this connection one may think of the Convention on the contract for the International Carriage of Goods by Road (CMR) and of the Hague Maintenance Enforcement Convention 1973.

The literature is divided over the question which convention prevails when the special convention also stipulates that other conventions shall remain unaffected. It has been argued that the particular prevails over the general, but a citizen shall retain the right to rely on the convention which provides a more favourable solution for him. The system of various conventions being used simultaneously has been rejected. According to the literature, an exception to this rule could apply if the convention chosen in the first instance does not contain a complete arrangement. This view was recently confirmed by the Court of Justice in the decision *Cargo-owners of cargo on board vessel Tatry* v. *owners vessel Maciej Rataj* (ECJ 6 December 1994, Case 406/92, [1995] ECR 5439 (Tatry); Lloyd's Maritime and Commercial Law Quarterly 1995, p. 161 note Briggs; *see* sections 3.2.15 and 3.4.2).

3.1.9. THE BRUSSELS CONVENTION

Since the Brussels Convention may be regarded as the most important convention concerning international jurisdiction, recognition and enforcement, the remainder of the chapter on international procedural rules of law will only deal with this convention. The system of the Convention will be discussed in brief, regarding both jurisdiction and recognition and enforcement. For the purpose of the rules of jurisdiction in the Convention a diagram has been included at the end of this chapter, which shows in which sequence the court must apply the Brussels Convention. In addition, diagrams have been included representing the system of recognition and enforcement under the Brussels Convention.

It should be noted that the interpretation of the convention is streamlined in all Brussels Convention States as a result of the relevant jurisdiction of the European Court of Justice. In those cases in which the European Court of Justice has not yet given a judgment, the courts will be obliged to interpret in accordance with the objectives of the convention rather than holding on to domestic procedural viewpoints. Anything set out hereafter about the Brussels Convention applies to all Contracting States. Only inasmuch as the

Brussels Convention leaves matters to the Contracting States will there be room for domestic law.

The following will be based upon the San Sebastian version of the Brussels Convention. Whenever the previous version, Brussels Convention 1982 (virtually identical to the version of 1978) deviates, this will be indicated. In view of the close relationship between the Lugano Convention and the Brussels Convention, any deviations of the Lugano Convention in respect of the Brussels Convention will also be touched upon.

3.2. Jurisdiction

3.2.1. SCOPE OF THE BRUSSELS CONVENTION

Article 1 Brussels Convention provides that the Convention shall apply in civil and commercial matters whatever the nature of the court or tribunal by which these matters are heard. According to the European Court of Justice the term *civil and commercial matters* shall be explained autonomously in the light of the objectives of the Convention. The Court decided in its judgment *Sonntag* v. *Waidmann* (ECR 21 April 1993, Case 172/91 [1993] ECR 1963, NILR 1994, p. 333 note Vlas; IPRax 1994/1, p. 10 note Heß, Rev. Crit. 1994, p. 96 note Gaudemet-Tallon) that a claim for damages filed by a private person in a criminal court against a teacher in a state school, who during a school trip owing to wrongful and culpable neglect of his duties as supervisor caused damage to a pupil, falls within the Brussels Convention. This also applies if rules of public law can be relied upon. A teacher in a state school is not a government body acting in the discharge of government power.

Excluded from the scope shall be (*sub* 1) the status or legal capacity of natural persons, the rights in property arising out of a matrimonial relationship, wills and intestacy (however, claims of maintenance do come under the convention); (*sub* 2) bankruptcy, composition and analogous proceedings (claims not resulting directly from the bankruptcy but directly related to it also do not fall under the Brussels Convention); (*sub* 3) social security; and (*sub* 4) arbitration. In the case *Rich* v. *Impianti* (ECJ 25 July 1991, Case 190/89, [1991] ECR 3855) the European Court has pronounced judgment on the significance of art. 1(4) Brussels Convention concerning arbitration. It decided that proceedings before a national court concerning the appointment of an arbitrator fall outside the scope of the Brussels Convention by virtue of art. 1(4).

3.2.2. MAIN RULE: *FORUM REI*

The main rule of the Brussels Convention is that anybody who is domiciled in the Convention's territory can only be sued in the courts of the State in which he is domiciled. There are several exceptions to this concept of protection of the defendant, which will be discussed later.

It has to be determined whether the domicile of the defendant or the seat of a legal person is situated in one of the Contracting States (art. 2 Brussels Convention). In order to determine the domicile, the court shall apply the domestic law of the Contracting State in which this domicile is situated (art. 52 (1) Brussels Convention).

In the Netherlands art. 1:10(1) BW applies; in Belgium arts. 102-111 BW; in France art. 43 NCPC; in Germany §13 ZPO; in Italy arts. 2505 and 2509 CC and in England s. 41 Civil Jurisdiction and Judgments Act 1982. In Luxembourg the domicile of a natural person is the place of his principal establishment.

In order to determine the seat of a legal person, however, the court shall apply its rules of private international law (art. 53(1) second sentence Brussels Convention). The rule of private international law applicable in the Netherlands is based on the Act of 25 July 1959, Stb. 1959, 256, concerning the execution of the Convention on the recognition of the legal personality of foreign companies, associations and foundations (The Hague, 1 June 1956, Trb. 1956, 131; did not enter into force). This Act on enforcement, which has come into force, provides that the Netherlands is not a country which honours the system of the actual place of business (the 'siège réel' or effective or actual seat as being the administrative centre of the company). Reasoning *a contrario* leads to the conclusion that the Netherlands adheres to the system of the registered office (statutory seat). One of the consequences of this is that in the Netherlands the place where the registered office is, determines where a legal person is based, irrespective of the place of actual business or management (this is confirmed in the Netherlands Wetsvoorstel Conflictenrecht Corporaties, TK 1994-1995, 24 141).

In Belgium, however, the court uses the place where the actual seat of the legal person is situated; this is also true in France, Luxembourg and Germany. In England there is no workable rule to satisfy the concept of seat. For the Brussels Convention special rules, adapted to continental concepts, have been included in s. 42(2) Civil Jurisdiction and Judgments Act 1982. A legal person has its seat (and pursuant to art. 53 in conjunction with art. 2 Brussels Convention, its domicile) in England if it has been incorporated or formed under English law and has its *registered office* or any other official address in England or if its management (the actual seat) is exercised in England (s.

42(3)). Italy uses the statutory seat doctrine for Italian companies (art. 2509 CC) and the actual seat doctrine for foreign companies (art. 2505 CC).

Article 3 Brussels Convention excludes the application of exorbitant rules of jurisdiction by the Contracting States in the case where a person has his domicile in the Convention's territory (*see* section 3.1.7).

3.2.3. DOMICILE OUTSIDE BRUSSELS CONVENTION TERRITORY

If the defendant is not domiciled in a Contracting State, art. 4 Brussels Convention applies. This article refers to the domestic procedural rules of law of the Contracting States to determine jurisdiction. Exorbitant forums shall regain their effect in respect of persons domiciled outside the Convention's territory. It must be noted that there are certain rules of jurisdiction in the Convention whose application does not depend upon whether or not a person is domiciled in a Contracting State.

3.2.4. SPECIAL JURISDICTION

If a person is domiciled within Brussels Convention territory, he may be sued, at the plaintiff's choice, either before the courts of the State of his domicile or before a court which has jurisdiction pursuant to art. 5 or 6 Brussels Convention, inasmuch as these provisions lead to jurisdiction of courts in *another* Contracting State than the one designated by art. 2.

A special feature of these rules is that the competent court is directly appointed and not merely the country whose courts are competent, according to national criteria. The alternative jurisdictions rules cut right across national procedural rules of law.

3.2.5. JURISDICTION IN MATTERS RELATING TO A CONTRACT

Article 5(1) provides that in matters relating to a contract a defendant *may* be sued 'in the courts for the place of performance of the obligation in question. In matters relating to individual contracts of employment, this place is that where the employee habitually carries out his work, or if the employee does not habitually carry out his work in any one country, the *employer* may also be sued in the courts for the place where the business which engaged the employee was or is now situated'.

Article 5(1) contains rules for two kinds of cases. On the one hand, the jurisdiction in disputes arising from contracts of employment (and other contracts relating to employment) is regulated. On the other hand, jurisdiction is provided for all other contracts. In a series of decisions the Court of Justice has solved various points in question. Part of this case law only matters to the 1982 Brussels Convention. For a relevant discussion the reader is referred to the handbooks mentioned in sections 3.1.3 and 3.1.5.1.

In various decisions the Court has decided that the term 'contracts' in art. 5(1) must be interpreted autonomously. In its decision on the case *Handte* v. *TMCS*, the Court determined that art. 5(1) does not apply to a dispute between a subsequent purchaser and the manufacturer, who is not the seller, in respect of defects in the purchased good or its unsuitability for the purpose for which it was intended. The manufacturer cannot anticipate jurisdiction on the ground of art. 5(1), since he does not know who the buyer is and where the buyer acquired the product, so the ground of jurisdiction conflicts with the principle of legal security, according to the Court (ECJ 17 June 1992, Case 26/91, [1992] ECR I-3697, TVVS 1993/9, p. 248 note Vlas; NILR 1993, p. 497 note Vlas; Rev. crit. 1993, p. 485 note Gaudemet-Tallon). Hereby the Court rejects qualification pursuant to the applicable French law, under which the relationship would have been qualified as contractual.

Even if the existence of the obligation is in dispute, art. 5(1) can apply.

a. Contracts (excluding contracts of employment)

The defendant who is domiciled in a Contracting State can be sued in a court in *another* Contracting State if the place of performance of the obligation in question is situated within the territorial jurisdiction of the relevant court. Defendants domiciled in Luxembourg can refuse to submit to this jurisdiction pursuant to art. I of the Protocol annexed to the Brussels Convention and art. I of Protocol No. 1 annexed to the Lugano Convention.

The first question to arise is what the obligation in question is. In *De Bloos* v. *Bouyer* (ECJ 6 October 1976, Case 14/76) it was decided that this is the contractual obligation which forms the basis of the legal proceedings (the 1978 Brussels Convention has been amended in conformity with this decision and now the text explicitly mentions the obligation *in question*). If the seller wants to obtain payment, the payment will be the obligation in question. If the buyer demands performance of the delivery, or even compensation for damages on account of defective delivery, the delivery will be the obligation in question. In a dispute about the consequences of the violation of an exclusive distribution agreement by the grantor of a franchise, such as payment of damages or rescission of the agreement, the obligation in question consists of the obligation arising out of the contract on the part of the grantor, which consists of his enabling the franchisee to perform his obligations arising from the contract (*De Bloos* v. *Bouyer*).

Once the obligation in question has been established, the place of performance of this obligation will have to be found. Where must payment be made? Where must delivery take place? In 1976 the Court ruled that the court before which the matter is brought must determine the place of performance of the contractual obligation according to the rules of the law which governs the contract in question as determined by its own rules of private international law (ECJ 6 October 1976, Case 12/76, *Tessili* v. *Dunlop*). In the decision *Custom Made* v. *Stawa* (ECJ 29 June 1994, Case 288/92, [1994] ECR I-2913, NJ 1995, 221, TVVS 95/2, p. 54 note Vlas; Rev. crit. 1994, p. 696 note Gaudemet-Tallon; IPRax 1995/1, p. 13 note Jayme) the Court reiterated this view, even if the applicable law should not be a domestic legal system, but uniform law (such as the United Nations Convention on the International Sale of Goods (CISG) (Vienna 11 April 1980, Trb. 1981, 184; entry into force in the Netherlands on 1 January 1992). In *Custom Made* v. *Stawa* the precursor of the CISG, the Hague Uniform Sales Law, applied, but this does not detract from the principle. The CISG contains provisions determining both the place of delivery and the place of payment. In *Custom Made* v. *Stawa* the Court emphatically refused to review any connection between the dispute and the place of performance. To justify this refusal, the Court argued that, although such a connection had indeed been the underlying idea of art. 5(1), the literal text of art. 5(1) did not prescribe an actual review. In practice art. 5(1) will often lead to the *forum actoris*, the courts of the country where the plaintiff is domiciled.

The Court has also sanctioned arrangements of parties whereby they had in their contract determined the place of performance of the various obligations arising from it. The contract may stipulate that payment shall be made at a bank in Rotterdam and that delivery shall be performed at the building site. The Court has ruled that these clauses, which are veiled choice of forum clauses, do not need to satisfy the strict requirements of being in writing or evidenced in writing which are set for the choice of forum clause pursuant to art. 17 (ECJ 17 January 1980, Case 56/79 *Zelger* v. *Salinitri I*).

It happens frequently that there are two or more obligations in question. How must art. 5(1) then be applied? The Court of Justice ruled that in such a case the main obligation in question is the one which determines the forum. The other obligations follow from it and thus all obligations in question can be concentrated in one court (ECJ 15 January 1987, Case 266/85 *Shenavai* v. *Kreischer*).

b. Contracts of employment

The defendant (being the employer or employee) who is domiciled in a Contracting State can be sued in another Contracting State than the State of his domicile in the court of the place where the employee habitually carries out his work. If the work is performed in more than one State, the employee may turn to the second level of jurisdiction in art. 5(1). The employer may not invoke this jurisdiction. The second level of art. 5(1) indicates that the employee can turn to the court for the place of the business which engaged the employee. This forum may be important if this place of business is different from the place of business considered for art. 2 and if, in addition, art. 5(5) (branch) does not apply because the work is not performed for the benefit of the business which engaged the employee (*see* section 3.2.8). Article 5(1), second level, also applies if the performance of work within the Convention's territory is limited to one country, but work is also performed in one or more countries outside its territory. Even if the work is performed completely outside the territory of the Convention, and stretches over more countries, the second level of jurisdiction under art. 5(1) may be used by the employee. The purpose of art. 5(1) is to give as much protection as possible to the employee, who is regarded as the weaker party. Article 5(1) creates a number of options enabling the employee to institute legal proceedings in the country with which he is familiar through his domicile and/or place of work.

With respect to contracts of employment art. 5(1) uses a different approach than with respect to the other contracts if there are two or more obligations in question. In case of contracts of employment it does not matter what obligations are in question. The place where the employment is carried out or the place of the business which engaged the employee (only for plaintiff-employee) are available, irrespective of the number and nature of the obligations in question.

The current provision concerning contracts of employment did not yet occur in the 1982 Brussels Convention. The reason for including such a rule was the development in case law which art. 5(1) underwent with regard to contracts of employment. In *Ivenel* v. *Schwab* (ECJ 26 May 1982, Case 133/81), *Shenavai* v. *Kreischer* (ECJ 15 January 1987, Case 266/85), *Six Constructions* v. *Humbert* (ECJ 15 February 1989, Case 32/88) and *Mulox* v. *Geels* (ECJ 13 July 1993, Case 125/92, [1993] ECR 4075, TVVS 1995/1, p. 23 note Vlas; Rev. crit. 1994, p. 596 note Lagarde) art. 5 has been interpreted by the Court. Even in the last of these decisions, which was made after the text of the Lugano Convention was known, the Court did not anticipate art. 5(1) Lugano Convention, but gave an independent derogating rule.

The wording of art. 5(1) in the Lugano Convention differs from that in the Brussels Convention. If the employee does not habitually carry out his work in any one country, the forum which applies in addition to the one in the place where the employment is carried out, is the forum in the place of the business through which the employee was engaged (as in the Brussels Convention), but pursuant to the Lugano Convention both the employee and the employer can turn to this forum.

3.2.6. MAINTENANCE OBLIGATIONS

Although maintenance obligations have to do with the matrimonial relationship which is excluded in art. 1, they do come under the Brussels Convention. A separate provision has been included in art. 5(2) apart from art. 2. In addition to the courts of the defendant's own State, there is special jurisdiction for the courts of the place where the maintenance creditor is domiciled or habitually resident, or for the courts judging the divorce if the alimony is ancillary to the proceedings, unless that jurisdiction is based solely on the nationality of one of the parties. In the Netherlands this is never the case. Article 814(1) Rv bases jurisdiction on the Dutch nationality of *both* parties, or on the nationality of one of the parties in conjunction with a domicile requirement. In Belgium this problem cannot occur either. Article 628, 1° Ger.W./CJ does not attribute jurisdiction solely on the basis of the fact that one of the parties is a Belgian national. Jurisdiction of the English courts with respect to divorce is found in the Matrimonial and Family Proceedings Act 1973 (as amended by the Matrimonial and Family Proceedings Act 1984) s. 5 and is not based on the nationality of one of the parties. In the case of a French divorce, however, this condition can play a part. The jurisdiction of the French and Luxembourg divorce court may be derived from art. 14 CC, according to which only one party needs to be a French or Luxembourg national. In Germany, too, the jurisdiction of the court can be based on the sole German nationality of one of the spouses according to §606a(1), sub 1 ZPO. The same goes for Italy, where jurisdiction, apart from other grounds, may be derived from art. 32 (§1) of the Act of 17 May 1995, number 218.This article gives jurisdiction to the Italian court when at least one of the spouses is an Italian national, or when the marriage was concluded in Italy.

3.2.7. TORT, DELICT OR QUASI-DELICT

A person domiciled in a Contracting State may be sued in another Contracting State in matters relating to tort, delict or quasi-delict, if 'the place where the harmful event occurred' is situated in that country (art. 5(3)). Whether an action is 'related to tort, delict or quasi-delict' must be determined under the community meaning of the Convention, according to the judgment of the European Court of Justice in *Kalfelis* v. *Schröder* (ECJ 27 September 1988, Case 189/87): it must concern an action which seeks to establish the liability of a defendant and which does not form part of a contractual obligation within the meaning of art. 5(1). In the same judgment it was also decided that the court which has jurisdiction under art. 5(3) in a matter relating to tort, delict or quasi-delict does not also have jurisdiction in respect of other aspects of that action which have a different legal basis (e.g. actions resulting from a contract).

The controversial question as to what exactly is the *locus delicti* (i.e. the place where the 'harmful' event occurred) was answered by the European Court of Justice in 1976 for the special case of cross-border water pollution. In the *Reinwater* judgment (also known as the *Mines de Potasse* judgment) (ECJ 30 November 1976, Case 21/76) the Court interpreted this concept in favour of the plaintiff in such a way that both the place of the 'event giving rise to it' and the place 'where the damage occurred' apply. The plaintiff has a choice, if these places are not identical, to sue in the courts of either of those places.

The place where the damage occurred can only be interpreted as the place where the tort or delict had direct harmful consequences for the person directly affected. The place where indirect financial losses have been suffered by an indirect victim cannot be accepted as a place granting jurisdiction according to a judgment of the European Court of Justice in *Dumez* v. *Hessische Landesbank* (ECJ 11 January 1990, Case 220/88). In *Marinari* v. *Lloyd's Bank plc* (ECJ 19 September 1995, Case 364/93, not yet published) the Court ruled that art. 5(3) does not lead to the place where the direct victim suffers financial losses as a result of damage that has occurred in another State.

Another recent judgment of the Court concerned an action for libel, injury to the reputation of a natural person (ECJ 7 March 1995, Case 68/93, (*Shevill* v. *Presse Alliance*), not yet published). Mrs. Shevill had in a publication in the France-Soir been mentioned in such a way that it seemed as if, together with the exchange office also mentioned, she was involved in a network of dealers in drugs and engaged in laundering drug money. The publication was circulated by the French publisher Presse Alliance. The majority of the edition (230,000) appeared in France, a small part in England (230) and 15,000 copies in other countries. Shevill claimed damages before the English court which she deemed to have jurisdiction for the entire damages pursuant to art. 5(3). In Dumez the Court had drawn very sharp limits, but in this judgment the Court holds the view that the principles of the Mines de Potasse judgment can be applied to compensation for non-physical damage in case of defamation of a natural person by a publication. In such a case the place of the event giving rise to damage is the place where the publisher of the publication involved has his seat, inasmuch as this is the place from where the harmful event originates and from where the defamation has been expressed and spread. In the Shevill judgment this would have led to the French court having jurisdiction. In a case of defamation by the press, the places where the harm becomes manifest are those places where the publication is circulated, and where the victim alleges that his reputation has been damaged. The Court restricts this broad interpretation by ruling that the forum State only has jurisdiction for the harm which has occurred within its territory. This means that the English court can only award damages for any harm which has occurred in England, not for harm which has been suffered in France or somewhere else. There is a risk that different courts judge differently, but the plaintiff can overcome this problem by concentrating the claim before the court of the publisher, or of another defendant.

3.2.8. BRANCH

Article 5(5) Brussels Convention provides that, in respect of disputes arising out of the operations of a branch, agency or other establishment, the court of the place in which they are situated has jurisdiction. A decision on the interpretation of the term 'branch' was given by the Court in *Somafer* v. *Saar-Ferngas* (ECJ 22 November 1978, Case 33/78). The concept of branch, agency or other establishment 'implies a place of business which has an appearance of permanency as an extension of a parent body, with its own management and equipment so that it can negotiate business with third parties whereby the third party, although knowing that there may be a legal relationship with the parent body situated abroad, does not have to deal directly with the parent body but may transact business at the place of business which forms an extension'. In *Blanckaert* v. *Frost* (ECJ 18 March 1981, Case 139/80) it was added that the foreign parent body must have control of the establishment. Thus, establishments of a commercial agency or a distributor are not establishments or agencies in the sense of art. 5(5). The concept of 'operations' implies that it must concern disputes relating to the actual management of the branch and disputes relating to business entered into by the branch in favour of its mother company. The business does not have to be performed in the Contracting State where the branch is established (ECJ 6 April 1995, Case 439/93 (*Lloyd's Register of Shipping* v. *Campenon Bernard*), not yet published).

The Court has interpreted art. 5(5) quite broadly in the judgment *Schotte* v. *Rothschild* (ECJ 9 December 1987, Case 218/86). In this case the Court decided that the parent company in certain circumstances could be considered as a branch of the subsidiary company.

3.2.9. THE OTHER PARAGRAPHS OF ART. 5 BRUSSELS CONVENTION

Article 5(4) grants jurisdiction to the courts when a civil claim for damages is filed against a person against whom criminal proceedings have been instituted in respect of the same matter. The court before which the criminal proceedings are heard has jurisdiction, provided the relevant Contracting State's own law permits this joinder. This was the case in the decision *Sonntag* v. *Waidmann* (section 3.2.1), where the parents of the pupil who was killed, instituted civil proceedings before the Italian court which heard the criminal proceedings against the teacher, although both parties were domiciled in Germany.

Article 5(6) provides rules of jurisdiction in the case of a dispute regarding a trust. If the defendant is a settlor, trustee or beneficiary of the trust domiciled in the Convention's territory, the place in which the trust has its domicile determines the jurisdiction. According to art. 53 Brussels Convention the court shall determine where the trust is domiciled by applying its own rules of private international law. The countries from continental jurisdictions, where trusts are unknown, may find help in the Convention on the law applicable to trusts and on their recognition, The Hague 1985 (entered into force on 1 January 1992 for Australia, the United Kingdom and Italy; on 1 January 1993 for Canada and on 1 February for the Kingdom of the Netherlands (only for the Netherlands)).

Article 5(7) provides rules for special jurisdiction in addition to art. 2 in case of a dispute concerning the payment of a remuneration claimed in respect of the salvage of a cargo or freight. In such a case, jurisdiction is based on the place of attachment (*forum arresti*).

3.2.10. ARTICLE 6 BRUSSELS CONVENTION

Formal special grounds of jurisdiction may be found in art. 6. When there is a number of defendants, they may all be sued in the courts of the place where any one of them is *domiciled* (art. 6(1)), provided the various claims against the different defendants are connected in such a way that it is expedient to determine these claims together, according to the European Court of Justice in *Kalfelis* v. *Schröder* (ECJ 27 September 1988, Case 189/87).

In the case of a third party in an action on a warranty or guarantee or in any other third party proceedings, the court seized of the original proceedings has jurisdiction (art. 6(2)). Here a role is reserved for national procedural rules of law. We refer the reader to sections 3.4 of the chapters dealing with the procedural rules of law of separate countries. The European Court of Justice decided in *Kongress Agentur Hagen* v. *Zeehaghe BV* (ECJ 15 May 1990, Case 365/88) that national procedural rules determine the form and the time requirements in the cases referred to in art. 6(2) Brussels Convention, since article 6(2) too merely attributes jurisdiction. The Court did indicate that the national rules should not impair the principles of the Convention. It is not permitted to refuse third party proceedings merely on the ground that the third party resides or is domiciled in a Contracting State other than that of the court before which the original proceedings are heard and that this action may cause procedural delay.

In case of a counterclaim arising out of the same contract or facts on which the original claim was based, the court before which the original claim is pending has jurisdiction (art. 6(3)). The Court of Justice recently held that art. 6(3) does not cover counterclaims for set-offs. Article 6(3) is solely meant to cover counterclaims intended to obtain a separate judgment against the plaintiff. If the counterclaim is only raised as a defence, art. 6(3) is not applicable (ECJ 13 July 1995, Case 341/93, *Danvaeru* v. *Otterbeck*, not yet published).

Article 6(4) grants the court of the country in which the immovable property is situated (which has exclusive jurisdiction; *see* section 3.2.12) jurisdiction also in respect of a claim arising out of a contract relating to that property which may be combined with an action relating to rights *in rem* in that immovable property. Under the 1982 Brussels Convention such an action could quite often not be brought before the courts of the place where the immovable property was situated. Indeed, the defendant may be domiciled in a State other than the one in which the immovable property is located, which means that art. 2 designates a different country from art. 16. The place of performance of the obligation in question (art. 5(1)) does not need to coincide with the country in which the immovable property is situated either. Under the 1989 Brussels Convention the proceedings relating to rights *in rem* and proceedings relating to a contract may be concentrated before the same court, the court of art. 16(1).

3.2.11. JURISDICTION IN MATTERS RELATING TO INSURANCE AND CONSUMER CONTRACTS

In respect of a number of subjects the Brussels Convention has laid down the jurisdiction quasi-imperatively (under certain conditions parties may deviate from this jurisdiction by choosing a forum). As regards insurance cases and consumer contracts the underlying idea has been the protection of the weaker party.

The jurisdiction regarding disputes in insurance cases has been regulated imperatively in arts. 7-12A Brussels Convention. Article 4 (defendant domiciled outside a Contracting State) and art. 5(5) (branch) remain operative in addition to these articles. The basic idea is the protection of the defendant, not being the insurer. The defendant (policy-holder, insured or beneficiary) may therefore only be sued in the courts of the place where he is domiciled. A choice of forum can only appoint another court under special circumstances (art. 12). The insurer may be sued in the courts of the State where he is domiciled, and also in the courts of the State where the policy-holder is domiciled (art. 8). If the insurer is domiciled outside the Brussels Convention territory but does have a branch, agency or other establishment in one of the Contracting States, he shall, in disputes arising out of the operations of the branch, be deemed to be domiciled within the Convention's territory (art. 8). This is a derogation from art. 53 in conjunction with art. 4. *See Brenner and Noller* v. *Dean Witter Reynolds Inc.* (ECJ 15 September 1994, Case 318/93, [1994] ECR I-4275, TVVS 95/3 note Vlas), in which the Court held in respect of art. 13 (the counterpart of art. 8 in the section on consumer contracts) that the literal text had to be adhered to. The Court denounced a broader interpretation in favour of consumers (or insured). Article 4 is only disregarded if a defendant not domiciled in a Contracting State (usually governed by art. 4) has a branch or other establishment in a Contracting State and disputes arising out of the operations of that branch are concerned.

A similar system has been followed for consumer contracts. Consumer contracts under the Brussels Convention are contracts concluded by a person for a purpose which can be regarded as being outside his trade or profession and if it is a contract for the sale of goods on payment of instalments or for the financing of such a sale. Under certain conditions, other forms of supply of goods or services to consumers come under this article (art. 13 Brussels

Convention). In arts. 14 and 15 narrowly specified grounds are laid down for jurisdiction which are deemed to be favourable for the consumer. The idea is for the consumer to be able to sue in his own country. The advantage is that the costs will remain lower than when suing abroad and that proceedings can take place in the consumer's own language. With this end in view, the Court decided in the judgment *Shearson* v. *TVB* that a party which acts in its professional capacity and is therefore not a party itself in one of the consumer contracts mentioned in art. 13, cannot use the rules of jurisdiction laid down in the consumer section (ECJ 19 January 1993, Case 89/91, [1993] ECR 139, TVVS 1993/10 p. 275 note Vlas; NILR 1993, p. 501 note Vlas; Rev. crit. 1993, p. 320 note Gaudemet-Tallon; IPRax 1995/2, p. 71 note Koch).

Only if the consumer himself is a party to the contract and personally acts as a party in the proceedings, can the grounds of jurisdiction of arts. 14 and 15 be used. If the consumer transfers his claim, as had been the case, he loses his procedural protection.

3.2.12. EXCLUSIVE JURISDICTION; ART. 16 BRUSSELS CONVENTION

Article 16 Brussels Convention lays down rules for jurisdiction in respect of five subjects, including jurisdiction concerning immovable property and legal entities. The court seized of a claim shall examine of its own motion whether it has jurisdiction in respect of these matters (art. 19). For the subjects of art. 16 the idea was that the court appointed therein would be the appropriate court to judge the case, on account of the imperative law of *lex fori* often prevailing in these cases. In most cases this will lead to a '*Gleichlauf*' of the *lex fori* and the law applicable to the relationship.

A choice of forum (art. 17 (explicitly) or art. 18 (implicitly)) cannot be honoured if it contravenes jurisdiction based on art. 16.

a. Immovable property

Article 16(1a) appoints the courts of the country in which the immovable property is located as competent in proceedings which have as their object rights *in rem* in immovable property or tenancies of immovable property. The Court of Justice has recently decided twice on the scope of the concept of 'rights *in rem*'. In *Webb* v. *Webb* (ECJ 17 May 1994, Case 294/92, [1994] ECR I-1717, TVVS 95/3, p. 81 note Vlas; Rev. crit. 1995, p. 123 note Beraudo; Law Quarterly Review 1994, Vol. 110, p. 527 note Briggs) an action was brought by father Webb against son Webb for an order that the son should provide the necessary documents for and co-operate in the transfer of ownership of the holiday home in France. The house had at the time been purchased by the son with funds supplied by the father and the English judge held that there was a resulting trust. This meant that the son held the house in trust for the father, and could at a certain moment be forced to convey the home to the father. The Court, referring to its judgment in *Reichert I* (ECJ 10 January 1990, Case 115/88), stated that art. 16(1) only applied if the action was based on a right *in rem*. If the action is based on a right *in personam*, art. 16(1) does not apply, even if there is immovable property involved or if there is a link with immovable property (this is different in case of tenancies of immovable property). The Court subsequently established that father Webb did not claim that he already enjoyed rights to the property which he wanted to enforce against anyone (the characteristic of a right *in rem*), but that he only sought to assert his rights as against his son. The Court held that this constituted a right *in personam* and not an action *in rem* within the meaning of art. 16(1). Nor were considerations relating to the proper administration of justice underlying art. 16(1) applicable in this case. Indeed, the jurisdiction of the courts of the State in which the property is situated is justified, because actions concerning rights *in rem* in immovable property often involve checks, inquiries and expert assessments, for which this court is the most obvious choice.

The second decision, *Lieber* v. *Göbel* (ECJ 9 June 1994, Case 292/93, [1994] ECR I-2535, TVVS 95/4, p. 110 note Vlas; NILR 1994, p. 351 note Vlas; Rev. crit. 1995, p. 123 note Beraudo; IPRax 1995/2, p. 72 note Ulmer), was rendered one month later and also gives an interpretation of the concept 'rights *in rem*' in art. 16. The parties contended with each other on the question whether the court of the State where the apartment was situated, France, had exclusive jurisdiction in a claim for compensation for use of the apartment after the annulment of the transfer of ownership. The settlement had been declared void by the German court, yet the purchaser had already spent years in the apartment. The vendors claimed compensation for this use of the apartment - which later proved illegitimate. The Court decided that art. 16 was not applicable here. The vendor's claim for compensation for use could only be exercised against the purchaser, and thus constituted a right *in personam* and not a right *in rem*, at any rate where the purchaser did not dispute that the vendor had indeed remained the owner of the apartment. This was not disputed. In this case it was also attempted to range the constellation of facts under the concept of tenancies (16(1)), but the Court found that a tenancy relationship also involves rights and duties which are partly laid down in imperative domestic law, such as liability for maintenance and taxes. In the *Lieber* v. *Göbel* case this was out of the question.

The conclusion for art. 16 in respect of the term 'rights *in rem*' is that the courts of the State in which the property is situated have exclusive jurisdiction if the action is based on a right *in rem*. It is not sufficient that the claim has a link with a right *in rem* or with immovable property. This restriction of the scope is intended to protect the parties, who can pursuant to art. 16 be forced to bring proceedings outside their country of domicile. In addition, there is no choice of forum. Only actions tending to establish the size, the quality, the ownership or the possession of immovable property, and claims intended to guarantee rightful claimants protection of the powers connected with their title fall within the meaning of art. 16 (Reichert I). In such claims the locally imperative legislation and the property law system of the country where the property is situated are of crucial importance, which makes the local court eminently suited to judge the case.

Both judgments were made under an older version of the Brussels Convention, but the decisions are equally important to its present version.

Article 16(1.a) also attributes exclusive jurisdiction to the courts of the State where the property is situated if the dispute concerns tenancy. In *Lieber* v. *Göbel* (*see above*) the Court interpreted the term 'tenancy' in a strict sense. In the case of *Hacker* v. *Euro-Relais*, in which a private person, Hacker, domiciled in Germany, had booked a fully organised 2-week holiday in a holiday home with the travel organiser Euro-Relais, domiciled in Germany, the Court once again limited the scope of art. 16 Brussels Convention 1982 (ECJ 26 February 1992, Case 280/90, TVVS 1993/10, p. 277 note Vlas; NILR 1993, p. 505 note Vlas: Rev. crit. 1993, p. 74 note Droz; IPRax 1993/1, p. 18 note Jayme). Since the travel organiser had let the home, booked the travel arrangements, but was not the owner of the holiday home and charged the customer for the total package, this contract had to be regarded as a mixed contract, judged the Court. This meant that the courts of the country in which the holiday home was located, the Netherlands, did not have exclusive jurisdiction under art. 16 in respect of the claims of Hacker, which involved reduction in the cost of the holiday, damages for the cost of an extra room and damages for lost holiday enjoyment, because upon Hacker's arrival the holiday home turned out to be much smaller than had been promised, which, apart from her having been forced to rent a hotel room, resulted in the holiday being terminated prematurely by Hacker.

This judgment was also rendered under an older version of the Brussels Convention, but in this case, too, the decision is equally relevant to its present version. Pursuant to the present Brussels Convention the constellation of the facts would not lead to applicability of art. 16(1.b), because the proprietor is not a natural person (*see below*), so that the main rule of art. 16(1.a) applies, which is identical to the old art. 16.

Article 16(1.b) stipulates that in the case of tenancies of immovable property concluded for temporary private use for a maximum period of six consecutive months, the courts of the Contracting State in which the defendant is domiciled shall also have jurisdiction (i.e. as an alternative to art. 16(1.a)). However, the landlord and the tenant must be natural persons and must be domiciled in the same Contracting State. In fact such a dispute is an internal affair but for the fact that the foreign immovable property be abroad. Sub 1.b did not occur in the previous versions of the Brussels Convention. This addition in the 1989 Brussels Convention is the result of a judgment of the Court of Justice in the case *Rösler* v. *Rottwinkel* (ECJ 15 January 1985, Case 241/83) in which two Germans domiciled in Germany were forced to fight out their dispute concerning the holiday home in the country where it was situated, Italy. In addition, proceedings had to be instituted in Germany, since the Court decided that only disputes directly related to the use of the property let fell under the jurisdiction of the Italian courts. Compensation for loss of holiday enjoyment had to be obtained in a German court. The 1989 Brussels Convention requires that proprietor and tenant are domiciled in the same country and that both are natural persons. The Lugano Convention is less strict in this respect. Article 16(1.b) Lugano Convention only requires that the tenant is a natural person and that neither party is domiciled in the Contracting State in which the property is located (*see*, however, the French reservation under art. Iter Protocol to the Lugano Convention).

b. Legal persons

In respect of certain disputes relating to companies or other legal persons or associations of natural or legal persons, art. 16(2) appoints the courts of the Contracting State in which the company or other legal person or association is situated. The seat is determined by the court under its own rules of private international law (art. 53 Brussels Convention; *see* section 3.2.2). Theoretically two courts could decide they had exclusive jurisdiction if the actual seat and the registered seat are situated respectively in a country which applies the actual seat criterion and one which applies the registered seat criterion. Article 23 Brussels Convention provides for this. The court seized later in time shall decline jurisdiction.

c. Other paragraphs

Article 16(3) provides that in respect of proceedings which concern the validity of entries in public registers the courts of the Contracting State in which the register is kept shall have jurisdiction. Article 16(4) concerns the registration or validity of patents and the like. The courts of the Contracting State in which the deposit or registration has been applied for, shall have jurisdiction. Article 16(5) lays down rules relating to enforcement disputes. In these cases the courts of the state of enforcement have jurisdiction.

3.2.13. CHOICE OF FORUM

Under the Brussels Convention, parties are at liberty to choose a court in a Contracting State to have jurisdiction. The choice may be made in advance and will have to comply with the requirements of art. 17. If, however, lack of jurisdiction is not invoked before submitting a defence (although it is permissible to submit a conditional defence on points of substance), the parties thereby automatically grant jurisdiction to the court seized (without prejudice to art. 16). This is the implied choice of jurisdiction of art. 18 Brussels Convention. Parties can thus still deviate from a prior written choice of forum. It is not clear whether the defendant, or at least one of the parties, must be domiciled in a Contracting State in order for art. 18 to apply. If the parties appear, the court will – of its own motion – only need to test against art. 16. It does not seem to matter, then, where the parties are domiciled. It is, however, imperative that the dispute should be international and come within the scope of the Brussels Convention.

A prior agreement concerning the choice of the forum must take into account the restrictions laid down by arts. 12 and 15 (insurance and consumer contracts). A choice made in contravention of the courts exclusively appointed by art. 16 shall have no legal force.

Article 17 requires that one of the parties (plaintiff or defendant) is domiciled in a Contracting State. The agreement conferring jurisdiction must be in writing or in a form which is in accordance with practices established between the parties. If one of the parties is domiciled in Luxembourg, the choice of forum only applies if this person has expressly and specifically so agreed (Art. I, Protocol I Brussels Convention). In international commerce a form is valid which accords with usage, is widely known in international commerce, and is regularly observed by, parties to contracts of the type involved in the particular commerce concerned. This formulation is slightly different from the one in art. 17 1982 Brussels Convention. It appears from the judgment *Powell Duffryn* v. *Petereit* that the European Court of Justice considers a choice of a forum in the articles of a company to be within the scope of art. 17 (ECJ 10 March 1992, Case 214/89, TVVS 1993/11, p. 305 note Vlas; NILR 1993, p. 508 note Vlas; Rev. crit. 1993, p. 528 note Gaudemet-Tallon; IPRax 1993/1, p. 19 note Koch; Common Market Law Review

1993, p. 406 note Polak). The formal requirements laid down in art. 17 Brussels Convention must be deemed to be complied with in regard to any shareholder, if the clause conferring jurisdiction is contained in the articles of the company and those articles are lodged in a place to which the shareholder may have access or are contained in a public register, according to the Court. Whether a legal relationship has been sufficiently specified, will depend on the formulation of the clause conferring jurisdiction contained in the articles. Such legal relationship must be explainable as referring to the disputes between the company and its shareholders as such. The exact interpretation is left to the national court. However, such a clause conferring jurisdiction must not derogate from the jurisdiction under art. 16(2) Brussels Convention.

A special arrangement has been made for trusts and contracts of employment. For contracts of employment the conferring of jurisdiction is only effective if this was done after the dispute arose or if the employee invokes this in order to bring proceedings in other courts than those which he may choose under arts. 2 and 5(1) Brussels Convention. The second possibility does not exist under the Lugano Convention. These provisions did not occur in the 1982 Brussels Convention.

3.2.14. DEFENDANT DOES NOT ENTER AN APPEARANCE

If the defendant does not enter an appearance, the court must examine its jurisdiction under the Convention. If it cannot derive jurisdiction from the Convention, it must declare of its own motion that it has no jurisdiction (art. 20 Brussels Convention). Whether the defendant has been able to receive the document instituting the proceedings in sufficient time to enable him to arrange for his defence, must be established pursuant to art. 15 of The Hague Convention of 15 November 1965 on the service abroad of judicial and extrajudicial documents in civil or commercial matters, since the Netherlands, Belgium, Germany, France, Italy, Luxembourg and the United Kingdom are parties thereto (art. 20 Brussels Convention). Article 15 of this Convention provides that judgment shall not be given until it is established that -

a) the document instituting the proceedings was served by a method prescribed by the internal law of the State in which the defendant is domiciled;
b) the document was delivered to the defendant personally in another manner provided for in the Convention; or

c) the document was served by another method provided for by this Convention (arts. 2-10 of the Hague Convention of 15 November 1965).

As long as this has not been established, the court must of its own motion stay the proceedings.

3.2.15. *LIS PENDENS* AND RELATED ACTIONS

Articles 21-23 provide how the courts of different Contracting States may or shall act when there is litigation pending in several courts of different Contracting States. National procedural rules of law play an important part in this connection. The time at which proceedings have been brought is established by national procedural rules of law. In the Netherlands, according to the Supreme Court, the time at which the writ has been issued is decisive (*see* 8.4.2b). In England the Court of Appeal decided that for the application of arts. 21-23 the time of the service of the writ is decisive. In Luxembourg (*see* section 6.4.2b) it is the date of service of the writ if the case has been entered on the *rôle* of the court in time. France uses the moment when the writ is deposited at the Registry (art. 757 NCPC; section 5.4.2b). In Belgium proceedings have commenced on the date of the service of the writ if the case has been entered on the *rôle* in time (*see* section 7.4.2b). In Germany proceedings have commenced at the moment when the writ (*Klageschrift*) is issued (§ 253(1) ZPO; *see* section 9.4.2b). The same goes for Italy (*see* section 10.4.2b).

Where proceedings involving the same cause of action and between the same parties are brought in the courts of different Contracting States, any court other than the court first seized (i.e. the second court seized) must of its own motion stay its proceedings until such time as the jurisdiction of the court first seized is established (art. 21 Brussels Convention). In its judgment *Overseas Union Insurance Ltd* v. *New Hampshire Insurance Company* (ECJ 27 June 1991, Case 351/89) the European Court of Justice made some decisions on art. 21 Brussels Convention. Firstly, the Court decided that the domicile of the parties is irrelevant to the application of art. 21 Brussels Convention. In the judgment *Tatry* (*see below*) the Court has meanwhile held that if in the two actions pending the parties on either side are not exactly identical, the proceedings can be continued between the parties which do not participate in both proceedings. The reference then applies only to the parties that are litigating in both actions. Secondly, in *Overseas* v. *New Hampshire* the Court was of the opinion that the second court seized must not examine the jurisdiction of the first court seized. This examination must be left to the first court seized and the second court seized must only of its own motion stay the proceedings until the first court seized has established or declined its jurisdiction. Article 21 states that the second court seized must of its own motion decline jurisdiction when the first court seized has accepted jurisdiction for the proceedings referred to it by the second court seized. To be perfectly clear: arts. 21-23 do not create jurisdiction. The first court must be able to independently derive its jurisdiction for the proceedings referred to it from the Brussels Convention, possibly via art. 4 Brussels Convention. The formulation in art. 21 1982 Brussels Convention deviated slightly.

In the judgment *Tatry* (ECJ 6 December 1994, Case 406/92, *see* section 3.1.8) the Court ruled on the terms 'the same cause of action' and 'the same object'. In *Maciej Rataj* the shipowner sought a declaration from the Rotterdam district court that he was not (fully) liable for alleged damage to the cargo (contamination of soya bean oil with *inter alia* diesel oil) during transport by his vessel *Tatry*. Subsequently the various cargo-owners in England arrested another ship, the *Maciej Rataj*, owned by the shipowner of the vessel *Tatry*, and sought damages before an English court for contamination of the cargo. The Court held that art. 21 must be construed thus 'that an action seeking to have the defendant held liable for causing loss and ordered to pay damages has the same cause of action and the same object as earlier proceedings brought by that defendant seeking a declaration that he is not liable for that loss.' This means that the two sides of the same coin relate to the same cause of action and the same object. That is an important decision, for if it had been held that they did not have the same object and the same cause of action, then the proceedings can be continued before the different courts and there is a risk of the courts reaching conflicting decisions, which in a liability action gives rise to very strange consequences and also renders enforcement of the judgment in each other's States almost impossible. Whether the claims pending before the different courts are qualified by the one as actions *in rem* and by the other as actions *in personam* or a mixture of these is irrelevant to the application of art. 21, as held by the Court in the judgment *Tatry*.

As far as related actions are concerned which are pending at first instance, the second court seized may stay its proceedings (art. 22 Brussels Convention). On application of one of the parties this court may also refer the case, provided its law permits the consolidation of related actions (*see* sections 3.4 in the discussion of the different countries) and the first court seized has jurisdiction over both actions (art. 22). The first court seized (to which the case has been referred) must be able to derive its jurisdiction for the second action independently from art. 2 Brussels Convention *et seq.*

The term 'related' is defined in art. 22, so that there is no room left for national interpretations of related actions. This has been confirmed in the judgment *Tatry*. The Court held that if one group of cargo-owners, for whom separate but identical bills of lading apply, have in one country brought an action seeking damages against the shipowner and in the other country an action seeking damages has been brought against the shipowner by the owners of another part of the cargo, who have identical bills of lading for their part of the cargo (which has been transported under identical conditions as the other part of the cargo), the actions are already related when 'the separate trial and judgment of those actions would involve the risk of conflicting decisions, without necessarily involving the risk of giving rise to mutually exclusive legal consequences.' Indeed, if the court in one country allows damages and the court in the other country does not allow them or not to the same extent, these decisions are admittedly conflicting, but they do not mutually exclude legal consequences.

Article 23 provides for the situation where two courts have exclusive jurisdiction. As stated before, the first court seized shall have priority.

In a judgment *Owens Bank Ltd* v. *Bracco SpA*, the Court has given its opinion on the formal scope of arts. 21-23 (ECJ 20 January 1994, Case 129/92, [1994] ECR 117, 1 All E.R., 2 February 1994, p. 336 note Toulmin; TVVS 1995/7, p. 198 note Vlas; NILR 1994, p. 355 note Vlas; Rev. crit. 1994, p. 377 note Gaudemet-Tallon). The Court decided that arts. 21-23 of the Brussels Convention do not apply to procedures brought in different Contracting States in which the enforcement of a judgment of a non-Contracting State is in dispute.

3.2.16. PROVISIONAL MEASURES

Article 24, the final article of the title on jurisdiction, provides for the jurisdiction of a court in a Contracting State where provisional or protective measures are applied for. These measures may be applied for in the courts of the State under whose law such measures are available. The Netherlands Supreme Court has posed the question to the Court of Justice whether the provisional hearing of witnesses before litigation has started (art. 214 Netherlands CCP *et seq.*) can be regarded as a measure falling under art. 24 (HR 24 March 1995, RvdW 1995, 71C, *Forbo* v. *Sauressig*). This is possible even if, pursuant to the rules of jurisdiction of the Brussels Convention, another court has jurisdiction in respect of the substance of the matter. The decisions under art. 24 must be recognised and enforced in all Contracting States inasmuch as they can stand the test of arts. 27 and 28 (*see* section 3.3.5). The literature is divided on the question whether art. 24 should require that the defendant, or at least one of the parties, shall have his domicile in a Contracting State. Another point of view holds that the court of the place where the measure is to take effect shall have jurisdiction, irrespective of the domicile of the parties.

3.2.17. INTERNATIONAL JURISDICTION UNDER TRADITIONAL RULES

If the Brussels Convention (or any other convention) does not apply, or refers to the traditional procedural rules of law, it must be investigated whether the court can assume jurisdiction pursuant to any provision of traditional procedural rules of law. The general opinion in the Netherlands is that if there is a court with relative jurisdiction in the Netherlands, this allows international jurisdiction, the so-called 'distribution is attribution'-principle (*see* section 8.3.2b). In some articles of Netherlands law international jurisdiction of the Netherlands court is explicitly provided for (*see* arts. 814 and 767 Rv). It should be noted that a radical change of *inter alia* the rules of international jurisdiction of the Netherlands court is imminent. A separate division of the Code of Civil Procedure will provide for the international jurisdiction of the Netherlands court, whereas domestic relative jurisdiction will be determined on the basis of rules which also apply in national cases. In practice there will not be any major changes in comparison with the present grounds of jurisdiction, which are partly accepted on the basis of case law. The introduction of these rules is expected to take place in 1997. In Germany (*see* section 9.3.2b) a dual function of the relative jurisdiction rules also applies in international cases. In Belgium (*see* section 7.3.2b) the communal jurisdiction in international cases can be found in arts. 635-638 Ger.W./CJ (with reference to defendants of foreign nationality), art. 15 BW (when the defendant is a Belgian national) and arts. 624-634 Ger.W./CJ (relative jurisdiction is international jurisdiction). France and Luxembourg have arts. 14 and 15 CC (*see* sections 5.3.2b and 6.3.2b) for all international cases outside treaties. In England the rules are (for actions *in personam*) that service of a writ on a person resident in England gives the English court jurisdiction (*see* section 4.3.2b and the Civil Jurisdiction and Judgments Act 1982). In special cases this jurisdiction of the English courts may be extended if the plaintiff is allowed leave by the English court to serve the writ abroad on a person resident in the relevant foreign country. The cases in which this is permitted are set out in the Rules of the Supreme Court (RSC) Ord. 11, r. 1. In Italy the international jurisdiction may be derived from Title II, arts. 3-12 of the Act of 17 May 1995, number 218. (*Riforma del sistema italiano di diritto internazionale privato*). The Italian courts have jurisdiction in case there is relative jurisdiction. If the defendant is not domiciled within the territory of the Brussels Convention, but the case does come within the scope of this Convention, the rules of jurisdiction of the Convention apply to determine the international jurisdiction of the Italian court (*see* section 10.3.2b).

In all the countries mentioned a prorogating or derogating choice of forum is possible under certain conditions. In the Netherlands this was confirmed in the judgments *Piscator* (HR 1 February 1985, NJ 1985, 698 note Schultsz) and *Harvest Trader* (HR 28 October 1988, NJ 1989, 765 note Schultsz). In the judgment *Esmil* (HR 17 December 1993, NJ 1994, 348 and 350) the *Hoge Raad* decided that the *forum arresti* of art. 767 (old) Rv does not create jurisdiction if the parties have made an exclusive choice of forum. This decision was confirmed in HR 16 June 1995, RvdW 1995, 139 C in respect of art. 767 (new) Rv. This is even the case when the choice of forum has been made before the court of a country with which the Netherlands has no enforcement convention, so that the judgment obtained in that country does not yield a title which is capable of execution in the Netherlands. The Netherlands court does have jurisdiction to make protective attachment inasmuch as there are assets situated in the Netherlands, but this attachment will not be converted into enforcement measures until the foreign judgment has been converted into a Netherlands decision pursuant to art. 431 (2) Rv. In general there will be no inquiry into the facts, because the jurisdiction of the foreign court was based on a choice of forum, assuming that there have been proper proceedings (*see* section 3.3.14).

3.3. Recognition and Enforcement

3.3.1. GENERAL REMARKS

Title III lays down rules for recognition and enforcement. Article 25 states that for the purposes of the Convention a judgment is any judgment given by a court or tribunal of a Contracting State, whatever the judgment may be called. In the judgment *Solo Kleinmotoren* v. *Boch* (ECJ 2 June 1994, Case 414/92, [1994] ECR I-2237, NILR 1994, p. 359 note Vlas) the Court indicates how the term 'judgment' must be construed. In order to be a 'judgment' for the purposes of the Convention the decision must emanate from a judicial body of a Contracting State deciding on its own authority on the issues between the parties. That condition is not fulfilled in the case of a settlement, even if it was reached in a court of a Contracting State and brings legal proceedings to an end. Settlements in court are essentially contractual in that their terms depend first and foremost on the parties' intention. This construction is in keeping with the fact that the enforcement of court settlements has been regulated in a separate provision (art. 51 Brussels Convention).

The Brussels Convention has a fast procedure for the recognition and enforcement of judgments falling within its scope and given in a Contracting State. The relevant provisions may be found in arts. 26 *et seq*. Brussels Convention. It is evident from the judgment *Owens bank Ltd.* v. *Bracco* (ECJ 20 January 1994: *see* section 3.2.15) that a judgment whereby leave has been granted for recognition *casu quo* enforcement of another judgment (in the case of a State which has not acceded to the Brussels Convention), cannot in its turn be recognised or enforced again under the Brussels Convention. If a German judgment which is already being enforced in France, is also required to be enforced in the Netherlands, the Brussels Convention procedure needs to be applied again, this time by the Netherlands court.

It must be noted that the judgment to be recognised (or to be enforced) must be within the scope of art. 1 Brussels Convention. The court before which recognition is sought must examine independently whether it concerns a subject within the scope of the Convention. It may therefore occur that the court which has given the judgment was of the opinion that the subject did fall within the scope of the Brussels Convention, but that the second court thinks differently. The interpretation by the court must respect the autonomy of the Convention, but marginal differences cannot be completely excluded.

Considering Title III it will become clear that jurisdiction will only be examined by the court before which recognition or enforcement is sought in highly exceptional cases, so that judgments which at first instance were only regarded as an internal case or judgments given under art. 4 Brussels Convention pursuant to the national rules of jurisdiction or under art. 57 pursuant to the rules of a convention on a particular matter, qualify for recognition and enforcement on the same basis as judgments which, as regards jurisdiction, are explicitly founded on jurisdiction under a Convention. Indeed, the court before which recognition and enforcement are sought may not examine the grounds of jurisdiction.

3.3.2. ARTICLE 26 BRUSSELS CONVENTION: RECOGNITION

Judgments given in a Contracting State must be recognised without any special procedure being required. If objections are made against recognition, the party interested in the determination of recognition as a principal matter, may use the rules laid down for enforcement (Title III, sections 2 and 3 Brussels Convention). If in the Contracting State where the decision was given an ordinary appeal has been lodged against the judgment whose recognition is sought, the court before which recognition is sought may stay the proceedings (art. 30 Brussels Convention).

The concept of *recognition* is not further explained in the Brussels Convention. The Jenard report states that judgments must have the authority and the effect which they have in the Contracting State where they were given. The Court of Justice decided in the case *Hoffmann* v. *Krieg* (ECJ 4 February 1988, Case 145/86) that a judgment from Contracting State D (State where Decision was given) must have the same effects in state R (State in which Recognition is sought). Thus, it may have a wider effect than such a judgment would have had in State R without this rule. It is also possible that this judgment has an even wider effect than a comparable judgment of State R would have had in a national case.

3.3.3. GROUNDS FOR REFUSAL

Recognition may be refused if any of the situations referred to in art. 27 or 28 Brussels Convention occurs. According to the literature these articles must be applied by the court of the State in which recognition is sought (State R) of its own motion.

a. Article 27 Brussels Convention

Article 27 provides for the following grounds of refusal:

(1) Conflict with international public policy.

The Brussels Convention does not indicate under what circumstances international public policy will be violated. The judgment itself may not be reviewed in respect of its substance (art. 29), so that only recognition can be contrary to international public policy. The European Court of Justice has in a number of judgments given its opinion on this paragraph. The Court has taken the view that conflicts with international public policy must be interpreted very strictly, which is in accordance with the Jenard report. Moreover, art. 27(1) does not apply if any of the other paragraphs of art. 27 already apply.

(2) Where judgment was given *in default of appearance*, if the defendant was not duly served with the document which instituted the proceedings or with an equivalent document in sufficient time to enable him to arrange for his defence.

The phrase a 'document which instituted the proceedings or an equivalent document' refers to the document, or the documents, whose due and timely service or notification enables the defendant to assert his rights, before an enforceable judgment is given in the original State (see judgment *Minalmet* (*below*) and ECJ 13 July 1995, Case 474/93, *Hengst Import BV* v. *Campese*, not yet published). On these grounds the Italian *decreto ingiuntivo* (payment order; *see* section 10.7.2) together with the request had to be regarded as a document which instituted the proceedings in the sense of art. 27(2).

The Court indicated in the decision *Sonntag* v. *Waidmann* (ECJ 1993; *see* section 3.2.1) that non-recognition and/or enforcement of a judgment for the reasons set out in art. 27(2) is possible only where the defendant was in default of appearance in the original proceedings. Where the defendant entered an appearance in the original proceedings, art. 27(2) may no longer be relied upon in the recognition and/or enforcement stage.

If judgment is entered against the defendant in default of appearance, and the court under art. 20 Brussels Convention had to examine of its own motion whether its jurisdiction is derived from the provisions of the Convention and whether the documents instituting the proceedings had been duly served *and* in sufficient time, a second examination is required by art. 27(2). The court of the State in which recognition is sought (State R) must examine independently whether the document was served in due form *and* in sufficient time, whereby the court is bound by the finding of the actual circumstances under which service has taken place, as ascertained by the court of the State which has given the judgment (State B). The Court of Justice in its judgment on the case *Lancray* v. *Peters* (ECJ 3 July 1990, Case 305/88) decided that the court of State R must base its evaluation of these facts and its decision whether or not the document had been served in due form on the rules as they apply in State B, including any relevant international agreements applicable in State B. Further evidence to show that the Court of Justice regards due service as an extremely important guarantee in default cases, is presented by its judgment in the case *Minalmet GmbH* v. *Brandeis Ltd.* (ECJ 12 November 1992, Case 123/91; TVVS 1993/11, p. 307 note

Vlas; NILR 1993, p. 512 note Vlas; Rev. crit. 1993, p. 81 note Droz; IPRax 1993, p. 376 note Rauscher). In this case the Court decided that an English judgment given in default of appearance could not be recognised in Germany, since the original writ had not been served on the party domiciled in Germany in accordance with German requirements, even though this party was later informed of the English default judgment and could at that time have lodged an appeal in England against the judgment, but failed to do so. The Court took the position that the lodging of an appeal against a judgment cannot be compared to a defence on the principal issue. The service of the document must under all circumstances have taken place in due form.

Apart from the requirement of due form, service must also have been effected in sufficient time for the defendant to arrange for his defence. The court of State R can assess this independently, whereby the court is not bound by periods prescribed in its own State or in State D. Exceptional circumstances after service in sufficient time may give rise to the court of State R concluding that service has not been effected in sufficient time, according to the European Court of Justice in the case *Debaecker* v. *Bouwman* (ECJ 11 June 1985, Case 49/84).

(3) If a judgment given in State D is irreconcilable with a judgment given in State R between the same parties, the first judgment must not be recognised.

It should be noted that the question whether there is a conflict is assessed at the moment when recognition is sought. The judgment of State R may therefore have been given at a later stage than the judgment of State D in relation to which recognition is sought. In the decision *Solo Kleinmotoren* v. *Boch* (ECJ 1994; *see* section 3.3.1) the Court favours a strict interpretation of the term 'judgment' in art. 27(3). This term must be interpreted identically in arts. 25 and 27(3).

(4) The judgment given in State D must not be recognised if the court of State D, in order to arrive at its judgment, has decided a preliminary question concerning the status or legal capacity of natural persons, rights in property arising out of a matrimonial relationship or wills or intestacy and in doing so violated a rule of the private international law which State R would have applied. This does not apply, however, if the judgment of State D reached the same result as would have been reached on the basis of the (different) rules of private international law of State R.

Here it concerns the situation in which the court of State D has decided a preliminary question which is not covered by the Convention (*see* art. 1(1) Brussels Convention), but which preliminary question decided the main question which did come under the Convention. This could, for example, occur when the court of State D deems a person to be a minor and consequently resolves an international agreement of sale to which this person was a party and grants compensation. Whether a person is a minor may be decided by one system of private international law on the basis of the rules of law of the country of nationality, but another system may decide on the basis of the rules of law of the country of domicile. A judgment in respect of an international agreement of sale falls within the scope of the Brussels Convention and can therefore be recognised. The court of State R will therefore examine whether the court of State D applied the rules of private international law as used by State R to the question of minority, which determined the validity of the entire agreement. If the court of State D did not apply the same rules as the court in State R would have done, recognition must be refused, unless the person would be a minor both under State D's and under State R's rules of private international law.

(5) The judgment from State D must not be recognised if the following case presents itself: the judgment from State D is irreconcilable with an earlier judgment given in a non-Contracting State involving the same cause of action and between the same parties, provided that this latter judgment fulfils the conditions necessary for its recognition in State R.

It is thereby necessary that the judgment in the non-Contracting State has been given earlier than the one in State D. If the judgment from the non-Contracting State is capable of recognition in State R, this judgment is as it were attributed to State R and can therefore be in conflict with a judgment of State D which is given later and in relation to which recognition is sought in State R. The earlier judgment (not from a Contracting State but recognised by such a State) in this case prevails over a later judgment from a Contracting State.

b. Article 28 Brussels Convention

Article 28 sets out the following grounds for refusal:

(1) conflict with the provisions of Chapters 3, 4 and 5 of Title II (insurance, consumers and art. 16). If the court of the State which delivered the

judgment assumed jurisdiction in violation of the exclusive jurisdiction rules of these Chapters, the judgment cannot be recognised.

(2) in a case provided for in article 59 (a judgment by a court in a Contracting State under art. 4 Brussels Convention against a defendant domiciled in a third State, when the Contracting State in which recognition is sought is under an obligation to that third State by virtue of a convention not to recognise such judgments as are based on the *forum actoris*).

The court before which recognition is sought is bound by the findings of fact on which the court of State D has based its jurisdiction. Examination of the grounds of jurisdiction may only take place on the basis of those facts and only for the jurisdictional rules mentioned in art. 28. Otherwise any examination of jurisdiction is absolutely forbidden. Jurisdiction wrongly assumed by a court of State D cannot, in case of recognition in State R, impede this recognition, other than in the cases stated in art. 28. Therefore it is irrelevant whether the jurisdiction was directly based on the Brussels Convention or (possibly via art. 4) on internal grounds for jurisdiction.

In order to prevent examination of jurisdiction in any other way, art. 28 states that the rules relating to jurisdiction do not concern the test of international public policy referred to in art. 27(1).

3.3.4. GROUNDS FOR REFUSAL UNDER THE LUGANO CONVENTION

Examination under the Lugano Convention runs almost completely parallel to the Brussels Convention, but there are two additional grounds for refusal in the former. Article 28 Lugano Convention provides in its second paragraph that recognition of a judgment may be refused if it conflicts with the provisions of art. 54B (3) or art. 57(4) Lugano Convention.

Article 54B (3) provides that if a ground of jurisdiction on which the judgment is based differs from Title II Lugano Convention and recognition is sought against a party domiciled in an EFTA-Lugano Convention State (i.e. an Lugano Convention Contracting State from an EFTA country), such recognition may be refused. If it is possible for this EFTA-Lugano Convention State to recognise the judgment on any other ground (e.g. under traditional rules) recognition is permitted. From the Jenard/Möller report (no. 16) it appears that this article concerns the case whereby a court in an EU-Lugano Convention Contracting State (i.e. a Lugano Convention Contracting State from the EU territory) assumed jurisdiction on the basis of a ground of jurisdiction not known in the Lugano Convention. This would protect persons domiciled in EFTA-Lugano Convention States against recognition of a decision rendered by a EU-Lugano Convention court which mistakenly based its jurisdiction on a ground which does not exist under the Lugano Convention. Only mistakes made by an EU-Lugano Convention court qualify for consideration, according to the explanation.

Article 57(4) Lugano Convention provides that if State R is not a contracting party to the special convention and the person against whom recognition is sought is domiciled in State R, recognition and enforcement may be refused, unless State R is able to recognise the judgment under other rules of law (*see* section 3.4.2).

3.3.5. FURTHER RULES REGARDING RECOGNITION

There are no circumstances in which art. 29 allows a judgment to be reviewed as to its substance.

Article 30 provides that the court of the Contracting State (State R) *may* stay the recognition proceedings if an ordinary appeal against this judgment has been lodged in the Contracting State where the judgment has been given (State D). Meanwhile, however, the court may test the judgment against arts. 27 and 28 Brussels Convention. The Court has ruled that the term 'ordinary appeal' must be interpreted autonomously (ECJ 22 November 1977, Case 43/77, *Industrial Diamonds Supplies* v. *Riva*). The expression 'ordinary' appeal must be understood as meaning any appeal which can lead to the setting aside or amendment of the judgment to be recognised or enforced in accordance with the Brussels Convention; and of which the use in State D is bound by the law to a specific period of time which starts to run by virtue of the actual decision. The United Kingdom (and the Republic of Ireland) do not distinguish between ordinary and extraordinary appeal, which is why art. 30(2) stipulates a separate provision for that purpose. Provisional judgments, too, (e.g. under art. 24) may be recognised. A summary judgment may qualify for recognition because the defendant has been *summoned to appear*. This was required by the European Court of Justice in *Denilauler* v. *Couchet Frères* (ECJ 21 May 1980, Case 125/79).

3.3.6. ENFORCEMENT

Enforcement is provided for in art. 31 *et seq*. Here, too, only very limited examination is permitted.

Article 31 provides that judgments given in Contracting State D and enforceable in that State (they need not have become *res iudicata*), can be enforced in another Contracting State if leave for enforcement of such judgments has been granted there.

3.3.7. COURT WHICH HAS JURISDICTION IN CASE OF ENFORCEMENT

Article 32 provides to which court of the Contracting States an application for enforcement shall be submitted.

In the Netherlands the relative jurisdiction lies with the President of the *arrondissementsrechtbank* in whose district the person against whom enforcement is sought is domiciled. In Belgium the application must be submitted to the *tribunal de première instance*, in Germany to the presiding judge of a chamber of the *Landgericht*, in France to the presiding judge of the *tribunal de grande instance*. In England and Wales the application must be submitted to the High Court of Justice (in case of a maintenance judgment to the Magistrates' Court through the *Secretary of State*). In Italy the application must be submitted to the *corte d'appello* and in Luxembourg to the President of the *tribunal d'arrondissement*.

If a party against whom enforcement is sought is not domiciled in the State in which enforcement is sought, jurisdiction must be determined on the basis of the place of enforcement.

3.3.8. PROCEDURAL REQUIREMENTS OF AN APPLICATION FOR ENFORCEMENT

Article 33 provides that the law of the State in which enforcement is sought determines the procedure of an application for enforcement. The Contracting States must indicate in their domestic laws which provisions apply.

For the Netherlands the Act enforcing the Brussels Convention (Act of 4 May 1972, Stb. 1972, 240 as amended on 25 October 1989, Stb. 490 and on 3 December 1991, Stb. 607) sets out the requirements for this application. The requirements in Rv (ss. 985-990) have been set aside (s. 2 Act enforcing the Brussels Convention). In Germany the requirements for the application have been laid down in the *Anerkennungs- und Vollstreckungsausführungsgesetz* of 30 May 1988 (Bundesgesetzblatt 1988 I 662). This German Act provides rules for such procedures in respect of the Brussels Convention and some bilateral conventions. In England the requirements can be found in section 4(1) Civil Jurisdiction and Judgments Act 1982 and in RSC Ord. 71, rr. 25-34 (registration with the English court which has jurisdiction). Belgium and France have no enforcement legislation. In France the procedural requirements can be found in art. 493 *et seq.* and 812 *et seq.* NCPC. In Belgium arts. 1025-1034 Ger.W./CJ apply (unilateral application; *see* sections 7.5.1 and 7.5.2). In Italy the Brussels Convention is enforced by the Act of 21 June 1971, no. 804 (*legge di applicazione della convenzione di Bruxelles*).

The European Court of Justice decided in its judgment *De Wolf* v. *Cox* (ECJ 30 November 1976, Case 42/76) that it is not possible to seek enforcement of a judgment given in a Contracting State and covered by art. 1 Brussels Convention in any other manner than through the Brussels Convention. Bringing new proceedings on the basis of the same disputed case is not allowed.

An applicant must give an address for service of process within the area of jurisdiction of the court to which he makes the application or, if the law of the State in which enforcement is sought does not provide for the choosing of such an address, the applicant must appoint a representative *ad litem*.

The following documents must be attached to the application:

- a certified copy of the judgment which establishes its authenticity;
- in case of a judgment given in default: a document which confirms that the party in default was served with the document instituting the proceedings. If such document cannot be submitted, art. 48 Brussels Convention offers a solution;
- a document confirming the enforceability and service of the judgment; and
- a document confirming that the applicant is in receipt of legal aid. Here, too, art. 48 applies if a proper document cannot be produced.

In no case may legalisation be required in respect of the documents referred to in arts. 46, 47 and 48 (art. 49 Brussels Convention).

The court deciding on an application for enforcement *may* require a translation of the documents referred to in arts. 46 and 47 (art. 48(2)).

3.3.9. GROUNDS FOR REFUSAL OF ENFORCEMENT

Article 34 compels the court to which an application for enforcement is made to give its decision without delay.

The party against whom enforcement is sought will not be heard at this stage of the proceedings.

The reasons for refusal specified in arts. 27 and 28 apply in the same way as in respect of recognition (*see* section 3.3.3). In the case of enforcement, too, the foreign judgment may under no circumstances be reviewed as to its substance.

3.3.10. ENFORCEMENT IS AUTHORISED

The appropriate officer of the court must without delay notify the applicant of the decision given on the application in accordance with the procedure laid down by the law of the State in which enforcement is sought. In the Netherlands this has been laid down in art. 3(4) Act enforcing the Brussels Convention. Notification by letter suffices.

The party against whom enforcement is authorised may appeal against the decision within one month of service thereof. The time for appealing is two months if this party is domiciled in a Contracting State other than the State in which the decision allowing enforcement was given (art. 36 Brussels Convention). No extension of time on account of distance will be granted.

Article 37 Brussels Convention provides that an appeal against the decision authorising enforcement must be lodged in accordance with the rules governing procedure in contentious matters in the court appointed in that article.

The judgment given on the appeal may be contested in ways which differ in the Contracting States. In the Netherlands, Belgium, Italy, Luxembourg and France an appeal in cassation may be lodged. In Germany *Rechtsbeschwerde* may be lodged and in England it may only be contested by a single further appeal on a point of law (art. 37). The Court has ruled in various decisions that art. 37(2) must be interpreted restrictively. In the decision *Sonntag* v. *Waidmann* (*see* section 3.2.1) the Court therefore held that an interested third party cannot lodge an appeal against the decision given on appeal under art. 36, since the interested third party is not mentioned as such in art. 36. It only stipulates that the party against whom enforcement is authorised may appeal against the decision, and consequently this party is the only party which may, in case such appeal is rejected, appeal against that decision too. It is immaterial that the national rules of procedure do allow an interested third party to lodge an appeal, as in *Sonntag* v. *Waidmann*, where under the applicable German rules of procedure the interested third party could lodge the recourse of *Rechtsbeschwerde*.

Article 38 contains a procedure whereby, at the request of the party who appeals against the judgment of enforcement, the proceedings as to whether the appeal will succeed may be stayed if an ordinary appeal (*see* section

3.3.5 for the explanation of this term) has been lodged against the judgment in the State in which that judgment was given (or if the time for lodging such an appeal has not yet expired). The court may also make enforcement conditional on the provision of security. This article gives the court discretionary power.

The European Court of Justice decided in its judgment *Van Dalfsen* v. *Van Loon* (ECJ 4 October 1991, Case 183/90) that only a judgment given on the appeal may be contested by an appeal in cassation. The decisions which may be taken by the court pursuant to art. 38 Brussels Convention (stay, security) and may be contained in the same judgment as the decision under art. 37 are not open to cassation.

If enforcement is authorised, protective measures may be taken against the property of the party against whom enforcement is sought (art. 39 Brussels Convention) during the time specified for an appeal (art. 36). The procedure laid down in art. 24 Brussels Convention may not be followed in this case. Article 39 provides that the decision allowing enforcement must carry with it leave to obtain protective measures.

3.3.11. ENFORCEMENT IS REFUSED

Article 40 Brussels Convention provides that if at first instance an application for enforcement of a decision given in another Contracting State has been refused, an appeal can be lodged.

In that case, the party against whom enforcement is sought, shall for the first time in these proceedings be summoned to appear before the appellate court. Article 20(2) and (3) Brussels Convention (*see* section 3.2.14) apply in case of non-appearance, irrespective of the party being domiciled in a Contracting State or not.

Article 41 provides that an appeal may also be lodged against a judgment given on an appeal against the original judgment which refused the application for enforcement. For the Netherlands, Belgium, Italy, Luxembourg and France this can only be a cassation appeal. In Germany the only option is the *Rechtsbeschwerde* and in England the second judgment may be contested only by a single further appeal on a point of law (art. 41 Brussels Convention).

3.3.12. ARTICLES 42-51 BRUSSELS CONVENTION

Enforcement may also be allowed for part of the judgment (art. 42).

Article 43 allows enforcement of a judgment ordering a penalty payment, provided the amount of the payment was determined by the courts of the State in which the judgment was given.

Article 44 contains rules on proceedings by applicants of limited means. Article 45 forbids the *cautio iudicatum solvi* for an enforcement pursuant to the Brussels Convention.

In art. 50 provisions are contained regarding the enforcement of authentic instruments. Article 51 declares these provisions applicable also to settlements approved by courts.

3.3.13. RECOGNITION AND ENFORCEMENT UNDER THE LUGANO CONVENTION

Articles 25 to 51 inclusive of the Lugano Convention contain similar provisions as the Brussels Convention. Article 28(2) represents an exception, in that it contains two additional grounds for refusal. These grounds were discussed in section 3.3.4.

The Netherlands Act enforcing the Lugano Convention (Act of 26 March 1992, Stb. 1992, 141; entered into force on 1 June 1992, Stb. 1992, 235) refers to the Act enforcing the Brussels Convention, so that procedures pursuant to the Brussels and the Lugano Convention are identical. For the implementation of the Lugano Convention in the United Kingdom, the Civil Jurisdiction and Judgments Act 1982 has been amended by the Civil Jurisdiction and Judgments Act 1991, which includes the Lugano Convention. Italy has laid down its enforcement legislation in the Act of 20 February 1992, number 198. The other countries use the same method as for the Brussels Convention (*see* section 3.3.8).

3.3.14. RECOGNITION AND ENFORCEMENT UNDER TRADITIONAL RULES

In the countries discussed in this book the recognition and enforcement of foreign judgments under traditional rules of law runs largely parallel as far as the intrinsic examination of the case is concerned. Recognition of a foreign decision may take place in all these countries without any extra procedural steps. Enforcement of a foreign decision requires new proceedings in the Netherlands (art. 431(2) Rv). In Belgium, Italy, France, Luxembourg and Germany no more is needed than proceedings to obtain an exequatur. In England there are two ways, namely enforcement under common law and registration. The common law procedure means that an action is brought before the English Courts by the party in whose favour the decision was given in order to realise fulfilment of the obligation of the 'condemned party' resulting from the foreign judgment. This may be done by way of an ordinary action (RSC Ord. 11), but also by means of a summary judgment (RSC. Ord. 14; *see* section 4.7.2). The registration procedure mainly takes place under the Foreign Judgments (Reciprocal Enforcement) Act 1933 and can only concern judgments delivered in a country named in this Act, e.g. the Netherlands, Belgium, France, Italy and Germany. It should be made clear, however, that the Civil Jurisdiction and Judgments Act 1982 (enforcement of judgments under the Brussels Convention), rather than this Act, will usually apply as far as judgments given in the countries discussed in this book are concerned.

Despite the fact that procedures differ slightly, the intrinsic requirements for recognition (and possible enforcement) can still be said to run parallel. In the Netherlands these requirements are laid down in case law. In Belgium they may be found in art. 570 Ger.W./CJ. In France art. 509 NCPC and art. 2123 CC apply. In Germany they are found in §§ 328 and 722 ZPO. In England the unwritten rules of common law apply and the written requirements of the Foreign Judgments Act 1933, which almost completely correspond. In Italy the requirements are laid down in arts. 64-71 of the Act of 17 May 1995 (Title IV).

The court before which recognition is sought will examine firstly whether the foreign court is deemed to have international jurisdiction. In this connection it is not the foreign court's own procedural rules of law which provide the criteria. The domestic rules of jurisdiction are interpreted in the light of acceptable international rules, and rules of jurisdiction laid down in conventions will in general be deemed internationally acceptable outside these conventions too. Exorbitant jurisdiction will often not be regarded as internationally acceptable. In Italy the Italian grounds of jurisdiction are used as a criterion for the jurisdiction of the foreign court. In case of voluntary submission to a foreign court through a choice of forum or as a result of not invoking a formal exception of lack of jurisdiction, it is assumed that the requirement of international jurisdiction has been met. In Belgium one specific interpretation has been given to the concept of 'international jurisdiction', which is that jurisdiction on the basis of the plaintiff's nationality is insufficient to assume international jurisdiction. In England the Foreign Judgments Act 1933 provides exactly when a foreign court shall be deemed to have international jurisdiction, which provision corresponds with the requirements of common law and with what other countries regard as proper international jurisdiction.

Secondly, the defendant must have been properly summoned and regular proceedings must have taken place, in which the principle of hearing both sides plays an important part.

Thirdly, the decision must not contravene international public policy of the country in which recognition is sought. In Belgium this means *inter alia* that it must not conflict with any Belgian judgment. In Germany and Italy conflict with an earlier or later German respectively Italian decision is a separate requirement and consequently does not come under the concept of international public policy. A separate requirement stipulated in England is that the foreign judgment must not have been obtained by fraud. It appears to me that the other countries will consider this to form part of the public policy rule. Germany uses the principle of reciprocity, which implies that no judgments are recognised from countries which do not recognise German judgments. Since it is difficult to establish whether a country from which a judgment originates will be prepared to recognise a German judgment, the consideration in the literature is that this rule can only be applied if it is already clear that one or more German judgments have not been recognised.

None of the countries will review a foreign judgment as to its substance.

When a judgment is capable of recognition, it will be possible to issue an exequatur in Belgium, France and Germany or to grant registration in England. In the Netherlands, recognition will imply that the Netherlands court will pass judgment in conformity with the foreign decision, and in England in the common law procedure an English decision will follow, giving an order for compliance with the foreign decision. In Italy new proceedings must be brought against the defendant (art. 796 Cpc).

In family law cases and cases introduced by a petition, other procedures may sometimes apply. The formal review remains identical, although in family law cases a conflict-of-laws check is used at times (*see* art. 27(4) Brussels Convention) for cases that fall under the Brussels Convention.

3.4. The Demarcation Between the Brussels Convention (and the Lugano Convention) and Other Conventions

3.4.1. GENERAL CONVENTIONS

The Brussels Convention needed to contain provisions for the demarcation between the Brussels Convention and older conventions. A number of different situations can occur.

Conventions already in existence at the moment when the Brussels Convention entered into force lose their effect between the Contracting States if they concern the same matters as the Brussels Convention (art. 55 Brussels Convention). The Conventions covered by this article are enumerated in art. 55.

Judgments given before the Brussels Convention came into force will continue to have effect pursuant to the older conventions (art. 56(2) Brussels Convention). The conventions set out in art. 55 shall also continue to have effect in relation to matters to which the Brussels Convention does not apply. For the Netherlands and Belgium one may think of the Convention between Belgium and the Netherlands on Jurisdiction, Bankruptcy and the Validity and Enforcement of Judgments, Arbitration Awards and Authentic Instruments of 1925 which continues to have effect in matters of personal and family law, successions and bankruptcies. The convention can no longer be applied to matters covered by the Brussels Convention.

The Lugano Convention contains similar provisions in arts. 55 and 56.

3.4.2. SPECIAL CONVENTIONS

a. Brussels Convention

The situation differs in respect of conventions which deal with a special matter, which, unlike the Brussels Convention, are not general conventions on civil and commercial matters, but only deal with e.g. collision or maintenance ('special conventions'). Article 57 Brussels Convention provides that the Brussels Convention does not affect these special conventions, irrespective of the time at which they became effective (before or after the Brussels Convention came into force). In order to guarantee a uniform interpretation of art. 55(1), paragraph (2) prescribes how this article is to be applied.

The following applies in respect of jurisdiction:

a. if a Brussels Convention State is a party to a special convention and may assume jurisdiction by virtue of that special convention, the Brussels Convention State may base its jurisdiction on that convention. This also applies when the defendant is domiciled in another Brussels Convention State which is not a party to that special convention. In this case the Brussels Convention permits a deviation from art. 2 Brussels Convention. The court hearing the action must in any event apply art. 20 Brussels Convention, if the defendant does not enter an appearance.

The following applies as to recognition and enforcement:

b. judgments given in a Brussels Convention State by a court whose jurisdiction is based upon a special convention shall be recognised and enforced in the other Brussels Convention States in accordance with the Brussels Convention.

When both the State of origin and the State in which recognition is sought are parties to the special convention and this convention provides rules for recognition or enforcement of judgments, those rules shall apply (i.e. not the Brussels Convention rules). The Brussels Convention rules of procedure may, however, be applied. In the judgment *Tatry* (ECJ 1994; *see* sections 3.1.7 and 3.2.15) the Court of Justice held that art. 57 only determines that if a Brussels Convention State is also a party to a special convention governing jurisdiction, this special convention only excludes the applicability of the Brussels Convention with respect to the jurisdictional rules provided for by the special convention, not in cases not provided for by it. In this case the International Convention for the Unification of certain rules relating to the Arrest of Sea-Going Ships (signed at Brussels on 10 May 1952; the Netherlands and the United Kingdom are both parties to this convention) did not contain any provision concerning *lis pendens* and related actions, as provided for in arts. 21-23 Brussels Convention. The Court allowed these Brussels Convention provisions to be used, in spite of the applicability of the Arrest Convention.

Article 57(3) provides a special rule to prevent conflicts with regulations made by the Institutions of the European Communities regarding jurisdiction, recognition and enforcement. The EC regulations are to prevail, even when they are contained in national laws implementing such regulations. The Brussels Convention shall not be applied.

b. Lugano Convention

In the negotiations on the Lugano Convention art. 57 has also been the subject of lengthy discussions. In respect of jurisdiction the Lugano Convention uses the same system as the Brussels Convention. Article 57 Lugano Convention, also, allows an exception to the principle of *forum rei* of art. 2 Lugano Convention; the defendant from a Lugano Convention State may be sued in another Lugano Convention State where the court has jurisdiction by virtue of a special convention. If the defendant fails to appear, the court must establish under art. 20 Lugano Convention (which is identical to art. 20 Brussels Convention) whether service of the document was effected in sufficient time and in due form.

The provisions concerning recognition and enforcement contain a ground for refusal not included in the provisions applicable to the Brussels Convention. Recognition or enforcement may be refused on the grounds set out in Title III (recognition and enforcement), but they may also be refused if the Lugano Convention State in which recognition is sought is not a party to the special convention and the party against whom recognition or enforcement is sought is domiciled in this Lugano Convention State. Recognition or enforcement may be granted if this is possible on other grounds under the law of the Lugano Convention State in which recognition is sought (art. 57(4) Lugano Convention). The Jenard/Möller report states in no. 82 that the reason for this difference between the Lugano Convention and the Brussels Convention is that, in contrast to the former, the latter applies between Member States of the same community (*see* section 3.3.4).

Article 57(3) Brussels Convention has not been copied in the Lugano Convention. This item was awkward for the Lugano Convention States because in principle they have nothing to do with the EC regulations. In Protocol 3 annexed to the Lugano Convention concerning the applicability of art. 57 the Contracting States have declared that provisions governing jurisdiction in acts of the Institutions of the EU shall be treated in the same way as the special conventions referred to in art. 57(1).

c. Summary

The situation is therefore that recognition or enforcement of a judgment given in a Brussels Convention State or Lugano Convention State, based on jurisdiction by virtue of a special convention, must be tested in another Brussels Convention State or Lugano Convention State against:

- Title III Brussels Convention or Lugano Convention; or
- if both are parties to the special convention: the rules provided by the special convention (this may not be imperative; *see* the judgment *Tatry*).

Only if the Lugano Convention applies to recognition or enforcement, is the exceptional additional ground for refusal of art. 57(4) Lugano Convention to be applied (at the discretion of the court).

3.4.3. CONVENTIONS WITH THIRD STATES

Article 59 Brussels Convention deals with the case in which, by convention, a Brussels Convention State has committed itself towards a third State to a certain policy on recognition (and/or enforcement) with respect to judgments against defendants domiciled in that third State. If judgment has been given in a Brussels Convention State (State D) against a defendant domiciled in a State with which the Brussels Convention State in which recognition of this judgment is sought (State R) has a convention on enforcement, and the jurisdiction of State D could only be founded on art. 4 Brussels Convention in conjunction with an exorbitant ground of jurisdiction as referred to in art. 3 Brussels Convention, then State R may refuse recognition. State R is not required to violate its conventional obligations to the third State, in view of the fact that the defendant against whom the judgment had been given was domiciled in the territory of the third State. The power of Brussels Convention States to conclude conventions with third States which give rise to such obligations, is limited by two situations.

Recognition or enforcement in one Brussels Convention State of a judgment given in another Brussels Convention State against a defendant domiciled in a third State may not be refused if in State D the jurisdiction was founded on the presence of property within that State, or on the seizure of property situated there, if

- the action brought is related to the property;
  or
- the property constitutes security for a debt which is the subject-matter of the action.

3.5. Transitional Provisions and Concurrence of the Brussels and Lugano Conventions

3.5.1. ENTRY INTO FORCE OF THE 1989 BRUSSELS CONVENTION

Pursuant to art. 16 of the Convention on Accession of 1989, art. 54 Brussels Convention has been substituted by a new text in which the transitional provisions from the Conventions on Accession of 1978 and of 1982 have been incorporated. Article 54 applies to transitional situations occurring as a result of the entry into force of the Conventions of 1968, 1978 and 1982 consecutively. In addition, each Convention on Accession contains its own transitional provisions for when the Convention on Accession enters into force. In the 1989 Convention on Accession the transitional provisions are contained in art. 29. It reads as follows:

1. The 1968 Convention and the 1971 Protocol, as amended by the 1978 Convention, the 1982 Convention and this Convention, shall apply only to legal proceedings instituted and to authentic instruments formally drawn up or registered after the entry into force of this Convention in the State of origin and, where recognition or enforcement of a judgment or authentic instrument is sought, in the State addressed.
2. However, judgments given after the date of entry into force of this Convention between the State of origin and the State addressed in proceedings instituted before that date shall be recognised and enforced in accordance with the provisions of Title III of the 1968 Convention, as amended by the 1978 Convention, the 1982 Convention and this Convention, if jurisdiction was founded upon rules which accorded with the provisions of Title II of the 1968 Convention, as amended, or with the provisions of a convention which was in force between the State of origin and the State addressed when the proceedings were instituted.

Paragraph (1) states that the 1989 Brussels Convention shall be applied by the court of a State if the 1989 Brussels Convention has entered into force for that State. As far as jurisdiction is concerned, this rule is easy to apply. In recognition and enforcement cases the court of the State in which the 1989 Brussels Convention already has effect shall examine whether or not the judgment was given by a court from a State where the 1989 Convention had already entered into force at the time when the proceedings were commenced. If this is the case, paragraph (1) prescribes the application of the 1989 Convention and there shall not be an examination of jurisdiction except for the cases referred to in art. 28, 1989, Brussels Convention. If proceedings were instituted in the Netherlands after 1 February 1991 and recognition of the Netherlands judgment is sought in France on 1 September 1992, the 1989 Brussels Convention is applied both in respect of jurisdiction and of recognition. At the time when the proceedings were instituted, the 1989 Brussels Convention had entered into force in France and in the Netherlands.

If the 1989 Brussels Convention had not yet entered into force in the State in which judgment was delivered, at the moment when the proceedings were instituted, the court must determine pursuant to paragraph (2) whether the 1989 Brussels Convention should be applied to recognition and enforcement. It is, of course, impossible for a court of a State for which the 1989 Convention has not yet entered into force to apply the 1989 Brussels Convention to recognition or enforcement.

Paragraph (2) determines the case where proceedings were instituted *before* entry into force of the 1989 Brussels Convention between State D *and* State R, but judgment was given *after* entry into force of the 1989 Brussels Convention between State D *and* State R. For recognition or enforcement of these judgments the 1989 Convention shall be applied if the ground of jurisdiction applied by the court of State D:

- is in accordance with a ground of jurisdiction laid down by the 1989 Brussels Convention;
  or
- is based on a convention which was in force between State D and State R at the time when proceedings were instituted.

If proceedings were instituted in Portugal (Member State from 1 July 1992) on 1 December 1991, the judgment was given on 1 August 1992 and its enforcement was sought in the Netherlands on 1 September 1992, the Netherlands court will have to examine whether the jurisdiction of the Portuguese court was in accordance with Title II 1989 Brussels Convention. There was no Convention on jurisdiction in force between the Netherlands and Portugal on 1 December 1991.

The Portuguese court could have founded its jurisdiction on the fact that the defendant was domiciled in Portugal, which means that the 1989 Brussels Convention does apply to enforcement.

3.5.2. CONCURRENCE OF THE BRUSSELS AND LUGANO CONVENTIONS

Courts of the Brussels Convention States can be confronted with the question whether they must in a given case apply the Brussels or the Lugano Convention. In most cases there will not be much difference, but in matters of employment or of tenancy for several months it may lead to a different outcome. Article 54B Lugano Convention provides a solution for this.

I. Paragraph (1) shows that the application of the Brussels Convention is honoured. It states that the Brussels Convention shall continue to be mutually applied by its Contracting States. We may think of a case in which a national from a Brussels Convention State, France for example, is summoned to appear before the court of another Brussels Convention State, let us say the Netherlands. The nationality and the domicile of the plaintiff are irrelevant. In the enforcement stage, a judgment given in a Brussels Convention State (England) pursuant to the Brussels Convention will be enforced in another Contracting State (France) pursuant to the Brussels Convention.

The Brussels Convention is also applicable where a defendant domiciled outside the Convention's territory or the Lugano Convention's territory is summoned to appear before a Brussels Convention court under art. 4 Brussels Convention. In these three cases, the European Court of Justice is entitled pursuant to the 1971 Protocol on the interpretation to express its opinion on the interpretation of the Convention (*see* no. 15 Jenard/Möller report).

II. Paragraph (2) states that the Lugano Convention *shall* in any event be applied above the Brussels Convention (this applies to the EU-Lugano Convention States; they have a choice between Brussels Convention and Lugano Convention):

a in matters of jurisdiction:
   1 if the defendant is domiciled in an EFTA-Lugano Convention State;
   2 if art. 16 confers jurisdiction on a court of an EFTA-Lugano Convention State; or
   3 if art. 17 confers jurisdiction on a court of an EFTA-Lugano Convention State

b in relation to *lis pendens* and related actions:
   – when proceedings are instituted in the courts of an EU-Lugano Convention State and an EFTA-Lugano Convention State; and

c in matters of recognition and enforcement:
   – if State D and/or State R is an EFTA-Lugano Convention State.

Paragraphs b and c appear to be self-evident. It would be illogical to suppose that an EU-Lugano Convention State would want to apply the Brussels Convention provisions for related actions where the case has to be referred to an EFTA-Lugano Convention State, in which State only the Lugano Convention applies. The EFTA-Lugano Convention State does not even have the option of applying the Brussels Convention to the referral. In cases of recognition it also stands to reason that an EFTA-Lugano Convention State can only apply the Lugano Convention to the recognition and *vice versa*, that an EU-Lugano Convention State will automatically apply the Lugano Convention to a judgment given in an EFTA-Lugano Convention State. The Jenard/Möller report therefore indicates that paragraphs (b) and (c) of art. 54B (2) have only been included to remove all uncertainty. The following example may illustrate these rules. A person domiciled in Denmark lets an immovable property situated in Switzerland to a person domiciled in the Netherlands. The landlord brings an action for performance against the tenant. Which court has jurisdiction? The Netherlands court? No, it has no jurisdiction, since art. 16(1.a) Lugano Convention designates the Swiss courts. The Danish court? No, the property is situated outside Brussels Convention territory, but the defendant is domiciled within the Brussels Convention territory, so that the Danish court has no jurisdiction either (all things considered, the Danish court has nothing to do with the Lugano Convention, since Denmark is not a party to that Convention yet). Special jurisdictions yield no solution. The Swiss court? Yes, the Swiss court has jurisdiction under art. 16(1.a) Lugano Convention. The Swiss court cannot choose between the Brussels Convention and the Lugano Convention.

Suppose the Swiss court gives judgment. Is enforcement thereof possible in the Netherlands? Yes, pursuant to art. 54B(2)(c) Lugano Convention in conjunction with art. 34 Lugano Convention. The judgment originates from an EFTA-Lugano Convention State, so that enforcement will also be effected pursuant to that Convention. Is enforcement possible in Denmark? Not under the Lugano Convention. Perhaps there is another convention in force between Denmark and Switzerland, so that enforcement can still occur.

Next diagram on jurisdiction is based on the assumption that the defendant enters an appearance. If the defendant fails to appear, the court must of its own motion examine its jurisdiction (steps 1 up to and including 9); *see* art. 20 Brussels Convention.

JURISDICTION

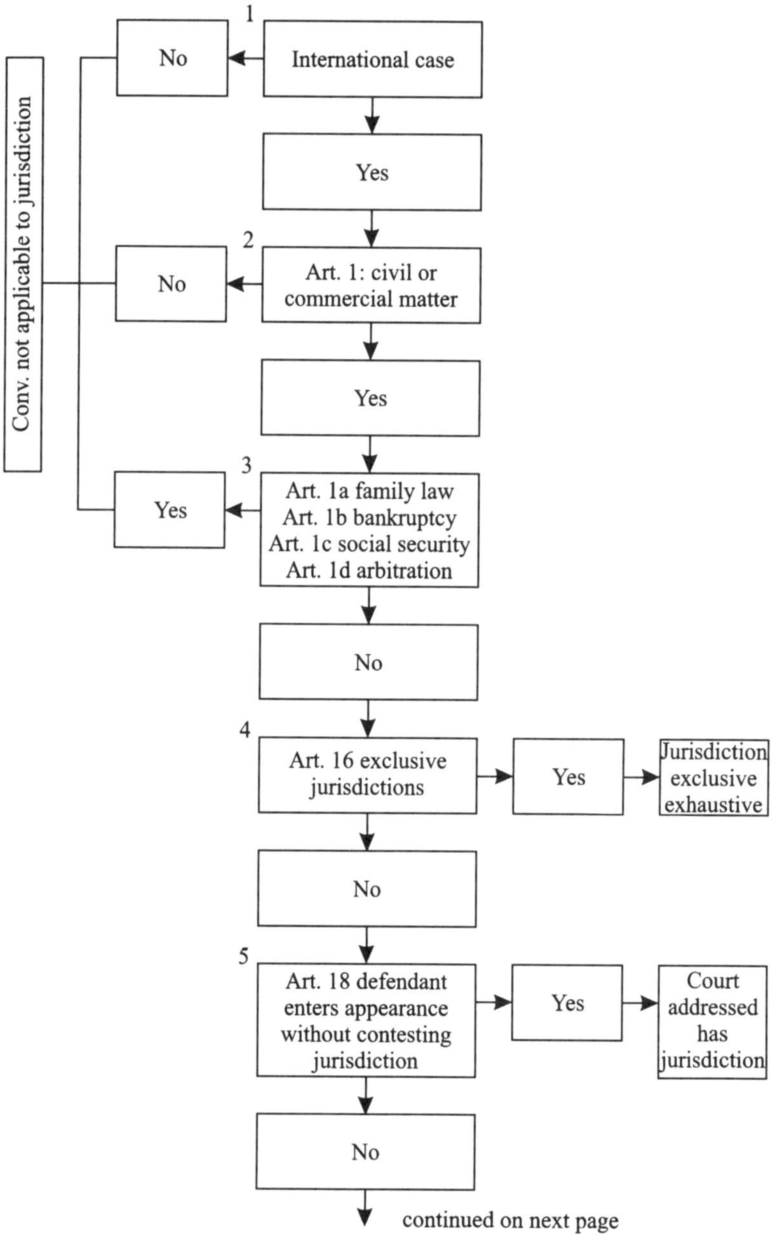

continued on next page

continuation of previous page

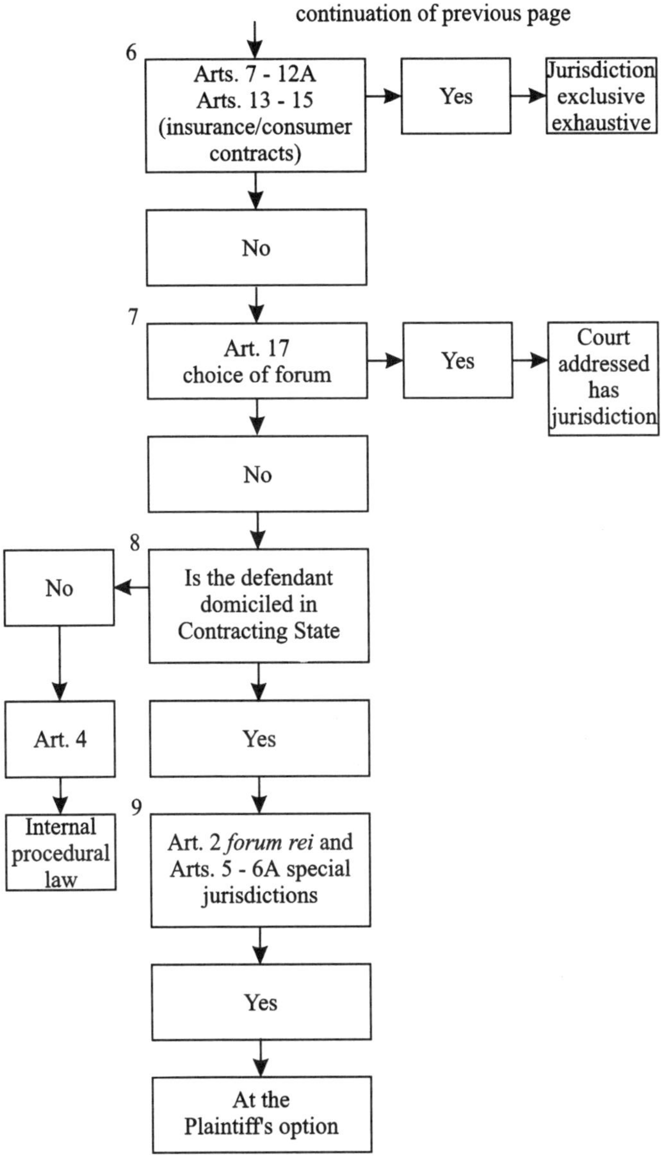

RECOGNITION

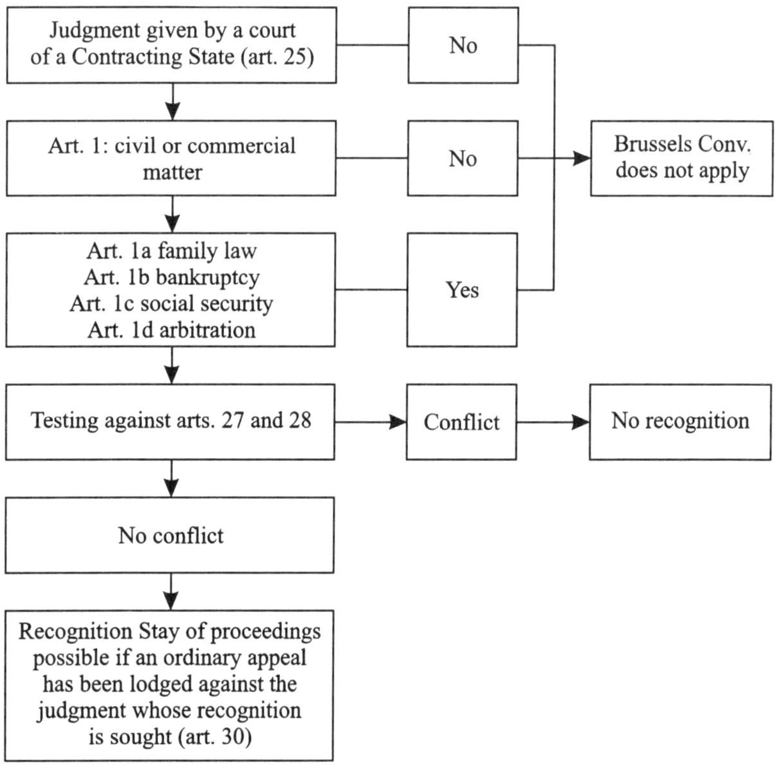

ENFORCEMENT

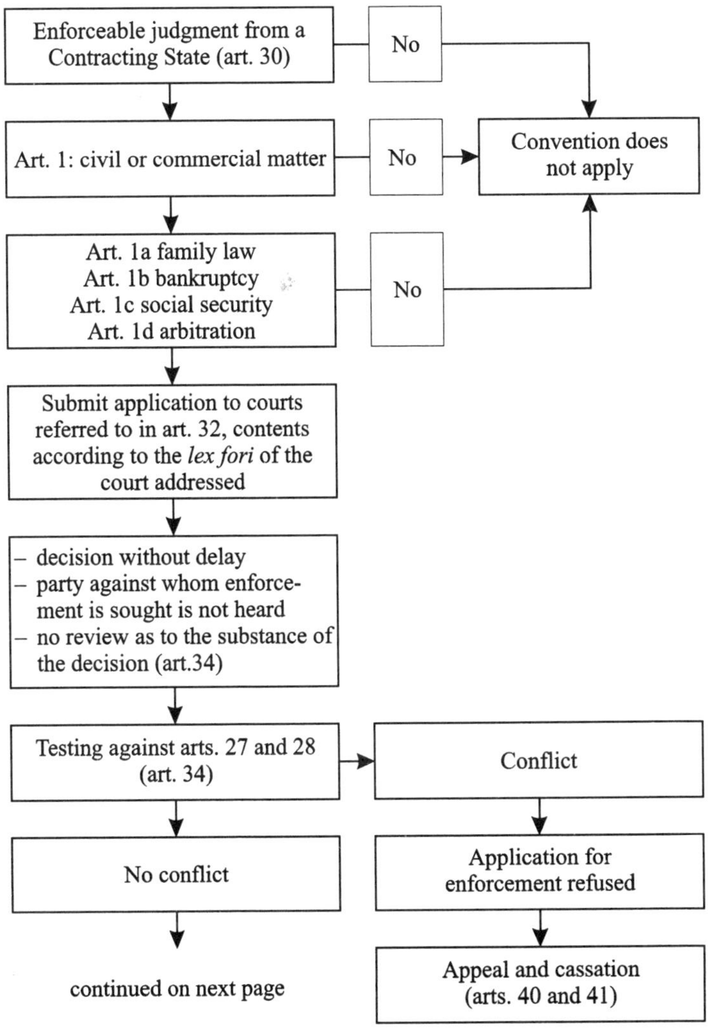

continued on next page

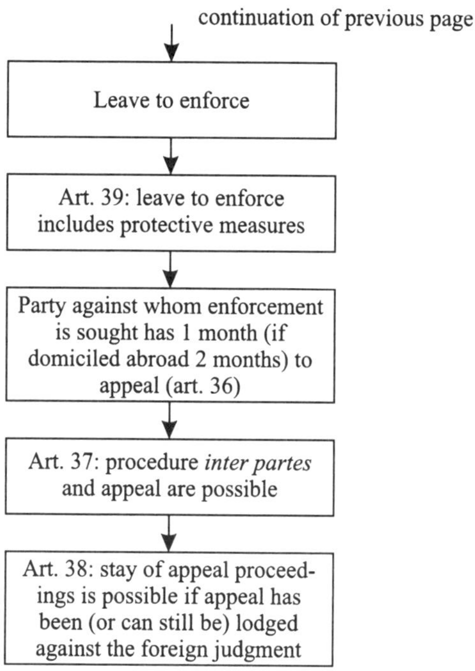
continuation of previous page
Leave to enforce
Art. 39: leave to enforce includes protective measures
Party against whom enforcement is sought has 1 month (if domiciled abroad 2 months) to appeal (art. 36)
Art. 37: procedure *inter partes* and appeal are possible
Art. 38: stay of appeal proceedings is possible if appeal has been (or can still be) lodged against the foreign judgment

4. English Civil Procedure

J. Henriëtte van Dam-Lely and Rob J.P. Kottenhagen*

4.1. Overview/Sources

4.1.1. INTRODUCTION

This chapter will only discuss English civil procedure (which also applies in Wales). In England a distinction is made between civil procedure, which refers to the procedural aspects of legal action, and civil litigation, which includes all aspects of legal action in general. Civil procedure in Ireland and Scotland materially differs from English civil procedure and will not be discussed further.

It may be useful to begin with a short characterisation of English law, in view of certain conspicuous differences from continental legal systems. The first striking feature in contrast to the other systems of law described in this book is that there is no overall codification of the main areas of law in England; a Civil Code or Code of Civil Procedure is unknown. On the other hand, there are a great number of specific laws (Statutes), relating to numerous areas of the law. A number of these Statutes will be discussed as far as they are relevant to the subject.

Through the centuries the lack of codification has led to a second characteristic of English law: the fact that prior judicial decisions are binding on the courts. In England the doctrine of precedent prevails in the narrowest sense of the word. According to this doctrine, decisions from the highest courts, the House of Lords and the Court of Appeal, are binding on all inferior courts. The Court of Appeal is always bound by its own previous decisions and by jurisdiction from the House of Lords. Only the House of Lords may reconsider its own previous decisions. This power has only been in existence since a 1966 Practice Direction (*see* section 4.1.2) issued by the House of Lords itself.

Such a system could eventually lead to complete stagnation of the law. Only in highly exceptional cases are proceedings continued up to the House of Lords; at all other levels the court is obliged to follow existing precedent, even if this were to lead to an unfair outcome. For that reason a technique has been developed to escape from the binding force of precedent. The term

* Thanks are due to Ms. H.A. Zebregs (solicitor, London).

used in that connection is 'distinguishing'; for only in a legally identical case is one bound by precedent.

Apart from the question whether two cases may be considered to be identical, there is another problem. English judicial decisions are not published as one decision by the court, but all the opinions are published, both concurring and dissenting ones. Consequently it is often quite difficult to ascertain what exactly is the *ratio decidendi* - the binding part or the principle of law - of a decision, and in fact a lot is left to the interpretation by the courts in later cases. The part of the decision without binding force is called *obiter dictum*.

A final characteristic of English law explains the naming of the different divisions of the courts and their competence. This concerns the fact that for many centuries there have actually been two legal systems in England existing side by side: common law and equity. Initially (since 1066, the time of William the Conqueror) justice was administered on behalf of the King by a council (*Curia Regis*, i.e. council of vassals) presided over by the Lord Chancellor. This Curia consisted of different courts (for example the King's Bench Division) and since the *Magna Carta* (1215) these have been located in London. This is still the present situation. The proceedings were (and still are) commenced by a writ: initially this was an order from the King to one of his subjects to comply with the plaintiff's claim (the plaintiff being the person who had invoked the King's help), unless he (the defendant) could justify himself before the court. The legal system which developed from this practice is called the common law. However, since 1258 the creating of new writs was curbed pursuant to the Provisions of Oxford, because the law became increasingly difficult and complicated. Naturally this prohibition caused some degree of rigidity in the law, which resulted in greater injustice under the regime of the common law. In order to ensure that justice was done, the citizen could now invoke the King's mercy, as a fountain of justice. This function was delegated to the Lord Chancellor and this was the beginning of the Court of Chancery. At this stage decisions were given in equity - to correct the unfairness of the common law - and from this equity developed, alongside the common law. Not until the Judicature Acts of 1873-1875 was this distinction lifted and have law and equity been applied by the same courts; the old courts of common law and the Court of Chancery have been replaced by the Supreme Court of Judicature. The Judicature Acts were consolidated in 1925 in the Supreme Court of Judicature (Consolidation) Act and today the Supreme Court Act 1981 is operative. In these Acts the organisation of the judicial powers of the Supreme Court is described (*see* section 4.3.2).

4.1.2. ACT AND CONVENTION

There is no Code of Civil Procedure in England. Work is, however, in progress on a uniform procedural code for the High Court and the county courts. English procedural law is derived from different sources. The (original) source is statute law. Statutes provide for the organisation, the jurisdiction and the appointment of judges. Some of the most relevant Acts in this connection are the Supreme Court Act (SCA) 1981, the Civil Jurisdiction and Judgments Act (CJJA) 1982 and 1991 and the County Courts Act (CCA) 1984. These Acts concern the competence of the various courts and the method of proceedings. In addition, the Courts and Legal Services Act (CLSA) 1990 must be mentioned; this Act contains regulations in relation to the main figures discussed in more detail below (judges and lawyers) and the legal services (e.g. a regulation with respect to the Legal Services Ombudsman; this matter will not be discussed any further).

As regards legal aid, the Legal Aid Act 1988 and the Legal Aid Regulations must be mentioned, in which the foundation is laid for a Legal Aid Scheme (*see* section 4.9.3a). Finally, there are special statutes, for example the Arbitration Acts 1950 and 1979 and the Civil Evidence Act 1968.

Typical of English procedural law are the Rules of Court, which govern the method of proceeding. Highly relevant to the subject under discussion are the Rules of Supreme Court (RSC), drawn up by a rule committee consisting of at most eight eminent judges and four practitioners (barristers/solicitors), currently authorised to do so under the Supreme Court Act 1981, sections 84 to 87 inclusive. The rules are also called judgemade (or delegated) legislation and may be consulted in a publication whose official title is: *The Supreme Court Practice*, London, Sweet and Maxwell, in which the rules are accompanied by elaborate comments. In practice one speaks of the '*White Book*'. The rules consist of orders (Ord.), subdivided into rules (r.). A new edition of the *White Book* is published every two years and in the intervening period a cumulative supplement is published several times a year. The latest edition dates from 1995, published in September 1994

Similar rules have been developed for the county courts: the County Court Rules. They can be found in *The County Court Practice*, which is known as the '*Green Book*'. These rules are also drawn up by a rule committee, which is again appointed by the Lord Chancellor. The committee consists of five judges, two barristers, two registrars and two solicitors. The legal basis for this is (currently) provided by the CCA 1984, s. 75 and the CLSA 1990, s. 16.

Both the *White Book* and the *Green Book* are in practice also called codes of procedure, but they do not constitute any codification of rules in the sense in which continental jurists understand it.

In addition to the rules, the *Practice Directions* may be mentioned as important sources; these are rules for legal practice, issued by the judges themselves: statements to guide the courts and the legal profession on matters of practice and procedure. The *Practice Directions* are published in the collections of legislation referred to in section 4.1.3.

Of course international conventions are also relevant to English procedural law. It must be added, however, that such conventions can in principle only be invoked if they have been implemented in the national system of laws. *See* for exceptions to this principle Dicey and Morris, *The Conflict of Laws*, Sweet and Maxwell, London 1993, Chapter 8, commentary on rule 17. In this connection the reader must be referred to the CJJA of 1982 and 1991, into which the European Convention on Jurisdiction and the Enforcement of Judgments in Civil and Commercial Matters and the EFTA-EC Convention on Jurisdiction and the Enforcement of Judgments in Civil and Commercial Matters (*see* sections 3.1.1 and 3.1.5) have been incorporated. The New York Convention of 1958 on the Recognition and Enforcement of Foreign Arbitral Awards (entry into force 23 December 1975) has been incorporated into the Arbitration Act of 1975. Furthermore, mention must be made of the Hague Convention on the Service Abroad of Judicial and Extrajudicial Documents in Civil or Commercial Matters of 1965 (entry into force 10 February 1969) and the Hague Convention on the Taking of Evidence Abroad in Civil or Commercial Matters of 1970 (entry into force 14 September 1976). England is also a party to the ECHRFF (entry into force 3 September 1953) and the CCPR (entry into force 20 August 1976). Although the ECHRFF has no direct effect in England, as it has not been implemented in English law, the courts are bound by it. An action before the ECHR for violation of the ECHRFF is bound to be admissible. Other conventions which apply are the European Convention on Information on Foreign Law of 1968 (entry into force 17 December 1969) and the European Agreement on the Transmission of Applications for Legal Aid of 1977 (entry into force 18 February 1978).

In RSC Ord. 114 the procedures are found that must be followed when a preliminary ruling is asked from the European Court pursuant to art. 177 EC Treaty.

4.1.3. LITERATURE AND CASE LAW

It goes without saying that case law is also a highly important source for the reasons stated before. It may be found in the Law Reports. Recommendable are the *Weekly Law Reports* (WLR) and the *All England Law Reports* (All E.R.). Apart from these collections, case law may be found in the data banks to be named below.

As regards the literature the *White Book* - containing extensive commentaries on Orders and rules - is the most authoritative work of reference. Apart from this there are a number of books in the area of civil litigation, such as Langan and Henderson, *Civil Procedure*, Sweet and Maxwell, London 1988, J. O'Hare and R.N. Hill, *Civil Litigation*, Longman Practitioner Series, 1993, *Odgers on High Court Pleading and Practice*, Sweet and Maxwell 1991, D. Barnard and M. Houghton, *The New Civil Court in Action*, Butterworths, 1993 and finally Walker & Walker, *The English Legal System*, Butterworths 1994. In this survey we would not wish to forget mentioning *The Fabric of English Justice*, Hamlyn Lectures 1987, Stevens, by the legendary Sir J.I.H. Jacob. Important for legal practice is *Atkin's Encyclopaedia of Court Forms in Civil Proceedings* (Second edition, Butterworths, 1992 Issue, 41 vols.), which includes examples of forms required for a large number of actions with an explanation of the requirements which must be met.

An important review to be mentioned for procedural practice is *Current Law*, which provides a useful means of keeping up to date. Furthermore, important developments in the main fields of law are discussed in the following reviews a.o.: the *Law Quarterly Review*, the *Cambridge Law Journal*, the *Modern Law Review* and the *New Law Journal*, which are intended more for academic purposes rather than for legal practice.

Other books than *The White Book* are hardly used by the legal practitioner. The main source of civil litigation is the *White Book*, significantly called 'the litigator's bible'. Therefore only sporadic references to literature will be given in the separate sections below.

4.1.4. DATA BASES

For the very reason that case law is so important in England, it is included in a data bank named Lexis. The full text of all case law from the highest instances - including material which is not published in the Law Reports - is included.

There is also the data bank Lawtel, containing abstracts of judgments since 1979. In addition, concise information on legislation is included and a cross-referenced index.

4.2. Fundamental Principles

4.2.1. INTRODUCTION

It is not customary in handbooks on English procedural law to present an enumeration of the fundamental principles. However, the following principles may be mentioned (derived from Sir Jack I.H. Jacob, *The Fabric of English Justice*, Hamlyn Lectures 1987, Stevens). These principles partly result from art. 6 ECHRFF and art. 14 CCPR. English legal principles such as the principle of orality (3.2.4), the principle of immediacy (3.2.5) and the principle of specialisation (3.2.7) as such cannot be found in art. 6 ECHRFF and art. 14 CCPR.

4.2.2. ADVERSARIAL SYSTEM

In principle the English court is passive to a high extent. It cannot, for instance, of its own motion appoint experts and cannot question witnesses. As opposed to this passivity of the court the parties have an active role. In this role we can distinguish the following aspects:

- party control (the parties decide the subject of the proceedings, they interrogate the other party and witnesses, they determine which witnesses are summoned and so on);
- party prosecution (the parties themselves determine whether proceedings will be fast or slow); and
- party autonomy (at each stage of the proceedings the parties are entitled to settle the case without requiring the court's approval).

The adversarial system is under growing pressure, by the way. Modern and efficient litigation requires an increasing influence from the judge on the development of the procedure (*see also* section 4.2.4). *See* for further information C. Glasser, *Civil Procedure and Lawyers. The Adversary system and the Decline of the Orality Principle*, Modern Law Review 1993 pp. 307-324.

4.2.3. FAIR TRIAL

The principle of a fair trial is also fundamental in English law. It is clearly manifest in the rules concerning the pleadings, discovery and the trial and has a direct relation with the adversarial system.

4.2.4. PRINCIPLE OF ORALITY

Initially the emphasis of the proceedings was on the oral treatment (trial). In principle all written documents which are submitted during the proceedings are read out at the trial. The judgment is also given orally. Recently, however, a tendency may be observed to terminate proceedings in the pretrial phase, if possible (this will be discussed in more detail in section 4.4.1), by encouraging parties to settle their case after having been given the opportunity to consider the other party's position.

4.2.5. PRINCIPLE OF IMMEDIACY

The principle of immediacy is closely connected to the principle of orality. The trial is the heart of the proceedings. All documents, statements concerning the facts as well as the applicable precedents and other legal sources are discussed at the trial.

4.2.6. PRINCIPLE OF FINALITY (*LITES FINIRI OPORTET*)

This principle is based on the idea that proceedings must come to an end sometime (*lites finiri oportet*). Appeal courts in the English system adhere to the principle that the decisions by lower courts are correct until proven incorrect. As a result, England has fewer appeal cases than the European continental countries; indeed, the system of leave to appeal, which will be discussed below, works like a sieve in this connection.

4.2.7. PRINCIPLE OF SPECIALISATION

This principle may be found back in the judicial organisation and the organisation of lawyers. The judicial organisation has a great number of specialised courts (*see* section 4.3.2).

As regards the lawyers, there is a difference between barristers and solicitors (*see also* below under principal characters, section 4.3).

4.2.8. PRINCIPLE OF PUBLICITY

The proceedings are in principle public (SCA 1981, s. 67) There are two important exceptions:

1. The hearing of pretrial proceedings in chambers; only parties and their counsel are present, the public and the press are excluded from the session (RSC Ord. 32); and
2. The hearing of proceedings in Camera; the court may decide before or during the public proceedings, both in the pretrial and in the trial phase, that the court must be cleared; the public and the press are removed (RSC Ord. 33, r. 4/3).

As regards the first exception, there have been pleas to abolish it, except of course in cases in which art. 6 ECHRFF also allows administration of justice in camera.

4.2.9. PRINCIPLE OF INDEPENDENCE AND IMPARTIALITY

Administration of justice by an independent court is a fundamental principle in England, too; this is illustrated *inter alia* by the fact that judges are appointed for life.

4.3. Principal Characters

4.3.1. INTRODUCTION

The principal characters such as the judge, the lawyers and the parties will be discussed in detail below. First, we look at two persons who also play a part in English civil procedure, the sheriff and the bailiff.

In each county the Crown appoints a sheriff. The sheriff deals *inter alia* with the enforcement of High Court judgments and he is assisted by bailiffs, persons appointed by him to serve writs, draw up official reports and enforce both High Court and county court judgments. County court bailiffs are appointed by the Lord Chancellor.

The territory coming under the jurisdiction of a sheriff or bailiff is called a bailiwick.

4.3.2. THE JUDGE

a. Introduction

In the area of civil law the following institutions are distinguished: the county courts, the High Court, the Court of Appeal and the House of Lords (*see* the diagram below).

Judges are appointed for life and are selected from the ranks of barristers (*see below*) who have a certain minimum of years' standing (for High Court Judges this is 10 years, SCA 1981 s. 10). Since the right of audience for solicitors before the High Court has now been extended, under certain conditions they too may now be appointed as judges (CLSA 1990, s. 27).

The judges in the county courts and in the High Court are *unus iudex* and in the Court of Appeal they sit in a panel of 2 or 3 judges (SCA s. 54). In the House of Lords a court usually consists of five judges (Administration of Justice Act (AJA) 1968).

The Judicial Committee of the Privy Council, or Privy Council for short, will not be discussed further in this chapter. It is the highest court of appeal for the Dominions or the Dependencies of England, such as Australia. In respect of domestic affairs, the Privy Council is an appeal court for decisions from certain professional organisations, for example the General Medical Council, in particular in matters concerning the expulsion of members from the organisation.

In respect of the different judges the following terminology is used. Head of the House of Lords is the Lord Chancellor (AJA 1968), assisted by 11 Lords of Appeal in Ordinary (also referred to as the Law Lords). Head of the Court of Appeal (i.e. of the civil division) is the Master of the Rolls (SCA 1981, s. 3(2)), assisted by the Lords Justices of Appeal (SCA 1981, s. 2(3)). In the High Court one speaks of puisne judges, more commonly referred to as Justices of the High Court (SCA 1981, s. 4(2)). The county courts, finally, consist of Circuit Judges (CCA 1984, s. 5).

An important role in the pretrial phase is played by the master. He is in charge of procedure in the pretrial phase, which means that he makes all necessary decisions about the progress of the procedure and the way in which litigation is conducted and that he delivers judgments, for example in summary proceedings (*see* section 4.7.2). The equivalent of the master in the District Registries of the High Court and in the county courts is the district judge (CLSA 1990, s. 74). Before the CLSA 1990 came into force the district judge was called district registrar or county court registrar. Masters are appointed from the ranks of barristers or solicitors (*see* the CCA 1984, ss. 6-12 and SCA 1981 s. 89). The master adjudicates alone. Interlocutory applications to the master may be filed in several different ways: e.g. *ex parte* (without hearing the opposing party), by summons (summons for hearing) and by motion (especially for interlocutory injunctions), as discussed below. *See* for a more general discussion of the role of the judge in the Commonwealth: B. McLachlin, *The Role of Judges in Modern Commonwealth Society*, Law Quarterly Review 1994, Vol. 110, pp. 260-269.

b. International jurisdiction, with the exception of jurisdiction arising from treaties

To the extent that the jurisdiction of the English court is not governed by the Civil Jurisdiction and Judgments Act (CJJA) 1982 (implementing the Brussels Convention on Jurisdiction and Enforcement of Judgments in Civil and Commercial Matters), the court decides on its jurisdiction pursuant to the rules which had been developed in case law before the CJJA 1982 entered into force. A well-known rule is that the English court has jurisdiction if the defendant resides in England at the time of the commencement of proceedings (presence within the territorial limits). If the defendant resides outside England, the English court may in some cases nevertheless have jurisdiction. Sometimes leave is required, sometimes it is not (leave to serve out of jurisdiction RSC Ord. 11).

c. Jurisdiction of the non-civil courts

The crown courts and the magistrates' courts are criminal courts. The crown court may act as court of first instance, but minor criminal offences are mostly dealt with at first instance by courts consisting mostly of lay judges, the magistrates' courts. The appeal instances are the Criminal Division of the Court of Appeal and finally, the House of Lords.

For administrative matters there is no separate administrative court system. Such disputes are brought before the High Court (judicial review, RSC Ord. 53). Special cases may sometimes be brought before certain Administrative Tribunals.

d. Absolute jurisdiction

Until recently the jurisdiction of the county courts (the lowest instance) was governed by the County Courts Act 1984 (CCA 1984) and some special Acts. In the Courts and Legal Services Act (CLSA) 1990 the jurisdiction of the county courts has been widened. The Lord Chancellor has been granted jurisdiction to provide rules by Order concerning *inter alia* the allocation of business between the county courts and the High Court (CLSA 1990, s. 1). The relevant rules have been laid down in the High Court and County Courts Jurisdiction Order 1991 (in force since 1 July 1991). Unless there is special statutory jurisdiction, the county court has jurisdiction for claims not exceeding £25,000 and the High Court for claims exceeding £50,000. Claims between £25,000 and £50,000 fall within the jurisdiction of either the High Court or the county court. Claims not exceeding £1,000 are automatically dealt with by arbitration, whereby a registrar (CCR Ord. 19, *see* section 4.7.3) acts as arbitrator. As can be seen in section 4.10.3 on arbitration, it is noteworthy that a court official acts as arbitrator and that no arbitration agreement has been concluded between the parties.

Apart from these rules concerning general jurisdiction, county courts are designated as the competent court in a large number of special acts (such as the Sex Discrimination Act 1975, s. 66, the Rent Act 1977, s. 141 and the Landlord and Tenant Act 1954, s. 63).

Finally there is the possibility of jurisdiction by agreement. Parties can mutually agree to initiate proceedings before a county court, even if this court had no competence to adjudicate the case by virtue of general rules of jurisdiction. In order to do so, a memorandum must be drawn up signed by the parties or their respective solicitors (CCA 1984, ss. 18 and 24).

The Supreme Court Act 1981, s. 53 provides rules for the distribution of business in the Supreme Court of Judicature which consists of the High Court and the Court of Appeal (the Crown Court, a criminal instance which is not discussed here further, is in theory a division of the High Court).

The High Court consists of three divisions (SCA 1981, ss. 5 and 6): the Chancery Division, the Queen's Bench Division and the Family Division.

In the Chancery Division - presided over by the Vice-Chancellor - decisions are made especially regarding trusts, mortgages, bankruptcies, company matters, partnership matters, wills and probate. Furthermore the Companies Court (RSC Ord. 102) and the Patents Court (Patents Act 1977, s. 96(1) and RSC Ord. 104) form part of this Division.

The Family Division - presided over by the President of the Family Division - deals with issues regarding matrimonial causes, guardianship, adoption and such like (Family Proceedings Rules 1991).

The Queen's Bench Division - presided over by the Lord Chief Justice of England - mainly deals with cases regarding claims in connection with contracts and torts. In addition it is a remainder division. Two specialised courts form part of the Queen's Bench Division: the Admiralty Court (cases regarding maritime law; *see* RSC Ords. 74 and 75) and the Commercial Court (cases regarding commercial actions; *see* RSC Ord. 72).

The SCA 1981 s. 61 provides for the allocation of business among these three divisions; this allocation is based on Schedule 1 to the SCA 1981 s. 61. In principle, they all have equal jurisdiction, but they have wide powers to transfer a case to another division or to retain a case, even though it was started in the wrong division. The cases are brought in the Royal Courts of Justice in London or, elsewhere in England, in the District Registries, at the plaintiff's choice. These registries, which can be described as the country branches of the High Court, are set up by the Lord Chancellor (SCA 1981, ss. 99-104). In practice, they are usually situated in places where there is already a county court. In addition, there are trial centres in the major provincial cities (RSC Ord. 33, r. 1). These are permanent civil trial centres (25 at present), which have taken over the role of the former Assizes (a system whereby touring judges held periodical sessions in specific places in the country). However, High Court judges still go on circuit from London to these centres. In this way, the advantages of a centralised legal system - such as unity and certainty of the law - are guaranteed.

Appeal from decisions of the High Court and the county court lies to the Court of Appeal (SCA 1981, ss. 16-18, CCA 1984, ss. 77-82, CLSA 1990, s. 7 and RSC Ord. 59), following which in special cases appeal lies to the House of Lords (Administration of Justice (Appeals) Act 1934, s. 1 and the RSC 16.001-16-116 and Ord. 59, r. 1/56. *See* the diagram on p. 97.

e. Relative jurisdiction

Jurisdiction lies with the county court of the district in which the defendant resides or carries on business or the court of the district in which the cause of action wholly or partly arose (CCR Ord. 4, r. 2), depending on the plaintiff's choice. If an action has been commenced in the wrong county court, this court may nevertheless deal with the case or transfer it to the appropriate court (CCR Ord. 16, r. 2). There are approximately 290 county courts.

The High Court, the Court of Appeal and the House of Lords are all based in London, so that questions as to relative jurisdiction do not arise. Insofar as the High Court holds sessions elsewhere in the country (the District Registries, *see above*) the plaintiff can choose where the action is to be commenced.

DIAGRAM JUDICIAL ORGANISATION IN CIVIL CASES IN ENGLAND AND WALES

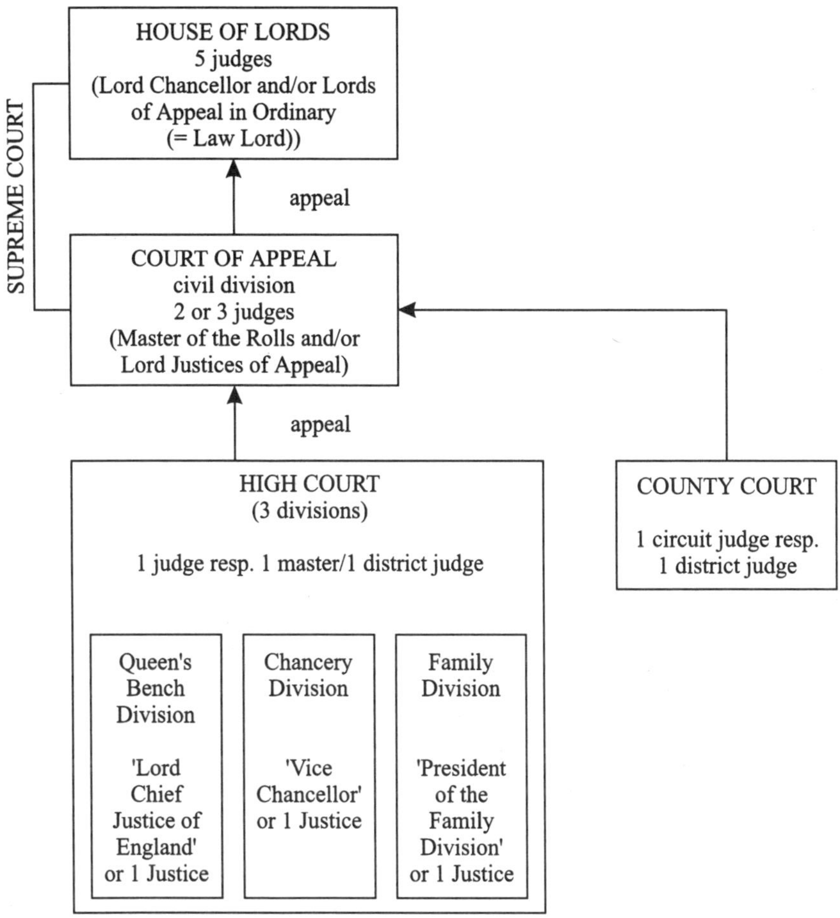

4.3.3. THE LAWYERS

Representation *ad litem* is not mandatory for natural persons, unless they are under a legal disability. Legal persons must be represented by a solicitor (RSC Ord. 5, r. 6).

Generally speaking, solicitors advise the parties, prepare proceedings for trial, negotiate and so on, while barristers, also referred to as counsel, actually plead the case in court. Barristers obtain their instructions from solicitors and parties have no direct access to barristers: contact between client and barrister is via the solicitor, although, in practice, barrister and solicitor increasingly work as a team together with the client, particularly in complicated and time-consuming cases. Barristers usually draw up the pleadings (e.g. statement of claim, defence, counterclaim), especially in complicated procedures, but this may also be done by solicitors (which is only recommended if they have adequate experience, *see* Ord. 18/A). At an early stage of the proceedings, the barrister's advice on evidence is often asked. The barrister may represent the client in pretrial hearings before the Master and will conduct the trial (*see* section 4.4.2c).

This only applies to the Supreme Court; a solicitor can therefore conduct the entire proceedings before a county court (CCA 1984, s. 60). In the High Court the solicitor may act in proceedings before the Master. However, solicitors with special authority can now also deal with the entire proceedings before the High Court (by virtue of the CLSA 1990, s. 27).

As stated above, there is no mandatory representation *ad litem* for natural persons in England. They may therefore conduct proceedings unassisted, but they are not allowed to appoint another person by proxy to represent them.

The Law Society (since 1831), of which most solicitors are members, provides for the admission of solicitors (Solicitors Act 1974, ss. 1 and 28). For such regulations it needs the permission of the Lord Chancellor, the Lord Chief Justice and the Master of the Rolls. In order to qualify as a solicitor, one either needs a law degree or, failing that, one needs to do a one-year law course followed by an examination. After that, all candidates must attend another, more practical law course and sit an examination. Finally, they are required to do two years of articles with a practising solicitor. The Law Society also provides rules on the running of a practice (such as the duty to have a separate account for monies of third parties, a so-called client account) and rules on conduct and etiquette. A solicitor not only has obligations to his client but also to the court, for he/she is an officer of the court. Solicitors often work together in partnerships. At the moment there are over 37,000 solicitors working in England.

Subject to the exceptions set out above, barristers possess a monopoly over pleading in the High Court, the Court of Appeal and the House of Lords.

In order to become a barrister a Bar examination must be passed. At the moment the Council of Legal Education under the supervision of the Bar Council provides the training for this examination (*see below*). In addition, a student is obliged to keep terms for a period of two years, i.e. to dine a number of times in one of the four Inns of Court (hence the expression 'to eat and drink your way to the bar'), after which a senior barrister (bencher) calls him to the bar. He can only act as an independent barrister if he has practised under the supervision of another barrister for a year - the first six months of which are unpaid - (pupillage) and if he has been offered a place in a set of chambers. A set of chambers is a suite of rooms in one of the Inns of Court - more on which will be said below - where 15 to 25 barristers conduct their practice. Barristers have their own practice and are only paid for their own cases. However, the costs of running the chambers are shared among the barristers. The organisation of each set of chambers is in the hands of a barrister's clerk. He also negotiates the amount of a barrister's fee with the solicitor. A solicitor decides which barrister he wants to use, but the clerk may suggest that the case be handled by another barrister.

Barristers belong to one of the four Inns of Court. These Inns - Inner Temple, Middle Temple, Lincoln's Inn and Gray's Inn - are actually associations with the authority 'to call persons to practice at the Bar'. In addition, the Inns also have disciplinary supervision over the barristers. The Senate of the Inns of Court and the Bar - also called the Bar Council - is the central governing body of the profession of the Bar. The training of barristers is supervised by the Bar Council.

After a barrister has successfully practised for a number of years, he may request the Lord Chancellor to be given the title of Queen's Counsel (QC). A QC is also called a silk because he is entitled to wear a black silk gown. A Queen's Counsel will be instructed in important cases and is always assisted by a junior counsel (a barrister who is not yet a QC).

A barrister must be instructed by a solicitor and cannot receive instruction directly from a client. The solicitor is liable for the barrister's fee.

At present there are approximately 6,000 practising barristers.

Literature: Morison and Leith, *The Barrister's World. And the Nature of Law.* Philadelphia 1992, 1st edition; R. Abel, *The Legal Profession in England and Wales*, Blackwell 1988. *See further* for a survey of recent literature: R.C.A. White, *The Legal System: Knowledge, Scholarship and Policy*, Oxford Journal of Legal Studies, Vol. 14 pp. 99-109.

4.3.4. THE PARTIES

Natural persons and legal persons can be parties in proceedings (companies and other corporate bodies). If a party is not authorised to act as a party in the proceedings, the proceedings were and always have been a nullity and should be struck out.

Partnerships (these are not legal persons) can summon or be summoned under the firm's name, but as such they are not party to the proceedings. They can be forced to disclose the names and addresses of the partners, which is important in connection with enforcement.

Minors (Family Law Reform Act 1969, s. 1 and RSC Ord. 92, r. 5/5) and mental patients can act as plaintiffs (RSC Ord. 80), but must be represented by a so-called next friend and as defendants by a guardian *ad litem*. It is usual for a parent or family member to be appointed as next friend or guardian.

Two or more plaintiffs and two or more defendants may without leave of the Court be joined together in one action, if the claims concern some common question of fact or law and the different claims arise out of the same transaction(s); *see* RSC Ord. 15, r. 4 (joinder of parties). In any other case leave of the Court is needed, but seldom granted. Plaintiffs must be represented by the same solicitor and barrister and cannot have conflicting interests.

A group of known plaintiffs may be represented by one plaintiff. Not all members of the group need to give explicit permission, but they are all bound by the judgment. All members of the group are required to have the same interest, e.g. they are all party to one contract (representative action RSC Ord. 15, r. 12).

These requirements are interpreted strictly, and it is therefore not allowed to bring an action to protect the general interest. In this respect we refer to the relator actions (Ord. 15, r. 11): somebody who wants to act against the violation of a general interest without having been damaged himself, may request the Attorney-General to institute proceedings. Such an action may only be brought by the Attorney-General, in this case in relation to X (the relator). The Attorney-General decides whether or not he will institute proceedings, against which decision there is in principle no recourse (Ord. 15, r. 11/2).

4.4. Basic Procedure for Contentious Jurisdiction at First Instance

4.4.1. INTRODUCTION

A distinction can be made between the pretrial stage and the trial itself, a distinction which is not made in any continental system of law. The trial is the (oral) treatment of the case itself. The pretrial stage, which will be discussed below, precedes the trial and is comprised of:

1. commencement of proceedings; e.g. issuing the writ or originating summons (*see* section 4.5.2);

2. parties and causes of actions; here the central question is who proceeds against whom and on what grounds;
3. pleadings;
4. discovery; and
5. directions for trial.

The proceedings can also end at the pretrial stage (*see* section 4.7).

4.4.2. HIGH COURT PROCEDURE

a. Introduction

Following the procedure used by all handbooks on English litigation the High Court proceedings will now be discussed in detail, followed by a brief survey of the county court proceedings (*see* section 4.4.3). After discussion of the ordinary proceedings in which there are always assumed to be two parties - plaintiff and defendant - section 4.4.2e will deal with a number of particularities.

If at the beginning of or during the proceedings the Rules of Supreme Court are not complied with, this does not nullify the proceedings. Under Ord. 2, r. 1 the Court may set aside such proceedings either wholly or partly, as well as any step taken in those proceedings or any document, judgment or order therein, or exercise its powers to allow such an amendment to be made or to make any order it thinks fit. A party's application to the Court to set aside proceedings for an irregularity on the part of the opposing party is only allowed if it is made within a reasonable time and before the party applying has taken any fresh step after becoming aware of this irregularity (RSC Ord. 2, r. 2). A fresh step is a step sufficient to constitute a waiver of the irregularity (RSC Ord. 2, r. 2/3).

b. Commencement of proceedings

Generally speaking, contentious proceedings begin by the issue of a writ (*see* RSC Ord. 5, r. 2 and Ord. 6). In exceptional cases, e.g. when the proceedings only relate to a point of law, they may be commenced by originating summons (*see* section 4.5.2). If commencement was by the wrong form, for example an originating summons instead of a writ, this does not render the action a nullity or set aside the proceedings (RSC Ord. 2, r. 1). *See* e.g. Ord. 28, r. 8 when a matter is commenced by originating summons instead of by writ. The Court may then order the proceedings to continue as if they had been commenced by writ.

The way in which the writ must be drawn up is prescribed exactly by RSC Ord. 6. Obviously, the writ must state the plaintiff's and the defendant's name and address, as well as the name and address of the plaintiff's solicitor. The writ also contains the claim and the grounds upon which it is based (the statement of claim) may be indorsed on the writ (i.e. set out on the back of the writ), *see* RSC Ord. 6, r. 2. The plaintiff may also confine himself to merely stating the nature of his claim without specifying the grounds upon which it is based, provided he serves a separate statement of claim on the defendant (RSC Ord. 18, r. 1) either when the writ is served on the defendant, or within 14 days after the defendant has given notice of intention to defend (RSC Ord. 12).

We should also refer to RSC Ord. 15, r. 1 (joinder of causes of action), by virtue of which the plaintiff may claim relief against the defendant in respect of more than one cause of action. This possibility has been created to avoid a multiplicity of legal proceedings; *see* SCA 1981, s. 49(2) for the relevant particulars.

The issue of the writ is effected when the Court seals and dates the writ, i.e. when the Court seal (which includes the date) is stamped on the writ. The proceedings begin once the writ is issued. The writ must be served within 4 months after its issue. The Court may extend this term by a maximum period of 4 months (RSC Ord. 6, r. 8). If the Court has been convinced that service of the writ cannot take place within this further period of four months, it may grant a maximum extension to twelve months after the date of issue. An extension to twelve months is reserved for very rare cases and even an extension by four months is not easy to obtain.

The writ may be served in two ways:

1. personal service (RSC Ord. 10, r. 1): the writ must be served personally on a defendant and this is usually effected by an inquiry agent instructed by the solicitor or by a county court bailiff (RSC Ord. 65, r. 2); or
2. service by post (RSC Ord. 10, r. 1 (2)): the usual means of service is by post. A sealed copy of the writ is sent by first class post or deposited in the defendant's letterbox. The writ is deemed to have been served on the 7th day after its having been posted or (as the case may be) deposited in the letterbox (RSC Ord. 10, r. 1(3)).

The writ states that the defendant must either settle the claim or return the acknowledgment of service accompanying the writ.

c. Proceedings

After the writ or statement of claim has been served on the defendant, he must within 14 days (RSC Ord. 12, r. 1) complete and return the form for the acknowledgment of service to the Central Office (if the proceedings take place in London) of the High Court or the District Registry. In his acknowledgment of service the defendant indicates whether or not he wants to defend the proceedings (RSC Ord. 12).

If the defendant intends to defend the proceedings, he will serve his defence upon the plaintiff.

The following documents (called pleadings) may be exchanged:

- statement of claim (RSC Ord. 6, r. 2 and Ord. 18, r. 1);
- defence (RSC Ord. 18, r. 2), counterclaim (RSC Ord. 15, r. 2), set-off (RSC Ord. 18, r. 17); and
- reply and, where appropriate, defence to counterclaim (RSC Ord. 18, r. 3).

In the pleadings the grounds are laid for the actual trial; the pleadings serve to establish the issues in dispute. This only concerns the establishment of the facts (RSC Ord. 18); no evidence is produced and no legal arguments are put forward in the pleadings. All facts relevant to the claim or the defence must be stated.

The statement of claim contains the factual grounds of the claim, as well as the claim itself. In his defence the defendant may plead a counterclaim or set-off (*see* 4.4.2e(4)).

All pleadings must be served on the other party. After the exchange of the above pleadings the pleadings are closed. Then the second part of the pretrial stage follows, which takes place before the master.

If parties actually want to take the proceedings to trial (*see below* for the possibilities of terminating proceedings before trial (section 4.7.2), the plaintiff will issue a summons for directions. This must be done within one calendar month after the close of pleadings (RSC Ord. 25, r. 1). Parties are obliged to submit all relevant documents to the master and to give all necessary information. The object of the summons is to apply for measures to keep the trial itself as short as possible, to limit costs by dealing directly with as many matters as possible and to give directions on the further course of the proceedings. The directions for the trial are laid down in an order for directions. In personal injury cases there are automatic directions: within fourteen days after close of pleadings (and sometimes before that) discovery takes place (RSC Ord. 25, r. 8). *See further* below on the discovery.

If the case calls for the appointment of experts, the order for directions will provide how many experts either party may appoint and at which point in the pretrial stage expert reports will be exchanged between the parties (Ord. 38, rr. 35-43).

In the order for directions the exchange of witness statements is also provided for in accordance with RSC Ord. 38, r. 2A. Since 1992 parties have been obliged to exchange witness statements before the trial. These statements must contain all the evidence which the party hopes to adduce at the trial. Unless with leave of the court, a witness can only give evidence at the trial if his statement had previously been exchanged. This is a crucial stage in the proceedings, for through these statements and the documents submitted in the discovery (*see below*), the parties have an opportunity to assess each other's strong and weak points and they can judge their chances of success.

In this stage, too, an application for security for costs may be made in the case of a foreign plaintiff litigating in England (*see* section 4.9.3a.).

In English litigation, great importance is attached to discovery (RSC Ord. 24). The parties are obliged to produce all documents (including audiotapes and videotapes) which are relevant to the action and which are in their possession, custody or power. This even applies if the documents are disadvantageous to the party concerned or cause him to lose the case! Documents which come into the parties' possession, custody or power later, during the proceedings, must also be discovered. The solicitor is under an obligation towards the Court to inspect his client's documents himself in order to ensure that his client has given full discovery. If his client disallows this, the solicitor must withdraw from the case. There are three exceptions to the principle that all relevant documents must be discovered (i.e. documents privileged from production):

1. legal professional privilege (RSC Ord. 24, r. 5/6): correspondence between solicitor and client and correspondence between solicitor and third parties when litigation was contemplated or pending;
2. documents whose discovery may harm the public interest (RSC Ord. 24, r. 5/15); and
3. documents which may render the relevant party or his spouse liable to criminal prosecution in the United Kingdom (the privilege against self-incrimination; RSC Ord. 24, r. 5/14).

Discovery normally takes place by the parties exchanging lists of all relevant documents (where required, supported by affidavit). An affidavit is a document whose authenticity is confirmed on oath before a solicitor (Ord. 41).

In this list it is indicated in respect of which documents the party invokes one of the privileges. The opposing party may request copies of the documents which are not privileged. In any event, documents may be inspected at the solicitor's or his client's office. If necessary, a party may obtain an order for discovery.

Discovery may only be ordered between the parties to the action, so in principle it is not possible for discovery to be ordered against third parties. This is called the 'mere witness' rule, to which there are two exceptions. In certain cases of personal injuries and death a party may, even before the action, apply to the court for an order for disclosure of certain documents by a third party (e.g. a hospital). *See* SCA 1981, s. 34, CCA 1984, s. 53. The second exception was made in the case of *Norwich Pharmacal* v. *Customs and Excise* [1974] AC 133, which concerned infringement of a patent. The defendants obtained an order for disclosure in respect of certain documents which would enable the plaintiff to find out who the persons infringing the patent really were.

See further on discovery Matthews and Malek, *Discovery*, Sweet and Maxwell 1992.

Another way to obtain more information from the opponent is through interrogatories (RSC Ord. 26), whereby one party asks written questions of the other party. These questions must be answered in an affidavit (i.e. under oath). The party due to answer the questions may, within 14 days after the interrogatories have been served on him, apply to the court for an order to amend or withdraw the interrogatories. If there is no reply to the interrogatories, the party asking the interrogatories may request the court to give judgment in default against the party who has failed to reply.

A party may also serve a notice on the other party requesting him to admit the facts specified in the notice (a so-called notice to admit facts). This is done to prevent unnecessary production of evidence (RSC Ord. 27, r. 2).

When a party is of the opinion that there are facts missing in the opposing party's pleadings and/or that certain facts should be added, he may file a request for further and better particulars (of pleading) (RSC Ord. 18, r. 12/3, Ord. 6, r. 7 and Ord. 9, r. 11). Before an application for further and better particulars is made to the Court, a request must be made by letter to the opposing party. Usually a request for particulars is complied with voluntarily. If, however, the opposing party is not prepared to comply with the request, an application for further and better particulars (usually at the same time as the summons for directions) is made before the master who may subsequently give an order for further and better particulars.

In preparation for the trial, counsel is asked to give advice on evidence. In order to do so, counsel will need to consider the pleadings, the written statements from the client and any witnesses (proofs of evidence), the witness statements, any expert reports and the correspondence in the case.

Within the time-limit stated in the order for directions (RSC Ord. 25, r. 1) the plaintiff then sets the action down for trial (RSC Ord. 34) by delivering the documents to the Court and notifying the defendant within 24 hours after setting the action down for trial (RSC Ord. 34, r. 8).

The trial (the hearing of the whole case in open court) takes place in a set way. First the party on whom the burden of proof lies (usually the plaintiff) holds his opening speech, in which he states the facts and legal grounds upon which his claim is based and explains the points at issue. The plaintiff examines 'his' witnesses, who can then be cross-examined by the defendant. The defendant then holds his opening speech and calls his witnesses. These are examined by the defendant and cross-examined by the plaintiff (*see also* section 4.4.5). The defendant makes his final speech, followed by the plaintiff (RSC Ord. 35, r. 7). The plaintiff has therefore the last word. These final speeches can be a very important means of convincing the Court which party is in the right.

See about the pleadings system: O. Hartwieg, *Die Kunst des Sachvortrags im Zivilprozeß, Eine rechtsvergleichende Studie zur Arbeitsweise des Englischen Pleadings-Systems*, Heidelberg 1988.

d. Judgment

The Court usually gives an oral (reasoned) judgment immediately. In difficult cases judgment is not pronounced immediately, but within a period varying from one day to several months in highly complex cases.

The court associate certifies the judgment, whilst the plaintiff sees to it that the judgment is drawn up and submitted to the Court for approval. He also ensures that the judgment is entered in the court's records. *See further* on this RSC Ord. 42.

With regard to the awarding of costs the Court usually makes a separate order immediately after the judgment. The relevant provisions may be found in RSC Ord. 62 (*see* section 4.9.3).

In this connection the default judgment must also be mentioned, against which lies the recourse of setting aside. *See below* under non-appearance (e.1).

Judgments which are not final are called orders, e.g. orders for direction.

e. Special aspects of procedure

1. Non-appearance

If the defendant 1) does not return the acknowledgment of service; 2) fails to give notice of intention to defend; or 3) does not serve a defence in time, judgment in default may be given. *See* CCR Ord. 9 and RSC Ords. 13 and 19.

In most cases no evidence needs to be produced in order to enter judgment. In the cases mentioned under 1) and 2) the plaintiff only needs to file an affidavit of service. In the third case the plaintiff places an indorsement on one of the copies of the judgment to the effect that the defendant has not contested the proceedings in time. No judicial decision is required; it is merely an administrative act. The default judgment may be enforced, but no appeal lies against it. It is, however, possible for the judgment to be set aside, if there is reason to do so (Ord. 13, r. 9 and Ord. 19, r. 9). There is no time-limit for an application to set aside a default judgment (*see further* section 4.4.2). If neither party appears at the trial, the Court may strike the action out of the list. If one party fails to attend, the trial will be continued in that party's absence. The judgment so obtained may be set aside by the Court on the application of the party who was absent, provided such application is made within seven days after the trial. The relevant provisions may be found in RSC Ord. 35, rr. 1 and 2.

2. Third parties in the action

RSC Ord. 16 determines the way in which third parties may become involved in the action. There are four ways for the defendant to involve a third party:

- a claim for contribution;
- a claim for indemnity (e.g. a claim by the defendant against his insurance company to compensate for damages claimed against him in the main action);
- a claim for a remedy which is similar to the remedy the plaintiff claims and which arises out of the same facts as the plaintiff's claim (e.g. the defendant, who is asked to pay damages resulting from a road accident which was caused by a defect in his car, claims damages against the seller of the car for negligence); and
- a claim to have any question or issue arising out of the plaintiff's claim decided not only as between the plaintiff and the defendant but also as between either or both of them and the third party (e.g. A seeks to obtain an order against B to refrain from manufacturing certain goods. If the

order is made, B will be negligent in respect of C. B can now involve C in the action in order to ensure that C is also bound by the judgment between A and B).

If the defendant issues a third party notice before he serves his defence on the plaintiff, no leave is required (Ord. 16, rr. 1 (2) and 2). When the third party gives notice of intention to defend, the defendant must issue a summons for third party directions, whereupon the master will decide whether the third party proceedings are admitted (Ord. 16, r. 4). The master can make several decisions regarding the position of the third party in the action and regarding the continuation of the proceedings. For instance: dismissal of the summons, adding the third party as a defendant in the main action, substituting the third party as a defendant or giving leave to defend, orders for third party pleadings (e.g. third party defence) or discovery.

Apart from these third party proceedings, there are other ways of involving third parties in the action. The Court has ample powers to strike out, add or substitute parties to the proceedings (misjoinder and non-joinder, RSC Ord. 15, r. 6). A third party may be added as a plaintiff only if he agrees to this. However, a third party may always be involved as a defendant in the action, even if the plaintiff in the original proceedings disagrees. Furthermore, in some cases a person may be allowed to join an action at his own request.

Finally, the interpleader proceedings must be mentioned (RSC Ord. 17 and CCR Ord. 33): a person who holds property or money, in which he has no interest himself, but which is claimed by two other persons, may apply to the Court for relief by way of interpleader proceedings, in order that the Court may decide the dispute between the two persons who both claim the property or money. The interpleader himself is not a party to the proceedings.

3. *Amendment of claim*

The writ may be amended once without leave of the Court before the pleadings are closed. In any other circumstances leave is required. Parties may without the Court's leave amend their pleadings once, before the pleadings are closed. Obviously, the opposing party may ask the Court to disallow the amendment of claim. Amendments are possible at any stage of the proceedings if the opposing party agrees in writing (RSC Ord. 20).

4. Counterclaim

A defendant may make a counterclaim (RSC Ord. 15, rr. 2 and 3). It need not be of the same nature as the original claim; the counterclaim does not need to be connected to the claim. When the defendant claims a sum of money by way of a defence against the plaintiff's claim, this is called a set-off. The defendant may make this claim of set-off either in his defence or in a separate counterclaim (RSC Ord. 18, r. 17).

5. Production of evidence

Some remarks about evidence have been made in section 4.4.2c. The rules regarding evidence have been laid down in RSC Ords. 38 to 41. The party on whom the burden of proof lies, must present his witnesses first (in accordance with the provisions of RSC Ord. 35, r. 7). The Court decides where the burden of proof lies on the basis of substantive law and the way in which the parties have pleaded.

Evidence may be given by means of witnesses, production of documents and by showing real evidence to the Court.

Witnesses are put forward by the parties and in principle are heard under oath at the trial (RSC Ord. 38, r. 1). Examination of the witnesses is done by the barristers of both parties. A witness first gives his evidence on the basis of questions asked by the barrister who has called the witness (examination in chief). This barrister is not allowed to ask leading questions. The barrister of the opposing party is then allowed to cross-examine the witness and may ask leading questions. After cross-examination the witness's own barrister may question him once again (re-examination). Examination of witnesses is therefore conducted by the parties.

At the pretrial stage written witness statements have already been exchanged and without the Court's or the opposing party's permission evidence may only be adduced if it appeared in the witness statement, unless it relates to new facts which have arisen during the trial.

Hearsay evidence is admitted under certain conditions (Civil Evidence Act 1968 and 1972 and RSC Ord. 38, rr. 20-34).

Experts may also be heard, but only after their reports have previously been produced to the opposing party (RSC Ord. 38, r. 37). If the Court deems it necessary, it may at the request of a party (i.e. not *ex officio*), also appoint experts itself (RSC Ord. 40). In practice, however, this occurs seldom.

Written evidence is adduced by the production of documents which formed part of the discovery. The party to whom discovery has been made (i.e. on whom the list of documents to be produced has been served) is deemed to admit their authenticity unless he denies such authenticity (RSC Ord. 27, r. 4).

Real evidence may be brought to the trial. This concerns material objects which may be further inspected by the Court. This form of evidence also comprises the site inspection by the Court (RSC Ords. 38 and 39).

Evidence in the pretrial stage is given by affidavit. An affidavit is a written statement drawn up in a prescribed form, the authenticity is sworn before a solicitor or court official (RSC Ord. 41).

It is worth mentioning that in case foreign law applies (i.e. non-English substantive law) the rules of evidence play an important role. Foreign law must be pleaded and proven just like any other fact. If the court finds the evidence insufficient, it applies English law. Evidence is usually produced by legal experts. It is not sufficient to submit texts of foreign law and to quote foreign literature. *See* Dicey and Morris, *The Conflict of Laws*, Sweet and Maxwell, London, 1993, Vol. 1, Ord. 18.

6. Settlement

Settlement out of court is possible at any stage of the proceedings. Apart from a number of exceptions which do not require further discussion here, the Court has no powers to try and reach a settlement between parties; ordering the parties to appear in person in chambers to attempt to reach a settlement is out of the question.

When discussing settlements, we must refer to the English concept of the payment into court (RSC Ords. 11 and 22). At any stage in the proceedings the defendant may, without admitting liability, pay a certain amount into court (part of the claim). The amount is paid to the Court Funds Office in London or the relevant District Registry and the defendant must send the plaintiff a notice of payment into court. The Court hearing the case must not be informed of the payment. If the plaintiff accepts the payment, the proceedings are terminated. If he does not, litigation is continued and if the amount which is finally awarded to the plaintiff is lower than the amount of the payment into court, the plaintiff will be ordered to pay the costs of the proceedings incurred since payment in.

The costs thus to be paid by the plaintiff include the costs of the preparation for trial and of the trial itself (which will be substantial). If a payment into court is made, the plaintiff with his solicitor and barrister must therefore consider very carefully whether it is likely that he will be awarded more if litigation is continued and the case is decided by the Court.

See in general about innovations in the procedure: C. Glasser, *Civil Procedure and Lawyers, The Adversary System and the Decline of the Orality Principle*, Modern Law Review 1993, pp. 307-324.

4.4.3. COUNTY COURT PROCEDURE

There are several ways to commence proceedings before a county court. Although the terminology in the county court differs considerably from that used in the High Court, a comparison can still be made with the High Court procedure.

In the county court the equivalent of the High Court writ is called the summons. This summons should not be confused with the originating summons procedure in the High Court, which is done by originating application in the county court. Finally, in the county court one may file petitions or requests for entry of appeal, which are comparable to petitions and originating notices of motion in the High Court.

The actual procedure in the High Court is largely determined by the way in which proceedings were commenced. To a certain extent this is also true for the county courts, but in the County Court Rules a number of special rules have been included concerning the way of proceeding which may differ depending on the nature and subject of the case. Thus a distinction is made between the frequently occurring default actions (CCR Ord. 3, r. 2), fixed date actions (CCR Ord. 9), originating applications (CCR Ords. 43 and 47), actions for the recovery of land (CCA 1984, s. 21 and CCR Ords. 4 and 6), rent action (CCR Ord. 24), the small claim procedure (CCR Ord. 19) and the interpleader proceedings (CCA 1984, s. 38 and CCR Ord. 33).

The above subject matter is so specialised that we must refrain from treating it in greater detail.

Finally, it should be noted that, when proceedings have been commenced in an incorrect manner, the court itself decides whether the proceedings may be continued on the basis of a wrong form, or whether the case will only be taken into consideration once the correct requirements have been complied with (CCR Ord. 37, r. 5).

Literature: *Sweet and Maxwell's County Court Litigation*, ed. Eric Owen, 1995.

4.5. Basic Procedure for Voluntary Jurisdiction at First Instance

4.5.1. INTRODUCTION

Procedures can be commenced by writ but also by originating summons, originating motion and petition (RSC Ord. 5). The nature of these procedures (originating process) can be described as voluntary jurisdiction.

4.5.2. ORIGINATING SUMMONS

The originating summons procedure (RSC Ord. 5, r. 4 and Ord. 28) is suited particularly for administrative procedures (e.g. the appointment of a trustee, *cf.* the receiver). It is most commonly used in the Chancery Division, but can also be used in the Queen's Bench Division. In addition, it is used for procedures not based on a dispute of fact (RSC Ord. 5, r. 4), or where matters of construction of, for instance, Acts or contracts are concerned.

The procedure by originating summons is simpler than the procedure by writ and often takes place in chambers. There are no pleadings. Evidence is produced by affidavit. Discovery only takes place if the judge so orders (upon request). Usually no witnesses are heard.

The originating summons is issued in the same way as a writ and within 14 days after acknowledgment of service the plaintiff must file with the office of the Court affidavit evidence on which he intends to rely and must serve a copy of the affidavit on the defendant. This is followed by a hearing before the Master. In some cases the Master can try the case himself. The case can also be transferred to a judge and then there will be a hearing before the judge. The judge will usually have read the documents in advance, which will accelerate the hearing. After the consideration of the case the judge will make a decision, which is called an order.

4.5.3. ORIGINATING MOTION

Proceedings by originating motion are mainly applications and appeals to the High Court under various statutes (RSC Ord. 5, r. 5 and Ord. 8).

4.5.4. PETITION

The petition (RSC Ord. 5, r. 5 and Ord. 9) is (*inter alia*) used in divorce cases and the person filing it is called the petitioner. An originating petition is used when prescribed by statute, for example the bankruptcy petitions under the Insolvency Act 1986. In such cases the Chancery Division nearly always has jurisdiction. Decisions are made by order.

4.6. Means of Recourse

4.6.1. INTRODUCTION

There are various means of recourse in English procedure, of which the application to set aside orders or judgments and the appeal are the most important.

Before discussing these means in greater detail, we must briefly mention the slip rule and the possibility of requesting a rehearing, both of which must be distinguished from the above means of recourse (for correction/rectification *see also* sections 1.2 and 1.6).

The slip rule and the rehearing are no means of recourse in the usual sense of the word. The slip rule is intended to amend the text of an order or judgment without affecting the position of the parties under that order or judgment (RSC Ord. 20, r. 11 and CCR Ord. 15, r. 5). Apparent mistakes may thus be corrected by the court in order to avoid the necessity of appeal against the order or judgment.

A request for the application of the slip rule is made by motion or summons.

By requesting a rehearing the parties may correct errors. Rehearing means that the evidence is judged afresh, but without repeating the complete trial. In the county courts the judge conducting the trial may order a rehearing of the trial or any part of it (CCR Ord. 37). The High Court does not have that power 'where no error of the Court at the hearing is alleged'.

4.6.2. TO SET ASIDE ORDERS OR JUDGMENTS

This recourse can be taken against a default judgment (*see* section 4.4.2e) to the court that has delivered the default judgment (RSC Ords. 13 and 19). It may also be used to vary or depart from previous orders.

There is no fixed time-limit for the application to set aside, but in case of a judgment which was obtained irregularly the defendant must make his application within a reasonable time and before taking any further steps (RSC Ord. 2, r. 1). The order or judgment will be set aside, if the manner in which it was obtained is irregular or, in case of a default judgment, if the defendant can prove in an affidavit that he had some defence against the claim. The new judgment is binding and there is no appeal from it; it immediately acquires the authority of *res iudicata*.

4.6.3. APPEAL

a. Appeal from orders of masters and registrars

Appeal from orders (*see also* section 4.4.2d) of masters and registrars usually lies to a judge in chambers (of the same court), in accordance with the rules laid down in RSC Ord. 58. In special cases an appeal may lie to the Court of Appeal (RSC Ord. 58, rr. 1 and 2). Appeal from a judgment of a judge in chambers lies to the Court of Appeal (RSC Ord. 58, r. 6). Under SCA 1981 s. 18(1)(h) (appeal against interlocutory order/judgment) leave to appeal is usually required.

b. Appeal from decisions by the county courts

Against orders and judgments by a county court appeal lies to the Court of Appeal (Civil Division). The time-limit for appeal is 4 weeks after the date of the judgment. For an appeal from an order by the registrar to the county court judge the time-limit is fourteen days. Leave to appeal is related to the value of the claim in the proceedings.

Rules for the appeal procedure are laid down in the County Court Appeals Order 1991 and RSC Ord. 59 (*County Court Practice 1993,* p. 455).

c. Appeal from decisions by the High Court

Appeal from judgments and orders by a High Court judge lies to the Court of Appeal. The Registrar of Civil Appeals is responsible for the procedure in civil appeals and parties may apply to him either *ex parte* or by summons for decisions on procedural aspects of the appeal (RSC Ord. 59, r. 14). The SCA 1981 s. 18 determines when leave to appeal is required (*see also* RSC Ord. 59). Rules for leave to appeal are also laid down in RSC Ords. 59/1/28-59/1/49. The time-limit for appeal is four weeks after the date of the judgment (RSC

Ord. 59, r. 4). If leave is required, an application must first be made to the judge who gave the order; if he refuses, an application may be made to a single judge of the Court of Appeal (*ex parte*). If this decision is given in open court it is irrevocable.

The parties in appeal are called appellant and respondent. The appeal is instituted by serving a notice of appeal on the defendant which notice must specify the grounds of appeal and the decision which the appellant seeks from the Court of Appeal (RSC Ord. 59, r. 3). Within seven days after service of the notice the appellant must set down his appeal by lodging a copy of the order appealed from and two copies of the notice of appeal. The respondent may serve a respondent's notice within 21 days after the service of the notice of appeal (RSC Ord. 59, r. 6). In the respondent's notice the respondent may contend by way of cross-appeal that the decision of the court below was wrong. The notices may be amended without leave until they appear in the List of Forthcoming Appeals and after that, only with leave (RSC Ord. 59, r. 7). The appeal will usually be considered exclusively on the documents. The appellant may request that the entire order be reviewed, whereby the appeal judge is not bound by the grounds of appeal raised by the parties in their notices; an appeal to the Court of Appeal shall be by way of rehearing (RSC Ord. 59, r. 3(1)). New facts and legislation may be considered in the decision (RSC. Ord. 59, r. 10). The appeal may relate both to the law and to the facts. The appeal judge will assume the correctness of the decision of the court below; the burden of proving that the decision was wrong lies with the appellant. The appeal judge will not easily allow the parties to adduce new arguments and new evidence which could have been adduced at first instance.

The Court of Appeal may also order a new trial, for instance on the basis of a misdirection by the judge at first instance where a substantial wrong or miscarriage has been thereby occasioned (Ord. 59, r. 11). An appeal does not stay the execution, unless the court of first instance or the Court of Appeal decides otherwise (RSC Ord. 59, r. 13).

4.6.4. APPEAL TO THE HOUSE OF LORDS

Leave to appeal is always required and usually the Court of Appeal when it pronounces its judgment will be asked for leave to appeal, but an application for leave may also be made to the House of Lords (Administration of Justice (Appeals) Act 1934). Leave is rarely granted. In proceedings relating to an important point of law, leave may be asked to appeal to the House of Lords directly from the High Court (the leapfrog procedure (AJA 1969, ss. 12-15)).

Normally, however, appeal to the House of Lords lies from a decision by the Court of Appeal.

4.7. Special Procedures

4.7.1. INTRODUCTION

Only a small number of procedures reach trial. Below the different procedural methods are discussed which may lead to the procedure being terminated in the pretrial stage or being restricted in the trial stage.

4.7.2. SUMMARY PROCEDURES

RSC Ord. 14 and CCR Ord. 9, r. 14 allow a plaintiff to obtain summary judgment against a defendant. Subject to a number of exceptions, a plaintiff may, if he is of the opinion that the defendant does not have a genuine defence, apply for summary judgment, in order to save time and money. This procedure is used frequently, especially in actions involving monetary claims. The plaintiff makes such application by summons to the Master, after the defendant has issued a notice of intention to defend. The summons must be supported by affidavit verifying the facts on which the claim is based and stating that in the deponent's belief there is no defence to the claim. The defendant may file an affidavit stating that there is an issue or question in dispute which ought to be tried or that there ought for some other reason to be a trial of that claim (RSC Ord. 14, r. 3). Unless the defendant manages to satisfy the Master, the Master must find for the plaintiff (RSC Ord. 14, r. 3). If the defendant does succeed in convincing the Master, the latter will give the defendant unconditional leave to defend (RSC Ord. 14, r. 4). If the chances of success of a defence are questionable, but there is a triable issue, the Master may give conditional leave to defend, requiring the defendant to give security or make a payment into court.

Any decision from the Master is subject to appeal to the judge in chambers and from this judge to the Court of Appeal. Appeal to the Court of Appeal sometimes requires leave (e.g. in the case of an appeal against an order by the Master to give leave to defend). In the last few years Order 14, except in cases of straightforward monetary claims, has become less popular since the Master is more inclined to order the plaintiff to pay the costs of the application if he does not succeed in his application under Order 14.

Since February 1992 it has been possible for the plaintiff to obtain summary judgment in relation of questions of law and construction (RSC Ord. 14A). Under this new Order summary judgment may be given if it concerns questions of law which may be answered without trial and if the decision on the relevant question of law will terminate the action. Another possibility to limit the extent and costs of the trial is a trial of preliminary issues pursuant to Ord. 33, r. 3. The Court may order certain issues, whether of law or fact, to be tried before the main trial. This may induce the parties to reach a settlement.

In addition to summary judgment proceedings the interlocutory injunction deserves to be discussed here. An application for an interlocutory injunction (RSC Ord. 29) may be made before or during the main proceedings. It is an order whereby a party will be compelled (mandatory injunction) or forbidden (negative injunction) to perform certain acts. If the injunction is given after the trial, it is final. In order to decide whether or not an injunction will be granted a weighing of the interests of the parties takes place, for which weighing guidelines have been formulated in case law. In the case *American Cyanamid Co.* v. *Ethicon Ltd.* ([1975] A.C. 396) the House of Lords ruled that the only test which the court must apply is the balance of convenience: the question is whether the plaintiff would suffer more without the injunction than the defendant would suffer under it: RSC Ord. 29, r. 1(3). Except if the injunction is final, the plaintiff must on every injunction give an undertaking as to damages, i.e. must promise to pay damages to the defendant if the court finds against the plaintiff. As the damages suffered by the defendant as a result of an injunction may be considerable, the plaintiff must consider carefully before he applies for an injunction whether he is prepared to give such an undertaking. Special interlocutory injunctions - the Mareva injunction to prevent dissipation of assets - and the Anton Piller Order will be discussed in sections 4.8.3 and 4.8.2 respectively.

Mandatory injunctions (i.e. injunctions to do something) are rare. An application for this type of injunction is usually made to a judge (not a master). In urgent cases the application is made *ex parte* (i.e. without the opposing party being heard), otherwise *inter partes*. Breach of an injunction leads to contempt of court, whereby the person in breach will be criminally liable.

For the sake of completeness we should mention the statutory demands and the winding up petition as an indirect way of ordering a debtor to pay. The creditor demands payment within 21 days, failing which the creditor may petition that the debtor be adjudicated bankrupt. One of the conditions is that the debt is undisputed. In case of misuse of the bankruptcy proceedings the creditor will be liable for the damage thereby caused (Insolvency Act 1986, s. 117 *et seq.* and s. 267 *et seq.*).

Finally, there is the possibility of an interim payment: at any moment in the period between service of writ and acknowledgment of service the plaintiff may request the High Court to make an order for the defendant to make an interim payment to the plaintiff, in anticipation of the outcome of the proceedings. The plaintiff must prove that the defendant has acknowledged liability or that it is certain that an order to pay damages will follow (RSC Ord. 29, r. 8/2 - Ord. 29/18).

See also A.A.S. Zuckermann, *Quality and Economy in Civil Procedure, The Case for Commuting Correct Judgments for Timely Judgments*, Oxford Journal of Legal Studies (1994) Vol. 14, no. 3.

4.7.3. SMALL CLAIMS PROCEDURES

The small claims procedures (CCR Ord. 19, r. 2.4) allows small claims up to a maximum amount of £1,000 to be tried by a Registrar of the County Court. The procedure is also referred to as arbitration (*see also* section 4.10.3) and is especially suited for consumer cases. It is an informal procedure, often in chambers, whereby it is common for the parties to appear in person without legal representation. The strict rules of evidence do not apply.

4.7.4. SECTOR PROCEDURES

Here we shall briefly consider procedures in divorce and employment law cases.

Pursuant to the Matrimonial Causes Act 1973 divorce proceedings can be commenced before the Family Division of the High Court or before a Divorce County Court, a county court especially designated by the Lord Chancellor (Domicile and Matrimonial Proceedings Act) 1984. The rules of proceedings are set down in the Family Proceedings Rules 1991. The proceedings are commenced by a petition.

Employment law proceedings are commenced before industrial tribunals. The legal basis for this is provided by the Employment Protection (Consolidation) Act 1978 (s. 128). In each of the approximately 75 tribunals a barrister or solicitor functions as Chairman, assisted by two lay judges.

Appeal from a decision by a tribunal lies to the Employment Appeal Tribunal. The Tribunal consists of a Judge and two to four appointed members. Appeal to the Court of Appeal is possible if leave to appeal is obtained.

4.8. Protective Measures and Enforcement Measures

4.8.1. INTRODUCTION

In English law protective measures form part of pretrial remedies. The Mareva injunction and the Anton Piller order are injunctions and are either interlocutory (given before trial) or final (after trial). Other protective measures are interlocutory receivership orders (to appoint a receiver) and orders to keep and examine litigious properties.

As regards the names of the persons involved in the enforcement it must be noted that the person seeking enforcement is called the judgment creditor and the person against whom enforcement is sought judgment debtor.

Enforcement measures by attachment are the writ of *fieri facias* and the charging order on land/securities. Garnishee proceedings are intended to compel the debtor of the judgment debtor to pay directly to the judgment creditor and will be discussed below as part of the enforcement measures. A special form of garnishee proceedings is the attachment of earnings, whereby the judgment debtor's employer is compelled to pay the judgment debtor's earnings directly to the judgment creditor. Oral examination of the judgment debtor is an enforcement measure whereby the judgment debtor must declare to an official of the court which assets he possesses and where they are situated. An application for specific performance in respect of immovable property is made by writ (warrant, in the county court) of possession and in respect of movable property by writ (warrant, in the county court) of delivery, using force if necessary. Enforcement of injunctions (whether final or interlocutory) takes place by committal proceedings. Breach of an injunction leads to contempt of court for which the condemned person may be sentenced to imprisonment (committal proceedings). English law does not attach a penalty clause to injunctions. The attachments and measures aforementioned will be explained in greater detail below.

Whether foreign judgments can be enforced in England is determined by the Administration of Justice Act 1920 (part II), the Foreign Judgments (Reciprocal Enforcement) Act 1933 and the Civil Jurisdiction and Judgments Act 1982 (CJJA 19182). The provisions of these Acts are worked out further in RSC Ord. 71. Money judgments and other judgments from judicial institutions of the EC member states may be registered with the High Court. Under CJJA 1982 the grounds for refusal of registration are limited. After registration a judgment may be enforced in the same manner as an English judgment from the Court in which the foreign judgment was registered.

4.8.2. PROTECTIVE MEASURES OTHER THAN ATTACHMENT

The Anton Piller order is a kind of mandatory injunction (*see* section 4.7.2) and its purpose is to safeguard things and documents which form the basis of the claim (e.g. unauthorised copies of videotapes in copyright actions). The defendant will be compelled to hand over certain goods or documents whereby he is usually required to permit the plaintiff's solicitor to search the defendant's house or office, in the presence of an independent solicitor whose duty it is to explain the effect of the order to the defendant in plain English and who will supervise its execution. This order allows a party to gather information and evidence for the trial. Inasmuch as the order compels the defendant to hand over material which is detrimental to his case, it shows a resemblance to protective measures by attachment. Since the order is very far-reaching for the defendant, strict guarantees are attached to the order, *inter alia* an undertaking by the plaintiff as to damages.

Just like the Mareva injunction, this order has arisen in case law (*Anton Piller KG* v. *Manufacturing Processes Ltd.* [1976] All E.R. 779). RSC Ord. 29, rr. 2 and 3 also empower the court to take this kind of protective measure during the procedure, but the use of an order based on Ord. 29 is limited, as it can only be issued after an *inter partes* hearing. The purpose of the Anton Piller order is to prevent goods or documents which are the subject matter of the plaintiff's action from being destroyed. That is why it is essential that the defendant should not be notified of the plaintiff's application for an Anton Piller order. The order is therefore made after an *ex parte* application, if necessary before the writ has been issued. The plaintiff must show that he will be seriously prejudiced if the Anton Piller order is refused. The ECHR decided in its judgment of 30 March 1989 NJ 1991, 522 that the Anton Piller order was not in conflict with art. 8 ECHRFF.

As set out above in this section and in section 4.7.2, by virtue of Ord. 29 the High Court has the power to grant interlocutory injunctions if required. These measures may also have the effect of attachment; for instance Ord. 29, r. 2 provides for the safekeeping of litigious properties. RSC Ord 29, r. 3 provides for the taking of samples (*cf.* the Anton Piller order above), and r. 4 for the sale of perishable property whereby Ord. 30 makes it possible to appoint a receiver. In urgent cases this application may be made *ex parte*.

4.8.3. PROTECTIVE MEASURES BY ATTACHMENT

The purpose of a Mareva injunction is to restrain a party from dissipating assets. The legal basis of this injunction can be found in SCA 1981, s. 37(3);

the matter is further worked out in RSC. Ord. 29, r. 1 (20-23). Case law had already developed the basis of the Mareva injunction (*Mareva Compania Naviera SA* v. *International Bulk Carriers SA 'The Mareva'* [1980] All E.R. 213). The Mareva injunction has boomed and is applied very frequently. The application is made to a judge *ex parte* and may be made before the trial (even before the writ is issued). The injunction may also be used after trial for enforcement of a judgment (*see* section 4.8.4). There are four conditions:

(1) The plaintiff must have a good arguable case as to a specified or approximate sum;
(2) There are some grounds for believing the defendant has assets within the jurisdiction;
(3) There is a real risk that the defendant, if not restrained, will remove his assets from the jurisdiction or dissipate them within it; and
(4) It is just to grant the injunction in all the circumstances, and, in particular, bearing in mind any prejudice which granting it might cause to the defendant, his business or third parties.

The plaintiff must give an undertaking as to damages (*see* section 4.7.2) to the defendant as well as an undertaking to third parties upon whom notice of the injunction is served in respect of expenses they may incur as a result of this injunction. The Mareva injunction may also be used in respect of monies held by a third party, such as a bank. The injunction is not effective until the person in possession of the monies or goods has been given notice of the injunction. The third party is then no longer allowed to dispose of the assets. If he does, he may be guilty of contempt of court (*see* section 4.8.5).

4.8.4. ENFORCEMENT MEASURES BY ATTACHMENT

The result achieved by the writ of *fieri facias* (writ of *fi fa*, Ords. 46 and 47) following an order for payment by any person of money is comparable to enforcement measures by attachment of movable property. The writ is in the form of a royal direction to the sheriff of the county to seize goods to satisfy the judgment debt plus interest and costs (in the county court this is done by warrant of execution), whereupon the sheriff (of the High Court) or the bailiff (of the county court) sees to the actual execution. High Court judgments may be enforced through the High Court itself or through a county court. A judgment from the county court of which £2,000 or more is to be recovered, may be enforced through the High Court. In general, execution by the sheriff is more effective than by the bailiff. It appears that sheriffs more often succeed in obtaining payment from the debtor. Subject to a number of important exceptions, no leave is required for the issue of the writ. Examples of such exceptions are: six years have elapsed since the date of the judgment or after the judgment a change in the state of the parties has taken place. *See further* RSC Ord. 46, r. 2. Execution is effected by the sheriff seizing such of the debtor's property as may provide enough to recover the sum owed. The items seized are then sold by public auction. Certain goods, such as clothing, cannot be seized.

The charging order on land and securities is enforcement by attachment of immovable property and securities respectively. The legal basis for this order can be found in the Charging Orders Act 1979, RSC Ord. 50 and CCR Ord. 31. Subject to certain exceptions, the High Court only has jurisdiction if the charging order is for an amount exceeding £5,000. In deciding whether the charging order can be granted to the creditor, the judge (master or registrar) also considers the position of any other creditors. If the charging order is granted, the creditor obtains a charge which is enforceable in the same way as a mortgage.

Finally, as set out above in section 4.8.3, an application for a Mareva injunction can also be made after judgment has been obtained and can therefore also be classified as a means of enforcement.

4.8.5. ENFORCEMENT MEASURES OTHER THAN ATTACHMENT

If a judgment debtor has a claim against a third party, the judgment creditor (garnishor) may request the master or registrar to order the third party (garnishee) to show cause, i.e. to appear before the master or registrar: if the garnishee disputes his liability to the judgment debtor, the master will either determine the issue (summary judgment, *see* section 4.7.2) or transfer the case to trial. If the garnishee does not appear or dispute his liability, the Court may order the garnishee to pay his debt direct to the judgment creditor, unless, for example, the judgment debtor is on the brink of bankruptcy and the garnishor would therefore be unreasonably preferred over other creditors of the judgment debtor. Garnishee proceedings may be commenced either in the High Court (RSC Ord. 49) or in the county court (CCR Ord. 30). The Mareva injunction (*see* section 4.8.3) may be used prior to the garnishee proceedings in order to prevent misappropriation of funds. The same applies to the attachment of earnings proceedings below.

Attachment of earnings (Attachment of Earnings Act 1971 and CCR Ord. 27) is a specific type of garnishee proceedings, whereby the employer of the judgment debtor is ordered to pay part of his salary direct to the judgment creditor. Attachment of earnings applications are made to the county court, except in certain procedures which fall under the jurisdiction of the High Court Family Division. Attachment of earnings is only allowed if the judgment debtor has sufficient means of existence and, when earnings are attached, the judgment debtor will be left an amount at subsistence level.

In order to enforce a judgment it is important for the judgment creditor to know which property the debtor has and where it is located. To that end the judgment creditor may apply *ex parte* to the court in which the judgment or order was obtained for an order that the judgment debtor attend court for an oral examination (RSC Ord. 48 and CCR Ord. 25). The order may include an order to produce relevant documents. If the judgment debtor fails to attend he may be committed to prison for contempt of court. In practice this hardly ever happens; the threat of committal proceedings will usually make the debtor appear! The debtor is examined and cross-examined before a master (in the High Court), or a district judge (in the county court) or - more often - before a senior officer of the High Court Central Office or the county court in the debtor's place of residence. The debtor is often allowed to give a written statement, in the county courts on a standard form.

In English law there is specific performance for the enforcement of judgments for the possession of land (RSC Ord. 45, r. 3 and CCR Ord. 26, r. 17) and for the enforcement of judgments for the delivery of goods (RSC Ord. 45, r. 4 and CCR Ord. 26, r. 17). In High Court procedures the sheriff's officer is entitled to enforce possession or delivery (using force if necessary) if he has a writ of possession (for land) or a writ of delivery (for movable property). In the county court the bailiff is entitled to enforce, if he has a warrant of possession (land) or a warrant of delivery (movable property). A writ of possession can only be issued with leave from the master, except in mortgage actions, whereas in case of a writ of delivery leave is only required in special cases. Leave to issue a writ of possession is not given unless it is shown that those who actually possess the land have had the opportunity to apply for relief.

Final and interlocutory injunctions may be enforced by committal proceedings (RSC Ord. 52 and CCR Ord. 29). If the judgment debtor fails to comply with the injunction he will be committed at the creditor's request. If he still fails to obey, he risks being convicted for contempt of court and imprisoned for a maximum of two years. The court may order this period to be shortened. Committal proceedings may be regarded as an indirect way to enforce. The conviction for contempt of court is a criminal conviction.

RSC Ord. 45, r. 8 provides for judicial authorisation: pursuant to this rule the plaintiff may be allowed to do an act himself which the disobedient party was ordered to do or to have it done at the cost of the disobedient party.

4.9. Duration and Costs

4.9.1. DURATION

The period between issuing proceedings and the judgment after trial is at the moment on average three years.

In the county courts the duration depends on the question before which court the proceedings are brought. In some courts it may be less than 30 weeks, in others it may be as much as 75 weeks.

Proceedings before the Court of Appeal or the House of Lords usually take less than two years (*see* McIntosh and Holmes 1991, p. 87).

4.9.2. COSTS

RSC Ord. 62 lays down the rules for costs. Below we will discuss costs and legal aid.

a. Costs

If costs are not agreed between the parties, the general rule is that costs follow the event: the losing party will be ordered to pay the winning party's costs (and obviously his own). Normally the parties will try to agree the amount of costs to be paid to the winning party on the basis of a bill of costs drawn up by the winning party's solicitor or by a costs draftman instructed by him. If the parties fail to reach agreement, they proceed to taxation of the bill of costs (*see* part III RSC Ord. 62, rr. 12-35). Taxation is done in the High Court by a special taxing master (part IV RSC Ord. 62). There are two bases for taxation: the standard basis and the indemnity basis (RSC Ord. 62, r. 12) which relate to the question whether certain costs were reasonably incurred or whether the amount was reasonable. On the standard basis any doubt concerning the reasonableness is resolved in favour of the losing party (the winning party therefore obtains a lower amount of costs) and on the indemnity basis in favour of the winning party (who then receives more). Costs are usually taxed on the standard basis.

Since the winning party's solicitor will in general charge his own client costs on an indemnity basis and furthermore, taxation will not allow all costs, this means that the winning party will not be able to recover all his costs from the losing party and will therefore have to bear part of his costs himself. The judge may also order solicitors and barristers personally to pay costs by making a wasted costs order. In *Ridehalghe* v. *Horsefield* [1994] 3

All E.R. 848, the Court of Appeal discussed this wasted costs order in detail: wasted costs orders may be given 'where the legal representative acted improperly, unreasonably or negligently'. Wasted costs orders may also be given against lawyers of legally aided persons.

The master or judge in the pretrial stage will give orders for costs in respect of interlocutory application and may determine that costs will be borne by a certain party, regardless of the outcome of the main proceedings.

Normally the following costs may be charged:

1. solicitor's fees and expenses; these are disbursements (costs incurred by the solicitor e.g. costs of photocopying, travel expenses) and profit costs (based on the hours spent on the case); the total amount is subject to VAT;
2. barrister's fees; these are agreed beforehand between the solicitor and the barrister's clerk;
3. court fees; as set out in the Supreme Court Fees Order 1980 and other orders;
4. experts' fees and expenses; these differ from case to case;
5. witness expenses; these also differ from case to case; and
6. interest of 15 per cent *per annum* on the total amount of costs from the date of the judgment until payment.

There are no lists with fixed amounts for the fees of barristers and solicitors. Since 1988 the government has increasingly referred to the drawing up and publication of such lists: thus, Recommendation 57 of the Review Body on Civil Justice (a committee of recommendation set up by the Lord Chancellor in 1985) reads: 'Solicitors and barristers should be encouraged and expected to provide information to the public by way of stated rates per case or per hour and should be entitled to free publicity about those rates in lawyers' referral lists'. It is expected that this recommendation will come into effect within five to ten years. A first directive concerning the amount of these costs was included in the Legal Advice and Assistance (Amendment) Regulations 1992, Schedule 6.

For the time being, the amount is determined on the basis of the number of hours spent on the case and its difficulty and substance. The fees of barristers and solicitors are high compared to the fees of lawyers in other countries (*The Law Society's Gazette*, 7 October 1992, p. 4).

Appeal from a decision by a taxing master lies to a Judge in Chambers, assisted by assessors including another Taxing Master and an experienced legal practitioner.

As stated before, there is no mandatory representation *ad litem* in England. When a party proceeds without a solicitor, he may charge the opposing party for the costs which would otherwise have been incurred for and by a solicitor (Litigants in Person (Costs and Expenses) Act and RSC Ord. 62, r. 18).

Before a writ can be issued a writ fee of (currently) £100 is payable. This is a fixed amount which is not related to the amount claimed. If further summons are issued in the course of the proceedings, e.g. to call witnesses or experts, an amount of £20 is payable for each summons.

At the county court the court fees do depend on the amount of the claim; fees vary from £7 to £43. The County Court Fees Order and the Supreme Court Fees Order provide more details on fees.

Finally, RSC Ord. 23 provides for security for costs. If the plaintiff is a foreigner litigating in England, the defendant can at any time in the proceedings after he has appeared request the court to order the plaintiff to give security for the costs of the action. In assessing the request the court considers the actual circumstances of the case. If the plaintiff is domiciled in one of the EC member states, he may not be required to give security for costs because this may conflict with arts. 59 and 60 EEC Treaty; *Hubbard* v. *Hamburger*, (ECJ 1 July 1993). The plaintiff of an EC member state is covered by the CJJA 1982, on the basis of which the defendant's position is already more secure in respect of the enforcement of the judgment (*see* RSC Ord. 3, r. 1(1)(a)).

b. Legal aid

Legal aid is provided for in the Legal Aid Act 1988 and the Legal Aid Regulations 1989. Under these rules it is possible to litigate free of charge if a person's disposable income is less than £2,645 per year and his disposable capital less than £3,000. A contribution towards the costs may be payable when the disposable income is below £7,780 per year in personal injury cases or £7,060 per year in any other case. For the disposable capital the limit lies at £6,750 and at £8,560 in personal injuries cases (amounts in 1992; *see* the Civil Legal Aid (Assessment of Resources) (Amendment) Regulations of 1992, in force on 6 April 1992). The amounts mentioned are those applicable currently. They are adjusted regularly. The assessment of means is done by the Department of Social Security (DSS).

In addition, a merits test is carried out by the Area Director of the Legal Aid Board to ensure that proceedings are warranted.

The following persons may apply for legal aid:

1. anyone residing in England (the applicant need not be an English citizen);
2. British subjects who reside elsewhere; and
3. persons who are entitled to legal aid on the basis of certain international conventions. *See* on this subject the Civil Legal Aid (General) Regulations 1989, part II.

The legal aid system as laid down in the Legal Aid Act 1988 is administered by the Legal Aid Board; this board consists of 11 to 17 members appointed by the Lord Chancellor (LAA 1988, s. 3). The costs of legal aid incurred by a legally aided person - e.g. for advice from or representation by a solicitor - are paid by the Board directly to the solicitor (LAA 1988, s. 15). Any possible contribution by a legally aided person shall be paid by him to the Board and not to his solicitor (LAA 1988, s. 16). The costs incurred are paid from the Legal Aid Fund (LAA 1988, s. 6). A legally aided person is free to choose his own solicitor (LAA 1988, s. 32).

4.10. Proceedings Outside the Courts

4.10.1. INTRODUCTION

At this point arbitration in particular will be discussed, as other forms of proceedings outside the courts are rarely used in England.

4.10.2. ARBITRATION

The arbitration procedure is set out in the Arbitration Acts of 1950 (AA 1950), 1975 (AA 1975) and 1979 (AA 1979). The CLSA 1990 further supplements this legislation (ss. 99-103). Arbitrators' jurisdiction frequently arises from contracts, but there are also many statutes which provide for dispute resolution by way of arbitration. An arbitration agreement must be in writing (AA 1950, s. 32). If a party issues proceedings in a court contrary to an arbitration agreement, such proceedings may be stayed at the defendant's request (discretionary power, AA 1950, s. 4). A clause to the effect that another party relinquishes his right to ordinary proceedings before a civil court is void (in conflict with public policy). It may be agreed in a contract that the case shall first be submitted to arbitrators before parties may turn to the ordinary court. This is called a *Scott* v. *Avery* (1856, 5 H.L. Cas. 183) clause which may be held against the other party if he nevertheless issues proceedings. In such cases the court is requested, after the writ has been issued, to stay the proceedings. In domestic arbitrations a court has a choice whether or not to grant such a request (AA 1950 s. 4(1)); in non-domestic arbitration agreements (international arbitration), however, the court is obliged to stay the proceedings (AA 1975 s. 1(1)). An arbitration is domestic if the place of arbitration is in the United Kingdom and also if one of the parties is a national of, or habitually resident in, the United Kingdom (*see* AA 1975 s. 1(4)). The AA 1975 provides for the enforcement of arbitral awards in countries which do not form part of the United Kingdom but which have acceded to the New York Convention of 1958.

Legal aid will not be granted for arbitration. An indigent party may therefore be at a serious disadvantage if a question of law cannot be submitted to an ordinary court. However, this is not normally a ground for the court to stay the proceedings because of the arbitration agreement. An application for a stay will be granted, if the other party has been financially wrecked as a result of default by the plaintiff.

Anyone may be appointed arbitrator. High Court judges can appoint arbitrators, if the parties fail to reach agreement on the appointment of arbitrators (AA 1950, s. 10).

Unless otherwise agreed between the parties, English (procedural) law (including the rules of evidence) applies. Unless otherwise provided, the arbitrator has virtually the same powers as the ordinary judge to make orders for e.g. discovery, pleadings and witness examinations (AA 1950, s. 12). In certain cases the arbitrator may submit a question of law to the High Court (with leave of the court or with the consent of both parties; *see* RSC Ord. 73, r. 2(1)). Subject to these conditions, appeal lies to the High Court (RSC Ord. 73, r. 2(2)). These forms of judicial review are not possible if parties have entered into an exclusion agreement (AA 1979, ss. 1, 2, 3 and 4).

A decision by an arbitrator is called an award; it may be enforced with leave of the High Court (AA 1950, s. 26).

Appeal from an arbitral award lies to the High Court, unless parties have excluded appeal in an exclusion agreement. This is allowed if both parties have consented or - if they have not - if the court gives leave (AA 1979, s. 1(2)). This procedure is commenced by originating motion within 21 days after an award has been given by the arbitrator(s). The Commercial Court (part of the High Court) has jurisdiction (RSC Ord. 73, rr. 2(2), 5(2) and 6; *see further* RSC (Amendment no. 3) Rules 1979).

Finally, appeal from a judgment of the Commercial Court lies to the Court of Appeal, subject to two conditions. Firstly, the High Court or the Court of Appeal must have given leave and, secondly, the High Court must certify that it concerns a question of law of general public importance or another special reason (AA 1979, s. 1(7)).

Other forms of arbitration than those pursuant to the Acts 1950-1979, whereby the arbitrator is always obliged to apply the law in force, are seldom used in England. We should also refer to the small claim procedure before the county court which is called arbitration (*see* section 4.7.3). Its character is, however, fundamentally different. Firstly, this form of arbitration takes place within the context of an ordinary procedure before a public court and, unlike normal arbitration, there is no arbitration agreement between parties. Secondly, a judgment by a judge-arbitrator in a small claim procedure is an ordinary legal decision which is immediately binding on the parties. As stated, an award by a real arbitrator can only be enforced after leave of the High Court (AA 1950, s. 26).

As stated before, the AA 1975 applies in respect of enforcement of foreign (i.e. non-English) awards. This Act implements the provisions of the New York Convention of 1958.

4.10.3. VALUATION OR APPRAISEMENT

Valuation or appraisement concerns decisions by a third party, called valuer or appraiser, on matters such as the value of shares. Valuation must be distinguished from arbitration: there is no need for a hearing and usually it is about the prevention of disputes rather than the resolution of disputes, as is the case with arbitration.

Neither the Arbitration Acts nor any other rules apply.

5. French Civil Procedure[*]

Renée Y. Nauta and Gerard J. Meijer[**]

5.1. Overview/Sources

5.1.1. INTRODUCTION

In France civil litigation has always been called *procédure civile*, but is also referred to as *droit judiciaire privé* and *droit processuel privé*.

French law forms part of Roman-Germanic law, which is characterised *inter alia* by its Roman law origins. After the French Revolution in 1789, which was also aimed at the abuses in the administration of justice, civil procedure was changed drastically and was codified in the *Code de procédure civile* in 1806 during the reign of Napoleon.

The law is still the most important source of French civil litigation. The rules of French civil procedure have been laid down not only in formal laws, originating from the national assembly, but also in regulations based on the *pouvoir réglementaire* of the government. Thus the new Code of Civil Procedure (*Nouveau Code de procédure civile*) was passed by a decree, as well as part of the Code of the judicial organisation (*Code de l'organisation judiciaire*) (*see* section 5.1.2).

France is a party to many international conventions and these conventions also form an important source of civil procedure. Article 55 of the Constitution determines that international conventions shall prevail over national legislation.

Literature and case law are also important sources, in particular the judgments of the *Cour de cassation*.

5.1.2. ACT AND CONVENTION

The main legislation on French civil procedure is laid down in the *Nouveau Code de procédure civile* and the *Code de l'organisation judiciaire*.

---

* Thanks are due to R.F.M. Bijloos Master of Laws (avocat à la Cour de Paris, Office Lefèvre et Associés, Paris).

** This English edition of the original Dutch text was prepared by Ms. R.Y. Nauta alone.

The *Nouveau Code de procédure civile* (NCPC) is regarded as the most important source. Unless otherwise indicated, a reference to an article in this chapter will be to an article of this Code. The first two books of the Nouveau Code de procédure civile entered into force on 1 January 1976. Six years later, on 1 January 1982, Books III and IV followed. Book V (rules of enforcement), which had originally been planned, has not yet been introduced. Until recently Book V of Napoleon's *Code de procédure civile* (ACPC) was in force in respect of enforcement matters. A number of other provisions of the ACPC have so far not been replaced. In the registers of the law text editions published by Dalloz and Litec, these provisions are specified.

Book I of the *Nouveau Code de procédure civile* contains provisions which apply to proceedings in general. Book II lays down specific rules which apply to (the different procedures before) each separate court. Book III deals with the administration of justice of a distinct nature, such as the commercial courts, and Book IV with arbitration. Book V had been reserved for the rules of enforcement, but the Act of 9 July 1991, which entered into force on 1 January 1993, has as yet appeared as appendix 32 to the NCPC. Pursuant to art. 96 of the Act of 9 July 1991, codification will take place by decree of the *Conseil d'Etat* after advice from the *Commission Supérieure de Codification* (*see* section 5.8).

The second code which is relevant to these matters is the *Code de l'organisation judiciaire* (COJ) of 1978.

As stated in section 5.1.1, the COJ contains partly formal (*loi*), partly regulatory (*décret*) legislation. The difference in origin is reflected in the method of reference to the articles in the COJ: an article occurring in the procedural part of the COJ is preceded by an L, whereas an article in the regulatory part is preceded by an R. The number of an article in the COJ is formed in such a way that one can see at a single glance where the relevant article may be found: the first figure indicates the book, the second the title, the third the chapter and the fourth the number of the article in that series, e.g. art. L.121-1.

Finally, there are numerous regulations which do not form part of the aforementioned codes, such as the Act on Legal Aid (Act 91-647 of 10 July 1991; *see* section 5.9.3).

This and other legislation relevant to civil litigation are included in the law text editions published by Dalloz (red) and Litec (blue). Apart from the actual text of the law these volumes also contain extensive references to literature and case law per article.

France is a party to various international conventions in the area of civil procedure, for instance the European Convention on Jurisdiction and the

Enforcement of Judgments in Civil and Commercial Matters (*see* section 3.1.1 *et seq.*), the Conventions on Civil Procedure of 1905 and 1954 (entry into force 22 June 1959), the Hague Convention on the Service Abroad of Judicial and Extrajudicial Documents in Civil or Commercial Matters of 1965 (entry into force 1 September 1972), the Hague Convention on the Taking of Evidence Abroad in Civil or Commercial Matters of 1970 (entry into force 6 October 1974), the European Convention on Information on Foreign Law of 1968 (entry into force 11 July 1972) and the European Agreement on the transmission of applications for legal aid of 1977 (entry into force 22 January 1980). In respect of arbitration, the New York Convention of 1958 on the Recognition and Enforcement of Foreign Arbitral Awards (entry into force 24 September 1959) and the European Convention on International Commercial Arbitration of 1961 (entry into force 16 March 1967) are relevant. Finally, France has also signed the ECHRFF (entry into force 3 May 1974) and the CCPR (entry into force 4 February 1981).

5.1.3. LITERATURE AND CASE LAW

With the introduction of the NCPC in France, a number of general handbooks on civil procedure were published. *Procédure Civile*, Paris 1992 (Sirey) by G. Couchez provides a good introduction to the NCPC. More detailed are the books by L. Cadiet, *Droit judiciaire privé*, Paris 1992 (Sirey) and J. Vincent and S. Guinchard, *Procédure civile*, Paris 1991 (Dalloz). A proper and detailed consideration of the new rules of civil procedure can be found in a work by H. Solus and R. Perrot, *Droit judiciaire privé*, Tome I (Introduction, notions fondamentales et organisation judiciaire), 1961; Tome II (Compétence), 1973; Tome III (Procédure de première instance), 1991 (Sirey).

In *Institutions judiciaires* by R. Perrot, Paris 1992 (Montchrestien) the judicial organisation is discussed in detail. The same applies to a handbook by J. Vincent, S. Guinchard, G. Montagnier and A. Varinard, *La justice et ses institutions*, Paris 1991 (Dalloz).

The *Juris-Classeur de procédure civile* (J.-Cl. Proc. civ.) edited by R. Perrot and Cl. Giverdon is a French loose-leaf edition on civil procedure.

Case law of the *Cour de cassation* is published in the *Bulletin des Arrêts de la Cour de cassation* (Bull. civ.). Journals such as *Recueil Dalloz Sirey* (D.), *Gazette du Palais* (Gaz. Pal.), *Juris-Classeur Périodique* (Semaine Juridique/J.C.P.) and *Revue de l'arbitrage* (Rev. Arb.) contain articles and information on current topics as well as judgments by other courts.

Case law is cited by indicating the court (including the Chamber), date and year and place of citation. Civ. 2e, 16 December 1985, D. 1986 refers to a judgment by the second civil Chamber of the *Cour de cassation*, pronounced on 16 December 1985, to be found in *Recueil Dalloz Sirey* volume 1986.

5.1.4. DATA BASES

In France a policy by the national government has led to the creation of the National Centre for Computerised Legal Information, called CNIJ (*Centre national d'informatique juridique*), a commercial service attached to the Prime Minister's department. It produces data banks concentrating on laws and decisions of the Supreme Courts, while a private group has taken the responsibility to provide the decisions of the Appeal Courts. All these data banks are distributed by the company L'Européenne de Données and are combined under the name of JURIDIAL.

These data banks contain:

- all documents published in the French *Journal officiel* since 1987, and all the French codes in full text (LEGI-CNIJ);
- the references and abstracts of the laws and decrees published in the *Journal officiel* since 1936, in a separate file (called LEX);
- the full text of the European Community Law and the successive modifications of the instruments creating community law (CELEX);
- decisions of the *Cour de cassation* since 1960 (CASS);
- decisions of the *Conseil constitutionnel* since 1958 (CONSTIT);
- decisions of the *Conseil d'Etat* (JADE);
- decisions of the European Court of Justice since 1954 (CJCE);
- decisions of the *cours d'appel* (JURISDATA); and
- bibliographic references with abstracts to about 200 journals.

Apart from this data base set up by the state, there is LEXIS in France, marketed by Téléconsulte: it contains largely the same information as the JURIDIAL data bases mentioned above, although in practice both systems supplement each other.

One of the most evident characteristics of the French data banks is the technique of the 'enriched' full text. This adds to the full text of each document any necessary clarifications, like explanations of names, references or specific terms. Another particularity is the accessing of data banks through the MINITEL hardware, which is widely distributed in France.

All these data banks are in the French language.

Literature: C. Serkis Bischof, *Legal Databases in France, Switzerland and Italy*, International Journal of Legal Information, Vol. 21, no. 1, spring 1993.

5.2. Fundamental Principles

5.2.1. INTRODUCTION

'Civil litigation is governed only to a limited extent by fundamental legal principles, which would apply in all countries at all times and to all kinds of procedures', says a Dutch handbook on civil procedure (Hugenholtz/ Heemskerk, 1994, no. 5). Yet the European legal principles do not differ greatly from each other in this respect. This can be ascribed partly to the fact that France is a party to the ECHRFF and the CCPR, so that the principles laid down by these conventions also apply in France. Furthermore, the ideas from the French Revolution have been disseminated by the French domination of large parts of Europe. In 1789 a strong need was felt to guarantee the principle of equality of citizens before the court and the principle of (financial) independence of the judges. These principles, which refer in particular to the organisation and functioning of the judiciary, will be considered in sections 5.2.4 *et seq.* (*see also* Perrot, *Institutions judiciaires*, nos. 58 ff.; Cadiet, 1992, nos. 115 ff).

The *Nouveau Code de procédure civile* starts with a number of principles set out under the heading *'les principes directeurs du procès'* (arts. 1 to 24 inclusive). These provisions, however, only apply to contentious jurisdiction. Articles 25 to 29 inclusive provide rules for voluntary jurisdiction (*juridiction gracieuse*). The *principes directeurs* consist of two fundamental principles (the *principe dispositif* and the *principe de la contradiction*), from which all kinds of other principles are derived (*see* sections 5.2.2 and 5.2.3). The observance of the *principes directeurs* is safeguarded by the public nature of the court hearings and of the judicial decisions (*see* arts. 22 and 451).

Principles such as the motivation of a decision, (art. 455), mandatory legal representation in the proceedings and oral consideration of the case are only mentioned in French literature if relevant to the subject under discussion. Thus when considering the judgment, motivation is regarded as *'une garantie de bonne justice'* (Couchez, 1992, no. 400).

Literature: L. Cadiet, Droit *judiciaire privé*, Paris 1992 (Litec);

G. Couchez, *Procédure Civile*, Paris 1992 (Sirey);

Hugenholtz/Heemskerk, *Hoofdlijnen van Nederlands Burgerlijk Procesrecht*, W.H. Heemskerk, Utrecht 1994 (Lemma);

H. Motulsky, *Ecrits*, Tome I (Etudes et notes de procédure civile), 1973 (Dalloz);

H. Solus and R. Perrot, *Droit judiciaire privé*, Tome III (Procédure de première instance), Paris 1991 (Sirey).

5.2.2. PRINCIPLE OF PARTY AUTONOMY (PRINCIPE DISPOSITIF)

The civil proceedings are in principle the proceedings of the parties: it is they who decide *whether* proceedings will be instituted and what their extent will be. The party is *dominus litis*. In French law this idea is laid down in the *principe dispositif* (Cadiet, 1992, no. 870). The principle is expressed in arts. 1 and 4, first sentence. It is closely connected with the principle of the passivity of the judge. When establishing the facts, the court is bound pursuant to arts. 5, 6 and 7 by what the parties put forward. Exceptions to this principle may be found in arts. 8, 10, 11 and 12. Article 12, para. 1, determines that the court must of its own motion add grounds of law. Another exception is provided by art. 3, which, in the interest of a good (i.e. smooth) course of the proceedings, allows the court to prescribe time-limits for the proceedings (*see* section 5.4.2; Solus and Perrot, 1991, nos. 76 to 105 inclusive).

5.2.3. PRINCIPLE OF HEARING BOTH PARTIES (PRINCIPE DE LA CONTRADICTION)

The second fundamental principle laid down by the *Nouveau Code de procédure civile* is the principe de la contradiction. This principle is *inter alia* expressed in arts. 14-17 and 132-137, of which art. 14 in particular explicitly formulates the *audi et alteram partem*: *'nulle partie ne peut être jugée sans avoir été entendue ou appelée'* (no party must be judged without having been heard or summoned). Before delivering judgment the court must not only enable both parties to respond to each other's statements, it must also give parties the opportunity to express their opinion on the grounds of law which may be supplemented by the court of its own motion, according to the explanatory notes of art. 16: *'le juge doit, en toutes circonstances, faire observer et observer lui-même le principe de la contradiction'* (Cadiet, 1992, no. 869; Solus and Perrot, 1991, no. 119).

5.2.4. PRINCIPLE OF EQUALITY OF THE PARTIES (PRINCIPE DE L'ÉGALITÉ)

The *principe de l'égalité* signifies the equality of citizens before the court. Not only is any discrimination against citizens in this respect unacceptable, there must also be equal access to the courts for everybody, rich or poor, French or foreign. The provision of legal aid forms part of this principle (section 5.9.3).

5.2.5. PRINCIPLE OF COURTS FREE OF CHARGE (PRINCIPE DE GRATUITÉ)

Closely connected with the *principe de l'égalité* is the principle which determines that administration of justice must be free of charge (*gratuit*). Before the French Revolution, parties had to pay the judge, which meant that the less well off were from the very start deprived of justice. This principle is, however, unrelated to the rules concerning the costs of proceedings (*see* section 5.9.3). This principle also implies that the public judge is (financially) independent of the parties.

5.2.6. PRINCIPLE OF CONTINUITY OF THE COURTS (PRINCIPE DE CONTINUITÉ)

The *principe de continuité* implies that as a rule judicial institutions sit continually in permanent locations and that their hearings are not restricted to specific periods of the year (art. R.711-1 COJ). In the summer months the judicial institutions also continue their work, albeit with a more limited staff.

5.2.7. PRINCIPLE OF TWO INSTANCES (PRINCIPE DU DOUBLE DEGRÉ DE JURIDICTION)

The *principe du double degré de juridiction* refers to the opportunity the parties have to bring their case before a higher court (*cour d'appel*) after the proceedings at first instance, in order to have their case completely re-examined and decided afresh (art. 543 *et seq.*). A continuation of this principle is the *Cour de cassation*, whose duty it is as the highest court of law to supervise the lower courts and to ensure unity in the application of the law.

5.3. Principal Characters

5.3.1. INTRODUCTION

The parties, the judge and the lawyers are the principal characters of civil litigation and each will be considered below.

The bailiff also plays an important part: it is the *huissier de justice*'s duty to serve writs and to enforce judgments and deeds, whereas the *huissiers audienciers* operate during court hearings. The bailiff can only carry out his duties within a specific jurisdiction.

We must also mention the registrar (*greffier*, art. R.812-3 COJ), the mediator (*conciliateur*, Decree 78-381 of 20 March 1978, as amended by Decree 81-583 of 18 May 1981), the administrator (*administrateur judiciaire*) and the liquidator in bankruptcy (*mandataire-liquidateur*, Act 85-99 of 25 January 1985, as amended by Act 90-1258 of 31 December 1990 and Decree 85-1389 of 27 December 1985, as amended by Decree 91-1030 of 8 October 1991).

Literature: G. Bolard, *La déontologie des mandataires de justice dans les faillites*, D. 1988. Chr. 261.;

R. Perrot, *Institutions judiciaires*, 1992 (Montchrestien);

F. Ruellan, *Le conciliateur civil, entre utopie et réalité*, J.C.P. 1990.I. 3431.

5.3.2. THE JUDGE

a. Introduction

The organisation and the jurisdiction of the judiciary are governed by the *Code de l'organisation judiciaire* (COJ). A distinction is made between, on the one hand, the *juridictions de droit commun*, which have jurisdiction to try all actions which by law have not been assigned to another court, and, on the other hand, the *juridictions d'exception*, which only try cases which by law form part of their jurisdiction under the law. The Cassation court (*Cour de cassation*; arts. L.111-1 to 142-2 inclusive and arts. R.121-1 to 132-4 inclusive COJ) falls outside this classification.

To the *juridictions de droit commun* belong:

- *cours d'appel* (courts of appeal): arts. L.211-1 to 225-4 inclusive and arts. R.211-1 to 231-1 inclusive COJ;

- *tribunaux de grande instance* (district courts): arts. L.311-1 to 312-6 inclusive and arts. R.311-1 to 312-6 inclusive COJ; and
- *tribunaux d'instance* (cantonal courts): arts. L. 321-1 to 323-1 inclusive and arts. R.321-1 to 323-3 inclusive COJ.

To the *juridictions d'exception* belong, for example:

- *tribunaux de commerce* (commercial courts): arts. L.411-1 to 414-7 inclusive and arts. R.411-1 to 414-21 inclusive COJ;
- *conseils de prud'hommes* (industrial courts): arts. L.421-1 to 424-1 inclusive and arts. R.421-1 to 424-1 inclusive COJ; and
- *tribunaux paritaires des baux ruraux* (rural tenancies courts): arts. L.441-1 to 444-1 inclusive COJ.

If an action is brought before a court which does not have jurisdiction, then one of the parties may bring a motion to contest jurisdiction, before submitting any defence, thereby naming the court which does have jurisdiction, and if he does not comply with these rules, his motion will be inadmissible (arts. 74 and 75). The court itself may also declare of its own motion that it does not have jurisdiction, for instance if the defendant does not enter an appearance (arts. 92 and 93).

The *Cour de cassation* is composed of three, five (as a rule) or seven judges (art. L.131-6 COJ). The *cour d'appel* is composed of three judges (*conseillers*) (art. L.212-2 COJ). *See* art. 956 NCPC for the resolution of disputes by the president in summary proceedings on appeal. The *tribunal de grande instance* normally decides with three judges (*juges*) (art. L.311-8 COJ). Decisions may, however, be made by a single judge (*juridiction à juge unique*) (art. L.311-10 COJ). In the *tribunal d'instance* cases are tried by one judge (art. L.321-4 COJ), while in the *tribunal de commerce* decisions by more than one judge (*juridiction collégiale*) are the rule (art. L.412-1 COJ). The judges of the commercial court (*juges consulaires*) are not *magistrats de carrière* (career magistrates), but (elected) lay judges (art. L.413-1 *et seq.* COJ). The *conseil de prud'hommes* does not consist of *magistrats de carrière* either. It is a paritarian commission chosen by electoral colleges of employers and employees (art. L.511-1 *et seq. Code du travail*). Each *tribunal d'instance* has a type of rural tenancies division (*tribunal paritaire des baux ruraux*) which is assisted by four assessors of whom two are tenants and two are landlords (art. L.441-2 *et seq.* COJ).

b. International jurisdiction

By virtue of arts. 14 and 15 Code Civil the French court has jurisdiction to try cases which involve a French national. International jurisdiction of the French court based on the nationality of (one of the) parties is in principle applicable to all areas of civil law, subject to important exceptions such as claims relating to immovable property situated abroad and requests for measures of enforcement outside France. Neither do the French courts have jurisdiction pursuant to art. 14 Code Civil if the defendant is domiciled within the EC (art. 3 Brussels Convention; *see further* section 3.1.5).

c. Sectoral jurisdiction

Apart from the administrative courts there are the 'ordinary' courts, which may try either civil or criminal cases. The administrative courts normally decide cases against public bodies. Neither the criminal courts, nor the administrative courts will be discussed here.

Courts with sectoral jurisdiction in the area of civil law are, for example, the commercial courts, the industrial courts and the rural tenancies courts (*see* section 5.3.2a, under *juridiction d'exception*). In addition, arbitrators can also have jurisdiction.

Due to all these judicial bodies it is quite conceivable that a case is presented before the wrong court. If either party finds this a problem, he must before submitting any defence and with reference to the court which does have jurisdiction, raise the objection as to jurisdiction if this objection is to be admissible (arts. 74 and 75). Sometimes the court declines jurisdiction of its own motion, for example if a defendant does not show up (arts. 92 and 93). If the court deems itself incompetent to judge the case, it indicates the court which does have jurisdiction, which indication is imperative both for the parties and for the relevant court. When the national frontiers or the limits of the sectoral jurisdiction are crossed, i.e. when the case should be decided by a foreign court, an arbitrator, an administrative court or a penal court, the court confines itself to sending the parties away in order to *mieux se pourvoir* (art. 96).

If the court addressed has not given a judgment on the merit of the case, the *contredit* is in principle the only possible means to challenge this decision regarding (lack of) jurisdiction (art. 80 *et seq.*; *see* section 5.6.5).

d. Absolute jurisdiction (compétence d'attribution)

General rules on absolute jurisdiction (*compétence d'attribution*) can be found in art. 33 *et seq.*

The *tribunal de grande instance* at first instance has jurisdiction in all actions except those which by law belong to the jurisdiction of another court, on account of the nature of the legal relationship or the procedure involved (arts. L.311-2 and R.311-1 COJ). Thus the *tribunal de grande instance* has jurisdiction to try all personal matters or cases relating to movable property, if the value of the claim exceeds FF 30,000 (art. R.321-1 COJ). *See* arts. 35 and 36 on objective and subjective cumulation. In cases which belong to the exclusive jurisdiction of the *tribunal de grande instance* on account of the nature of the legal relationship, a limit of FF 13,000 applies to appeals (art. R.311-2 COJ). Article L.311-2 COJ includes a list of cases in which the *tribunal de grande instance* has exclusive jurisdiction (*see also* Couchez, 1992, no. 52).

The *tribunal d'instance* tries all personal matters and all claims relating to movable property, without appeal, if the claim does not exceed FF 13,000 and subject to appeal, if it does not exceed FF 30,000 (art. R.321-1 COJ). This court also has exclusive jurisdiction in a number of specially designated cases, in particular tenancy cases (*inter alia* art. R.321-2 *et seq.* COJ).

The *tribunal de commerce* has jurisdiction in all disputes concerning commercial acts (*actes de commerce*) (art. L.411-1 in conjunction with arts. 631, 632, 633, 638 and 639 C. Com.). In districts without a commercial court, the *tribunal de grande instance* has jurisdiction (art. L.311-3 COJ). Here a limit of FF 13,000 to appeals also applies. If the dispute concerns an *acte mixte* (i.e. an act which is a commercial act for one party but not for the other - e.g. a contract concluded between a merchant and a private individual) then the private individual may only be summoned before the *tribunal de (grande) instance*. If the merchant is the defendant, then the private individual may decide whether the merchant will be summoned before the *tribunal de commerce* or the *tribunal de (grande) instance*.

The *conseil de prud'hommes* has jurisdiction in all disputes resulting from a contract of employment. They must concern individual disputes between an employee on the one hand and an employer on the other hand. This court also tries disputes between employees. Any clause in the contract of employment deviating from these provisions is null and void (art. L.421-1 COJ). Appeal is not allowed if the value of the claim does not exceed FF 18,900 (art. L.511-1 Code du travail in conjunction with art. D. 517-1 Code du travail).

Pursuant to art. L.441-1 COJ all disputes between tenants and landlords concerning the application of the provisions of Titles 1 and 5 of Book VI of the *Code rural* belong to the exclusive jurisdiction of the *tribunal paritaire des baux ruraux*.

Appeal against *all* appealable judgments must be lodged with the *cours d'appel* (art. R.211-1 COJ).

These courts also pass judgment at the first and the highest instance in certain cases of challenging judges (*récusation*) (arts. 349, 359 and 364; *see also* art. 80 *et seq*. and art. 568). *See* the diagram on p. 143.

e. Relative jurisdiction (compétence territoriale)

The general provisions concerning relative jurisdiction (*compétence territoriale*) can be found in art. 42 *et seq*.

Subject to exceptions the main rule is that one is summoned before the court of one's domicile or residence (art. 42, para. 1 and art. 43; *see also* art. 102 Code Civil). Exceptions to this concern immovable property and *bona vacantia* (arts. 44 and 45). The plaintiff has a choice in the cases enumerated in art. 46.

Literature: G. Giudicelli-Delage, *Institutions judiciaires et juridictionnelles*, 1987 (PUF);

R. Perrot, *Le juge unique en droit français*, Revue internationale de droit comparé, 1977, 659;

R. Perrot, *Institutions judiciaires*, 1992 (Montchrestien);

A. Pouille, *Le pouvoir judiciaire et les tribunaux*, 1985 (Masson);

H. Roland and L. Boyers, *Institutions judiciaires*, 1983 (l'Hermès);

J. Vincent, S. Guinchard, G. Montagnier, and A. Varinard, *La justice et ses institutions*, 1991 (Dalloz).

5.3.3. AVOCAT AND AVOUÉ

Legal assistance is provided *inter alia* by *avocats*, *avoués à la cour* and *avocats à la Cour de cassation/au Conseil d'Etat*.

In France the legal profession has undergone drastic changes in the past 20 years (*see* the Acts 71-1271 of 31 December 1971, 90-1258 and 90-1259 of 31 December 1990, as well as the Decree 91-1197 of 27 November 1991. Thus, into effect from 1 January 1992 the activities of various types of lawyers have merged into the activities of the *avocat*. In view of the competition in Europe an *avocat* in private practice is now allowed to be employed by

DIAGRAM JUDICIAL ORGANISATION IN CIVIL CASES IN FRANCE

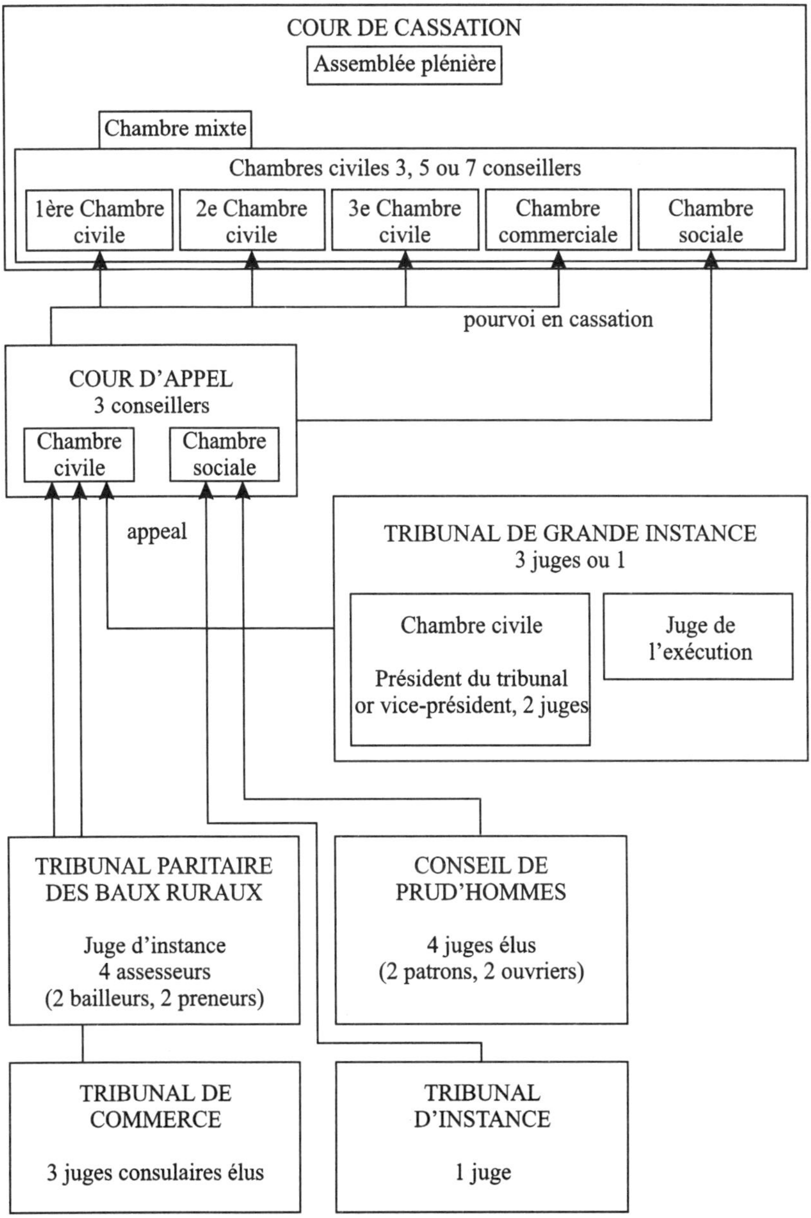

another lawyer in private practice or by a partnership of lawyers. The French new-style-lawyer is obliged to follow a three-year professional training/traineeship.

In principle *avocats* act before the courts of first instance as the parties' legal representatives in the proceedings. At this level the distinction between *avocat* and *avoué* has been abolished.

In the *tribunal de grande instance* legal representation in the proceedings (*mandat ad litem*) by a lawyer is obligatory. Except if the mandate is revoked, the lawyer cannot be compelled to show his mandate (arts. 416 and 418). As a mandatory representative *ad litem* a lawyer may only act before the *tribunal de grande instance* of his own district.

A lawyer is also the legal adviser of his client and is entitled to plead his client's case before the court: *mission d'assistance* (art. 412). A lawyer has a monopoly to plead the case before the *juridictions de droit commun*, without prejudice to the right of the parties to plead the case themselves (which pleading must not interfere with the mandatory representation *ad litem*: art. 18). When exercising his *fonction d'assistance* the lawyer is not bound to any district and can therefore plead his case before any court.

There is one exception to this rule: *avocats* are not allowed to plead cases before the *Cour de cassation* (*see below*).

Avoués (*see inter alia* Order 45-2591 of 2 November 1945, Decree 45-0118 of 19 December 1945 and Act 90-1258 of 31 December 1990) are the mandatory legal representatives *ad litem* in the *cours d'appel* (courts of appeal). The distinction between the function of representative *ad litem* (*représentation*) and of legal adviser (*assistance*) does still exist here, which means that parties in an action before a court of appeal must employ an *avoué* as well as an *avocat*. The *avoué* has a territorial mandate: he can only act before the *cour d'appel* where he is admitted. For a number of appeal procedures mandatory legal representation is not required (*see* art. 899 and art. 931 *et seq.*). Examples are the appeal procedure against judgments of the industrial court (art. R.517-7 - 517-9 Code du travail), the appeal procedure against judgments of the rural tenancies court (art. 892, para. 2) and the appeal procedure against certain judgments of the *tribunal de grande instance* (*see* e.g. art. 1163).

The *avocats aux Conseils*, who consist of the *avocats à la Cour de cassation* and the *avocats au Conseil d'Etat* (lawyers in the Court of Cassation and in the Council of State; *see inter alia* Act 90-1258 of 31 December 1990 and Decree 91-1125 of 28 October 1991) are both representatives *ad litem* and legal advisers of the parties. In principle there is mandatory representation *ad litem* (except for industrial cases). Altogether there are 60 cassation lawyers who constitute the Bar in the *Cour de cassation* (and the *Conseil d'Etat*).

Finally, it must be noted that *avoués* and *avocats aux Conseils*, as well as *huissiers de justice*, are ministerial officials, so-called *officiers ministériels*. The State grants this title to the above persons. Subject to State supervision, the *office ministériel* may be transferred.

Literature: G. Algazi, *La société d'exercice libérale: avantages et inconvénients*, Gaz. Pal. 1993, 317, p. 10;

Bacrot and Fontbressin, *Le nouvel avocat*, Gaz. Pal. 1992;

A. Bénabent, *Avocats: premières vues sur la nouvelle profession*, J.C.P. 1991.I.3499;

Eymard and Doucède, *Etude sur la représentation (ou assistance) obligatoire par un avocat*, Gaz. Pal. 1990, 332;

M. Jeantin, *Commentaire de la loi no. 90-1258 du 31 décembre 1990 relative aux sociétés d'exercice libéral*, J.C.P. 1991.I.3504;

Hamelin and Damien, *Les règles de la nouvelle profession d'avocat*, 7e édition (Dalloz).

5.3.4. THE PARTIES

Only natural and legal persons can act as plaintiffs in an action. The court will not admit an action brought by a company which is in the process of being incorporated and which does not possess legal personality in France. Persons who do not have legal capacity cannot be party to proceedings and must be represented in court by their legal representatives; minors will therefore have to be represented by their parents or guardian (*see* arts. 488 and 481 Code Civil).

An action cannot be admitted if the plaintiff has no interest in bringing it: *pas d'intérêt, pas d'action*. The interest must be already obtained and immediate. An action brought to prevent an impending violation of a right is in principle admissible (art. 31).

Representative actions (*actions des groupements*) may be brought by organised groups which represent a certain interest, provided it is an *intérêt collectif*. These organised groups may be trade unions or associations. Associations, however, have fewer rights than trade unions, who may institute proceedings in the interest of their members pursuant to art. L.411-11 Code du travail (*see also* art. L.123-6 and 135-4 Code du travail). Although certain associations are by law allowed to bring an action to defend their collective interests, the majority of actions brought by associations will be held inadmissible due to the lack of a collective interest. The following associations (*inter alia*) have by law been granted a direct right to institute proceedings with respect to collective interests: the *ligues anti-alcooliques* (art. 96 C. des boissons), the *associations de lutte contre le racisme* (art. 87 Act 87-588 of 30 July 1987), the *associations de lutte contre les discriminations 'sexistes'* (Act 85-772 of 25 July 1985), consumer organisations (art. 46 Act 73-1193 of 27 December 1973 and art. 1 Act 88-14 of 5 January 1988, Act 92-60 of 18 January 1992 and Decree 92-1306 of 11 December 1992) and nature and environmental associations (Act 88-1261 of 30 December 1988).

There is *pluralité de parties* when there are more than two parties in a dispute (arts. 323 and 324); starting-point is the independence of the different proceedings between the different parties to the proceedings (*divisibilité d'instance*): acts performed by or on behalf of one of the parties to the proceedings cannot benefit or harm others, with the exception of the provisions in arts. 474, 475, 529, 552, 553 and 615.

Literature: J. Calais-Auloy, *Les actions en justice des associations de consommateurs*, D. 1988, 193;

Coupet, *L'action en justice des personnes morales de droit privé*, thèse Aix, 1974;

F. Derrida, *La notion de partie dans les décisions relatives au redressement et à la liquidation judiciaire des entreprises*, D. 1989, 77;

S. Guinchard, *Le rôle et la participation des associations dans l'action en justice en matière civile en droit français*, Revue internationale de droit comparé 1989, 13;

S. Guinchard, *L'action de groupe*, Revue internationale de droit comparé 1990, 599;

J.-P. Moreau, *Les limites au principe de la divisibilité de l'instance quant aux parties*, LGDJ 1966, préface Cornu;

Paisant, *Lutte contre les clauses abusives*, D. 1988, 253;

G. Viney, *Un pas vers l'assainissement des pratiques contractuelles: la loi du 5 janvier 1988 relative aux actions en justice des associations agréées de consommateurs*, J.C.P. 88.I.3355.

5.4. Basic Procedure for Contentious Jurisdiction at First Instance

5.4.1. INTRODUCTION

Book I of the *Nouveau Code de procédure civile* contains provisions applicable to the method of proceedings in general. Book II (Titles 1-5) lays down a number of specific provisions for each procedure before a certain court. The basic procedure before the *tribunal de grande instance* will be discussed in detail. The other procedures, which will be discussed briefly, are those before the *tribunal d'instance* and the *tribunal de commerce*.

It must also be mentioned that, despite the formalistic nature of civil procedure, the *Nouveau Code de procédure civile* contains numerous provisions which relax rules which determine that violation of certain formal regulations (including regulations of substantive law and of public policy) leads to nullity and these provisions state that violation of such regulations does not lead to nullity unless the interests of the opposing party have been violated (*see* arts. 115 and 121; Cadiet, 1992, nos. 28, 881 and 1085; Couchez, 1992, nos. 4 and 188-198).

Literature: Dupeyron, *La régularisation des actes nuls*, LGDJ 1073, préface Hébraud;

Dymant, *Les nullités de forme et de fond en matière de signification d'acte*, Bulletin avoués 1985, 34;

E. Du Rusque, *Nature et régime des nullités pour vice de forme*, Gaz. Pal. 1979.1, doctr. p. 136;

D. Tomasin, *Remarques sur la nullité des actes de procédures*, Mélanges Pierre Hébraud, 1981, 853 (Toulouse).

5.4.2. TRIBUNAL DE GRANDE INSTANCE

a. Introduction

In an ordinary procedure before the *tribunal de grande instance* the parties are called *demandeur* (plaintiff) and *défendeur* (defendant). There is no requirement that an attempt to settle the case must be made before proceedings can be commenced.

b. Commencement of proceedings

The action is commenced by writ (*assignation*), which is issued by a bailiff. Article 648 lays down the requirements which the writ must satisfy. Pursuant to art. 56 in conjunction with art. 752 the writ must also contain the following in order to be valid:

- the name of the court which has jurisdiction;
- the subject of the claim with an explanation of the grounds; a brief account of the grounds does not suffice;
- the name of the plaintiff's lawyer; and

– the period within which the defendant must name his lawyer.

Pursuant to art. 755 the defendant must name his lawyer within 15 days after the writ. In practice, however, this can be done until the end of the examination. The case is pending when a copy of the writ has been deposited with the registry within a maximum period of 4 months after service. If this period is exceeded, the writ is invalid. The court must decide this of its own motion (art. 757).

Parties may also commence an action by means of a joint request (*requête conjointe*) (*see further* section 5.5.3).

c. Proceedings

After the case has been entered on the cause-list, the President of the court determines the date and the hour of the first hearing (arts. 758 and 796). The case is usually continued under the supervision of a cause-list judge: *le juge de la mise en état* (art. 762). His duties include supervising the exchange of written pleadings and the production of documents by the parties' lawyers. After exchange, copies of the written pleadings and of the documents must be deposited with the registry.

In article 763 *et seq.* the cause-list judge's task is set out; he must determine the time-limits for the lodging of written pleadings, he may hear the lawyers and the parties and can try to reach a settlement. The settlement may be recorded in an official report which is directly enforceable (*see also* arts. 127 *et seq.*). The decisions of the cause-list judge do not have authority of *res iudicata* and they cannot be set aside. Appeal or appeal in cassation against such decisions may in principle only be lodged together with an appeal or cassation against the (full or partial) final judgment.

As soon as the cause-list judge thinks that the case is ready to be decided, he gives an *ordonnance de clôture*, whereby he declares the examination closed. Then he refers the case to a hearing, the date of which is fixed by the President or by himself. The *ordonnance de clôture* does not need to be motivated and is in principle irrevocable (*see* arts. 782 and 784). After the examination is closed it is no longer possible to lodge written pleadings or to produce documents, subject to several specific exceptions (art. 783). The case remains under the supervision of the cause-list judge until the hearing where oral pleadings take place.

Article 430 *et seq.* provide rules for the oral pleadings (*débats*) which in principle are public. They are followed by the *délibérations*, unless judgment is pronounced immediately (art. 447 *et seq.*).

The above procedure is called the *circuit long* (*see* for a detailed description Cadiet, 1992, nos. 902-992; Couchez, 1992, nos. 246-273). On the other hand, there is the *circuit court*, whereby the President immediately refers the case to a trial hearing (*see further* section 5.7.2).

If the President is of the opinion that the case is virtually ready for trial, he may determine that the parties may exchange written pleadings or produce documents once more (the so-called *circuit moyen*). The President determines the time-limits for this and the date on which the lawyers must again appear before him. On that day the President will decide whether the case is indeed ready for trial. If this is so, he closes the examination and refers the case to the trial hearing. Referral may also take place at the request of either party if the opposing party has not complied (art. 761).

d. Judgment

Judgments (*jugements*) can be classified as judgments in adversarial proceedings (*jugements contradictoires*; art. 467 *et seq.*) and default judgments (*jugements par défaut*; art. 471 *et seq.*). French law also has final, partial and interim judgments (*jugements définitifs*, *jugements mixtes* and *jugements avant dire droit*; arts. 480-483). During proceedings the *juge de la mise en état* may make orders (*ordonnances*; art. 773; *see further* section 5.4.2c).

Article 454 prescribes the minimum requirements for each judgment. Together with the decision on the main claim, the court also decides on the costs of the proceedings (arts. 695-725; *see further* section 5.9.3). It may also pronounce the judgment to be provisionally enforceable (*exécution provisoire*), either fully or partly pursuant to arts. 514-526.

The judgment is pronounced in public (art. 451), must be motivated (art. 455, para. 1) and must be included in the *dictum* (art. 455, para. 2). Rectification of and additions to the judgment may be made in accordance with the provisions of arts. 462-464 (Cadiet, 1992, nos. 1072-1087; Couchez, 1992, nos. 396-404).

e. Special aspects of procedure

1. Non-appearance (défaut de comparution)

If a defendant does not enter an appearance (duly represented), a default judgment will not be pronounced automatically, but will only be pronounced if the judgment is given in the last instance *and* the summons has not been served on the defendant in person (art. 473). As a result of these two cumulative requirements, default judgments are in practice rather rare. In case the requirement of service has not been complied with, art. 471 allows the defendant to be called again. The default regulations apply to all civil procedures which is why they can be found in Book I.

2. *Third parties in the proceedings (intervention)*

Joinder (*intervention volontaire formée à titre accessoire*) and intervention (*intervention volontaire formée à titre principal*) are possible by virtue of arts. 328-330. *Intervention forcée* includes, for instance, indemnification, which is governed by arts. 331-338. These provisions are preceded by a number of general provisions (arts. 325-327), which apply to indemnification as well as to joinder and intervention.

3. *Amendment of claim (demande additionnelle)*

Each party may in the course of the proceedings amend his claim (arts. 4 and 65), on condition that there is sufficient connection (*lien suffisant*) between the original claim and the amendment (art. 70).

4. *Counterclaim (demande reconventionnelle)*

Book I allows the defendant to file a counterclaim (art. 63). This counterclaim must have a *lien suffisant* with the plaintiff's claim (art. 4 in conjunction with art. 70).

5. *Production of evidence (preuve)*

An important part of the rules of evidence can be found in the *Code Civil*. The *Nouveau Code de procédure civile* contains provisions on the formal rules of evidence (*administration judiciaire de la preuve*). Point of departure is art. 9, which states that it is up to the parties to prove the relevant facts. Article 6 imposes an obligation to produce *prima facie* evidence. Pursuant to art. 12, para. 1 the judge who decides the case must in principle apply foreign law if applicable; the party who invokes the application of foreign law must, however, prove the contents of the relevant rule of law. If the party does not succeed in doing this, French law will be applied as *lex fori*.

The way in which the above provisions must be effected, is stated in art. 132 *et seq.*:

- articles 132-142 contain provisions on the production of documents (*les pièces*). The court can order the parties or a third party to bring certain documents into the proceedings and if they fail to do so, parties may incur a penalty.

- articles 143-178 contain provisions on measures of inquiry in general, the enforcement of such measures and the invalidity of orders for such measures.
- articles 179-183 contain provisions on the first measure of examination: in any action the judge may personally verify the facts in dispute (*vérifications personnelles du juge*). Parties must be summoned thereto.
- the second measure of examination is the personal appearance of the parties (arts. 184-198). Article 198 is important and provides: *le juge peut tirer toute conséquence de droit des déclarations des parties, de l'absence ou du refus de répondre de l'une d'elles et en faire état comme équivalent à un commencement de preuve par écrit.*
- articles 199-231 provide rules for the giving of evidence by witnesses (*déclarations des tiers*). A distinction is made between written statements (*attestations*) and oral examination of witnesses (*enquête*).
- articles 232-248 contain provisions regarding expert examination (*mesures d'instruction exécutées par un technicien*). The law provides that this examination may be done by *constatations*, a *consultation* or an *expertise* (arts. 249-284-1).
- articles 285-316 provide rules for disputing written evidence: arts. 287-302 regard private documents, arts. 303-315 regard authentic documents.
- finally, arts. 317-322 contain provisions regarding the oath sworn before the court (which either can decide the proceedings or may be supplementary). *See also* art. 1357 *et seq*. Code Civil.

6. *Settlement (conciliation)*

In certain proceedings the law can provide for a compulsory attempt to settle the case (*see* section 6.4.3a). This does not apply to proceedings before the *tribunal de grande instance*. However, this does not mean that parties cannot, either of their own motion or on the court's initiative, settle the case during the proceedings (*see* art. 21 and arts. 127-131). Since provisions regarding settlement have now been included in Book I, it applies to all procedures.

Literature: Ph. Bertin, *Les règles communes à toutes les mesures d'instruction et l'enquête selon le décret du 17 décembre 1973*, Gaz. Pal. 1974.1, doctr. p. 252;

P. Estoup, *Le dossier de plaidoirie*, Gaz. Pal. 1990.1, doctr. pp. 202 and 251;

P. Estoup, *La pratique des jugements*, 1990 (Litec);

P. Estoup, *Une réforme souhaitable: l'assouplissement de certaines règles relatives à la motivation*, Gaz. Pal. 1990. 2 doctr. p. 413;

G. Flécheux, *Le droit d'être entendu*, Mélanges Pierre Bellet, 1991, 149 (Litec);

C. Giverdon, *La procédure devant les tribunaux de grande instance*, préface Jean Foyer, 1973 (Librairies techniques);

R. Legros, *Essai sur la motivation des jugements civils*, thèse Dijon, 1987;

H. Solus and R. Perrot, *Droit judiciaire privé*, Tome III (Procédure de première instance), Paris 1991 (Sirey);

5.4.3. TRIBUNAL D'INSTANCE

a. Introduction

The procedure before the *tribunal d'instance* is simpler than the one before the *tribunal de grande instance*. The proceedings before the *tribunal d'instance* are governed by arts. 827-847-2. Parties are called *demandeur* and *défendeur*. The first aim of instituting proceedings before the *tribunal d'instance* is to reach settlement of the case and only if this fails, to have the case tried by the court: if the plaintiff indicates to the registry either orally or by letter that he wants the court to attempt a settlement, such attempt will be made prior to the actual proceedings (arts. 829-835). Should this attempt prove successful, then at the parties' request the settlement may be laid down in an official report which is enforceable (art. 129 *et seq.*).

b. Commencement of proceedings

Leaving aside commencement by writ or by filing a joint petition, the case may also be commenced by the voluntary appearance of the parties or, in certain cases, by an oral declaration at the registry.

Apart from the requirements of art. 56 (*see* section 5.4.2b) additional provisions apply to the writ (art. 829 *et seq.*). The writ itself must be issued at least 14 days before the date of the first hearing, while a copy of the *acte introductif* by which the case is brought before the cantonal court must be lodged with the registry at least one week before that date. With leave of the court these two time-limits may be altered in urgent cases.

Article 57 governs the (filing of the) joint petition. According to art. 846 the case is commenced by lodging the petition with the court (*see also* section 5.5.3).

If parties together appear in person before the court, their claims will be recorded in an official report signed by the parties. In cases commenced by joint petition as well as in cases where parties voluntarily appear the court will always first try to settle the case between parties (art. 847).

By means of an oral declaration at the registry a claim not exceeding the appeal limit of the *tribunal d'instance* (FF 13,000) may be brought before the court (*see* art. 847-1 and 847-2).

c. Proceedings

If the attempt to settle fails, two options are open: either the case is ready for trial, or further examination is required, for which a new hearing date is determined. Article 843 stipulates that in principle these are oral proceedings.

Literature: M. Caratini, *A propos des tribunaux d'instance*, Gaz. Pal. 1989.2, doctr. p. 331;

P. Estoup, *La procédure devant le tribunal d'instance*, D. 1985, 246;

P. Estoup, *Le juge d'instance. Attributions et procédure*, Gaz. Pal. 1987.1, doctr. p. 67;

P. Estoup, *Le juge d'instance. Structures et organisation judiciaire. Les adaptations nécessaires*, Gaz. Pal. 1987.1, doctr. p. 197;

Pronier, *Le juge d'instance dans la société française*, 1993 (Economica).

5.4.4. TRIBUNAL DE COMMERCE

a. Introduction

The procedure before the commercial court can be found in art. 853 *et seq*.

b. Commencement of proceedings

According to art. 854 the case may be commenced in three different ways: by writ, joint petition and voluntary appearance of the parties.

To the writ the requirements of art. 56 (*see* section 5.4.2b) apply as well as some additional provisions (art. 855 *et seq.*). The writ itself must be issued at least 14 days before the date of the first hearing, while a copy of the *acte introductif* by which the case is brought before the court must be lodged with the registry at least one week before that date. With leave of the court these two time-limits may be altered in urgent cases. In maritime and aviation cases the writ may even be issued at an hour's notice, without the President's leave, where it concerns parties without domicile or urgent matters (art. 858).

It appears from arts. 859-860 that a case may also be brought before the commercial court by means of a joint petition. Such petition must comply with the provisions of art. 57 (*see further* section 5.5.3).

If parties together appear in person before the court, their claims will be recorded in an official report signed by the parties.

c. Proceedings

The proceedings are informal. Article 871 states that the procedure is oral, although written elements are not altogether excluded, for instance the writ or the joint petition.

At the first hearing it becomes apparent whether or not the case is ready for trial. If not, it may be adjourned to the next hearing without the necessity of a lengthy examination. If in view of the complexity of the case such examination is necessary, a so-called *juge-rapporteur* is appointed (arts. 862-869). His duties and powers resemble those of the *juge de la mise en état* (section 5.4.2c), although he is not authorised to declare the examination closed. Once the examination is finished, he refers the case to the court for further consideration.

Literature: P. Drai, *Le monde des affaires et ses juges*, Journ. agréés 1990, 329;

M. Jeantin, *Le juge-rapporteur*, J.C.P. 77, éd. CI, II, 12495;

D. Lebeau, J.-Class. Pr. civ., Fasc. 410-412;

G. Ripert and R. Roblot, *Droit commercial*, LGDJ, Tome 1, 1991, nos. 109-134.

5.5. Basic Procedure for Voluntary Jurisdiction at First Instance

5.5.1. INTRODUCTION

Voluntary jurisdiction may be translated as *juridiction gracieuse*. General provisions on this subject are found in Book I of the *Nouveau Code de procédure civile* (arts. 25-29, 60-62, 434, 454, 466, 543, 546, 547, 583, 587, 675 and 679). Book II contains special provisions for the different courts (arts. 797-800 and 950-953).

5.5.2. THE PROCEDURE COMMENCED BY PETITION

Voluntary jurisdiction procedures are normally commenced by petition. The petitioner is called *requérant* and any interested party is called *l'intéressé.*

As a rule the case is commenced by petition and is pending once the petition has been deposited with the registry of the relevant court (arts. 60 and 61). If it concerns a procedure before the *tribunal d'instance*, the case may also be commenced by the making of an oral declaration at the court's registry (art. 62).

Article 797 reiterates that a petition to the *tribunal de grande instance* must be filed by a lawyer (or, where applicable, by a ministerial officer).

In the *tribunal de grande instance* the President (of the relevant chamber) appoints a *rapporteur* to examine the case. By virtue of art. 26 the judge may base his decision on all facts relating to the case; this also includes facts not asserted by the parties. He may, even of his own motion, carry out any necessary examination. The judge may thereto, without any formalities, hear anyone, including persons whose interests may be prejudiced by the decision (art. 27). It is not possible to file a counter-petition.

The hearing takes place in chambers (art. 434) and is in principle not public (art. 436). At the trial there are no proper oral pleadings. Article 440 states the order in which the parties may speak during the hearing. Pursuant to art. 28 the judge may also make a decision without any pleadings having taken place.

In principle the decision is also not given in public (art. 451). This breach of the public nature of the administration of justice is somewhat alleviated by allowing third parties to inspect the file and to obtain a copy thereof in certain cases (art. 29). The decision must be served upon the petitioner (art. 675, para. 2). Service must also be effected upon possible third parties interested in the case (art. 454). These third parties can also lodge appeal against the decision (arts. 454, 546 and 547, para. 2). The decision does not have the authority of *res iudicata.*

5.5.3. THE PROCEDURE COMMENCED BY CONTENTIOUS PETITION

In the *Nouveau Code de procédure civile* the joint petition has been introduced as the normal way to commence proceedings in contentious cases. Although art. 54 puts the *requête conjointe* on a par with the writ, in legal practice this method of commencement of proceedings is not often used. Article 58 gives the parties the opportunity to request the court in such a petition to judge their case as an *amiable compositeur.*

In order to be admissible, the petition must satisfy the general provisions of art. 57. There are also different rules for the various courts. Thus, parties in a case before the *tribunal de grande instance* must also name a lawyer in their petition (art. 793). Usually proceedings are commenced by depositing the petition with the registry (*see* art. 795). For the procedure before the *tribunal de grande instance* art. 796 provides that arts. 759, 760 and 762 apply accordingly to the petition procedure, unless the case, if so requested, has been transferred to a single judge. *See also* sections 5.4.2-4.

Literature: J-L. Bergel, *La juridiction gracieuse en droit français*, D. 1983, 153;

J-L. Bergel, *Juridiction gracieuse et matière contentieuse*, D. 1983, 165;

Le Ninivin, *La juridiction gracieuse dans le Nouveau Code de procédure civile*, 1983 (Litec).

5.6. Means of Recourse

5.6.1. INTRODUCTION

Title XVI of Book I NCPC deals with the *voies de recours* (means of recourse). After distinguishing in art. 527 between ordinary and extraordinary means of recourse, the *Nouveau Code de procédure civile* continues with a number of provisions which apply to all means of recourse (arts. 528-537). Then follow provisions dealing with different means of recourse.

Appeal and the application to set aside a judgment in default are the ordinary means of recourse. In the case of contentious jurisdiction they must in principle be lodged within one month, in the case of voluntary jurisdiction within 14 days, after service of the judgment (art. 538). The ordinary means of recourse suspend enforcement of the judgment (art. 539), unless it has been pronounced provisionally enforceable (art. 514 *et seq.*). Extraordinary means of recourse are appeal in cassation, a third-party application to set aside a judgment in default and review. These means of recourse do not suspend enforcement (*effet suspensif*; art. 579).

Subject to a few exceptions, the time-limit for lodging a means of recourse starts to run from the moment of service of the judgment in dispute (art. 528). The judgment must be served on the parties themselves (art. 677). In case of mandatory legal representation the decision must first be served on the legal representatives, failing which service upon the parties is void (art. 678).

If no appeal has been lodged, the court may, at the request of either or both parties, explain its judgment (art. 461). The court is also allowed to rectify its judgment. French law goes to considerable lengths in this respect, for the rectification may not only deal with *'erreurs et omissions matérielles'* (art. 462), but also points in dispute on which the court has incorrectly failed to decide (art. 463), or points on which it has incorrectly made a decision (*ultra petita*; art. 464).

Literature: G. Almairac, *Du jugement d'un tribunal à un arrêt de la cour*, J.C.P. 78.I.2884;

B. Appert and R. Julliard, *Tableau des voies de recours du Nouveau Code de procédure civile*, D. 1976, chron. 14909 and 201;

Ph. Bertin, *A propos de la rectification des jugements: l'omission de statuer et l'ultra petita*, Gaz. Pal. 1984, 82;

Carel, *Au sujet des erreurs ou omissions matérielles affectant une décision judiciaire*, Gaz. Pal. 1973, 241;

Ph. Hoonakker, *L'effet suspensif des voies de recours dans le Nouveau Code de procédure civile: une chimère?*, thèse Strasbourg, 1988;

R. Lindon, *Perfection et imperfection de la décision judiciaire*, D. 1973, 143;

R. Lindon, *De deux innovations en matière de procédure*, J.C.P. 73.I. 2527;

A. Perdriau, *La pratique des arrêts civils de la cour de cassation*, 1993 (Litec);

G. Wiederkehr, *Le système des voies de recours en droit judiciaire privé français*, Revue internationale de droit comparé 1989, n° spéc., Vol. 11, 225.

5.6.2. THE APPLICATION TO SET ASIDE A JUDGMENT IN DEFAULT (OPPOSITION)

The application to set aside a judgment in default (*see* section 5.4.2e) is an ordinary means of recourse which is only open to the person against whom judgment was entered (art. 571). The court which delivered the judgment by default has jurisdiction to hear the application (arts. 572 and 573, para. 1). The case is commenced as prescribed by arts. 573-575. *Opposition sur opposition ne vaut*: the party who fails to appear in the application procedure and against whom a judgment in default is again delivered, cannot commence an application to set aside a second time (art. 578).

5.6.3. APPEAL (APPEL)

In principle appeal lies against all (contentious and voluntary) judgments at first instance. In cases of limited financial importance appeal is not allowed (*see* section 5.3.2d for the various financial limits). The *cour d'appel* has absolute jurisdiction. In ordinary proceedings (i.e. adversarial proceedings with mandatory legal representation), appeal is lodged by submitting a unilateral declaration signed by an *avoué*, to the registry of the *cour d'appel*. The parties are called *appelant* and *intimé*. Only the party who has an interest in the appeal is entitled to lodge an appeal, unless he has acquiesced in the judgment (art. 546, para. 1 and 556-558). In voluntary jurisdiction third parties on whom the judgment has been served may also appeal (art. 546, para. 2). *See further* arts. 547-555 *inter alia* on cross-appeal (*appel incident*) which may be lodged at any stage of the proceedings (art. 550). In that connection it must be noted that the appellate court can order the cross-appellant to pay damages if the appeal has been lodged late deliberately, for instance in order to delay the proceedings.

In art. 561 *et seq.* the devolutive effect of the appeal is expressed, which means that the whole case devolves from the court at first instance to the appellate court. The parties, however, determine the extent of the appeal in their grievances set out in the notice of appeal. The time-honoured rule *tantum devolutum, quantum appellatum* applies also in France (Cadiet, 1992, no. 1236; Couchez, 1992, no. 425).

The appellate court may in certain cases reconsider the whole case, despite the fact that the appeal was limited to certain grounds (*faculté d'évocation*; art. 568; *see further* Cadiet, 1992, no. 1243 ff.; Couchez, 1992, no. 428).

See for the further course of the appeal proceedings arts. 899-972.

Literature: O. Barret, *L'appel-nullité*, Revue trimestrielle de droit civil, 1990, 199;

G. Bolard, *L'appel-nullité,* D. 1988, 177;

P. Gerbay, *Les effets de l'appel voie d'annulation*, D. 1993, 143;

Le Royer, *Les effets de l'appel*, thèse Lyon, 1974;

Y. Lobin, *SOS contre un appel par déclaration au greffe*, D. 1975, 97;

Mas, *La portée de l'effet dévolutif de l'appel aux fins d'annulation d'un jugement sur le fond*, Univ. de Nice, 1988, préface Julien.

5.6.4. APPEAL IN CASSATION (POURVOI EN CASSATION)

It is remarkable that under French law appeal in cassation is an extraordinary means of recourse. The legislator of the *Nouveau Code de procédure civile* decided not to enumerate the grounds for cassation and restricted himself to the following vague description in article 604: *'Le pourvoi en cassation tend à faire censurer par la Cour de cassation la non-conformité du jugement qu'il attaque aux règles de droit'*. However, in practice the following grounds are recognised as grounds for cassation (Couchez, 1992, no. 451; Cadiet, 1992, nos. 1281-1284):

- breach of the law;
- lack of jurisdiction (the court has incorrectly decided that it had no jurisdiction);
- excess of (constitutional) jurisdiction;
- non-compliance with formalities which by law may lead to the decision being void;
- conflicting judgments (arts. 617-618); and
- lack of a legal basis (e.g. in case of an amendment of the law).

Appeal in cassation only lies against judgments given in the last instance (art. 605). It is lodged by submitting a declaration with the registry of the *Cour de cassation*, signed by an *avocat à la Cour*. No appeal lies if a judgment may be rectified pursuant to arts. 463-464 (art. 616). Only an appeal by parties who have an interest is admissible. Appeal in cassation may also be lodged in voluntary jurisdiction (art. 610). The *Cour de cassation* can punish abuse of the appeal in cassation by imposing a fine and damages (art. 628).

The Procurator-General in the *Cour de cassation* may in certain cases lodge cassation in the interest of the law. The same applies to the Minister of Justice.

The time-limit for cassation is two months (subject to certain exceptions; art. 612). For default judgments the time-limit begins to run on the day when an application to set aside judgment is no longer possible (art. 613).

The *Cour de cassation* only considers questions of law, not questions of fact (art. 604; *see also* L.111-2 COJ). The normal adversarial procedure with legal representation to be followed before the *Cour de cassation* is set out in arts. 974-983. The *demandeur au pourvoi* must in principle present the grounds for cassation within 5 months, failing which cassation will be inadmissible (art. 975, para. 2 in conjunction with art. 978). The *défendeur au pourvoi* must submit his statement of defence within three months in order to be admissible, as required by the recently amended art. 982. The *Cour de cassation* may also quash a judgment of its own motion, i.e. disregarding the grounds of cassation submitted (art. 620). Article 1015 requires special notice: pursuant to this article the president of the panel of judges is obliged to inform the parties of any grounds of cassation which the court may consider of its own motion and to give the parties the opportunity to react to such grounds within a specified period. *See also* art. 16.

In principle the Court must refer the case after its decision in cassation; in certain cases it may, however, give a final decision in the case (arts. 626 and 627). The court to which the case has been referred is not bound by the judgment of the Court. If new appeal in cassation (on the same grounds) is lodged against a subsequent judgment in the case, the case is considered by the *Assemblée plénière* of the *Cour de cassation*. The court to which the case may then be referred after cassation is, however, bound by the Court's judgment.

Literature: M.N. Bachelier and X. Bachelier, *La technique de cassation*, 1989 (Dalloz), préface Ponsard;

Ph. Blondel, *La Cour de cassation (Le traitement des affaires)*, in: Les juridictions suprêmes, du procès à la règle, 1991, 69 (Public. Univ. Saint-Etienne);

J. Boré, *Cassation (cour de)* 1994, *Encyclopédie Dalloz* (répertoire);

Cour de cassation, *Bicentenaire de la Cour de cassation*, La documentation française, 1991;

P. Drai, *Pour la Cour de cassation*, J.C.P. 89.I.3374;

Ferrand, *Cassation française et révision allemande*, thèse Lyon, 1990;

M. Jeantin, *Réformer la Cour de cassation*, Mélanges Pierre Hébraud, 1981, 465;

Kernaleguen, *L'extension du rôle des juges de cassation*, thèse Rennes, 1979;

A. Perdriau, *Réflexions désabusées sur le contrôle de la Cour de cassation en matière civile*, J.C.P. 91.I.3538;

M.-Cl. Rondeau-Rivier, *La Cour de cassation (L'accès)*, in: Les juridictions suprêmes, du procès à la règle, 1991, 15 (Public. Univ. de Saint-Etienne);

F. Zenati, *La saisine pour avis de la cour de cassation*, D. 1992, 247.

5.6.5. OTHER MEANS OF RECOURSE

Noteworthy is the *contredit*, which is provided for in arts. 80-91. It is a means of recourse against judgments in which the court only decides on its (lack of) jurisdiction (*see* section 5.3.2c). This type of appeal must be lodged within 14 days, counting from the day of the judgment, with the registry of the court *a quo*. Then the registry forthwith sends the file on to the competent *cour d'appel* (art. 83), which in turn fixes a date for the hearing as soon as possible. The parties are given the opportunity to submit *observations*. Subsequently there are two possibilities: the court first seized lacked jurisdiction; in that case the case is referred imperatively to the court which does have jurisdiction, unless it concerns an administrative, penal or foreign court or arbitrators (art. 96). The court first seized did have jurisdiction; then the case will be referred to that court (art. 86). Another possibility is that the *cour d'appel* itself decides the case (art. 89: *évocation*). In order to discourage parties from lodging frivolous appeals, art. 88 grants the *cour d'appel* authority to impose a fine of FF 100 to 10,000 on the appellant.

The other extraordinary means of recourse, third-party opposition (*tierce opposition*), governed by arts. 582-592, and review (*recours en révision*), governed by arts. 593-602, will not be discussed.

Literature: Barrère, *La rétraction du juge civil*, Mélanges Pierre Hébraud, 1, 1981 (Toulouse);

M. Eymard and M. Doucède, *L'incompétence - Voies de recours et juridiction de renvoi*, Gaz. Pal. 1987.2, doctr. p. 609;

Parmentier, *Les jugements mixtes au regard de la recevabilité du contredit et de l'appel*, Bulletin avoués 1984, 109;

R. Perrot, *Les aspects nouveaux de la tierce-opposition en droit judiciaire privé français*, Mélanges Segni, Tome III, 675;

P. Veaux and D. Veaux, *Les surprises de la tierce-opposition*, Mélanges Henri-Daniel Cosnard, 409, 1990 (Economica).

5.7. Special Procedures

5.7.1. INTRODUCTION

In addition to the basic procedures before the different courts as discussed in sections 5.4 and 5.5, there are several special procedures in French law. The special character of the proceedings may, for instance, be that the case is decided in accelerated proceedings, whether or not on the merits (section 5.7.2). A separate procedure was also created for frequently occurring, relatively simple matters, such as the judicial order for payment (section 5.7.3). Book III of the *Nouveau Code de procédure civile* provides special rules for procedures which are exclusively designed for a special kind of substantive law, for instance the divorce procedure (section 5.7.4).

5.7.2. SUMMARY PROCEDURES

Summary procedures include procedures in which the judge decides on the merits of the case and those in which a provisional decision is made. Both will be considered here.

a. Accelerated proceedings on the merits

There are two ways to decide a case before the *tribunal de grande instance* in accelerated proceedings.

Procédure de renvoi à l'audience/circuit court; when in the opinion of the President of the chamber the case does not require any examination and is therefore ready to be tried, it may be transferred directly to a hearing to be pleaded and decided. This particularly applies to simple cases (arts. 760 and 761). Transfer to a hearing may also take place if the defendant has not appeared and the case is ready to be tried, unless the President decides that the defendant must be summoned again.

Procédure d'urgence à jour fixe; this allows the plaintiff with leave of the President of the *tribunal de grande instance*, in a case of urgency to summon the defendant on a fixed date, whereby the defendant is under the obligation to name his lawyer before the first hearing (art. 788 *et seq.*). If the defendant has complied with this obligation, the case may be immediately pleaded orally. If necessary it may be adjourned to another hearing, or transferred to the *juge de la mise en état* (*'circuit long'*; section 5.4.2c). If the defendant has not named a lawyer, the *'circuit court'* is followed (*see above*).

b. Summary proceedings (référé)

In principle each court has its own judge dealing exclusively with summary proceedings. The general rules are laid down in arts. 484-492. For the *tribunal de grande instance* arts. 808-810 also apply, arts. 848-850 for the *tribunal d'instance* and arts. 872 and 873 for the *tribunal de commerce.*

In urgent cases the President of the *tribunal de grande instance* has jurisdiction if there are no summary proceedings available at another court (art. 810). *See also* art. 809, which does not require urgency in certain cases.

Usually the summary proceedings are commenced by writ. In urgent cases the judge in summary proceedings may fix a date for trial (if the day usually appointed for summary proceedings hearings is not suitable) which may even be a holiday (art. 485).

Having heard the parties, who appear either in person or by attorney, the President gives his decision as soon as possible. This *ordonnance* is a provisional decision (art. 484): it has no authority of *res iudicata* and is provisionally enforceable, possibly immediately. An application to set aside a decision in summary proceedings is possible to a limited extent. Appeal must be lodged to the *cour d'appel* within 14 days (art. 490).

Literature: P. Estoup, *La pratique des procédures rapides*, 1990 (Litec);

R. Perrot, *L'évolution du référé*, Mélanges Pierre Hébraud, 1981 (Toulouse);

F. Ruellan, *A propos de la représentation des parties devant le juge des référés du tribunal de grande instance*, Gaz. Pal. 1992.1, doctr. p. 119.

5.7.3. SMALL CLAIMS PROCEDURES

a. Judicial order for payment (injonction de payer)

Through a simple procedure a creditor can obtain a writ of execution against his debtor. This procedure is not limited to small claims, but is eminently suited for those. Article 1405 describes the kind of claims involved.

The *tribunal d'instance* or the *tribunal de commerce* of the defendant's domicile has jurisdiction. The creditor commences the proceedings by depositing a petition accompanied by the necessary documents with the registry. No means of recourse lie against the rejection of the petition. If the petition is allowed, copies of the petition and the decision are served upon the debtor, in which he is ordered to pay or to apply within one month to set the decision aside (*see further* arts. 1405-1425).

b. Judicial order to perform (injonction de faire)

Whereas the *injonction de payer* provides the creditor with a way to compel in particular an unwilling debtor to pay, the *injonction de faire* provides the consumer with a weapon to urge his debtor in a quick and simple way to perform his obligations.

In a way almost identical to the one described above under *a*, an interested party may ask the *tribunal d'instance* (within the restrictions of its jurisdiction) for the performance in kind of a contractual obligation (*see further* arts. 1425-1 *et seq.*).

Literature: S. Choppin Haudry de Janvry, *L'injonction de faire. Bilan d'une réforme*, Gaz. Pal. 1991.1, doctr. p. 73;

A. Crosio, *Le point sur l'injonction de payer*, Petites Affiches, 4 February 1987;

CTRC de Bretagne et SAF, *L'accès individuel et collectif des consommateurs à la justice*, Rev. jur. Ouest, 1990, numéro spécial;
Forestier, *De la procédure d'injonction de payer*, Rev. adm. 1983, 14;
Saint-Cricq, *La procédure d'injonction de payer*, thèse Paris II, 1977.

5.7.4. SECTOR PROCEDURES

There are also separate rules of procedure for certain areas of substantive law, for instance divorce (Book III, Title I, chapter V), industrial law (Book II, Title IV) and bankruptcy (Act 85-98 of 25 January 1985 *relative au redressement et à la liquidation judiciaires des entreprises* and the Decrees 85-1387/88 of 27 December 1985).

5.8. Protective Measures and Enforcement Measures

5.8.1. INTRODUCTION

On 1 January 1993 the new Act 91-650 of 9 July 1991 *portant réforme des procédures civiles d'exécution* entered into force. The Act provides rules for both protective and enforcement measures. Contrary to what was originally intended, this legislation does not form part of Book V of the *Nouveau Code de procédure civile.* In Decree 92-755 of 31 July 1992 the provisions of execution are contained (*see* annexe 32 *Code de Procédure civile*, 1993-1994 (Litec)).

The *juge d'exécution* plays an important part; pursuant to arts. L.311-312 *et seq*. COJ the powers of this judge, who in principle acts as *unus iudex*, are exercised by the president of the *tribunal de grande instance*, who may delegate these tasks. The *juge d'exécution* deals with disputes in respect of enforcement, applications for leave to attach goods, lifting attachments and the execution of the penalties. Attachment of earnings is explicitly excluded from the jurisdiction of the *juge d'exécution* and this comes under the jurisdiction of the *juge d'instance* (art. L.145-5 Code du travail).

Furthermore, art. 1244 Code Civil (as amended) allows the *juge d'exécution* to grant the debtor an extension of payment of a maximum period of two years in order to attempt to agree payment by instalments. During that period measures of enforcement are suspended and no penalties for late payment will become due.

Finally it is worth noting that the legislator has followed the principle that the creditor must first resort to the least far-reaching (which, however, are usually also the most effective) measures of enforcement, for instance attachment of bank balances and of the debtor's earnings. Having done this, he is then entitled to attach other property. In order to effect attachment of bank balances and of earnings, the *huissier* may in certain cases request the *procureur de la République* to find out where an unwilling debtor has his bank account and his job (art. 51 in conjunction with arts. 39 and 40 Act 91-650).

Literature: E. Blanc, *Les nouvelles procédures d'exécution*, 1993 (Montchrestien);

P. Julien, *Le juge de l'exécution*, Petites Affiches, 6 January 1993;

Numéro spécial de la Revue trimestrielle de droit civil 1993 (colloque des 28 et 29 janvier 1993);

R. Perrot, *Réforme des procédures civiles d'exécution*, 1993 (Sirey);

G. Taormina, *Le nouveau droit des procédures d'exécution et de distribution*, éd. Journal des notaires, 1993, préface P. Julien;

J. Vincent and J. Prévaut, *Voies d'exécution et procédures de distribution*, Précis Dalloz 1993 (Dalloz).

5.8.2. PROTECTIVE MEASURES OTHER THAN ATTACHMENT

Apart from attachment the law provides for the protective measure of *sûreté judiciaire* (judicial surety) of e.g. immovable property, shares and securities (arts. 77-79 in conjunction with arts. 67-73 Act 91-650). The creditor obtains a conditional right of pledge or of hypothec, which cannot be effected until the moment he obtains an enforceable title.

5.8.3. PROTECTIVE MEASURES BY ATTACHMENT

The *saisie conservatoire* may in principle be imposed on all the debtor's movable property (arts. 74 to 76 in conjunction with arts. 67-73 Act 91-650). The rules applying to attachment of immovable property have not yet been amended and can therefore be found in the *(ancien) Code de procédure civile* (art. 673 *et seq.*). *See* section 5.8.4 for the various kinds of attachment.

5.8.4. ENFORCEMENT MEASURES BY ATTACHMENT

The French legislator makes a distinction between attachment of a monetary claim (arts. 39-49 Act 91-650) and that of other property.

The basic form of attachment of a monetary claim is the *saisie-attribution*, which immediately transfers the claim to the garnishor (*attribution immédiate*, art. 43). If the third party is a banking institution, the special provisions of art. 47 also apply. Attachment of earnings (*saisie des rémunérations*) is provided for separately in art. 48 of the *Code du travail.*

Only if attachment of a monetary claim is impossible may the creditor proceed to attach other assets: *saisie-vente* (arts. 50-55) and *saisie des droits incorporels* (art. 59).

5.8.5. ENFORCEMENT MEASURES OTHER THAN ATTACHMENT

Another measure of enforcement is the penalty (*astreinte*), which may even be ordered of the court's own motion (art. 33 *et seq*. Act 91-650).

Enforcement by delivery of movable property is possible under article 56 of the Act 91-650.

With respect to *véhicules terrestres à moteur,* arts. 57 and 58 Act 91-650 contain separate measures of enforcement.

Articles 61-66 Act 91-650 provide rules for the vacating of immovable property or a dwelling.

5.9. Duration and Costs

5.9.1. INTRODUCTION

Within the framework of proper administration of justice, questions relating to the duration of legal procedures and the accessibility of courts must also be discussed.

5.9.2. DURATION

Although the term *'circuit long'* makes one fear the worst, the average civil case takes between 6 and 24 months (*see* McIntosh and Holmes, *Civil Procedures in EC Countries, an Industry Report*, London 1991, pp. 109 and 110). In this respect the *juge de la mise en état* has far-reaching powers to induce the parties to take the necessary action (*see* arts. 3, 780 and 781). In urgent cases the duration of the proceedings may be reduced to weeks, days or even hours.

Judgment is given relatively quickly: after oral consideration the judgment is usually pronounced within three to four weeks. The written judgment will usually follow within one week. The judge in summary proceedings will give his judgment as soon as possible, if necessary immediately.

However, the above course of affairs is not common in all districts. Thus, the consideration of ordinary civil cases before the *tribunal de grande instance* of Grasse would easily take 3 to 4 years (Adv.bl. 1995, p. 749).

5.9.3. COSTS

The principle of *gratuité* means that the parties do not have to pay *droits de greffe* (court fees), except in several special procedures. As a rule the losing party is ordered to pay the costs (*dépens*; art. 696). Leaving aside certain duties, these costs include costs of witnesses, expert reports and disbursements, fees of ministerial officials and lawyers' fees inasmuch as this is provided for. Thus the act of *postuler et conclure* is covered by the *dépens*, whereas the fee due for oral pleadings or for assistance in a procedure in which legal representation is not mandatory are not covered. On the grounds of fairness, however, the judge may order the losing party to pay part of these costs (art. 700). In practice a request pursuant to art. 700 is seldom rejected. However, the amount requested is often reduced. Article 708 *et seq.* provide special rules under which it is possible to oppose an order to pay costs before the president of the relevant court.

In order to make the court truly accessible to anyone, legal aid is also available in France. On 1 January 1992 new rules entered into force (Act 91-647 of 10 July 1991 *relative à l'aide juridique* and Decree 91-1266 of 19 December 1991; *see* Annexe 3 *Code de Procédure civile*, 1993-1994 (Litec)).

A person with a disposable income of less than FF 4,400 per month is eligible for full legal aid and a person with a disposable income of less than FF 6,600 per month for restricted legal aid. As of 1 January 1993 these amounts will be adjusted annually (art. 4 Act 91-647). The application, accompanied by the necessary documents, must be filed with a *bureau d'aide juridictionnelle* (art. 33 *et seq*. Decree 91-1266). These bureaus form part of the *tribunal de grande instance*. Separate bureaus have been established for the *Cour de cassation* and the *Conseil d'État*. A legally aided litigant is free to choose his lawyer, who in his turn must accept the applicant (in writing; art. 75 Decree 91-1266). The lawyer must also notify the president (*bâtonnier*), or the chairman of the Bar Council of his acceptance in view of the costs to be paid by the State at a later stage, which are calculated using a certain formula (art. 90 *et seq.* Decree 91-1266). Payments to lawyers are made through the *caisse des règlements pécuniaires* of the local court. All monies payable to third parties, with the exception of lawyers, are advanced by the State (art. 119 Decree 91-1266). However, these costs are in principle only refunded by a losing opponent to the State if they are *dépens* of art. 695. This order to award costs may also be opposed (art. 127 Decree 91-1266).

Literature: A. Damien, *L'article 700 et les honoraires de l'avocat*, Gaz. Pal. 1979.1, p. 134;

Chr. Larher, *Le recouvrement des frais et dépens*, Gaz. Pal. 1983.2, doctr. p. 402; and

Chr. Loyer-Larher, *L'article 700 du Nouveau Code de procédure civile et le remboursement des frais non compris dans les dépens*, D. 1977, p. 205.

5.10. Proceedings Outside the Courts

5.10.1. INTRODUCTION

A distinction traditionally made by French legislation is between *arbitrage contractuel* and *arbitrage juridictionnel*: In the first case a third party is allowed to add to or change a contract, in the second case a third party gives an arbitral award affecting the rights of the parties (the latter type is discussed in section 5.10.2).

5.10.2. ARBITRATION

This alternative form of dispute resolution is governed by Book IV of the *Nouveau Code de procédure civile*. A first distinction must be made between domestic (Titles I-IV) and international arbitration (Titles V and VI). Article 1492 states that *'est international l'arbitrage qui met en cause des intérêts du commerce international'*. Arbitration is possible in respect of disputes which are at the free disposal of the parties (arts. 1442 and 1447). *See also* arts. 2059 and 2061 Code Civil and art. 639 C. com.

An arbitration agreement may be concluded before a dispute arises (*clause compromissoire*) or afterwards (*compromis*). Although art. 2061 Code Civil declares an arbitration clause in principle null and void in order to protect the weaker contracting party, in practice this form occurs most. In order to be valid, an arbitration clause must be in writing (art. 1443). It must also state the (method of appointment of the) arbitrator(s). In respect of a *compromis* the subject of the dispute must also be mentioned, while the requirement of the written form only applies to evidence. In respect of international arbitration art. 1493 only refers to the *convention d'arbitrage* and the above distinction is irrelevant.

There must be an odd number of arbitrators according to arts. 1453 and 1454. Articles 1442-1480 only apply to international arbitration if the parties have not agreed otherwise (art. 1495). If they have agreed otherwise, they therefore do not have to comply with the above (national) provisions and an even number of arbitrators may consider their case. The autonomy and the liberty of the parties to organise the arbitration procedure as they think fit is paramount.

If either party seeks to rely on an arbitration agreement before a national court (*see* section 5.3.2a), the court must decline jurisdiction, unless the arbitration agreement is void (art. 1458). Arbitrators can make decisions on their own competence (art. 1466).

If the arbitration agreement does not specify a period, the arbitrators are appointed for a period of 6 months from the day when the (last) arbitrator accepted his mandate (art. 1456, the second paragraph of which allows an extension of this period).

Arbitral proceedings take place in the manner determined by the arbitral tribunal, unless the parties have agreed otherwise (art. 1460). Domestic arbitral proceedings are governed by the *principes directeurs du procès* (*see* section 5.2.1); they also apply to international arbitration, unless the parties have agreed otherwise (art. 1495 in conjunction with art. 1460). The principle of hearing both parties must never be violated; otherwise the arbitral award may be set aside. Arbitrators must decide in accordance with the rules of law, unless the parties in the arbitration agreement have given the arbitrators a mandate to decide as good men in equity (art. 1474 - *see also* art. 12, para. 3 which under certain conditions allows parties to give this mandate also to the national court). If the arbitrators decide as good men in equity, this implies that the parties do not have the right to appeal, unless they have explicitly reserved this right in their arbitration agreement (art. 1482).

Arbitral awards must be motivated (art. 1471). They can only be enforced after an exequatur has been obtained from the *tribunal de grande instance* in the district where the arbitral award was made (arts. 1477 and 1500). Appeal from the refusal to grant an exequatur lies to the *cour d'appel*. No appeal is possible against the granting of an exequatur. If anyone wishes to oppose this, they must file an application to set aside the arbitral award (*see below*).

A judgment given in a domestic arbitration case is neither open to opposition nor to appeal in cassation. Third-party opposition is possible (art. 1481).

The judgment is also open to appeal, unless the parties have agreed otherwise (art. 1482). If the parties have excluded appeal, then the only possible recourse, apart from *révision*, is setting aside. For international arbitration setting aside is the only option. This means of recourse can only be lodged on certain grounds laid down by law: art. 1484 for domestic arbitration and art. 1504 in conjunction with art. 1502 for international arbitration. It is remarkable that violation of the *principe de la contradiction* constitutes a separate ground for setting aside (*see* section 5.2.3). Appeal and the application for setting aside are lodged with the *cour d'appel* in the district where the arbitral award was made (arts. 1486 and 1505).

The recognition and enforcement of arbitral awards made outside France is governed by the same rules as French international arbitral awards: in the absence of an international convention or agreement arts. 1498 to 1500 in conjunction with arts. 1476 to 1479 apply.

As regards the enforcement of arbitral awards under conventions it is important to note that France is a party to the New York Convention of 1958 on the Recognition and Enforcement of Foreign Arbitral Awards, which provides rules for the recognition of arbitration agreements and the recognition and enforcement of arbitral awards.

Literature: P. Ancel, E. Loquin, M.-Cl. Rondeau-Rivier (dir. Rubellin-Devichi), *L'arbitrage*, 1992 (Litec);

F. Chartier, *L'arbitre*, Gaz. Pal. 1992.1, doctr. p. 135;

M. De Boisséson, *Le droit français de l'arbitrage*, 1990 (Joly);

Ph. Fouchard, *L'arbitrage judiciaire*, Mélanges Pierre Bellet, 1991 (Litec);

P. Lalive, *Avantages et inconvénients de l'arbitrage ad hoc*, Mélanges Pierre Bellet, 1991 (Litec);

E. Loquin, *Les voies de recours*, Rev. arb. 1992, 321;

R. Perrot, *L'application à l'arbitrage des règles du Nouveau Code de procédure civile*, Rev. arb. 1980, 642;

J. Robert, *L'arbitrage, droit interne, droit international privé*, 1993 (Dalloz).

6. Luxembourg Civil Procedure

Renée Y. Nauta*

6.1. Overview/Sources

6.1.1. INTRODUCTION

Luxembourg is one of the countries which has a civil law tradition. The present Luxembourg rules of civil procedural law actually date back to 1806. Indeed, it is the French *Code de procédure civile*, introduced by Napoleon, which (subject to a few minor amendments) is still in force in Luxembourg today.

Luxembourg may be a small country, but its international importance must not be underestimated, particularly in view of the international commercial and financial transactions frequently occurring in this country. Therefore an outline on the Luxembourg rules of civil procedure should form part of this book.

6.1.2. ACT AND CONVENTION

The French *Code de procédure civile* (CPC), which largely dates back to 1806, also forms the basis of the Luxembourg rules of civil procedure. In the past few years Luxembourg's neighbours Belgium and France have thoroughly revised their legislation in this area and entirely new Codes have been adopted. Luxembourg is following a similar path and is used to slightly updating its legislation now and then after the French model of the *Nouveau Code de procédure civile*. Since the *Code de procédure civile* can be regarded as the most important legal source, articles from the law that are not specified any further in this chapter will be from this Code.

When litigating commercial cases one should also consult the *Code de commerce* (CdC) dating from 1807; Book IV contains a number of supplementary provisions (arts. 631-648). Articles 1315-1369 of the *Code Civil* contain a number of provisions on evidence.

Finally, the *Loi sur l'Organisation Judiciaire* of 7 March 1980 provides for the organisation and jurisdiction of the judiciary.

---

* Thanks are due to Laura Molenkamp (avocat at the lawyers' office Wagener & Rukavina in Luxembourg).

All legislation is published in the *Mémorial* (Official Gazette). Practising lawyers usually turn to annotated texts of the codes. The *Pasinomie Luxembourgeoise* contains a summary of the most important texts.

Luxembourg is a party to several international conventions on civil procedure, such as the Brussels Convention (entry into force 1 February 1973; *see also* section 3.1.2 *et seq.*), the Hague Conventions on Civil Procedure of 1905 and 1954 (entry into force 12 April 1957), the Hague Convention on the Service Abroad of Judicial and Extrajudicial Documents in Civil or Commercial Matters of 1965 (entry into force 7 September 1975), the European Convention on Information on Foreign Law of 1968 (entry into force 15 December 1977), the Hague Convention on the Taking of Evidence Abroad in Civil or Commercial Matters of 1970 (entry into force 24 September 1977) and the European Agreement on the Transmission of Applications for Legal Aid of 1977 (entry into force 28 February 1977).

In respect of arbitration law, Luxembourg is a party to the New York Convention of 1958 on the Recognition and Enforcement of Foreign Arbitral Awards (entry into force 8 December 1983) and the European Convention on International Commercial Arbitration of 1961 (entry into force 24 June 1982). Since 1953 Luxembourg has been a party to the European Convention on Human Rights and Fundamental Freedoms. The Grand-Duchy has also ratified the CCPR (entry into force 18 November 1983).

6.1.3. LITERATURE AND CASE LAW

The limited size of the Grand-Duchy of Luxembourg and the fact that Luxembourg has followed its French neighbours as far as its legal system is concerned, account for the almost complete absence of legal literature dealing specifically with Luxembourg civil procedure. Belgian and particularly French legal literature are used avidly. The editions of the *Code de procédure civile* and the *Code de commerce* published by the Ministry of Justice contain conversion tables referring to the corresponding provisions in the (old) French and Belgian codes of procedure. French is the legal language.

Luxembourg's own case law does constitute an independent source of law. It can be found *inter alia* in the *Pasicrisie Luxembourgeoise*. In the editions of texts of law mentioned in section 6.1.2 above, summaries of decisions appear below the article of the Code to which they relate.

6.1.4. DATA BASES

It is possible to file an application with the documentation department of the *Cour Supérieure de Justice* for a search on CD-ROM for Luxembourg, Belgian and French case law and literature. Subsequently this department itself conducts the search. Payment is made per assignment. The local lawyers' offices are too small to be able to afford such data bases.

6.2. Fundamental Principles

Luxembourg civil procedural law has been and is still influenced strongly by French and Belgian civil procedure in particular. In addition, Luxembourg is a party to the European Convention on Human Rights and Fundamental Freedoms. The fundamental principles underlying its procedural law are therefore comparable to the principles in France and Belgium and these principles are therefore only mentioned here in brief. For further details the reader is referred to the relevant sections in the chapters on French and Belgian law (sections 5.2 and 7.2).

Fundamental principles which must be mentioned are the principle of party autonomy (*principe dispositif*; *see inter alia* art. 480 *sub* 3 and 4), the principle of consideration of each case in public and judgment in public (art. 87), the principle of motivation (art. 141), the principle of documentary and oral consideration of each case (*see* section 6.4.2), the *principe de gratuité*, the principle of hearing both parties and of accessibility (resulting *inter alia* from art. 6 ECHRFF). The *principe du double degré de juridiction* also exists in Luxembourg procedural law: subject to certain exceptions, appeal can be lodged against judicial decisions rendered at first instance (art. 451 *et seq.*) in order to have the case considered again by a superior court.

6.3. Principal Characters

6.3.1. INTRODUCTION

Due to the fact that Luxembourg civil procedure goes back directly to the old French laws of civil procedure, its principal characters are largely the same as their French counterparts. Here the mention of the main differences will therefore suffice; otherwise the reader is referred to section 5.3. Before discussing the judge, the lawyers and the parties, the function of the *huissier de justice* must be considered briefly.

The Luxembourg *huissier de justice* is an official whose main task is the service of judicial and extrajudicial documents and the enforcement of judicial decisions. His competence is limited to the district within which he has been appointed. Unlike his French counterpart he does not have any official task at court hearings, but he does provide legal assistance in cases before the *juge de paix*.

6.3.2. JUDGE

a. Introduction

In the small Grand-Duchy of Luxembourg there are only a few judicial bodies. The *Cour Supérieure de Justice* is situated in the city of Luxembourg (arts. 32-48 *Loi sur l'Organisation Judiciaire*). It consists of the *Cour de cassation*, which has one chamber, and the *cour d'appel* consisting 7 chambers. There are two *tribunaux d'arrondissement* (arts. 10-31 *Loi sur l'Organisation Judiciaire*), one in the city of Luxembourg and one in Diekirch. When the *tribunal d'arrondissement* convenes in a certain composition, it has jurisdiction over commercial matters (art. 29 *Loi sur l'Organisation Judiciaire*). Unlike France, then, Luxembourg does not have a separate *tribunal de commerce* (*see* section 5.3.2a). However, the *tribunal de commerce* is still referred to by that name in the older texts of law. In more recent legislation such as art. 645, which dates from 1983, reference is made to the *tribunal d'arrondissement (siégeant) en matière commerciale.* In three *circonscriptions* (the city of Luxembourg, Diekirch and Esch/Alzette) there is a *Juge de paix* (arts. 1-9 *Loi sur l'Organisation Judiciaire*), who also acts as a member of the judicial panel which decides employment matters, the *tribunal du travail* (art. 56-1 to 56-3 inclusive *Loi sur l'Organisation Judiciaire*).

Panel adjudication is the general practice. The *Cour de cassation* consists of five judges (one *Président*, two *conseillers à la Cour de cassation* and two *conseillers à la cour d'appel*), the *cour d'appel* of three (*conseillers*), as do the *tribunal d'arrondissement* and the *tribunal de commerce.* The *justice the paix* adjudicates alone. In the *tribunal du travail* he acts as president, assisted by two lay judges.

b. International jurisdiction

Pursuant to art. 2 Brussels Convention persons domiciled in the territory of a Contracting State can only be summoned to appear before the court of another

Contracting State under the provisions of the Brussels Convention. Articles 14 and 15 of the Luxembourg *Code Civil* can therefore not be used against such persons. *See further* section 3.1.

c. Sectoral jurisdiction

Within Luxembourg law a distinction is made between administrative law, criminal and civil law. The *Code de procédure civile* differentiates between civil and commercial law, which is subject to the special jurisdiction of the *tribunal du travail* and the *tribunal de commerce* respectively. The courts last named are otherwise characterised by the oral procedure; the exchange of pleadings occurring in the basic procedure is absent (*see* section 6.4.2c).

d. Absolute jurisdiction (compétence d'attribution)

The regulations providing for absolute and relative jurisdiction are not contained in a separate code; they precede Book I of the *Code de procédure civile* (arts. 1-43 *titre préliminaire*) in a chapter which was added in 1974. Book IV of the *Code de commerce*, entitled '*de la juridiction commerciale*', provides for special rules of jurisdiction in commercial cases.

The *Code de procédure civile* first determines the scope of the *compétence d'attribution* of the *justices de paix*. A *juge de paix* has jurisdiction over claims involving an amount up to LUF 200,000 (art. 2 *titre préliminaire*). This limit also applies to commercial cases. Articles 5 to 11, 20 and 21 *titre préliminaire* govern how the value of the claims must be calculated. The *justice de paix* also has jurisdiction over a number of specific cases irrespective of the amount in dispute, such as tenancy cases (art. 3 *titre préliminaire*) and certain disputes concerning maintenance obligations (art. 4 *titre préliminaire*). In employment cases (art. 22 *titre préliminaire*) he acts as president of the *tribunal du travail*.

Claims in excess of LUF 200,000 must be lodged with the *tribunal d'arrondissement/tribunal de commerce*. The *tribunal d'arrondissement* generally has jurisdiction in all cases not attributed to other courts (art. 17 *titre préliminaire*).

Appeal lies from judgments of the *justice de paix/tribunal du travail* if the original claim exceeds LUF 25,000. In principle the *tribunal d'arrondissement* is the appellate court for judgments of the *juge de paix* (art. 19 *titre préliminaire*). In commercial disputes the *tribunal de commerce* is the competent appellate court, provided the claim exceeds LUF 30,000 (*see* art. 16-1 *titre préliminaire* and arts. 631, 634, 635 and 639 CdC).

The *cour d'appel* decides appeals of judgments of the *tribunal d'arrondissement* (art. 19 *titre préliminaire*), the *tribunal du travail* (art. 473-7) and the *tribunal de commerce* (art. 644 CdC).

The *Cour de cassation* is the superior court. Appeal in cassation can be lodged only in case of a violation of the law and/or of a procedural defect, when no (further) appeal lies (art. 38 *Loi sur l'Organisation Judiciaire*). This applies following a decision on appeal of a judgment at first instance, or when an appeal is not available, e.g. in cases of limited value which have been dealt with by the *justice de paix* at first instance. The *Cour de cassation* does not consider facts but only points of law and decides exclusively whether the grounds adduced can lead to cassation. In case an appeal in cassation is deemed founded, the *Cour de cassation* refers the case to the *cour d'appel* or the *tribunal d'arrondissement* in order to have it judged anew by other judges. The *Cour de cassation* may also decide the case itself.

DIAGRAM JUDICIAL ORGANISATION IN CIVIL CASES IN LUXEMBOURG

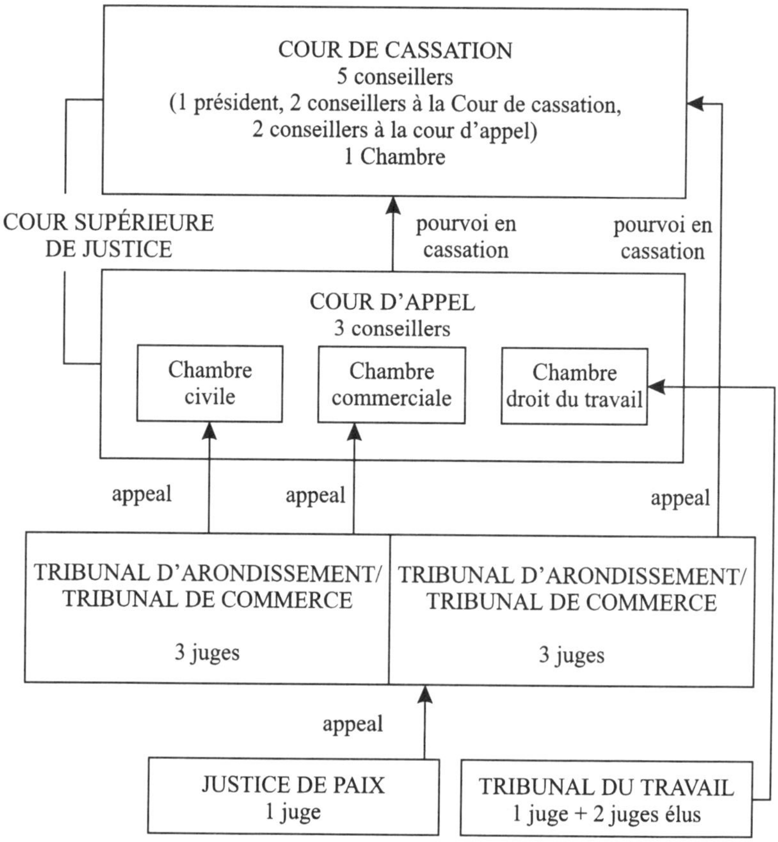

e. Relative jurisdiction (compétence territoriale)

The question which court has relative jurisdiction is usually decided in favour of the place of the defendant's domicile: jurisdiction mostly lies with the court of the defendant's (actual) domicile (art. 25 *titre préliminaire*) or, if the defendant is a legal person, his *siège social*, which means his registered office (art. 36 *titre préliminaire*). If there is a choice of domicile, another court may acquire jurisdiction (art. 26 *titre préliminaire*). An exception to this rule is, for example, the jurisdiction of the court in matters concerning immovable property: the court within whose territory the property is situated has exclusive jurisdiction (art. 28 *titre préliminaire*). In employment cases the court of the place where (the major part of) the work is performed has jurisdiction (art. 42 *titre préliminaire*).

6.3.3. AVOCAT AND AVOUÉ

The function of *avocat* is usually combined with that of *avoué*. As an *avocat* the lawyer advises his client and pleads his case in court; as an *avoué* he formally represents his client in the proceedings. In civil cases the *avocat* has a monopoly of pleading the case before the *tribunaux d'arrondissement* and the *Cour Supérieure de Justice*, whilst only the *avoué* is authorised to represent the parties. This monopoly does not exist before the *tribunaux de paix* (art. 9) and the *tribunaux d'arrondissement* in commercial cases (art. 414). There the parties have a choice whether or not to be legally represented, either by an *avocat* or by any other person who is not required to be legally qualified.

Anyone intending to be a lawyer in Luxembourg must study law at a university for at least 4 years. Since this is impossible in Luxembourg itself, this course is usually completed in Belgium or France, which countries share comparable principles of law with Luxembourg. The universities of Strasbourg, Brussels, Nancy, Paris and Aix-en-Provence are particularly favoured by Luxembourg law students. Then the aspiring *avocat* must attend a four-month course in Luxembourg law which is rounded off with exams. Subsequently he must swear an oath as an *avocat-stagiaire* (*avocat de la liste II*). This stagiaire period usually lasts 3 years. During that period he must work under the supervision of a fully qualified *avocat* (*avocat de la liste I: avocat-avoué*) and is entitled to perform all legal activities with the exception of those reserved for an *avoué*. This traineeship is concluded by the examination for *avocat-avoué*.

A new Act from 1991 regulates the profession of *avocat*. All *avocats* are members of the *Ordre des Avocats*, which is divided into two bars according to the geographical districts. The majority of *avocats* belongs to the Bar in the city of Luxembourg. Altogether there are some 400 *avocats*. As a result of the requirement by the European Court of Justice that the parties elect domicile at the seat of the Court, local *avocats* are often involved in proceedings before this court.

6.3.4. THE PARTIES

Both natural persons and legal persons can act as parties in proceedings. Separate rules apply to persons without legal capacity (arts. 488-515 CC) and bankrupt companies (*see* e.g. art. 440 CdC).

6.4. Basic Procedure for Contentious Jurisdiction at First Instance

6.4.1. INTRODUCTION

The *Code de procédure civile* begins in part I, Book 1 with the *justice de paix*. Book 2 deals with the *tribunaux inférieurs*, Book 3 with the *tribunaux d'appel*. For a description of the basic procedure for contentious jurisdiction the procedure before the *tribunal d'arrondissement* will be the point of departure. It falls under the *tribunaux inférieurs*. These regulations have recently been amended following the example of the French *Nouveau Code de procédure civile*.

6.4.2. TRIBUNAL D'ARRONDISSEMENT

a. Introduction

As in France, the parties in the most common court procedures are called *demandeur* and *défendeur*. Mandatory procedural representation by an *avoué* is standard practice.

b. Commencement of proceedings

The provisions concerning the writ and its service were amended by *Règlement Grand Ducal* 15 May 1991. At the plaintiff's request the *huissier de justice* issues the writ (*exploit d'assignation*). Articles 61-74 set out the relevant formal requirements for a writ (art. 69-7).

Service is preferably effected on the addressee in person, regardless where the *huissier* finds him (art. 68). If this is not possible, a copy of the writ can be handed to anyone who is over 14 years old and who is at the addressee's home, on condition that such person accepts the writ and gives his personal particulars to the *huissier*. If this person, who must not be the plaintiff/principal, refuses to accept the copy or if there is nobody home, the *huissier* leaves a copy of the writ in a sealed envelope. He also sends a copy to the relevant address through the post. The domicile of a defendant is the address as stated in the population register.

Article 61 prescribes the contents of a writ in order to be valid. However, in that respect art. 173-2 stipulates that the opposing party can only plead nullity of the writ if this party's interests have been damaged.

The summons period is 8 days, but may be shortened upon request (art. 72). In principle a longer period applies to persons not residing in Luxembourg (*see* arts. 73 and 74).

Within the above period the defendant must instruct an *avoué*, who through a formal document (*constitution d'avoué*) informs the plaintiff's *avoué* of his future appearance in the proceedings, even though these have not yet formally commenced (art. 75). The case only becomes pending once it has been entered on the *rôle* of the court (under a specific number).

If the defendant fails to appoint an *avoué* in time, the plaintiff can include this in so-called *conclusions de style par défaut* and ask for a judgment in default at the first hearing.

c. Proceedings

The civil proceedings are partly documentary, partly oral. Unlike in France, where a *juge de la mise en état* supervises the exchange of pleadings and the submission of documents, in Luxembourg this part of the proceedings is left to the parties and their *avoués*. Article 77, which compels the defendant to react in writing within two weeks after the appointment of the plaintiff's *avoué*, is not complied with in practice. When the plaintiff's *avoué* has been notified that the defendant will be duly represented, he usually takes the initiative by serving the *conclusions de style* on the opponent; in addition to the contents of the writ, they contain a summons (*avenir*) to appear before the court on a specific date. At least two days before the date specified the plaintiff's *avoué* must deliver a copy of these *conclusions* to the court so that the case may be entered on the list (*rôle*).

The defendant's *avoué* has fourteen days to react, by means of the *moyens de replique* (art. 77). If necessary, the plaintiff will be given an opportunity to reply to these in the *conclusions de réponse*, but he must not adduce any further grounds or lodge any further claims. In principle this concludes the exchange of pleadings. The *avocat-avoués* may by mutual arrangement deviate from the above time-limits.

On the first day of the hearing there is no oral consideration. The court determines whether the case is entered on the *rôle général* or whether it will be considered on a certain date. If the case has been referred to the list, the parties can proceed by exchanging documents until either of them serves an *avenir* on the other party inviting him to appear before the court so as to fix a date for the oral consideration. If the opponent thinks that the facts of the case have not been sufficiently established, he can ask the court for further inquiries to take place.

During the hearing, which in principle is public (*see* art. 88 Constitution and art. 87 CPC) the *avocat-avoués* read their pleadings before the full court, emphasising their arguments and the evidence in support. If the court finds that it has been informed sufficiently it may fix a date on which it will pass judgment. Otherwise the court will indicate, at the parties' request or on its own motion, which further inquiries are needed. In 1985, under the influence of the revision of French law of civil procedure, several drastic changes were implemented in Luxembourg law of civil procedure providing the court with means to accelerate proceedings (arts. 252-264). Thus it is now possible for the court at any stage of the proceedings to order *mesures d'instruction*, if it finds that there is insufficient material to reach a final decision (*see also* 6.4.2.e5). After this stage of the investigation, in which the parties are given another opportunity to comment, the court fixes a date for the last oral hearing. At that hearing there is usually merely a repetition of the main points already adduced in the pleadings. After this the court either gives its decision immediately or retires to chambers to give a judgment on a date to be fixed later (art. 116).

d. Judgment

Judgment is pronounced in open court (art. 89 Constitution and art. 116 CPC). Pursuant to art. 141 the judgment contains the names of the parties, their procedural representatives, the court, the names of the judges and the date of the judgment, a short summary of the evidence and of the parties' arguments, the actual decision (*le dispositif*) and the reasons (*les motifs*). Usually it also contains a costs award (*see* section 6.9.3). The judgment may be declared provisionally enforceable (arts. 134-137).

By filing a petition with the relevant court an interested party can have an apparent mathematical or clerical error in the judgment rectified or ask for the clarification of an obscure consideration.

Before a judgment can be enforced, it must be served on the *avoué* in order to be valid. In addition, a judgment whereby the losing party is ordered to do something must be served on the party himself (art. 147).

e. Special aspects of procedure

1. Non-appearance (défaut)

If the defendant has not notified the opponent's avoué in time that he has instructed an avoué, or if he fails to enter an appearance, the plaintiff can at the first hearing ask the judge to give judgment in default (arts. 149 and 150).

The default judgment can be enforced in the same way as an adversarial judgment, but usually such judgment is capable of being set aside (*opposition*; *see* section 6.6.2).

2. Third parties in the proceedings (intervention)

In the Netherlands, Belgium and France the original articles on *intervention* have been replaced. However, Luxembourg law still retains these provisions (arts. 339-341) relating to incidents when a third party can join the proceedings of his own motion. Article 339 states that such intervention must be made by a petition containing the grounds and pleadings. From art. 340 it can be deduced that this petition can be filed right until the moment when the case is ready for trial. *See further* art. 466 for appeal cases.

In case of compulsory intervention, a possible third party in third party proceedings is involved in such proceedings by means of a writ, pursuant to established case law.

3. Amendment of claim (demande additionnelle)

Like the French code, the Luxembourg code does not explicitly mention the amendment of claim. Case law accepts that a *demande additionnelle* is allowed, provided there remains sufficient connection with the original claim (*see* art. 337). To be valid, this additional claim must not be completely new. Article 464 stipulates that new claims are not allowed on appeal either. However, this article is not imperative, so that this may still be done by mutual consent of the parties, as the occasion arises.

4. Counterclaim (demande reconventionnelle)

With his written defence the defendant can file a counterclaim on condition that it is connected to the main claim. The actions on the original claim and the counterclaim are usually joined and are conducted as one action (arts. 11-13, 21 *titre préliminaire*). The original plaintiff may react to a counterclaim in writing.

5. Production of evidence (preuve)

The substantive rules of evidence are laid down in the *Code Civil* (arts. 1315-1369), whereas the *Code de procédure civile* (art. 188 *et seq.*) contains the formal rules of evidence. The rules of evidence are of a formal nature.

The *Code Civil* distinguishes five categories of evidence: documentary evidence (*la preuve littérale*), oral evidence (*la preuve testimoniale*), admissions (*aveu*), suspicions (*les indices*) and the decisive oath (*le serment litis-decisoire*). Legislation further prescribes certain types of evidence for specific cases.

The *Code de procédure civile* specifies in what way evidence may be produced. Thus, arts. 188-251 contain provisions regarding documentary evidence.

If a party wants to base his claim on foreign law, he must indicate this in his pleadings and prove its content. As a rule this is done by a declaration in writing (*certificat de coutume*) delivered by a qualified person. The rules as to what constitutes admissible evidence of foreign law are fairly liberal, which means that foreign conventions, handbooks or other documentary material are admitted in evidence.

The court may also of its own motion proceed to apply foreign law.

6. Settlement (conciliation)

The obligation to first try and reach a settlement has been abolished. Divorce proceedings form an important exception. Parties can, however, at any moment proceed to end their dispute through a settlement. Although the court is under no obligation to encourage a settlement, it is free to do so. Should the parties reach a settlement in such a case, the agreement is signed by the parties and by the judge and can be enforced like a normal judgment if provided with the *formule exécutoire.*

The parties can also agree to deal with existing or future disputes in a settlement out of court (*transaction extra-judiciaire*). This is only allowed for matters of which the parties can freely dispose. The settlement must be recorded in a document. No appeal lies from the result of such a settlement.

Another option is for the debtor-defendant to offer his creditor-plaintiff to pay what is due plus interest and costs in order to avoid further proceedings. In order to do so he can deposit a sum of money with the *Caisse des Consignations*, which releases him of his obligations. He is obliged, however, to inform the plaintiff in advance where and when the amount due will be paid.

6.5. Basic Procedure for Voluntary Jurisdiction at First Instance

No general rules apply to voluntary jurisdiction, but there are provisions stating explicitly that they apply to voluntary jurisdiction, such as art. 451, which contains the right to appeal.

In addition, there are various provisions in the CPC which prescribe that the judge must be addressed by means of a petition. A petition is also frequently used to commence proceedings in family law (*see*, for example, art. 875 (divorce), 881 (adoption), 882 (guardianship cases)). Employment law proceedings are also commenced by petition (art. 473-1 *et seq.*). Leave to enforce a foreign judgment is also requested by petition to the President of the *tribunal d'arrondissement* (art. 546-2 *et seq.*).

The effect of the above is that petition procedures can differ strongly from each other. Compare, for instance, art. 473-1 up to and including 473-9 regarding certain employment cases with arts. 875-880 for divorce cases.

6.6. Means of Recourse

6.6.1. INTRODUCTION

Under Luxembourg law there are ordinary and extraordinary means of recourse. Ordinary means of recourse include the application to set aside a judgment in default and the appeal, both of which suspend enforcement, unless the judgment *a quo* has been declared provisionally enforceable. Extraordinary means of recourse are the appeal in cassation, the third-party application to set aside a judgment in default and the revocation.

6.6.2. THE APPLICATION TO SET ASIDE A JUDGMENT IN DEFAULT (OPPOSITION)

This means of recourse (governed by arts. 157-165) may be invoked before the court which delivered the contested judgment and must be filed within 14 days, counting from the date of service of the judgment upon the defendant or his *avoué*. The period will not be extended in case the defendant lives abroad. Once the period for opposition has expired, the judgment can only be challenged by appeal.

If the *défaillant* has an *avoué*, the application is only admissible in a petition from *avoué* to *avoué*. Otherwise, it may be filed by a writ from a *huissier,* or by an informal declaration on the official report of the attaching bailiff. In the latter case, *opposition* must subsequently still be filed within 8 days by means of a bailiff's writ.

6.6.3. APPEAL (APPEL)

Appeal to a superior court lies in principle against all final judgments at first instance (art. 451). From judgments of the *tribunal de paix* appeal lies to the *tribunal d'arrondissement*, unless the claim is less than LUF 25,000. From judgments of the *tribunal d'arrondissement* appeal lies to the *Cour Supérieure de Justice, siégeant en matière d'appel* (*see further* section 6.3.2d).

On appeal the case is considered afresh as regards both facts and points of law and devolves to the appellate court (*effet dévolutif*). This means of recourse suspends enforcement (*effet suspensif*; art. 457)

The ordinary time-limit for appeal is 40 days from the date of service of the judgment on the defendant (art. 443). In case of default judgments this period starts to run from the end of the period within which the application to set aside must be filed (*see above* in section 6.6.2).

Appeal is lodged by service of a notice of appeal on the respondent (*l'intimé*) personally or at his domicile. To be valid, the respondent is summoned in this notice within the above periods for appeal (art. 456 in conjunction with art. 61). In principle the procedure develops like the procedure before the *tribunaux inférieurs* (art. 470).

If the conditions laid down by art. 473 have been satisfied, the appellate court has jurisdiction over the case (*droit d'évocation*).

6.6.4. APPEAL IN CASSATION (POURVOI EN CASSATION)

This extraordinary means of recourse only lies when there are no (further) means of appeal (*see* section 6.3.2d). It does not suspend enforcement. The *Cour Supérieure de Justice*, of which the *Cour de cassation* forms part, only considers questions of law. There are two grounds for cassation, i.e. breach of the law and/or non-compliance with procedural requirements (*see* art. 473-8 for employment cases). If the *Cour de cassation* quashes the contested judgment, it can either refer the case or give a final decision itself. The time-limit for cassation is two months.

6.6.5. OTHER MEANS OF RECOURSE

Third-party opposition (*tierce opposition*) and revocation (*requête civile*) are other extraordinary means of recourse. They do not suspend enforcement. The first means is governed by arts. 473-1 to 479-9 inclusive; the second, which may be lodged *inter alia* when a judgment has been obtained by improper means, is governed by arts. 480-504. The third extraordinary means of recourse mentioned by the *Code de procédure civile* is the possibility of redress against the court, for example in cases where it has misused its powers or refuses to do justice (arts. 505-516).

6.7. Special Procedures

6.7.1. INTRODUCTION

In addition to the basic procedure as described in outline in section 6.4, there are special procedures under the Luxembourg rules of civil procedure which can mainly be found in the second part of the *Code de procédure civile,* entitled *'procédures diverses'* (art. 812 *et seq.*) and which include family law and wills and intestacy. In section 6.7.3 only the divorce procedure will be discussed.

For employment and commercial cases there are special courts in Luxembourg, where special rules of procedure apply in addition to the general provisions. In principle these are laid down in the first part of the *Code de procédure civile*, which provides rules for the usual procedures before the different courts.

A special part of the rules contained in the first part of the *Code de procédure civile* in relation to the *justice de paix* concerns the *ordonnance de paiement*, which is discussed below under small claims procedures.

Finally, the summary procedures in the form of *référé* can also be found in the first part of the Code.

6.7.2. SUMMARY PROCEDURES

Title XVI of Book V on the enforcement of judgments consists of two sections: the first contains general provisions about the summary proceedings (arts. 806 to 811-2 inclusive), the second section governs the summary proceedings before the *tribunal du travail* (art. 811-3 to 811-10 inclusive).

As a rule the President of the *tribunal d'arrondissement* has jurisdiction to make interim orders (*ordonnances de référé*) in urgent cases. In addition, he has jurisdiction to judge enforcement disputes (art. 806). The President of the *tribunal du travail* has comparable powers.

Although summary proceedings are an excellent way to obtain injunctive relief in case of non-monetary claims, it is also possible to apply to the President in summary proceedings in case of monetary claims, where the obligation to pay is more or less determined. The creditor-plaintiff then obtains a provisional order for payment, which enables him to compel the debtor to pay part or all of the claim (arts. 807 and 811-4; *see* for small amounts the procedure before the *tribunal de paix* discussed in section 6.7.3).

Summary proceedings are commenced by summoning the opponent at a fixed hour on a fixed day. Before the *tribunal du travail* the plaintiff has a choice between a writ and a petition. In very urgent cases the judge in summary proceedings can allow a summons on shorter notice (arts. 808 and 811-5).

The judgment of the *référé* judge has no authority of *res judicata* and is provisionally enforceable, possibly pursuant to the original judgment (art. 811 and 811-7). The *ordonnance de référé* may be challenged by an application to set aside or appeal (art. 811-1 and 811-8). The appellate court is always the *cour d'appel*.

6.7.3. SMALL CLAIMS PROCEDURES

For monetary claims up to LUF 200,000 a creditor can apply to the *tribunal de paix* either orally or by submitting a simple form. If the claim appears justified, the *juge de paix* will have a provisional order for payment served on the debtor. The latter then has 14 days to oppose these proceedings (*former contredit*). If he fails to do so, the *juge de paix*, at the creditor's request, allows the order for payment to be enforced (arts. 48 to 58-5 inclusive).

6.7.4. SECTOR PROCEDURES

Part II of the *Code de procédure civile* provides rules for several proceedings, including the divorce procedure in arts. 875-880. It is commenced by petition, upon which the parties are ordered to enter an appearance before the President of the *tribunal d'arrondissement* in order to try to reach a settlement.

In employment cases the *tribunal du travail* has jurisdiction. It has separate rules of procedure, which were added to the first part of the *Code de procédure civile* in 1989 (art. 473-1 to 473-9 inclusive). Cases are commenced by petition.

In procedures before the *tribunal de commerce* special attention must be paid to the provisions in the *Code de commerce* (arts. 642-648 CdC) which differ from those in the *Code de procédure civile.* The *Code de commerce* also contains procedural rules applicable in bankruptcy cases (art. 437 *et seq.* CdC).

6.8. Protective Measures and Enforcement Measures

6.8.1. INTRODUCTION

To prevent assets from being dissipated, a party may apply to the court to obtain an order for protective measures.

Once the court has made such an order, enforcement cannot be effected until the judgment has been drawn up in the appropriate form. For that purpose the winning party's *avoué* files a certain document (*qualités*) (*see* art. 142 *et seq.*), drawn up by himself, with the court, requesting it to prepare a *grosse* or *expédition* (an enforceable copy of the judgment). The *qualités* document is served upon the opponent's *avoué*. The *grosse* itself must also be served on the opponent and his *avoué*. If the *grosse* is not served upon the *avoué*, the ensuing enforcement measures are void.

Enforcement disputes are usually brought before the President of the *tribunal d'arrondissement* in summary proceedings. The *juge de paix* decides on the enforcement of his own judgments, including attachment, such as attachment of earnings (art. 1*er titre préliminaire*), in contrast to the *tribunal de commerce*, which pursuant to art. 442 explicitly does not have this authority.

6.8.2. PROTECTIVE MEASURES OTHER THAN ATTACHMENT

Protective measures other than attachment are the sealing of an estate (art. 907 *et seq.*) and the making of an inventory (art. 941 *et seq.*).

6.8.3. PROTECTIVE MEASURES BY ATTACHMENT

Saisie conservatoire may be imposed pursuant to an authentic deed or a judicial order drawn up in the appropriate form (art. 557: *titre authentique ou privé*). If such a document is not (yet) available, attachment cannot be made until the President of the *tribunal d'arrondissement* or the President of the *tribunal de commerce* or the *juge de paix* has granted leave (*see* arts. 558, 417 and art. 1*er titre préliminaire*). Thereupon the *huissier* takes possession of the debtor's or a third party's property. If necessary a third person may be appointed to safeguard the property seized. The applicant/plaintiff must then summon the defendant within 8 days. The defendant cannot challenge the attachment by either *opposition* or an appeal against the President's order. He can, however, obtain the release of the attached property by providing alternative security (art. 567).

6.8.4. ENFORCEMENT MEASURES BY ATTACHMENT

If a debtor refuses to comply with an order, the *huissier* can effect one of the following kinds of attachment: attachment of personal property (*saisie-exécutoire*), of earnings (*saisie-salaires*), attachment of claims by the debtor against third parties (*saisie-arrêt*) or of immovable property (*saisie-immobilière*).

6.8.5. ENFORCEMENT MEASURES OTHER THAN ATTACHMENT

Pursuant to the Benelux Treaty of 26 November 1973 on the Uniform Law on penalties, in Luxembourg a penalty clause can be imposed. It functions as an indirect way of enforcement in cases where the court has ordered injunctive relief (*see* art. 811-2 allowing the President in summary proceedings to impose a penalty clause). The penalty cannot, as in France, be attached to a judgment to pay a sum of money. Civil imprisonment has been abolished.

6.9. Duration and Costs

6.9.1. INTRODUCTION

Before commencing civil proceedings one is well-advised to find out how much time and money will be involved. That is why these matters are briefly discussed in the following sections.

6.9.2. DURATION

On average the time between commencement of proceedings in a civil case before the *tribunal d'arrondissement* and judgment is two to three years. This long period can be partly explained by the considerable delay which is caused in proceedings when one of the parties has not submitted pleadings, so that the date appointed for the pleadings is not reached. If that happens, the new date for the hearing is usually moved a year ahead.

In the *tribunal de paix* and the *tribunal du travail* this is a period of months (three to six months), and the *tribunal de commerce* usually takes from six months to two years (McIntosh and Holmes, *Civil Procedures in EC Countries, an Industry Report*, London 1991, p. 213).

6.9.3. COSTS

In a legal procedure three different categories of costs are recognised: firstly, the *frais judiciaires*, comprising the fees of the *huissier* and the *greffier* (registrar); secondly, the *dépens*, the fees of the *avoué* in respect of each step taken by him in the proceedings; thirdly, the *honoraires*, which are the fees of the lawyer not comprised in the *dépens*, such as his assistance and representation during the proceedings.

The *frais judiciaires* must be paid by each party to either the court or the *huissier* at each time a step is taken for which payment is due. In principle the losing party is ordered to pay back the *frais judiciaires* and the *dépens* incurred by his opponent. Each party is, however, liable for the *honoraires* of his own lawyer. If a party succeeds only partly, a part of his costs must be paid by the losing party (*see* arts. 130-133).

For litigants of limited means there is legal aid. Under certain conditions Luxembourg citizens may in civil procedures be exempt (provisionally) from paying the *frais judiciaires* and the *dépens*. As regards the *honoraires*, litigants may apply to the president (*bâtonnier*) of the Bar Council, who may then appoint an *avocat-avoué* to represent the litigant. Only if, after proceedings have been concluded, it appears that the client's financial position has improved considerably may the lawyer charge him his fees.

6.10. Proceedings Outside the Courts

6.10.1. INTRODUCTION

Only since the beginning of the nineteen eighties, when Luxembourg ratified the New York Convention and the European Conventions of Geneva and drastically amended its domestic arbitration law, have proceedings outside the courts made a hesitant start. Consequently, the Grand-Duchy has no extensive legal tradition in this area, which accounts for the almost total absence of any relevant literature or case law. A convenient source may be the loose-leaf *International Handbook on Commercial Arbitration*. An appendix contains an English translation of the text of the relevant provisions of the *Code de procédure civile*. As far as we know there are no special regulations for binding advice, which therefore will not be considered here.

6.10.2. ARBITRATION

The rules on arbitration are contained in arts. 1003 to 1028-2 inclusive of the third book of the second part of the CPC. Unlike France, in Luxembourg no distinction is made between domestic and international arbitration.

The parties can agree to arbitration for those disputes of which they can freely dispose (arts. 1003 and 1004). They can do so before (*clause compromissoire*) or after a dispute arises (*compromis*). The form in writing is only relevant to the evidence (arts. 1005 and 1006). The formal requirements for the *clause compromissoire* and the *compromis* differ: in order to be valid, the *compromis* must state the issue in dispute and the names of the arbitrators (art. 1006), whilst this is not required in case of a *clause compromissoire*.

By agreeing arbitration, the parties exclude the national courts, with the exception of the *juge des référés*, who, for example, can order the defendant to pay an advance (*see* section 6.7.2), even though the actual dispute is subject to arbitration.

If either party should, notwithstanding the existence of an arbitration agreement, address the national court, the defendant will on pain of nullity have to raise the issue of the court's jurisdiction before submitting a defence.

In case of arbitration, an argument relating to the jurisdiction of arbitrators or to arbitrators exceeding their powers must be put forward in time; otherwise such argument cannot later be relied upon as a ground for an application to the *tribunal d'arrondissement* to set aside an award (art. 1023). Arbitrators can decide on their own (lack of) jurisdiction.

Any natural person of legal capacity may be appointed arbitrator. Article 1006 sets out the method of appointment of arbitrators, if the parties have not agreed on this or refuse to appoint any arbitrators. In emergencies either party can apply to the President of the *tribunal d'arrondissement* to appoint an arbitrator.

Failing a period of time specified in the arbitration agreement, the arbitrators' appointment lasts 3 months, commencing from the date on which the *compromis* was concluded (art. 1007).

The arbitration procedure progresses in principle along the same lines as a civil procedure before a national court. The parties are free, however, to agree other rules and time-limits (art. 1009). Usually arbitrators act jointly during the entire procedure (arts. 1011, 1014 and 1016). They are obliged to hear arguments from both sides, which may be presented orally and/or in writing.

Arbitrators can make an interim or a final award. The award must in principle be drawn up in writing, dated, motivated and signed by the arbitrators (art. 1016). They decide in accordance with the rules of law, unless the parties have ordered them to decide as *amiables compositeurs* (art. 1019). Arbitrators may, at the parties' request, also make an arbitral award on agreed terms. Until the expiry of the arbitrators' term of appointment, the parties may apply to the arbitrators to have any obscurities clarified or any omissions rectified. Article 1027 allows an additional award to be made, even after expiry of the term of appointment of the arbitrators. An arbitral award may be declared provisionally enforceable and may include an obligation to provide security (art. 1028).

Compulsory enforcement requires an exequatur, to be granted by the President of the *tribunal d'arrondissement* (art. 1020). As in France, it is only possible to appeal against a refusal of leave for enforcement. If a party wants to object against an exequatur being granted, proceedings to set aside must be commenced (*see below*). There is no appeal unless the parties have agreed to it. Any other remedies against arbitral awards were abolished in 1981 in order to increase the efficacy of this form of dispute resolution.

An arbitral award can only be set aside on the grounds stated in art. 1023, which remarkably includes violation of the right to defend a claim (compare art. 1704 of the Belgian *Gerechtelijk Wetboek/Code Judiciaire*). Proceedings to set aside are commenced by objecting against leave to enforce within a month after the service of the exequatur upon the parties. An arbitral award may be partly set aside (arts. 1024-1026).

In 1983 Luxembourg ratified the New York Convention on the Recognition and Enforcement of Foreign Arbitral Awards, subject to reciprocity. The Grand-Duchy has not signed any bilateral conventions in this area. A foreign arbitral award can be made enforceable upon application by either party to the President of the *tribunal d'arrondissement* (art. 1028-1). If the New York Convention does not apply, the President will refuse leave if any of the cases mentioned in art. 1028-2 applies.

7. Belgian Civil Procedure*

Gerard J. Meijer**

7.1. Overview/Sources

7.1.1. INTRODUCTION

In Belgium, civil procedural law is referred to in Dutch as *gerechtelijk privaatrecht* (judicial private law) and in French as *droit judiciaire privé.*

Sources of Belgian civil procedural law are legislation (the Constitution (Gr.w), the *Gerechtelijk Wetboek/Code Judiciaire* (Judicial Code; Ger.W./CJ) and numerous special laws) and conventions (e.g. the ECHRFF and the CCPR). Case law and doctrines are other important sources.

Belgium has a civil law tradition. Roman law is the foundation of civil procedural law in Belgium. The French *Code de procédure civile*, which dates back to 1806, served as the basis for the old Belgian Code of Civil Procedure, which was in force until 1970. It was replaced by the *Gerechtelijk Wetboek/Code Judiciaire*, which is operative at present and forms the most important source of Belgian civil procedure (*see* for the history of Belgian civil procedure R.C. van Caenegem, *History of European Civil Procedure*, especially nos. 2-64 ff. and A Kohl, *Romanist Legal Systems*, no. 6-83 in M. Cappelletti, *Civil Procedure*, Martinus Nijhoff Publishers, The Hague 1984).

7.1.2 ACT AND CONVENTION

The Constitution contains provisions relating to the judicial organisation and provisions into which a number of principles of procedural law have been incorporated. They are contained in arts. 13, 40 and 146-157 Gr.w of 17 February 1994, BS 17 February 1994, second edition (*see* section 7.2.1).

The Judicial Code may, as stated before, be regarded as the major source of Belgian civil procedure. The Judicial Code, which is called *Gerechtelijk Wetboek* in Dutch and *Code Judiciaire* in French, was introduced by the Act

* The original text for the first Dutch edition was written by G.J. Meijer in co-operation with T.J. van Gessel.

** Thanks are due to Prof. dr. P. Lemmens and S. Raes (professor and assistant respectively at the Faculty of Law of Leuven University. Both are lawyers at the Brussels Bar).

of 10 October 1967. This Code entered into force on 1 November 1970. Recently it has been thoroughly amended. In view of the backlog existing in the Belgian courts, a study group was set up in 1985 to adapt the Judicial Code. This led to a draft which was submitted to the Senate on 16 January 1991 (*Ontwerp van Wet tot wijziging van het Gerechtelijk Wetboek/Projet de loi modifiant le Code judiciaire*, Belgian Senate, Session 1990-1991, no. 1198-1, pp. 1-74, hereinafter called *Ontwerp*). In July 1992 the Senate and Chamber of Delegates approved the *Ontwerp* (the consideration by the Senate Commission for Justice of the *Ontwerp* has been recorded, Belgian Senate, Extraordinary Session 1991-1992, no. 307/2, pp. 1-140, hereinafter called *Verslag*). The Act amending the Judicial Code of 3 August 1992 (BS 31 August 1992) entered into force on 1 January 1993 and came into immediate effect; in principle, the regularity and consequences of actions commenced before that date will continue to be governed by the provisions of the old Act (art. 3 Ger.W./CJ) (G. Closset-Marchal, *Toepassing van de wet in de tijd - overgangsrecht, Het vernieuwd gerechtelijk recht* pp. 35-48 and J. Laenens and K. Broeckx, *Het gerechtelijk recht in een stroomversnelling*, RW, pp. 931-932). Recently arts. 747, 748 and 750 of the Judicial Code have been amended by the Act of 23 March 1995 (*Wet tot wijziging van de artikelen 747, 748 en 750 van het Gerechtelijk Wetboek/Loi modifiant les articles 747, 748 et 750 du Code judiciaire*, BS 5 May 1995) (entry into force 1 June 1995). *See* for the amendments in particular sections 7.3.2 (a) and (d), 7.4.2 (c), 7.4.3 and 7.6.3. Amendments have further been made in subsectors. In addition to incidental amendments concerning attachment law and the statute of bailiffs, mention must be made of the fundamental amendment of the rules for divorce procedures (*Wet van 30 juni 1994 houdende wijziging van artikel 931 Ger. W. en de bepalingen betreffende de procédures van echtscheiding/Loi modifiant l'article 931 du Code judiciaire et les dispositions relatives aux procédures du divorce*, BS 21 July 1994) (entry into force 1 October 1994).

The Judicial Code provides for the organisation of the courts, their jurisdiction and the administration of justice (art. 1 Ger.W./CJ). Furthermore the Code lays down rules for judicial offices, the bar and bailiffs (*see* arts. 288-555*quater* Ger.W./CJ). Thus in Belgium there is no separate act governing the judicial organisation, nor a separate act concerning the bar or bailiffs, as is the case in some other countries.

When listing the regulations in the area of civil procedure one must not forget the *Wet Taalgebruik Gerechtszaken/Loi concernant l'emploi des langues en matière judiciaire* (Act on the Use of Languages in Judicial Cases), which dates back to 1935. Furthermore, there is the Royal Decree of

30 November 1970 laying down a tariff of recoverable costs, referred to in art. 1022 Ger.W./CJ (concerning the costs of the administration of justice).

Belgium is a party to a number of multilateral and bilateral conventions in the field of international civil procedure. Relevant are the Brussels Convention and the Lugano Convention (*see* sections 3.1.1 and 3.1.5). Other multilateral conventions to which Belgium is a party are the Convention on Civil Procedure of 1954 (The Hague, entry into force 23 June 1958) and the Hague Convention on the Service Abroad of Judicial and Extrajudicial Documents in Civil or Commercial Matters of 1965 (The Hague, entry into force 18 January 1971). Reference should also be made to the European Convention on Information on Foreign Law of 1968 (London, entry into force 17 January 1974) and the European Agreement on the Transmission of Applications for Legal Aid of 1977 (Strasbourg, entry into force 11 June 1978). For arbitration the New York Convention of 1958 (*see* section 7.10.2) and the European Convention on International Commercial Arbitration of 1961 (Geneva, entry into force 7 January 1976) apply. The Hague Convention on the Taking of Evidence Abroad in Civil or Commercial Matters of 1970 has not yet entered into force in Belgium. Of major importance, furthermore, are the ECHRFF and the CCPR, which entered into force in Belgium on 14 June 1955 and 21 July 1983 respectively (*see further* section 7.2.1).

In the loose-leaf edition edited by M. Storme (Ghent), the Judicial Code, international conventions and special Acts and Decrees, stating case law and literature, have been included in French and Dutch. Further, there is *Burgerlijk en Gerechtelijk Recht*, annotated (in Dutch and French), Brussels. Convenient are the French paperback edition *Code Judiciaire*, Brussels and the Dutch paperback edition *Wetteksten Gerechtelijk Wetboek*, Antwerp-Apeldoorn.

7.1.3. LITERATURE AND CASE LAW

A relatively recent French handbook in the area of civil procedure is by A. Fettweis, *Manuel de Procédure Civile*, second edition, Liège 1987. An older work is by C. Cambier, *Droit Judiciaire civil*, Tome I (Fonction et organisation judiciaires) and Tome II (La compétence), Brussels 1974 respectively 1981. Other works which continue to be of interest are the volumes in the series *Précis de droit judiciaire* with contributions by A. Fettweis, II. La compétence, 1971, A. Le Paige, IV. Les voies de recours, 1973 and J.-L. Rens, V. Les procédures particulières, 1979, Brussels (also published in Dutch). Recent introductions to Belgian civil procedure are presented by C. Leclercq, *Eléments pratiques de procédure civile et modèles d'actes*, second edition,

Brussels 1993 and G. de Leval, *Institutions Judiciaires, Introduction au droit judiciaire privé*, Liège 1992. *See* in respect of the amendment of the Gerechtlijk Wetboek/Code Judiciaire *Le nouveau droit judiciaire privé. Commentaires*, Les dossiers du Journal des tribunaux, Vol. 5, Brussels 1994.

The *Commentaar Gerechtelijk Recht*, Antwerp (loose-leaf) is an important Dutch work in the area of judicial law. A recent Dutch book in the area of procedural law, with contributions from a number of procedural specialists, deals with the amendment of the Judicial Code, namely: *Het vernieuwd gerechtelijk recht, eerste commentaar bij de Wet van 3 Augustus 1992 tot wijziging van het Gerechtelijk Wetboek* (series Bibliotheek van Gerechtelijk Recht van het Interuniversitair Centrum voor Gerechtelijk Recht), Antwerp 1992 (hereinafter referred to as *Het vernieuwd gerechtelijk recht*). A clear survey, finally, is given in the collection of lectures by P. Lemmens, *Gerechtelijk Privaatrecht*, 3rd (revised) edition, Leuven 1994-95.

A concise English manual on Belgian private judicial law is given by P. Van den Neucker and J. de Vergnies in *Civil Procedures in EC Countries* (eds. D. MacIntosh and M. Holmes), London 1991, p. 37 ff., H. Callens and P. Verguts in *European Civil Practice* (eds. S. O'Malley and A. Layton), London 1989, p. 1169 ff. and C.S. Van den Kerckhove in *Trial and Court Procedures Worldwide* (ed. C. Platto), London/Dordrecht/Boston 1991, p. 104 ff.

A journal specialised in procedural law in the broad sense is *Proces & Bewijs* (Tijdschrift voor Procesrecht en Bewijsrecht), which has been published since 1993. Judgments from the *Cour de Cassation* are incorporated into the Dutch review *Arresten van het Hof van Cassatie* (Arr. Cass.) and into the French review *Pasicrisie belge* (Pas.). Other general legal reviews (*inter alia Journal des tribunaux* (JT), *Rechtskundig Weekblad* (RW) and *Tijdschrift voor Privaatrecht* (TPR)) regularly contain case law and/or literature in the area of civil procedure.

7.1.4. DATA BASES

The CREDOC (Bergstraat 34, 1000 Brussels, tel. 32-2-5116941) keeps data bases into which reviews and case law (BJUS) and legislation (BLEX) have been incorporated. Furthermore there is an edition of Kluwer on CD-ROM (JUDIT) containing literature and case law. Since 1992 there has been a separate CD-ROM (FBW) on which legislation is recorded, also produced by Kluwer. The Ministry of Justice in Belgium also has a data base (JUSTEL) which contains legislation and case law.

7.2. Fundamental Principles

7.2.1. INTRODUCTION

In Belgian civil procedure fundamental legal principles play an important role. They are embodied both in national and international law. In this respect art. 6(1) ECHRFF and art. 14(1) CCPR in particular are very important. These provisions have direct effect and prevail over domestic legal provisions.

The fundamental principles of Belgian civil procedure are the principle of hearing both parties, the principle of public court sessions and judgments, the motivation principle, the principle of party autonomy, the principle of an independent and impartial court, the principle of a reasonable time, the principle of documentary and oral consideration and the principle of access to the courts. They are also ranged under the doctrine of proper procedural order.

Belgium has no principle of obligatory procedural representation (*see further* section 7.3.3).

The principle of enquiry into the facts and judgment in two instances is usually not recognised as such in the Belgian literature. In principle, however, parties do have the right to have a full consideration of their case on appeal. Article 616 Ger.W./CJ provides that appeal lies against any judgment, but it allows for exceptions to that rule. The European Court of Human Rights (ECHR 23 July 1968) (Belgian language case), Publ. ECHR, Series A, vol. 6 (1968) and the Belgian Supreme Court (Cour de Cassation 21 January 1983, RW 1982-1983, pp. 2546-2549) have decided that the right to appeal is not a fundamental right of the parties.

Although in Belgium there is supervision of the administration of justice by way of cassation, this is usually not in itself regarded as a fundamental principle of Belgian civil procedure.

In respect of the principles of procedural law in general, *see* the contribution from M. Storme in *Algemene Rechtsbeginselen* (ed. M. van Hoecke), Antwerp 1991, pp. 158-195.

7.2.2. PRINCIPLE OF HEARING BOTH PARTIES

The principle of hearing both parties must never be lost sight of when applying other procedural standards (A. Fettweis, *Manuel de Procédure Civile*, p. 13).

The principle of hearing both parties is expressed *inter alia* in art. 702 Ger.W./CJ which provides for the due summoning of the defendant and art. 736 *et seq*. Ger.W./CJ, by virtue of which the parties must (in time) notify each other of the documents which they want to adduce in the proceedings. Article 747 Ger.W./CJ provides for the exchange of statements between the parties. If the court partly or fully rejects a claim on a ground which neither party has invoked, it must *ex officio* order the reopening of the proceedings, so that the parties may give their opinions on this point (art. 774 Ger.W./CJ).

7.2.3. PRINCIPLE OF PUBLICITY

The principle of publicity of the sessions of the court and judgment is anchored in arts. 148 and 149 Gr.w and is intended *inter alia* to prevent a biased administration of justice.

The Judicial Code phrases this principle thus: subject to exceptions provided by law, the pleadings, records and judgments are public (art. 757 Ger.W./CJ).

7.2.4. PRINCIPLE OF MOTIVATION

Under art. 149 Gr.w each judgment must be reasoned (*see also* art. 780 Ger.W./CJ). The court must indicate the facts and legal rules which underlie its decision. In addition, the court must address the grounds which the parties have adduced in their statements (P. Lemmens, *Gerechtelijk Privaatrecht*, third (revised) edition, Leuven 1994-95, p. 15).

7.2.5. PRINCIPLE OF PARTY AUTONOMY

By virtue of the principle of party autonomy the parties decide whether or not the court is addressed and what the subject of the proceedings will be.

The court cannot give a judgment on matters not pleaded or decide in excess of what was claimed (*see* art. 1138 *sub* 2 Ger.W./CJ). Furthermore, the court must decide all points of the claim (art. 1138 *sub* 3 Ger.W./CJ). In general, the court is not allowed to add facts. It is obliged, however, to add legal grounds (A. Fettweis, *Manuel de Procédure Civile*, pp. 21-23). Conflict of laws rules and foreign law also constitute law which must be applied *ex officio* (*see also* section 7.6.4, first paragraph). When foreign law is applied, in practice the court asks the parties for their co-operation because generally it is not familiar with that law. However, within that context the applicable foreign law must not be noted as a fact (*see* section 7.4.2 (e)(5)) (*see* in respect of the application of conflict of laws rules and foreign law F.

Rigaux, *Droit International Privé*, Tome I, Théorie Générale, second amended edition, Brussels 1987, nos. 435-441). Although an expert's report concerning legal questions is not allowed in Belgium pursuant to art. 962 in conjunction with art. 11 Ger.W./CJ, an exception to this rule is made for legal questions concerning foreign law (*see* the comparative legal note by J.B.M. Vranken to HR 2 February 1990, NJ 1991, 1, mentioning literature). In its investigation the court can also officially gain information abroad on the relevant foreign law under the European Convention on Information on Foreign Law, mentioned in section 7.1.2.

Party autonomy does not imply that the court must assume a passive role during the proceedings. Thus, the court may of its own motion order measures of inquiry (e.g. oral testimony (art. 916 Ger.W./CJ), personal appearance of the parties in court (art. 992 Ger.W./CJ) and site inspection (art. 1007 Ger.W./CJ)).

7.2.6. PRINCIPLE OF INDEPENDENCE AND IMPARTIALITY

With a view to his independence, a judge is appointed for life (*see* arts. 151-155 Gr.w). For the same reason judicial office is not compatible with any other office or profession (art. 292 *et seq*. Ger.W./CJ). Recently a new Act came into force which is intended to curb (party) political appointments in Belgium. There are now objective criteria for the appointment of judges (*Wet van 18 juli 1991 tot wijziging van de voorschriften van het Gerechtelijk Wetboek die betrekking hebben op de opleiding en de werving van magistraten/Loi du 18 juillet 1991 modifiant les règles du Code judiciaire relatives au recrutement et à la formation des magistrats* (Act of 18 July 1991 amending the rules of the Judicial Code relating to the training and recruitment of magistrates), BS 26 July 1991, whereby art. 259*bis*-259*quater* (Chapter V*bis*) has been added to the Judicial Code). *See* J. Sohier, *Les nouvelles règles du Code judiciaire relatives au recrutement des magistrats*, Journal des tribuneaux 1992, pp. 705-707 and J. Laenens and K. Broeckx, *Het gerechtelijk recht in een stroomversnelling*, RW 1993, pp. 897-906.

The judge must be impartial. If he is biased, he may be challenged (*see* art. 828 *et seq*. Ger.W./CJ). *See also* art. 648 *et seq*. Ger.W./CJ.

7.2.7. PRINCIPLE OF REASONABLE TIME

Everybody is entitled to have their case dealt with within a reasonable time. The amendments of the Judicial Code are intended to relieve the enormous backlog in the judicial system. *See further* sections 7.4.2c, 7.6.3 and 7.9.2.

7.2.8. PRINCIPLE OF WRITTEN AND ORAL CONSIDERATION OF THE CASE

In principle, Belgian civil procedure is based on both written and oral consideration of the case (*procédure écrite et orale*). Documents, such as writs, petitions and pleadings, mean precision. Oral consideration (the oral pleadings before the court in particular) supplements the written consideration of the case and creates the conditions for a dialogue between the judge and the parties (*see* A. Fettweis, *Manuel de Procédure Civile*, p. 12).

7.2.9. PRINCIPLE OF ACCESS TO THE COURTS

The right of access to the courts is also a fundamental principle of Belgian procedure. According to the European Court of Human Rights in the case of *Airey* v. *Ireland* (ECHR 9 October 1979, Publ. ECHR, Series A, vol. 32 (1980), the right of 'access to the courts' must be concrete and effective. Legal aid, for instance, may make access to the courts possible (*see also* section 7.9.3).

7.3. Principal Characters

7.3.1. INTRODUCTION

The principal characters in civil procedure are the judge, the clerk of the court, the lawyer, the parties to the proceedings and the court bailiff.

In this section the judge, the lawyer and the parties to the proceedings will be discussed in detail. *See* for the court bailiff arts. 509 to 555*quater* Ger.W./CJ.

7.3.2. THE JUDGE

a. Introduction

The courts which exercise judicial power in Belgium are the *vrederechters/juges de paix* (located in the main city of each judicial canton), the *rechtbanken van eerste aanleg/tribunaux de première instance*, the *arbeidsrechtbanken/tribunaux du travail*, the *rechtbanken van koophandel/tribunaux de commerce*, the *arrondissementsrechtbanken/tribunaux d'arrondissement* (which courts have their seat in the main city of each judicial district), the *hoven van beroep/cours d'appel* and the *arbeidshoven/cours du travail* (one of each in Brussels, Ghent, Antwerp, Liège and Mons) and the *Hof van Cassatie/Cour de Cassation*, which is located in Brussels (arts. 58 to 287 Ger.W./CJ).

Apart from the *vrederechters/juges de paix* there are judges sitting in the above-mentioned *rechtbanken/tribunaux*; they are called *rechters/juges*. Judges of the *hof van beroep/cour d'appel*, the *arbeidshof/cour du travail* and the *Hof van Cassatie/Cour de Cassation* are called *raadsheren/conseillers*.

The *vrederechter/juge de paix* sits alone (*unus iudex*). The panels of the *rechtbank van eerste aanleg/tribunal de première instance* usually consist of one judge (art. 78 in conjunction with art. 91, para. 1 Ger.W./CJ) and in exceptional cases of three judges (art. 78 in conjunction with art. 91, para. 6 and art. 92 Ger.W./CJ). For instance, a case is adjudicated by three judges if one of the parties requests this in time. Appeal against a decision of the *vrederechter/juge de paix* is always brought before a panel of three judges of the *rechtbank van eerste aanleg/tribunal de première instance* (art. 78 in conjunction with art. 92, para 1 *sub* 3 Ger.W./CJ). The panels of the *arbeidsrechtbank/tribunal du travail* consist of one judge in the *arbeidsrechtbank/tribunal du travail* and two or four judges in social matters. These judges are lay persons (arts. 81-83 Ger.W./CJ). The panels of the *rechtbank van koophandel/tribunal de commerce* consist of one judge in the *rechtbank van koophandel/tribunal de commerce* and two judges in commercial matters, who again are lay persons (arts. 84 and 85 Ger.W./CJ). The *arrondissementsrechtbank/tribunal d'arrondissement* consists of the presidents of the *rechtbank van eerste aanleg/tribunal de première instance*, the *rechtbank van koophandel/tribunal de commerce* and the *arbeidsrechtbank/tribunal du travail* (art. 74 Ger.W./CJ). The panels of the *hof van beroep/cour d'appel* in principle consist of three judges (art. 109*bis* § 1 paras. 2 and 3 and § 3 Ger.W./CJ) and in exceptional cases of one judge (art. 101, art. 109*bis* §§ 1 and 2 Ger.W./CJ). The *arbeidshof/cour du travail* sits with three or five judges (one professional judge and two or four lay judges) (art. 104 Ger.W./CJ). The *Hof van Cassatie/Cour de Cassation* considers cases with five judges (art. 128 Ger.W./CJ).

See also P. Lemmens, *Rechterlijke organisatie*, *Het vernieuwd gerechtelijk recht*, pp. 49-70. Absolute and relative jurisdiction are discussed in section 7.3.2 (d) and (e).

b. International jurisdiction

Whether a Belgian judge has international jurisdiction depends on arts. 635 to 638 Ger.W./CJ, art. 15 BW and, very important, any applicable conventions (*see inter alia* the Brussels Convention) (*see* section 7.1.2). Article 635 *et seq.* Ger.W./CJ determine in which cases a foreigner can be summoned to appear before a Belgian court. Article 15 BW is remarkable. It states that a Belgian national may always be summoned before a court in Belgium, even though he may live abroad. However, in cases where the Brussels Convention applies, art. 15 BW and art. 638 Ger.W./CJ do not apply (*see* art. 3 Brussels Convention).

c. Sectoral jurisdiction

The *Gerechtelijk Wetboek/Code Judiciaire* lays down rules for the organisation of the courts for both civil and criminal matters (art. 2 Ger.W./CJ). The criminal courts consist of the *politierechtbank/tribunal de police* (usually the *vrederechter/juge de paix*) (art. 60 *et seq.* Ger.W./CJ), the *correctionele rechtbank/tribunal correctionnel* (a division of the *rechtbank van eerste aanleg/tribunal de première instance*) (art. 76 Ger.W./CJ), the *hof van beroep/cour d'appel* (art. 101 Ger.W./CJ) and the *Hof van Assisen/Cour d'Assises* (*see* art. 114 *et seq.* Ger.W./CJ). Appeal in cassation may be lodged with the *Hof van Cassatie/Cour de Cassation* (art. 133 Ger.W./CJ).

There are also administrative courts, which in cases prescribed by law pass judgment in disputes concerning subjective political rights (e.g. the right to vote and liability for tax). The main administrative court is the *Raad van State/Conseil d'Etat* (Council of State), which has jurisdiction at first and last instance to decide on applications for the nullification of administrative decisions (*see* art. 160 Gr.w and art. 14 Acts on the Council of State), in addition to limited jurisdiction as a court of cassation or as a court of appeal over disputes concerning political rights.

The *Arbitragehof/Cour d'Arbitrage* has jurisdiction to annul statutes, decrees and orders pursuant to art. 142 Gr.w (*see also* the Act of 6 January 1989 on the *Arbitragehof/Cour d'Arbitrage*).

Civil courts with sectoral jurisdiction are the *rechtbank van koophandel/ tribunal de commerce*, the *arbeidsrechtbank/tribunal du travail* and the *arbeidshof/cour du travail*, which will be discussed in detail in the next section.

d. Absolute jurisdiction

Absolute jurisdiction (*materiële bevoegdheid/compétence matérielle*) is jurisdiction based upon the subject, the amount of the claim and, in certain cases, the urgency of the claim or the capacity of the parties (art. 9 Ger.W./ CJ). There are statutory rules to determine the amount of the claims in arts. 557-562 (*see also* art. 592 Ger.W./CJ in respect of claims of undetermined value). In the aforementioned amendment of the Judicial Code all limits for jurisdiction have been increased.

The *vrederechter/juge de paix* has absolute jurisdiction to hear claims not exceeding BF 75,000 (art. 590 Ger.W./CJ), with the exception of claims which by law must be decided by another court (arts. 569-571, 574, 578-583 and 590, para. 2 Ger.W./CJ) (*see also* section 7.7.3).

Irrespective of the amount of the claim, the *vrederechter/juge de paix* has exclusive jurisdiction in cases regarding the letting of immovable property and in the majority of maintenance cases (art. 591 *et seq.* Ger.W./CJ). These are rules of public policy.

By virtue of art. 568, para. 1 Ger.W./CJ the *rechtbank van eerste aanleg/ tribunal de première instance* hears all claims, apart from those which come under the direct jurisdiction of the *hof van beroep/cour d'appel* or the *Hof van Cassatie/Cour de Cassation*. The *rechtbank van eerste aanleg/tribunal de première instance* has a so-called 'conditional scope of jurisdiction'. It has jurisdiction to hear disputes which come under the jurisdiction of another court, if the defendant does not raise an objection before he submits his defence, unless the other court has exclusive jurisdiction. The *rechtbank van eerste aanleg/tribunal de première instance* itself has exclusive jurisdiction in the cases mentioned in arts. 569-571 Ger.W./CJ. In principle the *rechtbank van eerste aanleg/tribunal de première instance* hears appeals from judgments of the *vrederechters/juges de paix*, unless these judgments concern commercial acts (art. 577 Ger.W./CJ).

Regardless of the amount of the claim, the *arbeidsrechtbank/tribunal du travail* has jurisdiction to try all (individual) disputes relating to employment law, industrial injury law and social security law, and (individual) disputes arising out of the application of administrative sanctions in cases of breach of certain social laws (art. 590 Ger.W./CJ in conjunction with arts. 578-583 Ger.W./CJ). Collective employment law does not come under the jurisdiction of the *arbeidsrechtbank/tribunal du travail*, subject to certain exceptions (*see inter alia* art. 582 *sub* 3 and 4 Ger.W./CJ).

The *rechtbank van koophandel/tribunal de commerce* has jurisdiction to try disputes between merchants or traders (these terms are interchangeable) which involve acts which the law considers to be commercial acts and which do not come under the jurisdiction of the *vrederechter/juge de paix* (art. 573, para. 1 *sub* 1 Ger.W./CJ). The term 'merchant' is deemed to refer to all persons who professionally perform commercial acts (art. 1 K/C. comm.). Commercial acts are defined in arts. 2 and 3 K/C. comm. Irrespective of the parties' being merchants, however, the *rechtbank van koophandel/tribunal de commerce* has jurisdiction in respect of all disputes about bills of exchange and promissory notes if the claim exceeds BF 75,000. It also has jurisdiction in certain disputes between a non-merchant plaintiff and a merchant-defendant (art. 573, para. 2 Ger.W./CJ) and between non-merchants (art. 574 Ger.W./CJ). The *rechtbank van koophandel/tribunal de commerce* considers appeals of judgments given by the *vrederechter/juge de paix* in respect of commercial matters and bills of exchange. Unlike at first instance, both parties must always be merchants (art. 577, para. 2 Ger.W./CJ).

The jurisdiction of the president of the *rechtbank van eerste aanleg/tribunal de première instance*, the president of the *rechtbank van koophandel/tribunal de commerce* and the president of the *arbeidsrechtbank/tribunal du travail*, in *kort geding/référé*, will be discussed in section 7.7.2.

The only duty of the *arrondissementsrechtbank/tribunal d'arrondissement* is to solve questions of jurisdiction and to determine the competent court, pursuant to the rules of absolute and relative jurisdiction (*see* arts. 639 to 644 Ger.W./CJ). Hence, it cannot decide on the merits of the case. A case can only be transferred to the *arrondissementsrechtbank/tribunal d'arrondissement* when the defendant has raised the objection as to jurisdiction and the plaintiff has asked for the transferral (art. 639 Ger.W./CJ), or when the court has of its own motion raised the objection of jurisdiction (art. 640 Ger.W./CJ). On appeal the court itself must in principle decide if jurisdiction is contested (art. 643 Ger.W./CJ).

The *hof van appel/cour d'appel* tries appeals against judgments of first instance by the *rechtbank van eerste aanleg/tribunal de première instance* and the *rechtbank van koophandel/tribunal de commerce* and appeals against judgments by the presidents of these courts (art. 602 Ger.W./CJ).

The *arbeidshof/cour du travail* has jurisdiction to try appeals against judgments of first instance by the *arbeidsrechtbank/tribunal du travail* and against decisions by the president of the *arbeidsrechtbank/tribunal du travail* (art. 607 Ger.W./CJ).

The supreme court in Belgium, the *Hof van Cassatie/Cour de Cassation*, consists of three panels, the first dealing with civil and commercial matters, the second with criminal matters, and the third with matters of employment and social security. The *Hof van Cassatie/Cour de Cassation* gives judgment in civil cases about the appeal in cassation against any judgments given at final instance (art. 608 Ger.W./CJ).

If the defendant wishes to contest the jurisdiction of the court before which the case is brought, he must do so before he files a defence, unless jurisdiction rules of public policy are involved (art. 854 Ger.W./CJ). Thus, if jurisdiction is not of public policy, parties must contest jurisdiction before submitting any defence; the court cannot of its own motion declare that it has no jurisdiction, unless the defendant did not enter an appearance (*see* art. 630, para. 3 Ger.W./CJ). If, however, jurisdiction is of public policy, the court must of its own motion raise the objection as to jurisdiction; the issue of jurisdiction must be decided on as described above in this section. Most rules of absolute jurisdiction are of public policy. Not of public policy, for example, is the 'conditional scope of jurisdiction' of the *rechtbank van eerste aanleg/tribunal de première instance.*

See further on absolute and relative jurisdiction J. Laenens, *Overzicht van de rechtspraak, De bevoegdheid* (1979-1992), TPR 1993, pp. 1479-1615 and J. Laenens, *De bevoegdheid ratione summae, de aanleg en de regeling van bevoegdheidsincidenten, Het vernieuwd gerechtelijk recht*, pp. 71-79. *See* the diagram of the judicial organisation in civil cases on p. 206.

e. Relative jurisdiction

Relative jurisdiction (*territoriale bevoegdheid/compétence territoriale*) is the jurisdiction of a court in a particular area in accordance with the rules of law (art. 10 Ger.W./CJ). The court's relative jurisdiction is provided for in art. 622 *et seq*. Ger.W./CJ.

Pursuant to art. 624 Ger.W./CJ relative jurisdiction lies with the court of the place of domicile of the defendant or the court of the place where (one of) the obligations which are the subject of the dispute (has or) have arisen, or where these obligations are, have been or must be fulfilled.

Articles 627-629 Ger.W./CJ contain imperative rules which deviate from the main rule. For example, in respect of an action for a divorce based on certain facts, the court of the place of the last actual marital residence or of the domicile of the defendant has jurisdiction (art. 628 *sub* 1 in conjunction with art. 36 Ger.W.). Rules of imperative law may only be deviated from after the dispute has arisen (art. 630, para. 1 Ger.W./CJ).

DIAGRAM JUDICIAL ORGANISATION IN CIVIL CASES IN BELGIUM

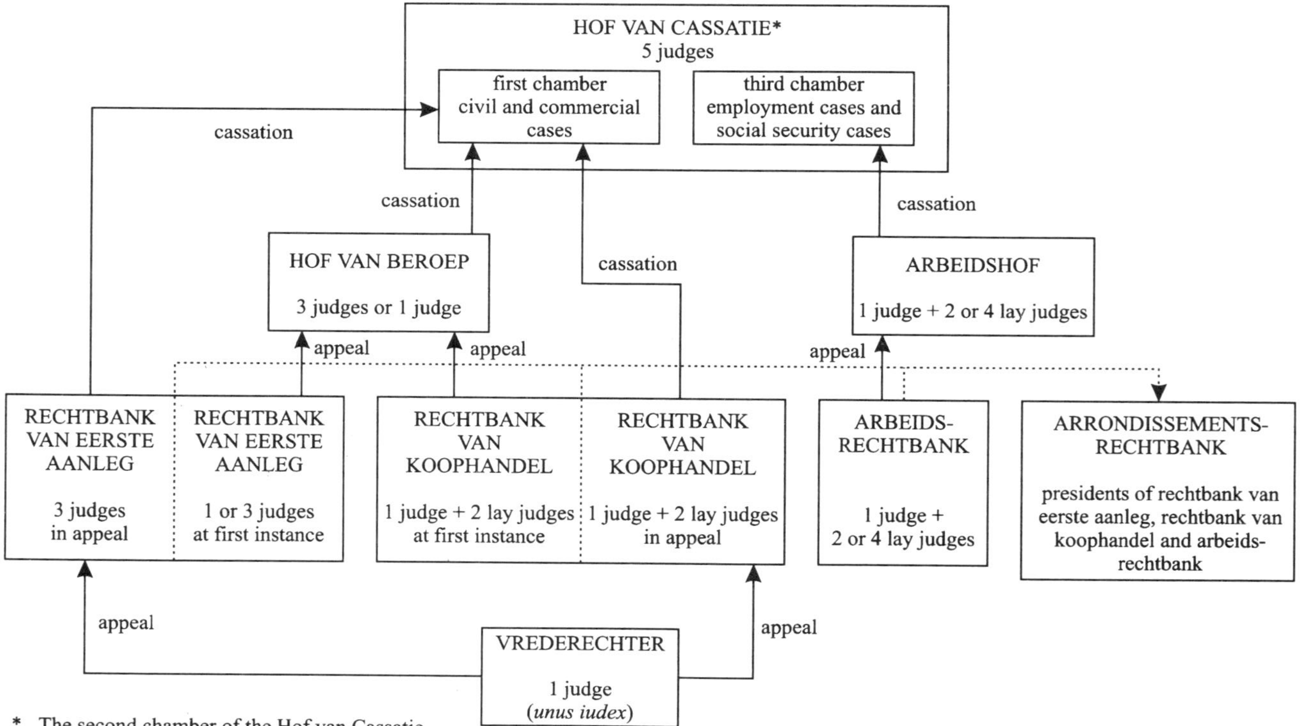

* The second chamber of the Hof van Cassatie need not be considered here.

** The French terms can be found in section 7.3.2d

Finally, arts. 631-633 Ger.W./CJ provide rules of public policy. Thus, claims in respect of protective attachment and of means of enforcement must in principle only be brought before the court of the place of the attachment (art. 633 Ger.W./CJ). In respect of immovable property the place of attachment is the place where the property is situated (*see also* art. 629 Ger.W./CJ). It is not permitted to derogate from rules of public policy.

See further section 7.3.2 (d) *in fine.*

7.3.3. THE LAWYERS

In principle there is no mandatory legal representation in Belgium (*see* art. 728 § 1 Ger.W./CJ). Parties may conduct their own proceedings if they wish to do so. Legal representation is obligatory in a certain respect before the *Hof van Cassatie/Cour de Cassation* and in procedures commenced upon an *ex parte* application. Then a lawyer (*advocaat*) is required (arts. 478-487, 1080 and 1092 resp. 1026 *sub* 5 and 1027, para. 1 Ger.W./CJ). In principle the *advocaat* has a monopoly of legal representation and oral pleadings (art. 440, para. 1 Ger.W./CJ), but there are exceptions to this monopoly (*see* for example art. 758 and art. 728 §§ 2 and 3 Ger.W./CJ).

The *advocaat* is entitled to act before all the courts of the State of Belgium (art. 439 Ger.W./CJ), except before the *Hof van Cassatie/Cour de Cassation* (*see* art. 478 Ger.W./CJ). At present only sixteen *advocaten*, appointed by the King on the recommendation of the *Hof van Cassatie/Cour de Cassation*, may act before the *Hof van Cassatie/Cour de Cassation* (*see* art. 478 Ger.W./CJ). No *advocaten-stagiairs* can act before the Council of State (art. 19 Acts on the Council of State).

The Belgian *advocaat* is both a legal adviser (a person who advises his clients on all aspects of their case) and a legal representative (a person who represents his clients in court).

The *advocaat* has a mandate *'ad litem'*. He does not need to produce a power of attorney, unless the law requires special authorisation (art. 440, para. 2 Ger.W./CJ). *See also* arts. 848-850 Ger.W./CJ concerning the disavowal of procedural acts (*désaveu*).

In order to practise as an *advocaat* in Belgium, one needs to be (a) either a Belgian national or a national of an EC State; (b) have a degree of either licentiate or doctor of law; (c) have sworn an oath; and (d) have been enrolled with the Bar or registered on the list of *stagiairs* as a trainee (art. 428 *et seq*. Ger.W./CJ). Before one can be enrolled with the Bar, there is an obligatory traineeship of at least three years (art. 434 Ger.W./CJ). Persons who are resident in one of the EC States and are entitled in that State to a title similar to that of a Belgian *advocaat*, may, under certain conditions, act as an *advocaat* in Belgium (*see* art. 477*bis et seq*. Ger.W./CJ).

See further A. Braun and F. Moreau, *La profession d'avocat*, Brussels 1985.

7.3.4. THE PARTIES

Article 17 Ger.W./CJ determines that a claim cannot be admitted if the plaintiff lacks the required capacity. Claims of persons who do not have legal capacity are inadmissible. In principle, minors must be represented in proceedings by their parents in their own name, but at the expense of the minor. Adults who have been certified incapable must be represented by their guardian. Pursuant to art. 452 K/C. comm. a person who has been declared bankrupt may not act as a plaintiff or defendant in court in respect of his commercial interests, subject to certain exceptions which are covered by special safeguards. The receiver represents a bankrupt person in court. Associations which do not have legal personality cannot appear in court.

An action is also not admissible if the party commencing the action has no interest (art. 17 Ger.W./CJ). The requirement of interest is defined in art. 18, para. 1 Ger.W./CJ: in principle the interest must already exist and must be immediate. The action is admissible, however, to prevent the infringement of a right which is under serious threat (art. 18, para. 2 Ger.W./CJ). Case law imposes a further condition: the interest must be personal and direct. The public interest does not qualify as interest within the meaning of art. 17 Ger.W./CJ. The *openbaar ministerie/ministère public* ensures the protection of the public interest (art. 138 Ger.W./CJ). On this basis it is presumed that group and representative actions are not admissible in the civil courts (*see* A. Fettweis, *Manuel de Procédure Civile*, p. 42 ff.). However, a number of organisations have by law been granted the right to bring group and/or representative actions (for example, professional and consumer associations, trade unions and associations to fight racism). In 1993 an Act entered into force whereby environmental associations can ask the president of the *rechtbank van eerste aanleg/tribunal de première instance*, in accordance with the procedure in *kort geding/référé* (summary judgment proceedings, *see* section 7.7.2), for an order to stop certain activities in order to protect the environment (*Wet van 12 januari 1993 betreffende een vorderingsrecht inzake bescherming van het leefmilieu/Loi concernant un droit d'action en matière de protection de l'environnement* (Act of 12 January concerning the right of action in cases relating to the protection of the environment, BS 19 February 1993)). Pursuant to this Act, art. 587 *sub* 4 Ger.W./CJ gives the president of the *rechtbank van eerste aanleg/tribunal de première instance* explicit jurisdiction to try such actions. *See further* J. van Compernolle, *Le droit d'action en justice des groupements*, Brussels 1975 and H. Bocken, *Schorsingsbevoegdheid milieuverenigingen* in *Procederen in nieuw België en komend Europa* (series Bibliotheek van Gerechtelijk Recht van het Interuniversitair Centrum voor Gerechtelijk Recht), Antwerp 1991, pp. 129-140 quoting case law and literature (hereinafter called *Procederen in nieuw België*).

7.4. Basic Procedure for Contentious Jurisdiction at First Instance

7.4.1. INTRODUCTION

Contentious proceedings are in principle commenced by writ. An adversarial petition may be used if the law explicitly allows or prescribes this in specific cases (in addition to contentious jurisdiction, an adversarial petition may also apply in voluntary jurisdiction) (*see* section 7.4.3). The *ex parte* petition procedure will be discussed in section 7.5 and is used not only in voluntary but also in contentious jurisdiction (e.g. in summary proceedings for orders of payment).

Since the introduction of the Judicial Code there has in principle been one type of procedure for nearly all courts (the *vrederechter/juge de paix*, the *rechtbank van eerste aanleg/tribunal de première instance*, the *rechtbank van koophandel/tribunal de commerce*, the *arbeidsrechtbank/tribunal du travail*, the *hof van appel/cour d'appel* and the *arbeidshof/cour du travail*); this principle is commonly known as *unité de procédure.*

In Belgium, as in other countries, there is also a strong tendency to deformalise the rules of procedure, e.g. in respect of void acts of procedure (*see* the amended art. 860 *et seq*. Ger.W./CJ discussed in the *Ontwerp*, p. 16 and R. de Corte and B. Deconinck, *Nietigheden na de wet van 3 augustus 1992, Toilettage of revolutie, Het vernieuwd gerechtelijk recht*, pp. 137-164).

7.4.2. THE PROCEDURE COMMENCED BY WRIT

a. Introduction

Main claims are in principle commenced by writ, without prejudice to the special rules concerning voluntary appearance and litigation commenced by petition (art. 700 Ger.W./CJ).

Voluntary appearance will not be discussed (*see* art. 706 Ger.W./CJ). From the reference in art. 700 Ger.W./CJ to special rules concerning litigation commenced by petition one must not deduce that art. 700 Ger.W./CJ recognises the adversarial petition along with the writ as a fully fledged notice of commencement of proceedings for all main claims (*see* section 7.4.3).

b. Commencement of proceedings

The writ must satisfy the formal requirements of art. 702 in conjunction with arts. 43 and 45 Ger.W./CJ. Otherwise it is void. The writ must, therefore, apart from personal particulars, state the subject and a short summary of the grounds of the claim. In addition, it must mention the court before which the claim is brought and the time (date and hour) of the initial hearing (art. 702 Ger.W./CJ).

It is the bailiff's duty to serve the writ. Service is effected by the bailiff upon the defendant in person. Service upon a person may take place at any place where the bailiff finds him (art. 32 *et seq*. Ger.W./CJ). If the bailiff fails to find the defendant, he leaves a copy of the writ at the defendant's place of domicile or residence (arts. 35, 38 and 39 Ger.W./CJ) (*see also* art. 40 Ger.W./CJ in respect of defendants living abroad and the Convention on the Service Abroad of Judicial and Extrajudicial Documents in Civil or Commercial Matters of 1965, referred to in section 7.1.2).

In principle, the minimum period stated in the writ for appearance is eight days (*see* art. 707 *et seq*. in conjunction with arts. 48-57 Ger.W./CJ). Failure to comply renders it void. The period stated in the writ may be reduced (art. 708 Ger.W./CJ) or extended (art. 709 in conjunction with art. 55 Ger.W./CJ). The period is counted from the day on which the writ was served and comprises all days, including Saturday, Sunday and public holidays (art. 52 Ger.W./CJ). The day of expiry is included in the period. If, however, that day is a Saturday, a Sunday or a public holiday, then the day of expiry is moved to the next working day (art. 53 Ger.W./CJ).

The case must be entered on the court's list (*rol/rôle*) (a register of cases) no later than the day prior to the date of the hearing set out in the writ (art. 716 Ger.W./CJ). Entry on the court's list takes place at the request of the bailiff who served the writ, of the interested parties or their lawyer or legal representation to the clerk of the court, who actually enters the case on the list, i.e. registers it. The case is pending on the date of the service of the writ if the case has been entered on the list in time. If the case has not been entered on the list (in time), it is of no value whatsoever (art. 717 Ger.W./CJ).

The clerk of the court keeps a file of each case which contains all important documents (art. 720 Ger.W./CJ).

c. Proceedings

The first time the case appears before the court, the clerk of the court calls the case (art. 727 Ger.W./CJ). A distinction must be made between the short proceedings (*korte debatten/débats succincts*) and the normal proceedings (*lange debatten*). The said *debatten* form the stage in the proceedings during which documents are (or may be) communicated and written and oral pleadings (may) take place.

If both parties appear in person before the court, cases requiring only short proceedings are either pleaded at this initial hearing or adjourned to be pleaded on a date to be fixed, whereby the duration of the proceedings is determined (art. 735 § 1 Ger.W./CJ). A dispute will be dealt with in short proceedings if it is not necessary to adduce grounds in writing. The legislator did not therefore only have urgent cases in mind (*Verslag*, p. 55).

The plaintiff may include a request for short proceedings in the notice which commences the proceedings (usually the writ), which request must state reasons (art. 735 § 1 Ger.W./CJ). The defendant may also make such a request (art. 735 § 1 *in fine*), but the law does not state how. Presumably, the defendant will do so either in writing or orally prior to or (no later than) at the first hearing before the court (*Verslag*, p. 56). The defendant will also have to motivate his request. The question is whether the court must grant a unilateral request for short proceedings. Opinions are divided on this (the common opinion, in line with practice, is that the court has an unassailable power to assess and to decide whether the request is adequately motivated; *see Ontwerp*, pp. 7-8, *Verslag*, p. 56 and J. Laenens and K. Broeckx, *Het gerechtelijk recht in een stroomversnelling*, RW 1993, p. 918; otherwise M. Storme, *De procedure van korte debatten: één zwaluw kan de lente maken...*, *Het vernieuwd gerechtelijk recht*, p. 95). Cases will at any event have to be considered in short proceedings if both parties so agree (art. 735 § 2 Ger.W./CJ).

Although written grounds are not actually required for the short proceedings, the parties are allowed to submit memoranda, notes and documents. This must be done before the closure of the proceedings, otherwise the court will exclude such documents (art. 740 Ger.W./CJ). Parties may also produce written pleadings (if required, with extension of time granted pursuant to art. 769, para. 2 Ger.W./CJ), but the court may pronounce judgment even if no written pleadings have been produced (art. 735 § 3 Ger.W./CJ).

The rules applying to short proceedings do not detract from the rules regarding non-appearance of the parties (art. 735 § 5 Ger.W./CJ). *See* section 7.3.2e1.

See further M. Storme, *De procedure van korte debatten: één zwaluw kan de lente maken..., Het vernieuwd gerechtelijk recht*, pp. 95-105.

We will now discuss the normal proceedings (*lange debatten*). Parties or their *advocaten* must appear at the initial hearing before the court (art. 728 Ger.W./CJ). *Advocaten* are instead allowed (only in the normal proceedings) to make a statement that they are acting in this case (art. 729 Ger.W./CJ). Pursuant to art. 735 § 4 Ger.W./CJ the case is referred to the (special) list (*rol/rôle*).

Parties must communicate to each other all documents (on evidence) which they wish to use, before they can actually use those documents (arts. 736-740 Ger.W./CJ). In practice such communication is provided amicably without formalities (art. 737 Ger.W./CJ). The plaintiff must communicate the documents within eight days after the first hearing. The defendant must communicate his documents along with his defence within a month after the plaintiff has communicated his documents (art. 736 Ger.W./CJ). All documents which have not been communicated at the latest when written pleadings were produced are excluded by the court from the proceedings (art. 740 Ger.W./CJ). If a party discovers a relevant new document before the day of the trial (*rechtsdag/date de l'audience*), he may request an extension of the period for written pleadings (art. 748 § 2 Ger.W./CJ). A distinction must be made between the above communication of documents and the submission of documents by order of the court (*see* arts. 877-882 Ger.W./CJ).

In the normal proceedings the parties in principle must produce written pleadings (art. 741 Ger.W./CJ). This implies that parties send their original pleadings, with their personal particulars and the court list number (*rolnummer /numéro au rôle*), to the court registry (or deposit them with the court registry) and at the same time send a copy to the opposing party or his *advocaat* (arts. 742-746 Ger.W./CJ). The defendant must produce a defence within one month after the plaintiff has communicated his documents. The plaintiff has one month to reply. The defendant then has fifteen days for his rejoinder (*see also* 868 Ger.W./CJ with reference to the 'concentration of defence' which the court can order). Parties can agree the time-limits between them (art. 747 § 1 Ger.W./CJ).

If one of the parties does not comply with the time-limits for the written pleadings as either prescribed by law or agreed between the parties, the opposing party may informally request the court to determine the periods for written pleadings (art. 747 § 2, para. 1 Ger.W./CJ) (strictly speaking this may also be requested before the statutory time-limit expires). The court is not allowed to determine periods of its own motion. If the court honours the request, it determines the time-limits and the date of the trial day (*rechtsdag/ date de l'audience*) (art. 747 § 2, para. 5 Ger.W./CJ). Written pleadings submitted outside these time-limits are excluded officially from the proceedings (art. 747 § 2, para. 6 Ger.W./CJ; art. 748 § 1 and § 2, para. 1 Ger.W./CJ allows three exceptions). On the day of the trial (*rechtsdag/date de l'audience*) either party may ask for an adversarial judgment, even if the opposing party does not appear (art. 747 § 2, para. 6 Ger.W./CJ). Article 747 § 2 Ger.W./CJ may thus provide a solution in case of delay of the proceedings.

When determining the time-limits the court, as stated before, also appoints a date for the day of the trial (*rechtsdag/date de l'audience*). The principle still remains the joint request by the parties to appoint a date for the trial (art. 750 §1, para. 1 Ger.W./CJ). In principle, all pleadings which have been deposited after the request of the parties has been made, are excluded officially from the proceedings (art. 748 §1 Ger.W./CJ). It may occur that a party refuses to cooperate in appointing a date for the day of the trial (*rechtsdag/date de l'audience*). In that case the recently introduced art. 750 § 2 Ger.W./CJ can provide a solution. Pursuant to this provision, a unilateral request to appoint a date for the day of the trial (*rechtsdag/date de l'audience*) may be made also. This can only be done, however, if all parties have deposited pleadings and the (pleadings) time-limit of art. 747 § 1, para. 3 Ger.W./CJ has expired (thus art. 750 § 2, para. 1 Ger.W./CJ). Pleadings deposited after the day of the trial has been determined pursuant to art. 750 § 2 Ger.W./CJ are in principle excluded from the proceedings (*see* art. 748 § 1, para. 1 Ger.W./CJ).

Pursuant to art. 751 Ger.W./CJ either party may request an adversarial judgment if the opposing party has not appeared at the initial or any later hearing before the court or has not produced written pleadings within the statutory (but not imperative) time-limits. The opposing party must be summoned and the summons must state that at the hearing referred to in the summons, an adversarial judgment will be requested. The opposing party may still be allowed to produce written pleadings within a certain period. If art. 747 Ger.W./CJ is applied systematically, art. 751 Ger.W./CJ will be superfluous (thus conclude J. Laenens and K. Broeckx, *Het gerechtelijk recht in een stroomversnelling*, RW 1993, p. 923).

In principle there are oral pleadings on the day of the trial. After the oral pleadings, the proceedings are closed (arts. 757 and 769 Ger.W./CJ). At the parties' request or of the court's own motion the proceedings may, however, be reopened (arts. 772-774 Ger.W./CJ).

See art. 755 Ger.W./CJ for the written consideration of cases at the parties' request.

See further G. de Leval, *De wet van 3 augustus 1992 tot wijziging van het Gerechtelijk Wetboek: het in staat stellen der zaken*, *Het vernieuwd gerechtelijk recht*, pp. 107-135.

d. Judgment

After the proceedings the judges deliberate. Judgment must be pronounced within one month after the closing of the proceedings. If the court postpones its deliberations for more than three months, it notifies the first President of the *hof van appel/cour d'appel* or of the *arbeidshof/cour du travail* (art. 770 Ger.W./CJ).

The *vrederechter/juge de paix* and the *rechtbanken/tribunaux* pronounce a *vonnis/jugement*. The *hoven/cours* (including the *Hof van Cassatie/Cour de Cassation*) pronounce *arresten/arrêts*.

We distinguish adversarial judgments and judgments in default (*see* arts. 802-806 Ger.W./CJ), which are discussed in section 7.4.2 (e)(1). A distinction is also made between final judgments (which conclude the jurisdiction of the court in respect of a certain issue, subject to any appeal) and interim judgments (judgments whereby the court makes an order for a provisional measure or for a measure of inquiry) (art. 19 Ger.W./CJ). Partial judgments are partly final, partly interim judgments. There are also decisions or measures of an internal nature, such as the decision whereby the date for the day of the trial is determined (*see* arts. 747 § 2 and 1046 Ger.W./CJ).

See for the provisional enforceability of judgments arts. 1397-1402 Ger.W./CJ (section 7.8.4) and for the award of costs arts. 1017-1024 Ger.W./CJ (*see also* section 7.9.3).

Every judgment must, if it is to avoid being nullified, apart from personal particulars, contain the reasons for the decision and a part in which the actual decision is set out (*see* the enumeration in art. 780 Ger.W./CJ). In addition, every judgment must in principle be pronounced in public (*see* section 7.2.3). Every final judgment has the authority of *res iudicata* from the moment when it is pronounced. The authority of *res iudicata* continues for as long as the decision has not been quashed (arts. 23-28 Ger.W./CJ).

A defective judgment can only be attacked by any of the legal means of recourse; a judgment cannot be automatically void (art. 20 Ger.W./CJ; *see* section 7.6).

Pursuant to arts. 793-801 Ger.W./CJ an obscure or ambiguous decision may be explained and clerical or computing errors in decisions may be corrected.

e. Special aspects of procedure

1. Non-appearance

If either party fails to appear at the first hearing before the court, that party may be declared to be in default of appearance and a default judgment may be requested (art. 802 Ger.W./CJ). If no default has been entered against that party, then at the request of the opposing party the party is notified by judicial letter to appear at the hearing to which the case has been adjourned or on a later appointed date (art. 803 Ger.W./CJ).

If either party fails to appear on a later appointed date or the date to which the case has been adjourned, a default judgment may be requested against the relevant party, even if that party had entered an appearance at the introductory session (art. 804, para. 1 Ger.W./CJ). If the relevant party appeared at the first hearing (pursuant to art. 728 or 729 Ger.W./CJ) and has submitted written pleadings prior to the later appointed hearing or the hearing to which the case has been adjourned, then the proceedings are adversarial (art. 804, para. 2 Ger.W./CJ).

It is possible to remedy a default of appearance (*see* art. 805 Ger.W./CJ).

A default judgment which is not served within one year loses its validity (art. 806 Ger.W./CJ).

Sometimes an adversarial judgment may be requested in case of non-appearance. *See* art. 753 in conjunction with art. 31 Ger.W./CJ (relating to more parties to the proceedings). *See also* arts. 747, 748 and 751 Ger.W./CJ (on which *see* section 7.4.2c *in fine*).

2. Third parties in the action

Rules for third party proceedings (compulsory intervention), joinder and intervention (voluntary intervention) are laid down in arts. 13 *in fine*, 15, 16, 811-814 Ger.W./CJ. *See also* arts. 563-566 and art. 634 Ger.W./CJ.

3. *Amendment of claim*

In an interim claim the plaintiff may amend his claim and file new claims, if the new written pleadings in adversarial proceedings are based upon a fact or deed alleged in the writ, even if the legal description thereof is different (art. 13 in conjunction with arts. 807-809 Ger.W./CJ).

4. *Counterclaim*

The defendant may file a counterclaim against the plaintiff (*see* art. 14 in conjunction with arts. 807-810 Ger.W./CJ).

5. *Production of evidence*

Rules regarding evidence have been included in arts. 870-1016*bis* Ger.W./CJ and arts. 1315-1369 BW/CC. In principle all parties are obliged to produce evidence of the facts they allege (art. 870 Ger.W./CJ and art. 1315 BW/CC). It must be noted that only the facts in dispute need to be proved. Facts of general knowledge do not need to be proved. Applicable foreign law does not constitute a fact for which, under the rules of the division of the burden of proof, such burden can come to lie on one of the parties, with all (evidentiary) risks this entails (*see* F. Rigaux, *Droit International Privé*, Tome I, Théorie Générale, second amended edition, Brussels 1987, no. 441) (*see further* section 7.2.5).

The court may of its own motion or at the request of a party order a measure of inquiry (*see* for instance arts. 916, 992 and 1007) (*see* section 7.2.5 *in fine*). In addition, the court may compel the parties to submit any evidence which they have at their disposal (art. 871 Ger.W./CJ).

The law does not give an exhaustive list of the ways in which evidence may be adduced. Although in Belgium the oath is still valid as a way of adducing evidence, it is no longer used.

See further R. Mougenot, *La preuve*, Brussels 1990 and N. Verheyden-Jeanmart, *Le droit de la preuve*, Brussels 1991.

6. *Settlement*

In certain cases the parties can try to reach a judicial settlement; sometimes an attempt at this is even obligatory (arts. 731-734 Ger.W./CJ). Such obligation exists in disputes before the *arbeidsrechtbank/tribunal du travail* covered by art. 578 Ger.W./CJ (art. 734 Ger.W./CJ).

Leaving aside the cases for which this is obligatory, an attempt to reach a judicial settlement at the request of one party or both parties is only possible if the case has not yet been introduced, the parties are capable of entering into a compromise and the case is capable of such solution (art. 731 Ger.W./CJ). If a settlement is reached, its wording is recorded in an official memorandum which can be issued with an enforcement form (art. 733 Ger.W./CJ).

It must be noted that a hearing whereby the parties appear in person in order to attempt to reach a settlement cannot be ordered. It is possible for the parties to request the court to enter *judgment* on the basis of an agreement reached by the parties, which agreement terminates the dispute between the parties (*see* art. 1043, para. 1 Ger.W./CJ).

Outside the court the parties can negotiate a settlement, unless matters of public policy are concerned. Pursuant to art. 730 Ger.W./CJ the case may be removed from the court's list (*rol/rôle*) with the consent of the parties. Since parties sometimes fail to request removal of the case, cases are in time removed from the court's list (*rol/rôle*) of the court's own motion in order to relieve the burden of the court's administrative offices (art. 730, § 2(a) Ger.W./CJ).

7.4.3. THE ADVERSARIAL PETITION

There is now a separate title with general rules for the proceedings commenced by adversarial petition, i.e. Title V*bis*, Part IV, Book II (art. 1034*bis*-1034*sexies*) Ger.W./CJ. These basic rules are intended to remove the past diversity of petition procedures (*Ontwerp*, p. 24).

A case is commenced by an adversarial petition if the law deviates from the general rule of commencement by writ and the claim is commenced by a petition of which the opposing party is notified (art. 1034*bis* Ger.W./CJ).

Article 700 Ger.W./CJ determines that cases are commenced by writ, subject to the *special* rules concerning the judicial proceedings commenced by petition. From this article it must be deduced that the adversarial petition is not, like the writ, recognised as a valid way to commence proceedings for all main claims (*see* on this J. Laenens and K. Broeckx, *Het gerechtelijk recht in een stroomversnelling*, RW 1993, p. 913) (*see also* art. 46 § 2, para. 1 Ger.W./CJ). The adversarial petition may therefore only be used when the law allows or prescribes this in a particular case (S. Raes, *Het verzoekschrift op tegenspraak*, *Het vernieuwd gerechtelijk recht*, pp. 82-83).

The rules concerning the proceedings commenced by adversarial petition are explicitly declared applicable in art. 1253*ter,* para. 3 Ger.W./CJ, which deals with claims of spouses concerning their matrimonial rights and duties and their property regime. This procedure can also be used pursuant to art. 1320 Ger.W./CJ (in respect of maintenance), 1337*bis* Ger.W./CJ (in respect of obtaining payment facilities for consumer credit), 1344*bis* Ger.W./CJ (in respect of hiring goods) and 1371*bis* Ger.W./CJ (in respect of a right of way).

Article 704, para. 2 Ger.W./CJ explicitly excludes the application of the general rules for adversarial petitions in respect of a number of cases commenced by petition before the *arbeidsrechtbank/tribunal du travail*. From art. 1034*bis* Ger.W./CJ it can be deduced that the rules only apply to main claims (art. 12 Ger.W./CJ) and not to interim claims (arts. 13-16 Ger.W./CJ). Consequently the general rules do not apply to a request for intervention (art. 813 Ger.W./CJ), a request for appeal (art. 1056 *sub* 2 Ger.W./CJ), a request for cassation (art. 1079 Ger.W./CJ) and a request from the respondent for a declaration of provisional enforceability on appeal (art. 1401 Ger.W./CJ) (*see* S. Raes, *Het verzoekschrift op tegenspraak, Het vernieuwd gerechtelijk recht*, pp. 85-87). The rules also do not apply to informal requests for decisions or measures of an internal nature (*Verslag*, p. 67), for instance, the request to determine the periods for written pleadings (art. 747 § 2 and 748 § 2 Ger.W./CJ) and the request for the reopening of proceedings (*see* art. 773 Ger.W./CJ and also art. 1046 Ger.W./CJ). *See* section 7.5.1 for the relationship to the *ex parte* petition.

The petition must satisfy the formalities of art. 1034*ter* Ger.W./CJ. The petition must be accompanied by a certificate of the domicile of persons to be notified (art. 1034*quater* in conjunction with art. 1034*ter sub* 3 Ger.W./CJ). The petition must be filed with the court offices (art. 1034*quinquies* Ger.W./CJ). The court officer notifies the parties by judicial letter to appear at a hearing determined by the court (if necessary, duties due in connection with the registration of the case must be paid prior to the notification). The notification is accompanied by a copy of the petition (art. 1034*sexies* Ger.W./CJ).

In case of a conflict between the general rules of art. 1034*bis*-1034*sexies* and specific rules, the latter take precedence (art. 1034*bis* Ger.W./CJ).

The rules of the adversarial petition only provide for the commencement of proceedings but not for the type of procedure. Subject to some exceptions, cases commenced by an adversarial petition proceed in accordance with the ordinary rules of the procedure (commenced by writ) (*see* e.g. arts. 1322 and 1261 Ger.W./CJ; *see* section 7.3.2c-e). Thus, the case must be registered on the court's list (art. 716 Ger.W./CJ; *see also* arts. 1034*sexies* and 1344*bis* para. 4 Ger.W./CJ).

7.5. Basic Procedure for Voluntary Jurisdiction at First Instance

7.5.1. INTRODUCTION

This section deals with the procedure for the *ex parte* petition. Without prejudice to statutory exceptions, arts. 1025-1034 Ger.W./CJ apply. The rules concerning the *ex parte* petition may only be used in cases explicitly provided for by law (this applies not only to voluntary, but also to contentious jurisdiction) and in those cases in which adversarial proceedings are impossible because of the absence of an opposing party (*see* e.g. arts. 585, 594, 1240 and 1288*bis* para 3 Ger.W./CJ).

The law may (explicitly) provide that a case must be commenced by petition, but may have failed to state whether the *ex parte* procedure or the adversarial procedure must be followed. In that case the type of procedure will have to be determined on the basis of the subject of the claim and the nature of the procedure to be followed. The main difference between the two procedures lies in the notice to any opposing parties. In the *ex parte* petition procedure any opposing party will not be notified in order to be heard by the court before a decision is made; in the adversarial petition procedure, however, this *is* done (arts. 1025 and 1034*bis* Ger.W./CJ; *see further* sections 7.5.2. and 7.4.3 respectively). Thus it is assumed that a claim commenced by petition to the President of the court in cases of extreme urgency proceeds in accordance with the rules applicable to the *ex parte* petition (*see* section 7.7.2); the extreme urgency justifies a breach of the right to hear the opposing party (*see* S. Raes, *Het verzoekschrift op tegenspraak*, *Het vernieuwd gerechtelijk recht*, p. 90 and A. Fettweis, *Manuel de Procédure Civile*, p. 331 ff.).

7.5.2. *EX PARTE* PETITION

To be valid, the *ex parte* petition must satisfy certain formal requirements. Thus, the petition must be signed by an *advocaat*; subject to exceptions, only an *advocaat* may file an *ex parte* petition (art. 1026 in conjunction with art. 1027, para. 1 *in fine* Ger.W./CJ).

The petition must be sent to the court which is due to decide the case and it must subsequently be deposited with the registry (the *advocaat* may also send it by letter to the registry). The petition is then recorded in the register of petitions and added to the litigation file (art. 1027 Ger.W./CJ).

The court examines the claim and may therefore notify the petitioner and any intervening parties (third parties may intervene pursuant to arts. 811-814 Ger.W./CJ) by judicial letter to appear before the court in chambers (art. 1028 Ger.W./CJ).

The judgment, a decision made in chambers, is provisionally enforceable by operation of law, unless the court decides otherwise (art. 1029 Ger.W./CJ).

Within three days after the decision the clerk of the court notifies the petitioner and the intervening parties of the decision by judicial letter. *Advocaten* receive a copy (art. 1030 Ger.W./CJ).

The petitioner and the intervening parties may lodge an appeal within one month after notification of the decision. The procedure on appeal continues *ex parte*, at least as long as there are no third parties intervening (art. 1031 Ger.W./CJ). In case of a change of circumstances, an amendment or withdrawal of the decision may be requested from the court which made the decision, without prejudice to any rights obtained by third parties (art. 1032 Ger.W./CJ). Aggrieved third parties may raise objections by means of third party opposition (arts. 1033 and 1034 Ger.W./CJ in conjunction with arts. 1122-1131 Ger.W./CJ).

7.6. Means of Recourse

7.6.1. INTRODUCTION

In Belgian law there are ordinary and extraordinary means of recourse (art. 21 Ger.W./CJ). Ordinary means of recourse suspend the enforcement of a judgment, subject to orders for provisional enforcement. Extraordinary means of recourse do not suspend enforcement (arts. 21, 1397, 1118 and 1137 Ger.W./CJ).

Ordinary means of recourse are the application to set aside a default judgment (arts. 1047-1049 Ger.W./CJ) and appeal (arts. 1050-1072 Ger.W./CJ). Extraordinary means of recourse, which usually can only be invoked after the ordinary means have been exhausted, are cassation (arts. 1073-1121 Ger.W./CJ), third-party opposition (arts. 1122-1131 Ger.W./CJ), revocation of *res iudicata* (arts. 1132-1139 Ger.W./CJ) and redress against the court (arts. 1140-1147 Ger.W./CJ).

The above means of recourse can be used in all cases commenced by writ or adversarial petition, regardless whether it involves contentious or voluntary jurisdiction (*see* section 7.5.2 for means of recourse against decisions on an *ex parte* request).

There are five general rules relating to means of recourse. There is no recourse against a judgment whereby the court confirms a settlement between the parties (art. 1043 Ger.W./CJ). Parties may (explicitly or implicitly) relinquish means of recourse which could have been used; if so, they acquiesce in the judgment (arts. 1044 and 1045 Ger.W./CJ). An application to set aside a default judgment or an appeal cannot be lodged against decisions or measures of an internal nature, such as allowing a delay in the written pleadings and the appointing of the trial day, or against a decision whereby the personal appearance of the parties is ordered (art. 1046 Ger.W./CJ).

Unless provided otherwise in arts. 1042-1147 Ger.W./CJ, the procedural rules at first instance apply to the means of recourse (art. 1042 Ger.W./CJ).

In principle the time-limit for lodging an application to set aside a default judgment, appeal or cassation begins to run when the judgment is served. In respect of foreign parties the time-limit begins to run when a copy of the judgment is put in the post or alternatively has been handed to the public prosecutor (*procureur des Konings/procureur du Roi*) (art. 57 Ger.W./CJ), unless service has been effected in accordance with a convention.

Below we shall only consider in detail the application to set aside a default judgment, appeal and cassation; the other means of recourse are only set out briefly. The rectification and interpretation of judicial decisions are discussed in section 7.4.2d *in fine*.

7.6.2. THE APPLICATION TO SET ASIDE A JUDGMENT IN DEFAULT

In principle the party who did not enter an appearance may apply to have any default judgment (both final and interim judgments) set aside, irrespective of the amount of the claim (art. 1047, para. 1 Ger.W./CJ). The case is then considered afresh by the court which entered the judgment in default (art. 1047, para. 2 Ger.W./CJ).

The time-limit for the application is in principle one month, which begins to run from when the judgment is served or, in exceptional cases, from the moment when the judgment is sent to the parties by the clerk of the court (art. 1048, para. 1 in conjunction with art. 792 Ger.W./CJ). In respect of foreign parties the time-limit is extended in accordance with art. 55 Ger.W./CJ (art. 1048, para. 1 Ger.W./CJ).

The application to set aside is served on the defendant in opposition by means of a bailiff's summons. Parties may also appear voluntarily. The memorandum supporting the application must contain the grounds of the plaintiff in opposition (art. 1047, paras. 2 and 3 Ger.W./CJ).

If the plaintiff in opposition fails to appear a second time, an application to set aside the second judgment in default is not admissible (art. 1049 Ger.W./CJ).

7.6.3. APPEAL

In principle appeal lies against any (final or interim) judgment. It may even be lodged against default judgments (art. 616 and art. 1050, para. 1 Ger.W./CJ). Appeal against decisions concerning the court's jurisdiction may only be lodged at the same time as an appeal against the final judgment (arts. 621, 1050, para. 2 and 1055 Ger.W./CJ).

Judgments by the *rechtbank van eerste aanleg/tribunal de première instance* and the *rechtbank van koophandel/tribunal de commerce* cannot be appealed, unless the amount of the claim exceeds BF 75,000. For the *vrederechter/juge de paix* an appeal limit of BF 50,000 applies (art. 617, para. 1 Ger.W./CJ). In the aforementioned amendment of the *Gerechtelijk Wetboek/Code Judiciaire* these appeal limits, as well as the limits of the purpose of jurisdiction, have been raised (*see* sections 7.1.2 and 7.3.2d). The amount of the claim is determined pursuant to arts. 618 and 619 Ger.W./CJ. For the *arbeidsrechtbank/tribunal du travail* there are no appeal limits.

The time-limit for appeal is in principle one month, starting from the service of the judgment in dispute (art. 1051 Ger.W./CJ).

Appeal (*principaal appel/appel principal*) is in principle lodged by bailiff's summons or petition (*see* art. 1056 Ger.W./CJ) (*see* section 7.4.3 about the petition). Compliance with art. 1056 Ger.W./CJ is not prescribed on pain of nullity. The respondent (*geïntimeerde/intimé*) may at any stage of the proceedings lodge a cross-appeal (*incidenteel appel/appel incident*), in written pleadings (which is the usual way) or by bailiff's summons (art. 1054 in conjunction with art. 809 Ger.W./CJ).

To be valid, the notice of appeal must, apart from the personal particulars, name the judgment against which the appeal is lodged. It must also explain the grievances against that judgment, unless appeal is lodged by written pleadings (art. 1057 *sub* 4 resp. 7 Ger.W./CJ). No detailed explanation is required, but the grievances must be formulated so as to enable the respondent to prepare his defence and to enable the judge to assess the scope of the grievances, in order that proceedings may be started as soon as possible, at the initial hearing or at a future hearing. The appellant may present new grievances at a later stage in the proceedings (*see* J. van Compernolle, *Het hoger beroep, Het vernieuwd gerechtelijk recht*, pp. 167-168 and J. Laenens and K. Broeckx, *Het gerechtelijk recht in een stroomversnelling*, RW 1993, p. 928).

The appeal has a devolutive effect (*see* arts. 1068-1072 Ger.W./CJ): the appeal judge considers the case in its entirety. Yet, in principle, the case is only considered on appeal if grievances have been filed against the judgment in dispute (A. Fettweis, *Manuel de procédure civile*, p. 531).

On appeal the case will also have to be registered on the court's list, before the date on which parties are due to enter an appearance on the basis of the notice of appeal, because otherwise the notice has no effect (art. 1059 in conjunction with art. 716 Ger.W./CJ).

On appeal the parties must appear at the initial hearing within fifteen days after the notice of appeal has been issued pursuant to art. 1056 Ger.W./CJ (art. 1062, para. 1 Ger.W./CJ). This time-limit may be extended in case of foreign parties (art. 1062, para. 3 in conjunction with art. 55 Ger.W./CJ). Pursuant to art. 729 Ger.W./CJ the *advocaten* of the parties in cases where short proceedings are not possible may by mutual agreement declare in writing beforehand that they will act in the matter; in that case there is no obligation to appear at the hearing (art. 1042 Ger.W./CJ).

Like the procedure at first instance, the case may be considered either in short proceedings or in normal proceedings.

Cases requiring only short proceedings are considered and pleaded at the initial hearing or a future hearing which must take place within at most three months (art. 1066, para. 1 Ger.W./CJ). Appellant and respondent may request consideration upon short proceedings (art. 1042 in conjunction with art. 735 § 1 *in fine* Ger.W./CJ). In a number of cases the matter must be considered upon short proceedings (e.g. in case of an appeal against a decision in summary proceedings). In fact this involves cases which are all urgent (art. 1066, para. 2 *sub* 1-6 Ger.W./CJ). The parties may nevertheless agree that the normal proceedings are followed even then (*see further* S. Lust, *De 'korte weg-procedure' in hoger beroep*, Jura Falconis 1993/1994, pp. 15-63).

If a case is not considered upon short proceedings, it is referred to the court's list (*rol/rôle*) (art. 1043 in conjunction with art. 735 § 4 Ger.W./CJ). In that case the parties must produce written pleadings. The respondent must file his pleading within a month after the case has been introduced. The appellant has one month to reply to the respondent; then the respondent must file his subsequent pleading within fifteen days (art. 1064 Ger.W./CJ). A trial day will then be appointed for oral pleadings of the case (art. 1065 Ger.W./CJ). Subsequently judgment is passed (art. 22 Ger.W./CJ).

Remarkable is the possible order for compensation in case of a provocative or reckless appeal on the merits, if the claim in such an appeal is rejected. Moreover, the court may *ex officio* impose a fine for a provocative or reckless appeal on the merits of a minimum of BF 5,000 and a maximum of BF 100,000 (art. 1072*bis* Ger.W./CJ) (*see* J. van Compernolle, *Het hoger beroep*, *Het vernieuwd gerechtelijk recht*, pp. 174-177 and J. Laenens and K. Broeckx, *Het gerechtelijk recht in een stroomversnelling*, RW 1993, pp. 930-931).

Otherwise the rules applying to proceedings at first instance also apply on appeal (art. 1042 Ger.W./CJ). It is explicitly stated that the rules on default and setting aside judgments apply on appeal. *See* sections 7.3.2 and 7.6.2.

See further A. Kohl, *L'appel en droit judiciaire privé*, Brussels 1990.

7.6.4. CASSATION

The *Hof van Cassatie/Cour de Cassation* decides on decisions made at final instance. Cassation is possible on the grounds of breach of the law, or of irregularity in substantive requirements or formalities prescribed on pain of nullity (art. 608 Ger.W./CJ). The *Hof van Cassatie/Cour de Cassation* does not review the facts (art. 147 Gr.w). Breach of applicable foreign law can be regarded as a ground for cassation pursuant to art. 608 Ger.W./CJ (*see* the discussion of relevant case law by F. Rigaux, *Droit International Privé*, Tome I, Théorie Générale, second amended edition, Brussels 1987, nos. 442-451) (*see further* section 7.2.5).

The time-limit for appeal in cassation is three months from service of the judgment in dispute or from the sending of a copy of the judgment, subject to any extensions, e.g. in case of foreign parties (arts. 1073 and 1074 in conjunction with art. 792 Ger.W./CJ). Cassation against interim judgments only lies from the final judgments (art. 1077 Ger.W./CJ).

The cassation proceedings are commenced by a petition which must be served upon the respondent and must be filed with the registry of the *Hof van Cassatie/Cour de Cassation* within fifteen days (art. 1079 Ger.W./CJ) (*see, however,* section 7.4.3).

To be valid, the petition must contain the grounds and the conclusion of the appellant, stating the legal provisions and rules of procedure which allegedly have been violated. The *Hof van Cassatie/Cour de Cassation* can only consider the parts of the judgment which are mentioned in the petition (art. 1095 Ger.W./CJ). The petition must be signed by an *advocaat* of the *Hof van Cassatie/Cour de Cassation* (art. 1080 Ger.W./CJ).

Once the petition is filed the registrar registers the case on the court's list (*rol/rôle*) (art. 1085 Ger.W./CJ). Within three months from the service of the petition the respondent must, on pain of default, put forward his arguments in a statement of defence, which must be served on the appellant and must be filed with the registry. The defence must be signed by an *advocaat* of the *Hof van Cassatie/Cour de Cassation* (arts. 1092 and 1093 Ger.W./CJ). In principle the appellant cannot reply to the statement of defence (*see also* art. 1094 Ger.W./CJ).

The President of the *Hof van Cassatie/Cour de Cassation* appoints a judge-reporter, who writes a draft judgment (art. 1104 Ger.W./CJ). An Advocate-General (*advocaat-generaal/avocat général*) then formulates an advisory opinion (art. 1105 Ger.W./CJ).

At a public hearing the judge-reporter reports; the parties are allowed to have their case pleaded orally by their *advocaten*, which right is seldom used in civil matters. Only the *openbaar ministerie/ministère public* (public prosecution) delivers its opinion orally (art. 1107 Ger.W./CJ) (*see* A. Fettweis, *Manuel de Procédure Civile*, p. 558).

We have now reached the deliberation stage of the judges. It is remarkable that the *openbaar ministerie/ministère public* in principle has the right to attend the deliberations (art. 1109 Ger.W./CJ). In a Belgian criminal case the European Court of Human Rights has decided that disallowing the parties' right to reply after the hearing of the *openbaar ministerie/ministère public* by the *Hof van Cassatie/Cour de Cassation*, considering the fact that the *openbaar ministerie/ministère public* participates in the deliberations of the Court in chambers, implies a breach of art. 6, para. 1 ECHRFF (ECHR 30 October 1991, Publ. ECHR, Series A, vol. 214 (1991)). The question remains whether the same applies in civil matters (*see also* J.M. Piret, *Het Parket van Cassatie*, RW 1994, pp. 490-494).

Whether or not the parties or their *advocaten* have entered an appearance, the judgments of the *Hof van Cassatie/Cour de Cassation* are always regarded as having been passed in adversarial proceedings (*see* art. 108 and 1113, para. 1 Ger.W./CJ and also art. 1113, para. 2 Ger.W./CJ).

If the *Hof van Cassatie/Cour de Cassation* quashes the judgment in dispute, it refers the case to a court of the same instance as the court which gave the original judgment. The case is commenced by writ in that court (art. 1110 Ger.W./CJ). The opinion of the *Hof van Cassatie/Cour de Cassation* does not bind the court. In case of a new appeal in cassation in the same case between the same parties, based on the same grounds, the *Hof van Cassatie/Cour de Cassation* must pronounce judgment with united chambers (art. 1119, para. 1 in conjunction with art. 131 Ger.W./CJ). This second judgment *is* binding on the court to which the case may be referred (art. 1120 Ger.W./CJ).

The Procurator-General (*Procureur-Generaal/Procureur-Général*) at the *Hof van Cassatie/Cour de Cassation* may of his own motion institute cassation in the interest of the law (art. 612 in conjunction with arts. 1089-1091 Ger.W./CJ).

7.6.5. OTHER MEANS OF RECOURSE

The third-party opposition

The extraordinary means of recourse of third-party opposition may be lodged by anyone who was not a party in the action or represented in it, against a decision which prejudices his rights (art. 1122 Ger.W./CJ). It must be lodged before the court which has made the judgment in dispute; the time-limit is three months from the service of the judgment in dispute upon the third party (arts. 1125 and 1129 Ger.W./CJ).

Revocation of *res iudicata*

The extraordinary means of recourse of revoking *res iudicata* may be lodged on the grounds mentioned in art. 1133 Ger.W./CJ against a judgment which has become *res iudicata* (arts. 1132 and 1136 Ger.W./CJ). A ground for revocation may be, for instance, withheld or false documents (art. 1133, para. 1, *sub* 2 and 4 Ger.W./CJ). The time-limit for applying for revocation is six months from the moment when the ground on which it is based was discovered (art. 1133 Ger.W./CJ).

Redress against the court

The extraordinary means of recourse of redress against the court may be lodged with the *Hof van Cassatie/Cour de Cassation* pursuant to art. 613 Ger.W./CJ, if one of the cases mentioned in art. 1140 Ger.W./CJ applies, e.g. if the court has perpetrated fraud in its judgment.

7.7. Special Procedures

7.7.1. INTRODUCTION

Apart from the basic procedure discussed in section 7.4.5, Belgian rules of civil procedure contain special rules for summary proceedings, small claims and sector proceedings. Especially worth mentioning are the summary proceedings in general (*kort geding/référé*), the small claims proceedings and the divorce proceedings.

7.7.2. SUMMARY PROCEDURES

The President of the *rechtbank van eerste aanleg/tribunal de première instance* may give a provisional judgment in summary proceedings (*kort geding/référé*) in cases which he deems urgent, except in those cases which by law are withdrawn from the judiciary (art. 584, para. 1 Ger.W./CJ). The Presidents of the *arbeidsrechtbank/tribunal du travail* and the *rechtbank van koophandel/tribunal de commerce* may give provisional judgments in summary proceedings (*kort geding/référé*), in cases which they deem urgent and which concern matters falling within their jurisdiction (art. 584, para. 2 Ger.W./CJ). Urgency is a requirement for jurisdiction (art. 9 Ger.W./CJ) and for the soundness of the claim (art 584, para. 1 Ger.W./CJ). The judge in *kort geding/référé* has relative jurisdiction if he would have had jurisdiction as a *bodemrechter/instance au fond* (judge dealing with the main proceedings) had the case been a *bodemzaak/principal* (trial on the main issue). However, claims in *kort geding/référé* may also be brought before the court of the place where a provision is urgently required or where the urgent problem occurs (*see* A. Fettweis, *Handboek voor gerechtelijk recht, II. Bevoegdheid*, pp. 330-331 and J. Laenens, *Overzicht van rechtspraak, De bevoegdheid* (1979-1992), TPR 1992, p. 1591).

The general rules of procedure apply, unless arts. 1035-1041 Ger.W./CJ provide otherwise. In principle the case is commenced by bailiff's summons before the judge in *kort geding/référé*. The summons period is at least two days (art. 1035 Ger.W./CJ and also arts. 55, 708, 1036 and 1037 Ger.W./CJ). The parties may also appear voluntarily (art. 706 Ger.W./CJ). If absolutely necessary, the case may be commenced by means of an *ex parte* petition (art. 584, para. 3 Ger.W./CJ in conjunction with arts. 1025-1034 Ger.W./CJ) (*see* section 7.5.1).

In general, litigation in *kort geding/référé* is by means of short proceedings (*see* J. Laenens and K. Broeckx, *Het gerechtelijk recht in een stroomversnelling*, RW 1993, p. 918). *See also* section 7.4.2, in which the procedure in short proceedings is explained.

The decision does not affect the main proceedings (art. 1039 Ger.W./CJ). The judge who decides on the main issue is not bound by the decision of the judge in *kort geding/référé*. It is possible, however, for the merits of the case to be considered in summary proceedings. The judge in *kort geding/référé* may examine the rights of the parties, on condition that he does not order any measures which might infringe these rights in a final and irrevocable manner (*Hof van Cassatie/Cour de Cassation* 9 September 1982, RW 1983-1984, pp. 1338-1340).

Unlike under the general rules of procedure, the decision in *kort geding/ référé* is always provisionally enforceable, which means that it can be enforced, notwithstanding the possibility of the application to set aside a default judgment and appeal.

The institution of means of recourse is in principle covered by the rules applying to ordinary proceedings. On appeal the case is considered in short proceedings, unless otherwise agreed by the parties (art. 1040, para. 2 in conjunction with 1066 *sub* 1 Ger.W./CJ).

See further P. Marchal, *Les référés*, Brussels 1992 and M. Storme and P. Taelman, *Het kort geding: ontwikkelingen en perspectieven* in *Procederen in nieuw België en komend Europa*, pp. 5-76, D. Lindemans, *Kort geding*, Antwerp 1985 and *De ontwikkeling van procedures 'zoals in kort geding'*, (eds. J. van Compernolle and M. Storme), Antwerp/Brussels 1994.

7.7.3. SMALL CLAIMS PROCEDURES

Here we will discuss the small claims proceedings.

Each claim falling within the jurisdiction of the *vrederechter/juge de paix* and involving a fixed debt of a sum of money not exceeding BF 75,000 may be lodged, considered and decided pursuant to the rules laid down by arts. 1338-1344 Ger.W./CJ. The limit of jurisdiction was raised when the *Gerechtelijk Wetboek/Code Judiciaire* was amended (*see* sections 7.1.2 and 7.3.2d). A further condition is that the claim must appear to be confirmed by a document issued by the debtor (domiciled or resident in Belgium) and that the petitioner (i.e. the creditor) has first reminded the debtor to pay, which reminder either has been served on the debtor by bailiff's summons or has been notified by registered letter (arts. 1338, 1339 and 1344 Ger.W./CJ). The period for payment is fifteen days from the date of service or posting of the letter (art. 1339 Ger.W./CJ). If no payment is made, the claim must within fifteen days after the expiry of this period be sent to the judge in *ex parte* petition in duplicate. The petition must be signed by an *advocaat* (art. 1340 Ger.W./CJ).

Within fifteen days after the lodging of the petition the *vrederechter/juge de paix* gives a decision in chambers. He may also grant suspension of payment (*see* art. 1342 Ger.W./CJ).

In case the petition is allowed either partly or completely, the decision by the *vrederechter/juge de paix* has the same effect as a judgment by default, which the debtor can apply to set aside. Contrary to art. 1047 Ger.W./CJ the application by the debtor to set aside may be lodged by adversarial petition. The parties are summoned by the court officer to appear at the session (art. 1343 § 3 Ger.W./CJ).

If the petition is rejected in the small claims proceedings, the claim may be brought in ordinary proceedings (art. 1343 § 4 Ger.W./CJ). In case of a partial rejection of the petition in the small claims proceedings the petitioner can neither apply to have the judgment set aside nor appeal. However, he may decide not to serve the decision given in the small claims proceedings but instead to bring the proceedings in the ordinary way (art. 1343 § 4, para. 2 Ger.W./CJ).

7.7.4. SECTOR PROCEDURES

The divorce procedure, which was drastically amended recently, is governed by arts. 1254 *et seq.* Ger.W./CJ. A distinction must be made between divorce based on certain facts, divorce by mutual consent, legal separation and the conversion of a legal separation into divorce (*see* arts. 1254-1310 and sections 7.4.3 and 7.5). There is also a provision for the separation of goods (arts. 1311-1318 Ger.W./CJ). *See further* J. Mellaerts, *Naar een hervorming van het echtscheidings-procesrecht*, Leuven 1991 and A.C. Oosterman-Meulenbeld, *Echtscheiden in de Euregio*, Echtscheidingsbulletin 1994, nos. 11 and 12, pp. 6-9.

Noteworthy are also maintenance proceedings pursuant to arts. 1320-1322 Ger.W./CJ (*see* sections 7.4.3 and 7.5.).

See for the special rules of procedure in relation to bankruptcy art. 574 *sub* 2 and 631 Ger.W./CJ with reference to the Commercial Code (*see* art. 437 *et seq.* K/C. comm.).

7.8. Protective Measures and Enforcement Measures

7.8.1. INTRODUCTION

Protective measures are: putting goods under seal (arts. 1148-1174 Ger.W./CJ), the making of an inventory (arts. 1175-1184 Ger.W./CJ) and protective attachment (arts. 1413-1493 Ger.W./CJ).

Enforcement measures provided for in the *Gerechtelijk Wetboek/Code Judiciaire* are *inter alia* the use of the police force (art. 139 Ger.W./CJ), the penalty (art. 1385*bis*-1385*nonies* Ger.W./CJ) and enforcement by attachment (arts. 1499-1675 Ger.W./CJ).

General provisions relating to protective and enforcement measures are laid down in arts. 1386-1412*bis* Ger.W./CJ.

See on the law of attachment in general G. de Leval, *Traité des saisies*, Liège 1988 and (by the same author) *La saisie immobilière*, J.-L. Ledoux, *Les saisies* - Chronique de jurisprudence 1983-1988, E. Dirix and K. Broeckx, *Beslag, Algemene Practische Rechtsverzameling*, Antwerp 1992 and E. Dirix and G. Van Haegenborgh, *Zekerheden en executierecht in 115 uitspraken*, Antwerp 1992.

7.8.2. PROTECTIVE MEASURES OTHER THAN ATTACHMENT

When a serious interest is involved, the *vrederechter/juge de paix* may be requested orally or by petition to seal objects belonging to the communal property of spouses, an estate or a joint tenancy (*see also* arts. 1148 to 1164 Ger.W./CJ). Article 1167 *et seq.* Ger.W./CJ provide for the unsealing of objects.

The making of an inventory is a protective measure intended to determine the extent of an estate or a joint tenancy (art. 1175 Ger.W./CJ). The persons mentioned in art. 1167 Ger.W./CJ who can prove that they have a serious interest in attachment may apply to the *vrederechter/juge de paix* for an authorisation to have an inventory made without prior sealing. In certain cases this authorisation is not required (*see* art. 1177 Ger.W./CJ).

7.8.3. PROTECTIVE MEASURES BY ATTACHMENT

Protective measures by attachment involve a temporary measure which restricts the power of disposal by the person whose property is attached.

Protective attachment is only allowed in urgent cases (art. 1413 Ger.W./CJ). In addition, the claim in respect of which attachment is made, must be certain, payable and fixed or capable of being estimated provisionally (art. 1415 Ger.W./CJ). Protective attachment may be made as security for a claim of periodic payments not yet due, when such payments are in jeopardy (art. 1415, para. 2 Ger.W./CJ).

Prior leave from the judge ordering attachment (at the *rechtbank van eerste aanleg/tribunal de première instance*) must be requested by an *ex parte* petition (arts. 1395 and 1413 in conjunction with arts. 1417 *et seq.* Ger.W./CJ). The judge ordering attachment delivers a decision within eight days pursuant to art. 1418 (*see also* section 7.5.2). If, however, the person who seeks attachment has already obtained a judgment against his debtor, this judgment is accepted as leave for making the protective attachment (art. 1414 Ger.W./CJ). The foregoing may be important pursuant to the provisions of arts. 1388 and 1495, para. 2 Ger.W./CJ.

The decision allowing or refusing protective attachment is open to appeal: article 1419 Ger.W./CJ declares that arts. 1031-1034 Ger.W./CJ apply accordingly (*see* section 7.5.2). The debtor can request withdrawal of the attachment (arts. 1419, paras. 2 and 3 and 1420 Ger.W./CJ). The debtor may obtain release of the property attached or prevent attachment by depositing a sufficient sum of money as security for the debt (*see* in connection with this *cantonnement* arts. 1403-1407 Ger.W./CJ).

The creditor on whose behalf protective attachment took place, may summon the debtor in order to obtain a decision on the claim itself (art. 1490 Ger.W./CJ). The law does not impose a time-limit upon the creditor for instituting the claim proceedings themselves. Protective attachment is in principle valid for three years (arts. 1425, 1436, 1458, 1459 and 1474 Ger.W./CJ). If a claim about the case itself is pending before the judge dealing with the main proceedings, this period is adjourned until the final decision acquires the force of *res iudicata* (art. 1493 Ger.W./CJ).

If the main claim is sustained, protective attachment is converted into enforcement by attachment (*see* art. 1491 Ger.W./CJ). A judgment whereby the main claim is rejected includes the decision to release the attachment (art. 1492 Ger.W./CJ).

The following kinds of protective attachment may be distinguished: attachment of movable property, attachment of immovable property, garnishment, distraint, attachment for reclamation, attachment of sea-going and inland navigation vessels and attachment of counterfeits (*see* art. 1422 *et seq*. Ger.W./CJ). In respect of attachment of vessels *see* the extensive account by W.P. Verstrepen, Lloyd's Maritime And Commercial Law Quarterly 1995, *Arrest and judicial sale of ships in Belgium*, pp. 131-154.

7.8.4. ENFORCEMENT MEASURES BY ATTACHMENT

Enforcement by attachment may only be made pursuant to an enforceable title on account of claims that are fixed, certain and payable (art. 1494 Ger.W./CJ and art. 1186 BW/CC). These terms are interpreted more narrowly than in case of protective attachment (A. Fettweis, *Manuel de Procédure Civile*, p. 633).

No judgment against the debtor can be enforced before its service upon the debtor (art. 1495, para 1 Ger.W./CJ) (*but see* art. 1495, para. 2 Ger.W./CJ).

For enforcement measures by attachment no prior leave is required, in contrast to protective attachment. However, the judge ordering attachment does have a task in solving problems during the enforcement (arts. 569 *sub* 5 and 1498 Ger.W./CJ).

Ordinary means of recourse suspend the enforcement, unless the judgment is (or has been) declared provisionally enforceable (art. 1398 *et seq.* Ger.W./CJ and A. Fettweis, *Manuel de Procédure Civile*, pp. 604-607) (but *see* art. 1388 Ger.W./CJ). Provisional enforcement takes place at the judgment creditor's risk (art. 1398, para. 2 Ger.W./CJ). In case of provisional enforcement the debtor can obtain release of the property that has been attached or he can prevent the attachment by depositing a sufficient sum of money as security for the debt (*see* in connection with this *cantonnement* art. 1404 Ger.W./CJ).

The following kinds of enforcement measures by attachment may be distinguished: enforcement by attachment of movable property, enforcement by attachment of fruits connected to branches or roots, enforcement by garnishment, enforcement by attachment of sea-going and inland navigation vessels and enforcement by attachment of immovable property (art. 1499 *et seq.* Ger.W./CJ). For enforcement by attachment of vessels the reader is referred to the account by W.P. Verstrepen mentioned before in section 7.8.3 *in fine*.

7.8.5. ENFORCEMENT MEASURES OTHER THAN ATTACHMENT

At the request of an individual the *openbaar ministerie/ministère public* may, at the enforcement of a judicial decision, order the use of the police force if necessary (art. 139, para. 1 Ger.W./CJ). It may also order the carrying out of work which is required for the enforcement of judgments, with an order to pay the usual price to the contractor of such work (art. 139, para. 2 Ger.W./CJ).

Article 1385*bis*-1385*nonies* provides rules for the penalty. On 1 January 1978 the Benelux treaty of 26 November 1973 on the uniform law concerning the penalty entered into force in Belgium. At the request of either party the opposing party may be ordered to pay a penalty in case of non-compliance with the main judgment. It is not possible to impose a penalty in case of a main judgment ordering the payment of a sum of money or in respect of claims concerning compliance with employment contracts (art. 1385*bis* Ger.W./CJ). The Benelux Court in Brussels ensures the uniform interpretation of the rules (art. 1 Convention on the institution and the rules of a Benelux Court).

As a result of the introduction of the *Gerechtelijk Wetboek/Code Judiciaire* imprisonment in civil proceedings in Belgium has been abolished. This used to be provided for in arts. 780-805 (old) Code of Civil Procedure.

See further J. van Compernolle, *L'astreinte*, Brussels 1992.

7.9. Duration and Costs

7.9.1. INTRODUCTION

In this section we shall discuss the duration and costs of civil litigation in Belgium. A lengthy procedure in particular can seriously harm the interests of litigants; it can undermine the credibility of the administration of justice (*Ontwerp*, p. 1). In order to deal with the backlog of the courts the *Gerechtelijk Wetboek/Code Judiciaire* was drastically amended recently (*see further* sections 7.1.2, 7.4.2c and 7.6.3).

7.9.2. DURATION

A case before the *vrederechter/juge de paix* usually lasts from six months to a year, before the *rechtbank van eerste aanleg/tribunal de première instance*, the *rechtbank van koophandel/tribunal de commerce* and the *arbeidsrechtbank/tribunal du travail* usually about two years and before the *hof van beroep/cour d'appel* it mostly takes three years before the judge passes sentence (*see also* P. Van den Neucker and J. de Vergnies in *Civil Procedures in EC Countries*, London 1991, p. 48).

It is said that these periods are often exceeded to enormous extents. The long duration of procedures may be caused by the enormous backlog of the courts due to an overload of cases on the one hand, and the rules of procedure that applied until recently which lent themselves to dilatory tactics, on the other hand (*see Ontwerp*, p. 1 and J. Hubin, *De recente hervormingen, Het vernieuwd gerechtelijk recht*, pp. 21-33).

It remains to be seen whether the recently introduced amendments will produce the desired effect (*see also* R. Van Camp, RW 1995, p. 667, who secretly hopes that the judicial reorganisation will benefit the procedural economy and nip dilatory tactics in the bud) (*see also* section 7.4.2c).

7.9.3. COSTS

In principle the losing party is ordered to pay the costs in every final judgment, even of the court's own motion. In interim judgments the decision on the costs must be delayed until the final judgment (art. 1017, para. 1 Ger.W./CJ). The court may set off the costs of both parties, provided each party lost part of the claim, or if it concerns spouses or certain relatives (art. 1017, para. 3 Ger.W./CJ). A party can always be ordered to pay useless or vexatious costs it has incurred (art. 1382 BW/CC). The provisions of art. 1017, Ger.W./CJ also apply on appeal. Article 1111 provides rules for the costs in cassation procedures.

In order for the costs to be taxed the parties must carefully specify the fees incurred in the litigation in their court documents (art. 1021, para. 1 Ger.W./CJ). If this taxation did not or only partly occur, it may still be ordered, at the request of either party, by the court which pronounced the judgment, if its judgment was not opposed (art. 1021, para. 2 Ger.W./CJ in conjunction with art. 750 *et seq*. Ger.W./CJ).

Article 1018 Ger.W./CJ provides a non-exhaustive enumeration of legal costs, for example (1) stamp fees, court fees and registration fees; (2) fees for judicial documents; (3) the costs of enforcement of a judgment; (4) costs relating to measures of inquiry; (5) travel expenses of magistrates and court officers (and in certain cases travel costs of parties) and the costs of documents drawn up exclusively for the litigation; and (6) the fees for (procedural) acts carried out by *advocaten*. Article 1022 Ger.W./CJ provides for payment for these (procedural) acts carried out by *advocaten*. This concerns the so-called fees in respect of the litigation (*rechtsplegingsvergoeding/ indemnité de procédure*) (*see* Royal Decree of 30 November 1970 to determine a tariff of recoverable costs as referred to in art. 1022 Ger.W./CJ). The fees in respect of the litigation are calculated as a fixed (and limited) tariff which depends *inter alia* on the court before which the case is pending, the nature and the value of the claim and the (procedural) acts performed by the *advocaat*. Apart from the said fees in respect of the litigation, the *advocaat*'s retainer is not part of the costs of the proceedings. The losing party cannot be ordered to pay this retainer. The order to award costs therefore covers only a fraction of the (actual) costs incurred by the winning party in connection with his *advocaat*.

Article 455-455*bis* Ger.W./CJ in conjunction with art. 664 *et seq*. Ger.W./CJ provide rules concerning legal aid and assistance to persons of limited means.

7.10. Proceedings Outside the Courts

7.10.1. INTRODUCTION

Arbitration and binding advice are two important forms of proceedings outside the courts in Belgium. The binding decision by a third party is mentioned in only a few rules of law (*see inter alia* arts. 1592, 1716 and 1854 BW). Arbitration is governed by Part IV *Gerechtelijk Wetboek/Code Judiciaire*. Belgium is the only country which has incorporated the European convention of Strasbourg on a uniform law concerning arbitration, Strasbourg 1966, into its Code (in Part IV just mentioned (arts. 1676-1723 Ger.W./CJ)). At the Belgian centre for the study and practice of domestic and international arbitration (CEPINA) there is at present a proposal for the reformation of Belgian arbitration law (CEPINA Newsletter, 1993, no. 7 (special edition) and G. Keugten, *Voor een hervorming van de Belgische Arbitragewet. Voorstellen van het CEPINA*, TPR 1994, pp. 789-806 and TvA 1994/2, pp. 67-77).

7.10.2. ARBITRATION

By agreement parties may submit to arbitrators existing and future disputes arising out of a certain legal relationship of which disputes they have freedom to dispose (on which they can reach a compromise) (art. 1676 Ger.W./CJ and arts. 2044-2058 BW). Certain employment cases, for instance, cannot be decided by arbitration (art. 1678, para 2 Ger.W./CJ).

The arbitration agreement must be included in a written document signed by the parties or in another document binding on the parties, in which they show their intention to submit a dispute to arbitration (art. 1677 Ger.W./CJ).

The judge before whom proceedings are commenced in respect of a dispute which is the subject of an arbitration agreement will decline jurisdiction, provided one of the parties invokes the (valid) arbitration agreement before submitting a defence (arts. 568, para. 3, 590, para. 2 and 1679 *sub* 1 Ger.W./CJ).

In reverse, the arbitral tribunal may also decide on its own jurisdiction and may therefore examine the validity of the arbitration agreement. Thereby the arbitration agreement must be separated from the main contract to which it relates (*see* art. 1697 Ger.W./CJ which also relates to the actions that may be instituted against the declaration of (lack of) jurisdiction of the arbitral tribunal).

The arbitral tribunal must not consist of an even number of arbitrators (art. 1681 *sub* 1 Ger.W./CJ). Rules concerning the composition, appointment and mandate of the arbitrators are provided in arts. 585 *sub* 1, 594 *sub* 1, 1678 and 1680-1689 Ger.W./CJ. It is possible to challenge a partial arbitrator pursuant to arts. 1690-1692 in conjunction with art. 828 *et seq.* Ger.W./CJ.

In principle the parties decide the rules governing the arbitral proceedings and the place of arbitration. If the parties have failed to make their intentions clear on these points, the arbitrators determine the rules and the place (art. 1693 *sub* 1 Ger.W./CJ). If the place of arbitration is located in Belgium, Belgian arbitration law applies (in this respect *see* art. 630, para. 2 Ger.W./CJ relating to the venue of the arbitral tribunal and art. 665 *sub* 1 Ger.W./CJ relating to legal aid to persons of limited means).

The principle of hearing both parties obviously also applies to arbitration (*see* art. 1694 *sub* 1 Ger.W./CJ). The statutory rules of evidence do not apply (art. 1696 Ger.W./CJ).

The arbitral tribunal decides in principle in accordance with the rules of law. However, pursuant to art. 1700 Ger.W./CJ the parties may agree otherwise.

Unless otherwise agreed, the award made by the arbitral tribunal is a final award against which no appeal lies (art. 1699 Ger.W./CJ). The award must be motivated (art. 1701 *sub* 6 Ger.W./CJ). Arbitrators may also order the provisional enforceability of their award (art. 1709 Ger.W./CJ), if necessary on the condition of providing security (art 1714 Ger.W./CJ). The award in principle has the authority of *res iudicata* (art. 1713 Ger.W./CJ).

The chairman of the arbitral tribunal sends a copy of the award to the parties, deposits the original with the court office of the *rechtbank van eerste aanleg/tribunal de première instance* and notifies the parties of this deposition (art. 1702 *sub* 2 Ger.W./CJ).

See arts. 1715 and 1716 Ger.W./CJ with respect to a settlement reached before an arbitral tribunal.

An arbitral award may be contested before the *rechtbank van eerste aanleg/tribunal de première instance* by filing an application to set aside. It may be set aside on limited grounds only (*see* art. 1704 Ger.W./CJ). In this connection art. 1717 *sub* 4 Ger.W./CJ requires special attention. This provision, which was introduced by the Act of 27 March 1985 (BS 13 April 1985), stipulates that an application for setting aside an arbitral award may only be filed if Belgian interests are at stake (*see also* section 2.10).

Compulsory enforcement of Belgian arbitral awards can only take place after an exequatur has been obtained from the president of the *rechtbank van eerste aanleg/tribunal de première instance*. The president refuses the application if the award or its enforcement is contrary to public policy or if the dispute was not capable of being decided by arbitration (art. 1710 Ger.W./

CJ). Foreign arbitral awards can also be enforced in Belgium (art. 1719 *et seq.* Ger.W./CJ). Together with more than 100 other countries Belgium is a party to the New York Convention of 1958 on the Recognition and Enforcement of Foreign Arbitral Awards (entry into force 16 November 1975), the most important convention in this area (*see* art. 1723 Ger.W./CJ for the enforcement of foreign arbitral awards outside conventions).

It must also be noted that Belgium is a party to the European Convention on International Commercial Arbitration of 1961 (already mentioned in section 7.1.2).

See further M. Storme and B. Demeulenaere, *International Commercial Arbitration in Belgium*, Deventer 1989, J. Linsmeau, *L'arbitrage volontaire en droit privé belge*, Brussels 1991 and G. Keugten, *Belgisch Centrum voor Studie en Praktijk van Nationale en Internationale Arbitrage (CEPINA)*, TvA 1993/2, pp. 59-69.

7.10.3. BINDING ADVICE

A binding decision by a third party may supplement or change a legal relationship between the parties and may resolve any dispute arising out of that legal relationship (*see* M. Storme, *De bindende derdenbeslissing of het bindend advies als middel ter voorkoming van gedingen; Een rechtsvergelijkend onderzoek op de grenzen van het contractenrecht en het procesrecht*, TPR 1984, p. 1250 ff. and, together with M. E. Storme, *De bindende derdenbeslissing naar Belgisch recht*, TPR 1985, p. 713 ff.).

See further A. Kassis, *Problèmes de base de l'arbitrage en droit comparé et en droit international*, Tome 1, Arbitrage juridictionnel et arbitrage contractuel, Paris 1987 and *De rechter buiten spel/Conflictregeling buiten de rechtbank om* (eds. B. Hubeau and S. Parmentier), Tegenspraak Cahier 10, Antwerp 1990.

8. Netherlands Civil Procedure*

Henk J. Snijders

8.1. Overview/Sources

8.1.1. INTRODUCTION

Netherlands 'Burgerlijk procesrecht' (Civil procedural law) is also called 'Burgerlijke rechtspleging' (*Civil dispensation of justice*) and 'Burgerlijke rechtsvordering' (*Civil action*). A drawback of the term 'Burgerlijke rechtspleging' is that it refers too strongly to the dispute in which parties participate and in which the court 'dispenses justice' or 'does justice' and too little to civil procedure apart from the dispute as it occurs in the preliminary stage and in the post-judgment stage. The term 'Burgerlijke rechtsvordering' refers too much to the days when civil proceedings were mostly commenced with a claim in a summons, whereas nowadays roughly half the number of civil procedures in the Netherlands commences with a request in a petition.

Most of Netherlands civil procedural law is governed by the *Wetboek van Burgerlijke Rechtsvordering* (Code of Civil Procedure; Rv) and the *Wet op de rechterlijke organisatie* (Judicial Organisation Act; RO). Both sets of rules were introduced in 1838 and have been repeatedly amended since then. The *Wetboek van Burgerlijke Rechtsvordering* is largely derived from the French *Code de procédure civile* which was in force in the Netherlands from 1811 until 1838. It must be said that the legislators increasingly provide rules for certain parts of civil procedure outside the *Wetboek van Burgerlijke Rechtsvordering* and the *Wet op de rechterlijke organisatie*, and even incorporate a lot of procedural rules into primarily substantive legislation such as the *Burgerlijk Wetboek* (Civil Code; BW). This fragmentation of civil procedural law is regrettable.

In the Netherlands there are two main kinds of civil procedure: the procedure commenced by writ and the procedure commenced by petition. The procedure commenced by writ is used for contentious proceedings. The pro-

---

* This contribution forms a summary of my *Inleiding Nederlands burgerlijk procesrecht*, third ed., Zwolle 1995. It is largely identical to my contribution 'Il diritto processuale civile olandese' in *La Giustizia civile nei paesi comunitari*, a cura di Elio Fazzalari, CEDAM, Padova 1994.

cedure commenced by petition is used for both voluntary (extrajudicial) and contentious proceedings.

Netherlands civil procedural law may, as a result of its historical but still ongoing relationship with French civil procedural law, be described as a Romanist system of procedural law, just like Belgian procedural law for example. Netherlands civil procedure has fewer links with German civil procedure. Differences from Anglo-Saxon systems of procedure are even greater.

As in other countries, no ideal system of judicial procedure has been produced in the Netherlands. This appears to be unattainable. Any such system is a compromise, since the desiderata are frequently at odds with each other. The quality of the treatment of cases in particular would be at the expense of simplicity, speed and affordability.

The major sources of Netherlands civil procedural law may briefly be described as Act and convention, case law and literature. Of the other sources the rules made by local courts are particularly of interest. Most courts in the Netherlands have their own tailor-made arrangements for the *rol*, which contain provisions on how to register cases, when a defence must be filed and so on. The procedures for obtaining leave for attachment of goods also vary depending on which President of which district court is addressed. The growing importance of these regulations of local courts also implies an influx of regional procedural law. The streamlining of local regulations should be possible at least. Unity of procedural law is too important to afford drastic regional differences. This applies *a fortiori* to a small country like the Netherlands. Fortunately, regional procedural law regarding urgent appeals in summary proceedings cases has meanwhile been uniformised by the *Gerechtshoven*.

Act and convention, respectively case law and literature will be discussed below in greater detail. It must be mentioned by way of introduction that various general doctrines have an important role to play in the practice of civil procedure. Thus the court frequently invokes the *goede procesorde* ('proper procedural order'). Often the court refers to one of the fundamental principles of civil procedure (*see* section 8.2). The court sometimes also refers to the 'procedural economy' (e.g. when refusing a request for an introduction of proceedings against a third party). The doctrine of 'abuse of procedural law' also forms part of the jurisprudence. It constitutes a variation of the general doctrine of abuse of the law, which has now been codified in art. 3:13 of the new *Burgerlijk Wetboek*. In particular, abuse of the right of execution is more than once punished by the court (e.g. in cases where the claimant's interest in the immediate execution of a judgment is disproportionately small compared with the defendant's interest to be spared execution for the time being). The doctrine 'no interest, no right of action' (*point d'intérêt, point d'action*) plays an important part in jurisprudence. It has now been codified in art. 3:303 BW. Whoever commences an action, either by writ or by petition, or initiates appeal proceedings without sufficient interest, is declared nonsuited for lack of interest. It stands to reason that the doctrine of '*res iudicata*' (art. 67(1) Rv) plays an important part in case law. Especially in view of the latter two doctrines, no place has been reserved in Netherlands civil procedure for the rule '*ne bis in idem*'. Doctrine also shows very limited support for the application of this rule. Finally, without a doubt, good faith plays an important part in procedural case law, albeit not often explicitly. Since the other general doctrines aforementioned apply, good faith in itself does not play an independent role in procedural law.

8.1.2. ACT AND CONVENTION

The importance of international conventions as a source of civil procedure is increasing quantitatively as well as qualitatively. Particularly important are the European Convention for the Protection of Human Rights and Fundamental Freedoms (ECHRFF (entry into force 31 August 1954)) with accompanying protocols, the International Covenant on Civil and Political Rights (CCPR (entry into force 11 March 1979)), the European Convention on Jurisdiction and the Enforcement of Judgments in Civil and Commercial Matters (Brussels Convention (entry into force 1 February 1973)) and the parallel convention to the Brussels Convention, the Lugano Convention (entry into force 1 January 1992). These conventions are particularly important since they are considered to be self-executing in the Netherlands. Dutch citizens can therefore invoke their application in the courts of law. Other conventions which apply in the Netherlands are the Hague Convention on the Service Abroad of Judicial and Extrajudicial Documents in Civil or Commercial Matters of 1965 (entry into force 2 January 1976), the Hague Convention on the Taking of Evidence Abroad in Civil or Commercial Matters of 1970 (entry into force 7 June 1981), the European Convention on Information on Foreign Law of 1968 (entry into force 2 March 1977), the European Agreement on the Transmission of Applications for Legal Aid of 1977 (entry into force 13 April 1992) and the Hague Convention on Civil Procedure of 1954 (entry into force 27 June 1959). For arbitration the New York Convention of 1958 must be mentioned (entry into force 23 July 1964).

Some of the articles contained in the Constitution are also relevant, for example art. 1 on equality and art. 17, which entitles every citizen to be heard by the courts. As there is no possibility to date in the Netherlands to test legislation created by government and parliament against the Constitution, the relevance of the Constitution for the practice of civil procedure is not particularly great, certainly not if one compares it with the significance of the ECHRFF and other regulations to be discussed below.

The *Wet op de rechterlijke organisatie* is of essential importance. It specifically provides for the absolute jurisdiction of the ordinary courts: *kantongerecht* (cantonal court), *arrondissementsrechtbank* (district court), *Gerechtshof* (Court of Appeal) and *Hoge Raad* (Supreme Court). The *kantongerecht* is the court of first instance for all civil cases involving an amount of up to Fl. 5,000 and also for tenancy and labour cases. The remaining cases are dealt with by the *arrondissementsrechtbank* as the court of first instance. The *arrondissementsrechtbank* is also the appeal court for *kantongerecht* cases, unless (roughly) they involve an amount of up to Fl. 2,500. The *Gerechtshof* is the appeal court for all cases dealt with by the *arrondissementsrechtbank* at first instance. The *Hoge Raad* is the court of cassation for all cases. There are hardly any exceptions to the appealability of cases before the *arrondissementsrechtbank* or the *Gerechtshof*.

The *Wetboek van burgerlijke rechtsvordering*, considering the many dozens of amendments since its entry into force, has become a patchwork code. The framework has remained intact, though, and an insight into its system will no doubt facilitate the study of procedural law. The current code is divided into four books. The contents of these books can be briefly summarised as follows: proceedings in general (I); right of execution (II); various proceedings before the national courts (III); and arbitration (IV).

Book I requires closest attention. This book contains provisions for the procedure commenced by writ and for the procedure commenced by petition, both at first instance and on appeal and in cassation. Other means of legal recourse than appeal and cassation are also provided for in this book. Book II regulates both enforcement proper (*exécution forcée*) and enforcement in its widest sense (*exécution par suite d'instance*). Certainly until 1 April 1995 Title III formed a fairly unsystematic if not chaotic part of the Code of Civil Procedure; since that date general provisions for family law have applied which substitute numerous provisions for specific subjects of family law, so the systematic sight has been improved. Nevertheless, Title III still contains countless exceptions to the general procedural rules for specific family law subjects such as divorce and maintenance allowance; furthermore, it contains provisions for other specific subjects such as protective attachments. Book IV, which was added in 1986, is entirely devoted to arbitration. Of the special acts one particularly worthy of mention is the *Wet op de rechtsbijstand* (Legal Aid Act) which came into force on 1 January 1994 and which succeeds the *Wet rechtsbijstand aan on- en minvermogenden* (Act on legal aid for persons of limited means) and which provides for the financing of legal aid (for those in need of such aid), and the *Advocatenwet* which rules professional legal assistance by *advocaten* and *procureurs* in general.

Books on legislation are published *inter alia* by Gouda Quint publishers in Arnhem, Kluwer publishers in Deventer and Vermande publishers in Lelystad.

Judicial organisation in the Netherlands is currently going through considerable change and is likely to continue to do so for the foreseeable future. In particular there is the serious but controversial intention to merge the *kantongerechten* and *arrondissementsrechtbanken* within the next few years. If this intention is realised, the Netherlands will have one court of first instance and only one kind of appeal court. The merger of *kantongerechten* and *Arrondissementsrechtbanken* implies the need for the integration of the ordinary rules of civil procedure for *arrondissementsrechtbank* proceedings at first instance and the extraordinary rules of civil procedure for *kantongerecht* proceedings (meanwhile, specific provisions for small cases will still be necessary; for instance, legal assistance will not be made mandatory). In the meantime a preliminary draft has been published which meets this need for integration.

8.1.3. LITERATURE AND CASE LAW

Case law in the area of civil procedure plays an important part both in quantity and in quality. In particular the case law of the Civil Chamber of *Hoge Raad* contains relevant judgments in the field of civil procedure year after year. Nevertheless statute is still by far the most important source for this area of law. The most relevant case law may be found in the reviews *Rechtspraak van de Week* and the *Nederlandse Jurisprudentie* (Tjeenk Willink, Zwolle) and the *Tijdschrift voor Arbitrage* (T.M.C. Asser Institute The Hague/Kluwer Deventer).

There is also extensive literature on civil procedure. The most elaborate commentaries have been classified according to article. They are the loose-leaf edition *Burgerlijke Rechtsvordering* (Kluwer, Deventer) and - slightly outdated - W. van Rossum/R.P. Cleveringa, *Verklaring van het Nederlands Wetboek van Burgerlijke Rechtsvordering* (Tjeenk Willink, Zwolle 1972). For procedural practice the loose-leaf *Vademecum burgerlijk procesrecht* was written. There are three current, systematic descriptions of Netherlands civil procedure which must also be considered as more or less comprehensive: W. Hugenholtz/W.H. Heemskerk, *Hoofdlijnen van Nederlands burgerlijk procesrecht* (17th edition Lemma, Utrecht 1994), P.A. Stein,

Compendium van het burgerlijk procesrecht (10th edition Kluwer, Deventer 1995) and H.J. Snijders, M. Ynzonides and G.J. Meijer, *Nederlands burgerlijk procesrecht* (Tjeenk Willink, Zwolle 1993).

Since 1993 the Netherlands has had a review for procedural practice: the *Tijdschrift voor Civiele Rechtspleging* (TCR). Other reviews also used to and still contain articles on civil procedure, such as the *Advocatenblad*, the *Tijdschrift voor de rechterlijke macht* (TREMA) and the *Tijdschrift voor Arbitrage* (TvA).

8.1.4. DATA BASES

The accessibility of sources in the area of civil procedure is continually becoming more problematic, as it is in many other countries. The amount of relevant information has increased exponentially over the past few decades. On the other hand, the information is now also accessible through media other than books and reviews.

Some decades ago *the* data base for case law and literature in the area of Netherlands (civil procedural) law was the card index of the review *Nederlandse Jurisprudentie*. In 1973 the review *Data Juridica* appeared, which gives summaries of articles from other reviews. Since then on-line data bases have become available, especially those of Kluwer in Deventer and Vermande in Lelystad. The CD-ROM has also made its entry. The compact disks of Kluwer Deventer which contain recent volumes of *inter alia* the *Nederlandse Jurisprudentie* and *Data Juridica*, are very accessible. Other more sophisticated data communication systems are in preparation.

8.2. Fundamental Principles

8.2.1. INTRODUCTION

The fundamental principles of civil procedure can be derived from the functions and desiderata as well as from the sources of civil procedure. Although in legal literature numerous differences in the formulation and division of those fundamental principles appear, there are no fundamental controversies. Most of those fundamental principles have also been incorporated into art. 6 ECHRFF, which provides a solid basis to test all kinds of national rules and actions against the fundamental requirements of procedural law and which has thus proved invaluable to the development of European judicial procedure over the past decades. The same applies to art.

14 CCPR, which we need not discuss here since the relevant text of that article is identical to art. 6 ECHRFF, whose effect is much greater in view of the far-reaching competences of the European Court of Human Rights. Those fundamental principles which are not incorporated into art. 6 ECHRFF have a national basis varying from fairly solid to very solid.

Traditionally one distinguishes the following fundamental principles: publicity, party autonomy, hearing of both parties, inquiry into the facts of the action in two instances, supervision of the administration of justice by means of cassation, mandatory procedural representation of the parties and a procedure not free of charge. By now those traditional fundamental principles call for some adjustment, *inter alia* because of the effect of the ECHRFF concluded in 1950. Indeed, from art. 6(1) ECHRFF a number of requirements for the proper administration of justice concerning 'the determination of civil rights and obligations' can be deduced. The following requirements are stated in this provision: 'a fair and public hearing within a reasonable time by an independent and impartial tribunal established by law' followed by a 'judgment' which 'shall be pronounced publicly'.

Fundamental principles, then, are understood to mean fundamental requirements which civil procedure in general fulfils and must fulfil.

Yet even such a fundamental requirement may call for exceptions, based on another fundamental requirement of procedural or other law.

The division of fundamental principles always remains slightly arbitrary. In this chapter a division is used into fundamental principles of good behaviour (8.2.2), the fundamental principle of control, unity and development (8.2.3) and the fundamental principle of external accessibility (8.2.4). Indeed, it may successively be argued that the participants in civil proceedings must behave properly in such proceedings, that their behaviour must be controlled and the law must be unified and developed, and that potential parties must be given the opportunity (with a lawyer if necessary) to participate effectively in the civil proceedings.

8.2.2. GENERAL PRINCIPLE OF GOOD BEHAVIOUR

The fundamental principles of good behaviour, which might be paraphrased as 'fair play', demand that all participants in civil proceedings act carefully.

What is good behaviour? Behaviour which is unlawful is not good at any rate. In more general terms good behaviour calls for care. Apart from this general requirement of care the main principles of good behaviour may be summarised as follows: a) duty to administer justice; b) hearing of both (all) parties; c) independence and impartiality; d) internal accessibility or simplicity; e) publicity of treatment and judgment; f) motivation; g) reasonable time; and h) party autonomy.

a. Duty to administer justice

Judges and other professional participants in the proceedings who are (virtually) in a monopoly position, have in principle a collective duty to administer justice: collective refusal of administration of justice and legal assistance is forbidden. There is a basis for this principle of duty to administer service in art. 6 ECHRFF but also in national provisions such as arts. 17-18 Constitution, art. 844 Rv and arts. 13 and 67 *Advocatenwet*.

b. Hearing of both (all) parties

The principle of hearing both (all) parties (*audite et alteram partem*) naturally applies in the Netherlands too. The court must hear all parties equally. In view of this right, parties must be duly summoned. The principle of hearing both parties has not been laid down in a general, national legal provision. Perhaps the most general provision is art. 45 Rv. Furthermore, art. 6 ECHRFF also requires both parties to be heard.

c. Independence and impartiality

The court must be independent of the parties and any third parties (including the state) and must hear parties without prejudice and with respect for their equality. *See* art. 6 ECHRFF and art. 117 Constitution, art. 8 *et seq*. RO and art. 29 *et seq*. Rv. The unwritten '*sub iudice* rule', which implies that media shall abstain from commenting on cases under judicial consideration, is being criticised in the Netherlands. This rule is in any case at odds with the right to freedom of expression and does therefore not apply unconditionally in any event. *See* art. 10 ECHRFF, on which *inter alia* the Sunday-Times judgment (ECHR 26 April 1977, CEDH, Series A, Vol. 30). Also relevant in connection with independence is the privacy of the judges' chambers (art. 28 RO): the internal deliberations of judges must be kept secret in view of their independence. Publication of dissenting opinions or concurring opinions is still regarded in the Netherlands as not desirable. There have been arguments in favour of allowing dissenting and concurring opinions without completely surrendering the privacy of judges' chambers and this should be possible after all.

d. Internal accessibility (simplicity)

The principle of internal accessibility, also called the principle of simplicity, may also be derived from art. 6 ECHRFF: given proceedings, there must be a minimum of barriers in order that proceedings may be as good and efficient as possible. From that perspective it must be noted that the Netherlands *Hoge Raad* increasingly remedies procedural defects which are not relevant in substance. In the case law of the *Hoge Raad* there is a distinct trend towards deformalisation. Whoever forgets, for example, to register a writ in time on the *rol* of a court, is given a chance to correct that during the fortnight following the original session date mentioned in the writ (*see* the *Hoge Raad* in judgments of 17 December 1982 and 27 February 1987, published in the *Nederlandse Jurisprudentie* of 1984, no. 59 respectively 1987, no. 559).

e. Public consideration and judgment

The principle of publicity is also honoured in the Netherlands, given art. 6 ECHRFF. Since this article is understood to mean that 'any judgment... shall be made public', the Netherlands requirement of publicity may still be interpreted in such a way that court sessions must in fact be public and judicial decisions must actually be given in public (although usually judges actually pronounce only a few words from the judgment). Of course there are exceptions in the Netherlands to the principle of publicity which exceptions are based on national provisions and are also known to art. 6 ECHRFF (*see* for example art. 121 Constitution, art. 20 RO, arts. 18, 62 and 429*g* Rv).

f. Motivation

Countless national provisions (art. 121 Constitution, art. 20 RO, arts. 59 and 429*k* Rv) point to a motivation duty of the court. The motivation duty referred to there can be deduced partly from the following main argument: the duty to provide grounds for a decision forms a guarantee of the quality of the administration of justice and a guarantee that the provision of justice by civil procedural law is realised. For the unity and the development of civil procedural law the motivation is also essential. Still, legislation has in the past few years allowed exceptions to the motivation requirement, in order to promote the efficiency of proceedings and to economise. Default judgments, in which the claim is either completely or partly allowed, no longer need to specify grounds (art. 76(2) Rv); a cassation judgment by the *Hoge Raad* no longer has to specify grounds if the *Hoge Raad* finds that a claim put forward cannot lead to cassation and does not prompt the answering of legal questions in the interest of the unity or development of law (art. 101*a* RO).

g. Reasonable time

Furthermore, parties are entitled to a hearing and judgment within a reasonable time, with regard to both the entire proceedings and the separate stages of the proceedings (art. 6 ECHRFF).

h. Party autonomy

The court is passive to the extent that it must respect the parties' autonomy. The court must not add to the facts (art. 48 Rv). The court may not adduce evidence for facts stated by one party and insufficiently contested by the other party (art. 176(1) Rv). The court may not base its decision on certain legal grounds which were not pleaded (such as a plea of limitation and a plea of the force of *res iudicata*). The court may not grant in excess of or differently from what was claimed or requested and must give a judgment on all matters submitted (for the procedure commenced by writ this may be deduced from art. 382 Rv). In general, the court in appeal and in cassation may only inquire into those parts of the contested judgment which have been attacked by a party by means of an objection in appeal or a cassation plea. There are numerous exceptions to the applications of party autonomy just mentioned, in particular when public policy is in dispute. Besides, Netherlands courts have increasingly come to realise that respect for party autonomy must not be identified with inactivity. At present Netherlands courts are very active in proceedings, for example by ordering, of their own motion, the hearing of witnesses, asking for experts' reports and the actual appearance of the parties in court, including questioning the parties, of course, and asking them to provide for relevant documents; if they refuse to answer questions or to produce documents, the judge may derive suspicions prejudicial to them from that. Particularly the appearance in court of the parties (art. 141a Rv) is extremely popular in the Netherlands. *See* section 8.4.2 for more details on this.

8.2.3. FUNDAMENTAL PRINCIPLE OF CONTROL, UNITY AND DEVELOPMENT

As is inevitable in any legal system, decisions are made by the Netherlands courts which are based on incorrect assumptions in respect of rules of law or the facts of a case. This is one reason for a certain degree of control by means of appeal. Self-control of the parties and their lawyers is also desirable: by means of appeal, they make their claims, propositions and defences perfect. The classic argument still applies that '*le droit accroît en plaidant*'. Moreover, unity and development of law call for a central instance of appeal, which can remove unevenness in case law and can develop the law logically and consistently. This theory is put into practice by a) the availability of two full instances followed by b) cassation.

a. Principle of two full instances

In principle, everybody is entitled to a second full consideration of his case following judgment at first instance. The legislator has given effect to this principle of two full instances by providing for the possibility of appeal (arts. 332, 345 and 429n Rv). Although in civil cases this principle may not be deduced from art. 6 ECHRFF, the Netherlands *Hoge Raad* does regard it as fundamental.

The *Hoge Raad* interprets exceptions to the principle of appeal in a restricted way.

b. Principle of cassation

As a rule, everybody is also entitled to cassation: a restricted third consideration of his case to decide whether an inferior court has misapplied the law or has not complied with procedural requirements (in particular the requirement of motivation; art. 118(2) Constitution, arts. 94 *et seq*. RO, 398 *et seq*. and 426 *et seq*. Rv).

8.2.4. FUNDAMENTAL PRINCIPLE OF EXTERNAL ACCESSIBILITY

The fundamental principle of external accessibility, like the principle of internal accessibility, may be deduced from art. 6 ECHRFF, in particular from the 'right of effective access to the court'. However well the civil procedure may be regulated internally, it must be accessible from the outside. In every civil case a judge and, where necessary, a lawyer must be available (in accordance with the aforementioned duty to administer justice).

It is difficult to deny that a principle of external accessibility applies. The only problem is how such accessibility may best be reached. Sometimes legal representation and legal aid for the financially less fortunate may be required, sometimes simplification of the procedure without legal representation may be the best recipe for external accessibility. High financial thresholds, like for example high court fees, seem to be fundamentally wrong in any event and will most probably not stand the test of criticism of the European Court of Human Rights.

8.3. Principal Characters

8.3.1. SURVEY

In the Netherlands there are several *dramatis personae* in civil procedure who do not appear in every EU country. This particularly applies to the *deurwaarder* (process server/bailiff) and to the *Openbaar Ministerie* (Public Prosecution Department) insofar as it acts in civil cases. The *deurwaarder* is a more or less independent official, whose duty it is to issue and serve writs and other summonses and to enforce judgments, e.g. by attachment. Particularly in civil cases before the *Hoge Raad* the *Openbaar Ministerie* plays an important role: in any civil case it gives obligatory advice to the *Hoge Raad*; if the parties do not appeal to the *Hoge Raad*, the *Openbaar Ministerie* may appeal itself, requesting that the attacked judgment be reversed in the interest of the law; in this case the parties' rights and duties pursuant to the attacked judgment remain unaffected. In all lower instances it may also act where it is required by public policy pursuant to the law and no-one else takes any action. Thus, the *Openbaar Ministerie* may file a petition for bankruptcy of a shady company or demand that an incestuous father is deprived of his custody. In the lower instances, however, the *Openbaar Ministerie* is not very active *in civilibus*.

Attention will now be devoted to the principal characters whom the Netherlands has in common with all other EC countries: the judge, the lawyers and the parties.

8.3.2. THE JUDGE

a. General remarks

On leafing through issues of Trema (the Netherlands Review for the Judiciary) one sees a judiciary which is in a state of flux: automation of the administration and improvement of efficiency and formation are just a few practical, topical issues. The most drastic reorganisation of the judiciary since 1838, briefly set out in section 8.1.2, calls for particular attention. It is based on the final report of a public committee, the conclusions of which have been mainly adopted by the government. At present the ordinary judiciary consists of the following courts: the *kantongerecht* (cantonal court: a court of first instance mainly for minor matters), the *arrondissementsrechtbank* (district court: court of first instance for any other cases and also the appellate court for judgments from the *kantongerecht*), the *Gerechtshof* (Court of Appeal: appellate court for *arrondissementsrechtbank* judgments) and the *Hoge Raad* (Supreme Court: the highest court, established especially for appeal against judgments from the *kantongerechten* against which no appeal lies and against judgments on appeal). The reorganisation, which should be completed before the year 2000, provides in particular for the extension of the *arrondissementsrechtbank* to an integrated court of first instance, in which the *kantongerecht* will be merged; the *Gerechtshof* will then be the only instance for appeal.

Apart from judicial-political developments, jurisdictional problems require attention. This rather complex issue can meanwhile be split up into seven separate questions. These questions concern constitutional jurisdiction (does a court have jurisdiction or are we dealing with a legislative or administrative question?), jurisdiction pursuant to public international law (the problem of the international immunity of jurisdiction), jurisdiction pursuant to private international law (which is laid down particularly by the Brussels and Lugano Conventions for the countries under discussion in this book), sectoral jurisdiction (does the civil court, the criminal court or the administrative court have jurisdiction?), the national court's jurisdiction (does jurisdiction lie with the national court or with an arbitrator?), absolute jurisdiction (which court has jurisdiction hierarchically speaking: the *kantonrechter*, the *rechtbank*, the *Gerechtshof* or the *Hoge Raad?*) and relative jurisdiction (which court has territorial jurisdiction: the court in Amsterdam or in The Hage?). It seems fairly pointless to consider these questions in great detail within the framework of this contribution. Therefore a very limited selection of conspicuous elements must suffice.

b. Constitutional jurisdiction

There is a constitutional basis for jurisdiction of the civil court if that court is addressed pursuant to a civil right. This right is not one determined by the court, but one whose protection is sought by the plaintiff. That is why the discussion in the Netherlands is not aimed at the question of constitutional jurisdiction as an issue of procedural law, but at the question how far the civil court can go in its relationship with legislation and administration in reviewing government actions. The courts are in principle not allowed to review whether or not legislation is correct. The court does have jurisdiction to test lower regulations against higher regulations and against the general principles of proper administration (such as the principle of equality). Statutes (regulations established by government and parliament together) cannot, however, be tested against the Constitution or against general principles of proper administration. Since statutes may be tested against self-executing rules of conventions, the significance of the prohibition to review the constitutionality of statutes (art. 120 Constitution) is not great. Judicial review of whether or not decisions of administration (e.g. issuing or refusing a driving licence) are correct is in principle forbidden, because the administration has considerable freedom in establishing its policy. If there are rules of law which prescribe a certain line of conduct for the administration, then the court may conduct a review against such rules. The court may always review administrative decisions against the general principles of proper administration.

c. Public international jurisdiction

Jurisdiction under public international law poses few problems in the Netherlands, even though there was once a decision by a Netherlands court of first instance declaring a state bankrupt (namely the state of Zaïre); obviously, the judgment was reversed on appeal. Indeed, in general the Netherlands court, too, does not have jurisdiction in respect of supranational bodies and foreign States. In the relevant case there was no reason for any exception to this immunity of jurisdiction.

d. Private international jurisdiction

Apart from the Brussels Convention and the Lugano Convention, jurisdiction under private international law in the Netherlands is mainly subject to the unwritten rule that distribution results in attribution, in other words: according to unwritten rules of law, relative jurisdiction also determines jurisdiction under private international law.

e. Sectoral jurisdiction

The answer to the question of sectoral jurisdiction again depends on the nature of the law under which the plaintiff/petitioner litigates. If proceedings are conducted involving rights pursuant to civil law, then a civil judge has jurisdiction (art. 112.1. Constitution); if they are conducted on the basis of administrative rights, then an administrative judge has jurisdiction. A civil judge may declare a plaintiff or applicant nonsuited, if he has not addressed another judge first. If a person addresses a civil judge for additional legal protection, following proceedings before an administrative or a criminal judge, then the outcome of the proceedings before the administrative or criminal judge is binding on the civil judge.

f. Jurisdiction national court

Since a citizen is in principle entitled to a public court (art. 17 Constitution), arbitrators will only have jurisdiction if parties have agreed to renounce the right to a public court in favour of arbitration.

g. Absolute jurisdiction

We should repeat that the reorganisation of the Netherlands judiciary which has now been commenced, provides for the integration of the *kantongerechten* and *arrondissementsrechtbanken*, which must end the problem of jurisdiction between the *kantongerecht* and *arrondissementsrechtbank* of first instance and between the *arrondissementsrechtbank* and *Gerechtshof.* Yet similar problems will continue to exist, in view of the fact that the distinction between proceedings in minor and major cases must remain intact. There is considerable resistance to the abolition of the *kantongerecht* - which is what the merger with the *arrondissementsrechtbank* boils down to. The *kantongerecht* - the Dutch equivalent of the French and Belgian *juge de paix* - enjoys a good reputation in the Netherlands. Due to the strong decentralisation of *kantongerechten* the *kantonrechter* is often familiar with the local particularities in his canton (such as traffic situations and housing problems). In the reorganisation of the judiciary the legislator does try to provide a solution for this disadvantage of the abolition of the *kantongerechten* by locating the judges of the new courts of first instance in former *kantongerecht* buildings. *See* the diagram on p. 254 for a clarification of the present judicial organisation in civil cases.

h. Relative jurisdiction

Relative jurisdiction usually lies with the court of the defendant's or the petitioner's domicile (art. 126 Rv).

i. Related admissibility matters

Connected with the issue of jurisdiction are three issues of admissibility. The first of them has already been briefly discussed above: problems of

DIAGRAM JUDICIAL ORGANISATION IN CIVIL CASES IN THE NETHERLANDS

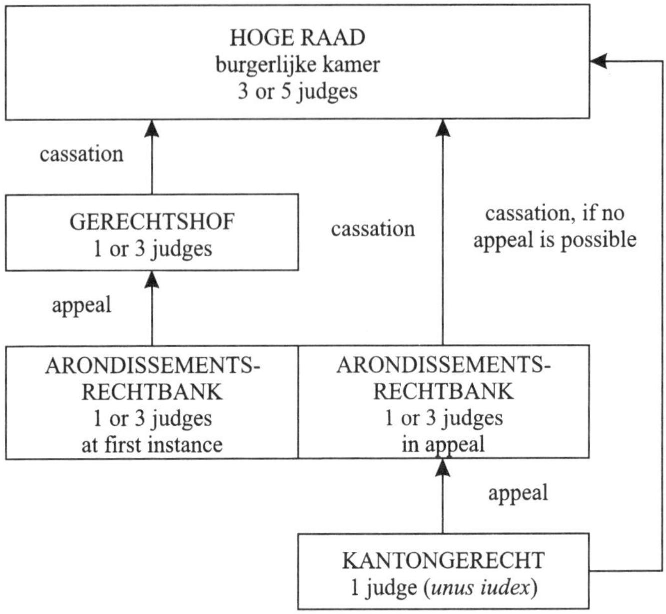

admissibility where administrative or criminal procedures are more appropriate.

A second admissibility problem occurs when the legislator has provided for an internal administrative procedure with adequate safeguards, e.g. duly organised administrative appeal against a decision by mayor and aldermen to the Provincial Executive. In such a case a party will also be declared non-suited unless he first followed the prescribed procedure.

A third admissibility problem arises in the case of a so-called binding advice. If parties have agreed to a binding advice, then they will have to follow that route before any claim is admissible before the ordinary court.

j. Staffing

Another interesting point is the number of judges per case. In the past few decades there has been a trend towards decreasing the number of judges being allowed per case. Around the turn of the century the situation was roughly as follows: the *Hoge Raad* adjudicated with seven judges, the *Gerechtshoven* with five, the *arrondissementsrechtbanken* with three and the *kantongerecht* was an *unus iudex* court (and still is). Nowadays the *arrondissementsrechtbanken* usually also adjudicate with one judge. Even the *Gerechtshoven* may in some cases (family matters) sit as an *unus iudex*. As a rule, however, *Gerechtshoven* adjudicate in panels of three judges. The *Hoge Raad* now usually sits with five judges, but in relatively simple cases three judges adjudicate. A reason for this trend may be the tendency to cut expenses particularly in a climate in which the Department of Justice is not very popular with the Treasury (with the exception of money spent on the fight against crime). This is all the more oppressing when one considers that the number of judges in the Netherlands per one hundred thousand inhabitants is substantially lower than in most surrounding countries.

It further seems important to point out that judges in the Netherlands are selected in two ways. One half of all judges is recruited from an internal training course which is open to selected young lawyers who have their 'doctoraal' examination in Netherlands law. The other half is recruited from jurists who have acquired at least six years of legally relevant practical experience. They are selected by an (independent) Commission for the recruitment of members of the judiciary. After a candidate has successfully finished the training or has been selected by the above Commission, he can apply to be appointed as a judge with one of the Netherlands courts.

Finally it must be added that the judge is assisted by a clerk. The clerk as manager of the court office has recently been replaced by a publicly appointed director of legal assistance for each district.

8.3.3. THE LAWYERS

Legal assistance in the Netherlands is provided *inter alia* by lawyers in private practice (*advocaat en procureur*) and corporate lawyers, trade union lawyers, bailiffs, legal advisers and debt-collection agencies. The *advocaat en procureur* are the providers of legal assistance in most cases. The *procureur* is the client's representative in the proceedings (he signs documents relating to the case and submits them to the court), the *advocaat* is his adviser (he advises clients, drafts pleadings and appears in court on behalf of clients). Most *procureurs* in the Netherlands are also *advocaten* and *vice versa*. The *procureur* may only act within his own district, so that a client who has an *advocaat* outside the district where the proceedings are brought, has to instruct another lawyer as *procureur* (which is usually done by his *advocaat*). The advantage of the system of *procureurs* is clear: the *procureur* is familiar with local regulations and practices. There is also an obvious drawback: it involves extra costs.

The *advocaten en procureurs* are still the main providers of legal assistance in the Netherlands, because of their training and the requirements for their enrolment as *advocaat en procureur* as well as the disciplinary law to which they are subject (ruled by the *Advocatenwet*).

8.3.4. THE PARTIES

Leaving aside some exceptions (such as the *vennootschap onder firma*, a type of partnership), only natural and legal persons may act as parties to proceedings. In general minors can act as parties to proceedings, but must be represented by their statutory representatives as 'formal parties' (parents or guardians).

In view of the costs of litigation and the limits on income and capital to qualify for legal aid set by the legislator, it is at present almost impossible for members of the middle-class to bring civil proceedings as plaintiff, defendant, petitioner or respondent. Civil proceedings are mainly brought by companies and institutions and persons who are either legally aided or rich.

It is interesting to note the acceptance by the civil court of representative actions, claims which are somewhat similar to the American class actions. This concerns actions brought by a specific person who acts on behalf of the general interest or a group interest. Over the past decades the Netherlands court has increasingly deemed plaintiffs in such actions admissible. Thus we have seen that actions were admitted to obtain an order to terminate dumping in the North Sea, to prohibit euthanasia of a comatose patient, to prohibit the clubbing of geese, which may be qualified as cruelty to animals, and to prohibit the deployment of Cruise Missiles in the Netherlands (admissibility in these cases does not imply that the claims were upheld, of course). Since 1 July 1994 Netherlands law has contained a general provision on the representative action in art. 3:305a-b BW. This provision requires that the interest group bringing the action be a legal person. The statutory object of the organisation must include the protection of the particular interests which are the subject of the proceedings. The law includes additional admissibility requirements such as the condition that a representative action on behalf of a group interest is only admissible if the individual interests which are grouped, can be qualified as homogeneous. In representative actions the difficult question is whether the persons whom the organisation represented are bound by the judgment in the representative action. In principle, as a point of law, that question must be answered negatively. The individuals involved were not a party to the representative action, so that the judgment does not have the authority of *res iudicata* for them (art. 67 Rv). Despite this, the effect of the judgment on third parties interested in the matter may be considerable, either in a negative or a positive sense.

8.4. Basic Procedure for Contentious Jurisdiction at First Instance

8.4.1. INTRODUCTION

The most important procedure for contentious jurisdiction in the Netherlands is still the procedure commenced by writ (provided for in Title III of Book I of the Code of Civil Procedure), as discussed in sections 8.4.2 and 8.4.3 below. In the last few decades, however, there has been a trend in the legislation to prescribe the procedure commenced by petition for contentious jurisdiction. Thus, either an employer or employee can file a petition for the rescission of a contract of employment, against which the other party may file a defence. Article 7A:1639w BW prescribes in this case the procedure commenced by petition. *See further* section 8.5 for the procedure commenced by petition in contentious cases.

8.4.2. PROCEDURE COMMENCED BY WRIT BEFORE THE ARRONDISSEMENTSRECHTBANK AT FIRST INSTANCE

a. Introduction

The procedure commenced by writ before the *arrondissementsrechtbank* at first instance may be classified as a fairly formal procedure (with the exception of the rules of evidence) which is mainly conducted in writing, although the personal appearance of the parties after the defence has been issued, as discussed below, has substantially reduced the differences with the fairly informal procedure commenced by petition to be discussed in section 8.5.2.

The procedure commenced by writ may be slightly reduced in time when, after leave by the court, the period for the writ is reduced (art. 7(2) Rv) or reply by the plaintiff and rejoinder by the defendant are omitted (art. 145 Rv). This is called an accelerated final procedure.

b. Commencement of proceedings

The *dagvaarding* (writ) is issued by the bailiff. Proceedings are generally deemed to have commenced on the date of service of the writ. Although the writ is subject to formal requirements, in particular those stated in art. 5 in conjunction with art. 91 Rv, it will nevertheless seldom be declared null and void. Netherlands law contains various mechanisms to prevent this, such as the possibility of a notification to remedy the defects in the writ (art. 92 Rv).

c. Proceedings

After the writ the normal proceedings are as follows: (1) a statement of claim by the plaintiff; (2) a defence by the defendant; (3) often a personal appearance of the parties ordered by the court; (4) a statement of reply by the plaintiff; and (5) a statement of rejoinder by the defendant. After these documents have been exchanged, the parties may plead their case orally before the court, which parties seldom do before the *arrondissementsrechtbank.* Upon a joint application by the parties the court may allow the parties to file a further statement each. Until the procedural documents have been submitted for judgment both parties may file a so-called *akte*, i.e. a brief written statement, whereby parties may produce evidence or enter documents into the dispute.

Both before and after proceedings are commenced, the court may at a party's request order a separate (which the legislator has somewhat misleadingly termed 'provisional') examination of witnesses, expert report, or site inspection (arts. 214-220 and 220-232 Rv), the results of which may be used in future or pending proceedings.

Undoubtedly the most interesting feature of Netherlands proceedings is the *comparitie na antwoord* (personal appearance of the parties after the statement of defence has been issued). The court has always had the power to order the personal appearance of the parties at any stage of the proceedings, also *ex officio*. What is new, however (and this is the codification of an institution which has developed in practice) is that the court of its own motion assesses each case, after the statement of defence has been issued, on its suitability for a personal appearance of the parties (art. 141 Rv). The purpose of this personal appearance is either to attempt a settlement between the parties or to obtain information. A third, frequently used purpose of the personal appearance may be described as obtaining clarity regarding the further way of dealing with the case. About ten years ago already in approximately 40 per cent of all cases commenced by writ (apart from family matters) a personal appearance of the parties was ordered by the court *ex officio*, out of which cases about 40 to 50 per cent were subsequently settled by the judge. This percentage appears not to have changed substantially since then. Although the use of the personal appearance may in general be characterised as positive, it is not entirely without risks. Parties must not be forced into a settlement when they appear before the court. Nor should parties commence proceedings in hopeless cases, on the off-chance that at the parties' personal appearance before the court a settlement will somehow be reached. The court should therefore not order the personal appearance of parties automatically. *See also* section 8.2.2h.

If proceedings have to be continued after this personal appearance of the parties, because settlement attempts have proved unsuccessful, it is possible for both parties to agree that no statement of reply and no rejoinder be exchanged, because during the personal appearance of the parties the court has obtained sufficient further information to pronounce judgment.

d. Judgment

If both parties have entered an appearance, a judgment is adversarial.

The so-called *minuut*, the original judgment, remains with the registry. The parties get a *grosse* of the judgment, a certified copy of the judgment drawn up in an enforceable form, which means that it commences with the words 'In naam der Koning(in)' (i.e. in the name of the King/Queen). The *grosse* is required for compulsory enforcement, the *executie* (art. 430 Rv). The parties can also get a non-enforceable but nevertheless certified copy of the judgment, the so-called *expeditie* (art. 62 Rv) which can be submitted, for example, when lodging an appeal.

The judgment may be an interim judgment or a final judgment. The final judgment may contain: nullification of the writ (arts. 90-96 Rv); a declaration that the court lacks jurisdiction (arts. 154-157b Rv); a declaration of inadmissibility of the plaintiff's claim (e.g. because the possibility of an administrative appeal or binding advice has been left unused); a decision whether the plaintiff's claim is allowed or refused. The declaration of inadmissibility and refusal of the claim are sometimes collectively referred to as denial. Furthermore, the final judgment can contain subordinate but nevertheless important additional decisions, such as an order to pay costs (*see also* section 8.9.3); a declaration of provisional enforceability; and leave or refusal of means of enforcement such as the penalty or civil imprisonment (*see* section 8.8.5).

A judgment is called constitutive if it ends or creates a certain legal status. A condemnatory judgment is a judgment which orders the defendant to do something. A declaratory judgment is one which determines a certain legal status. Many judgments combine certain features. Usually a judgment contains declaratory elements. Mostly, however, it is only called declaratory when it contains no constitutive or condemnatory elements.

e. Special aspects of procedure

Having so far considered the standard procedure before the *rechtbank*, now some special aspects of the procedure will be discussed.

1. Non-appearance

Non-appearance of the parties is a common occurrence: approximately half of all final judgments are default judgments. In nearly every case the court will give judgment against a party who failed to enter an appearance, since in such cases the court will usually conduct only a very summary examination of the grounds of the claims (art. 76 Rv). This judgment will be given after a writ and a statement of claim by the plaintiff.

2. Amendment of claim

It frequently occurs during the proceedings that the plaintiff amends his claim and the court allows this in many cases (art. 134 Rv). He can do this by statement or *akte* implying amendment of the claim. The defendant is allowed to make objections against this amendment in an akte. Only rarely are such objections successful.

3. Counterclaim

The defendant often issues a counterclaim which is allowed only in his statement of defence (arts. 250-253 Rv).

4. Production of evidence

The Netherlands rules of evidence laid down in arts. 176-232 Rv now, were amended considerably on 1 April 1988. The question upon which party the burden of proof rests has been answered by the legislator in art. 177 Rv which provides that the burden of proof lies upon the party who relies upon the legal consequences of facts alleged by him (according to the so-called objective legal theory), unless the requirements of reasonableness and fairness demand a change of burden of proof (according to the theory of fairness). This provides the court with ample room to arrive at a just division of the burden of proof. It should be added that the court often sets out from a presumption of the facts, which allows it, to put it rather bluntly, to ignore any rule in respect of the burden of proof and which at the same time increases the chances of reaching a solution in accordance with the factual circumstances of the case.

The question of admissibility of evidence is answered liberally in the Netherlands: all evidence, including evidence not laid down by law such as a film or a computer print-out, is in principle admissible (art. 179 (1) Rv), unless otherwise provided by the law. Evidence in a particular case may be disregarded by the court if it is unlawful. However, the civil court will not easily do so. Thus, the *Hoge Raad* determined that a tape-recording of a telephone conversation made without the permission of the other party to the conversation is in principle admissible in evidence (according to judgments of 16 October 1987 and 7 February 1992, published in the *Nederlandse Jurisprudentie* of 1988 under no. 850 and 1993 under no. 78). When assessing the evidence, the court will, however, be inclined to deal more cautiously with less reliable means of evidence such as tape-recordings. In principle the court is free in its assessment of evidence (art. 179(2)). Most evidence can be produced as appendices to statements and *akten* without prior judicial permission. For hearing witnesses or appointing judicial experts, the court must give an interlocutory judgment.

5. Other incidents

All kinds of incidents may occur in the proceedings which cannot be considered due to the restricted nature within the context of this contribution, e.g. third party proceedings, transfer and joinder of cases, joinder and intervention of persons and the extremely time-consuming procedure of the court officially requesting a foreign court to provide information on the law applicable in that country (art. 151 Rv in conjunction with the European Convention on Information on Foreign Law, Trb. 1968, 142 with the accompanying Act on enforcement). Further we must mention the challenge and excusal of a particular judge and, finally, the request for a preliminary ruling pursuant to art. 6 Benelux Court of Justice, art. 177 EEC Treaty or the Interpretation Protocol of the Brussels Convention; such a request also leads to enormous delay in the civil procedure.

f. Provisional production of evidence

Either before commencement of proceedings, or once they have been commenced, the court may at the request of an interested party order a separate (which the legislator has somewhat misleadingly called 'provisional') hearing of witnesses, expert's reports, or a separate ('provisional') site inspection (arts. 214-220 and 220-232 Rv). The results of any of these can be used in any future or parallel proceedings.

g. Evaluation

In summary, the procedure commenced by writ before the *arrondissementsrechtbank* at first instance can be qualified as a mainly documentary, decentralised and, rules of evidence apart, fairly formal procedure. However, the *comparitie na antwoord* (appearance of the parties before the court after the filing of their defence) has considerably reduced the differences with the rather informal petition procedure which is discussed in section 8.5

8.4.3. PROCEDURE COMMENCED BY WRIT BEFORE THE KANTONRECHTER

On a number of salient points the procedure commenced by writ before the *kantonrechter* (arts. 97-118 Rv), which was changed considerably with effect from 30 December 1991, differs from the procedure before the *arrondissementsrechtbank* at first instance. Thus, the writ may be issued by means of a form, delivered to the defendant through the office of the registrar. According to arts. 103-104 Rv, the bailiff will issue the writ in exceptional circumstances only. In practice, however, there appears to be a preference for the bailiff to issue the writ.

There is no legal obligation to exchange pleadings. Many *kantongerechten* will, however, prescribe an exchange of pleadings.

There is also no mandatory procedural representation, although many parties appoint someone to represent them in the *kantongerecht*; this may be a bailiff providing legal assistance or an *advocaat* (art. 101 Rv).

The procedure in the *kantongerecht* is clearly geared to minor cases. The *kantonrechter*, however, also decides some major disputes (particularly relating to employment and tenancy law) and for such disputes the procedure may be inappropriate, particularly in view of the fact that there is no mandatory legal representation *ad litem* (however, opinions on whether or not obligatory legal representation is desirable are actually divided).

8.5. Basic Procedure for Voluntary Jurisdiction at First Instance

8.5.1. INTRODUCTION

For voluntary jurisdiction (e.g. the appointment of a guardian for a minor after the parents' death) the one essential procedure is the procedure commenced by petition, which is the subject of this section. This procedure commenced by petition is also prescribed - and increasingly so - in certain types of contentious cases.

In general, the procedure commenced by petition at first instance and on appeal is governed by arts. 429a-t Rv and in cassation by arts. 426-429 Rv. Articles 429a-r have entered into force for the great majority of cases commenced by petition, but not yet for all such cases. Fortunately, the courts usually apply art. 429a-r indirectly by analogy, if it does not apply directly. Below it will be assumed that arts. 429a-r do apply.

8.5.2. PROCEDURE COMMENCED BY PETITION

The true litigation lawyer in the Netherlands has a kind of love-hate relationship with the procedure commenced by petition. The procedure is both the rascal and the pampered child of civil procedure.

The procedure commenced by petition is a 'rascal', since it plays all kinds of pranks. A great many subjects have not or have barely been provided for, so that parties frequently face surprises and uncertainties. For instance, there is no provision as to when and how exhibits can be submitted. The law also fails to provide for the right to adduce evidence by witnesses, although such right can be derived from art. 6 ECHRFF. It is also still unclear whether a decision in a procedure commenced by petition has authority of *res iudicata* and whether it is subject to the recourse of *request civiel* (revocation).

The procedure commenced by petition is also a 'pampered child'. Whoever tests it against *desiderata* such as speed, simplicity and cost-effectiveness will affirm this, in view of its informal, concentrated character.

In general, the procedure commenced by petition consists of the following parts: petition, defence, oral consideration and decision. Incidents of evidence only occur in exceptional circumstances. Oral pleadings and further written pleadings are excluded (but in exceptional cases, an additional petition or additional defence is filed).

It is not possible to lodge opposition against a judgment in default. It is the court's duty to ensure as far as possible that the defendant appears in the proceedings.

Amendments of the petition and counter-petition do occur regularly. They do not pose any technical procedural problems. In general the court will admit either. After a counter-petition is filed, the court will allow the original petitioner to file a written defence against the counter-petition, although this is not required by law. Again, art. 6 ECHRFF appears applicable. Incidents are rare in procedures commenced by petition.

The occurrence of so few complications in the procedure commenced by petition is not merely due to the fact that procedural law differs from the law in the procedure commenced by writ. It is also due to the nature of the matters, which causes fewer technical procedural difficulties. For instance, there is no or hardly any need for third-party notices in the procedure commenced by petition, whereas such notices may be useful in the procedure commenced by writ.

So far, it has been assumed that there is a petitioner and one or more opposing parties. There are also cases without an opposing party, which makes the procedure even simpler: the petition is then (possibly after an oral explanation) usually followed by an immediate decision.

There are numerous exceptions to the general rules applicable to the procedure commenced by petition (which rules are laid down in arts. 429a-t Rv).

8.6. Means of Recourse

8.6.1. SURVEY

Leaving aside the exceptional phenomenon of cassation in the interest of the law (a cassation instituted at the *Hoge Raad* by the *Openbaar Ministerie*, which cannot alter the rights and obligations of parties arising out of the judgments given by lower instances), Netherlands civil procedure has six means of recourse:

- the ordinary means of recourse of (1) application to set aside a default judgment; (2) appeal; (3) cassation; and (4) - only theoretically - review of decisions of the *Hoge Raad;*
  and
- the extraordinary means of (5) application by a third party to set aside a judgment in a proceeding in which he was not one of the parties; and (6) revocation (*request civiel*).

Instituting an ordinary means of recourse suspends execution, instituting an extraordinary means of recourse does not. In practice this difference between ordinary and extraordinary means of recourse is small because the court usually declares that its judgment is provisionally enforceable (art. 52 Rv), which implies that an ordinary means of recourse no longer suspends execution.

Ordinary means of recourse are subject to relatively short time-limits: for an action to set aside a default judgment two weeks after - in a nutshell - the defendant has been notified of a default judgment against him, for an appeal three months after the judgment in first instance and for cassation three months after the judgment on appeal or a non-appealable judgment. In cases commenced by petition the time-limits for appeal and cassation are in principle two months.

After expiration of the time-limit for lodging ordinary means of recourse, the judgment involved acquires the status of *res iudicata*.

The generally irrelevant means of recourse (4), (5) and (6) will not be discussed below. Further attention will now be given to the application to set aside a default judgment (8.6.2), appeal (8.6.3) and cassation (8.6.4).

As yet there are no statutory provisions for rectification of judicial decisions in the Netherlands, but case law does allow rectification in case of apparent clerical or mathematical errors.

8.6.2. THE APPLICATION TO SET ASIDE A JUDGMENT IN DEFAULT

A defendant against whom judgment is entered in default after a procedure commenced by writ may apply to have the judgment in default set aside and this is laid down in arts. 81-85 and 87 Rv.

The time-limit for this application is important. Time begins to run when the default judgment or a memorandum based on this judgment is served on the defendant in person and it ends fourteen days later. The time-limit also ends fourteen days after the person in default commits a *daad van bekendheid* (an action from which it is clear that the defendant is aware of the judgment in default) as referred to in art. 81(1) Rv. In all cases, the time-limit ends when the judgment has been enforced (arts. 81(2) Rv).

The application to set aside the default judgment continues like ordinary adversarial proceedings whereby the writ (the summons to set aside the default judgment) together with the first statement of the opposing party, has almost the same function as the defence in an ordinary procedure. Then a statement of defence in opposition by the original plaintiff and statement of reply in opposition by the original defendant usually follow (whose function is almost identical to that of the statements of reply and rejoinder in the ordinary procedure). Normally there is no statement of rejoinder in opposition.

Judgment in default proceedings commenced by petition cannot be set aside.

8.6.3. APPEAL

The rules for appeal in cases commenced by writ are laid down in arts. 332-357 Rv.

Appeal is lodged against less than 1 per cent of final judgments by the cantonal court and against no more than 5-10 per cent of final judgments in first instance by the *arrondissementsrechtbanken*.

If appeal is lodged, the chance of the decision against which appeal is instituted being reversed is as high as 50 per cent. Lawyers often act as a sieve and seem to be fairly effective in sifting out unjustifiable appeals.

Appeal is particularly intended as a means to control the courts but also to enable the parties to remedy and correct their own mistakes.

Having regard to the principle of a two-tier system, appeal is possible in nearly all cases. An exception is formed by judgments by the *kantongerecht* whereby the amount involved does not exceed Fl. 2,500 (art. 38 RO). Furthermore, the right of appeal against non-final judgments has been restricted by the legislator (arts. 337 and 429n(3)).

It is also inherent in the above principle that the appeal has a devolutive effect: in principle consideration of the case fully devolves to the superior court. On the other hand, appeal is subject to the so-called system of obligatory grievances: those parts of the decisions of the court of first instance against which a party does not appeal, remain intact in principle unless a respondent had heard the court at first instance rule completely in his favour in respect of the claim lodged. Consequently the Netherlands appeal procedure contains a mixture of the principle of the devolutive effect of an appeal and the adage *tantum devolutum, quantum appellatum*.

Leaving aside the above complications, the appeal procedure is technically fairly simple and the appeal procedure in the *arrondissementsrechtbank* from decisions by the *kantongerecht* is identical to the procedure in the *Gerechtshof*. After the service of a writ of appeal (which need not contain the grounds for the appeal) the appellant files a statement of grievances (which must contain such grounds). The respondent may subsequently file a statement of defence, which statement may contain a cross-appeal against the decision. In that case the original appellant is allowed to file a statement of defence in the cross-appeal. The parties are entitled to plead their case orally before the court, a right which is used relatively more in appeal proceedings than in proceedings before the *arrondissementsrechtbank* at first instance. At the request of both parties further statements may also be allowed by the court. *Akten* may be admitted until the parties have requested judgment. Evidence on appeal is produced in essentially the same manner as at first instance (art. 353r (1) in conjunction with 176-232 Rv). An amendment of claim is also possible on appeal and is frequently allowed by the appellate court, although, strictly speaking, this results in the loss of one instance. A new statement of counterclaim, however, cannot be lodged on appeal. Other ways of proceeding and procedural incidents are either not admitted, or even less used than at first instance.

The appeal procedure in cases commenced by petition is virtually identical to the procedure at first instance. The system of obligatory grievances also applies here, whilst there is also the possibility of a cross-appeal. The appellant's grievances must be contained in an appeal petition and those of the appellant in the cross-appeal in a statement of defence on appeal. Subsequently the respondent in the cross-appeal usually files a statement of defence on cross-appeal. A counter-petition on appeal is excluded.

8.6.4. CASSATION

The rules for cassation in cases commenced by writ is laid down in arts. 419 to 429 Rv.

Cassation in the Netherlands is of great private and public interest, in respect of both the provision of justice and the development and unity of the law. For the parties and their lawyers their private interest naturally weighs the most, for those not directly involved the public interest is paramount.

Having regard to the principle of cassation, it is obvious that, barring exceptions, appeal in cassation lies against all judgments of the highest factual instance. Cassation may even be lodged against judgments from the *kantongerecht* which are not subject to appeal, although in most cases the financial interest involved does not warrant an extra instance. Furthermore, the grounds for cassation to the *Hoge Raad* of judgments by the *kantongerecht* are more restricted than those for cassation against other judgments: grievances are mainly restricted to the absence of motivation. Cassation against judgments from other courts is also possible on the ground of a violation of the law. These grounds for cassation can be found in arts. 99 and 100 RO.

Although relatively speaking cassation is not instituted frequently, the *Hoge Raad* has had great difficulty in the past decade coping within a reasonable time with the growing number of cases. Nevertheless, it has so far succeeded, *inter alia* by introducing on a limited scale the three-judge bench and by relaxing the motivation requirements in those cases in which the *Hoge Raad* is of opinion that the ground for cassation is unfounded and does not raise any points which are interesting for the unity or development of the law (*see* sections 8.3.2j respectively 8.2.2f).

On the basis of art. 419 Rv the *Hoge Raad* generally restricts its consideration of the matter to the complicated grounds for cassation, at least in civil cases (unlike in criminal and fiscal cases). Therefore civil proceedings in cassation are not straightforward. Officially, the Netherlands may not have a bar which specialises in cassation, but *de facto* proceedings before the *Hoge Raad* are reserved for a few dozen lawyers in The Hague.

Cassation is instituted against an estimated 5 per cent of final appeal judgments only. The chances of the judgment being reversed in cassation are about 25 to 35 per cent.

Leaving aside technical problems of cassation relating to the question as to which aspects may be considered by the *Hoge Raad* in cassation, the procedure is not complicated. The writ of cassation (which includes the grounds for cassation) is followed by a defence, which may include a cross-cassation with the grounds for cross-cassation. If this occurs, the original appellant in cassation may file a statement of defence in the cross-cassation. If there is no cross-cassation, the statement of defence will not usually amount to much. The defence usually requests that the opposing party's claim should be held inadmissible in cassation, or at least that it should be disallowed. After the exchange of statements the parties may plead their case orally before the court. In order to reduce its overload, the *Hoge Raad* in consultation with the bar in The Hague, has developed a policy not to have the case pleaded orally but to confine matters to the submission of written explanations (*see* art. 408a Rv). If the lawyers insist on oral pleadings, they may still do so, but this opportunity is seldom used now. After the pleadings the *Openbaar Ministerie* at the *Hoge Raad* is under the obligation to submit its conclusion, which usually consists of a well-wrought written recommendation to the *Hoge Raad*, which plays a major part in the latter's deliberations. If the *Hoge Raad* disallows the cassation, the case is closed. If the *Hoge Raad* reverses the judgment below, it normally remits the case to a lower court for further decision.

The cassation procedure in cases commenced by petition is commenced with a petition for cassation, which specifies the grounds for cassation, followed by a much more elaborate defence in cassation. If this contains a cross-cassation, the original appellant in cassation may file a statement of defence in the cross-cassation. Subsequently, oral and written pleadings are allowed after permission by the *Hoge Raad*, but they do not occur much.

8.7. Special Procedures

8.7.1. INTRODUCTION

There are various special procedures in the Netherlands. They may be classified according to the reason for their speciality: urgency (8.7.2), minor interest (8.7.3) or a special subject matter (8.7.4)

8.7.2. SUMMARY PROCEDURES

Summary proceedings take place before the President of the *arrondissements-rechtbank* (in *kort geding*; arts. 289-297 Rv). The *kort geding* has over the years developed into an extremely important provisional judgment in urgent, civil disputes. Although in theory the judgment from the President in summary proceedings is provisional, in practice it is often considered by the parties to be final. It is also noteworthy that, although the President in *kort geding* often makes a decision in which he tries to anticipate the decision in the main procedure, it also happens that he allows or disallows a provision purely on the basis of a weighing of interests of the parties. The proceedings in *kort geding* are frequently used for the solution of strike conflicts, infringements of patents and for all types of representative actions mentioned in section 8.3.4. Nevertheless the number of judgments pronounced in *kort geding* is still relatively small compared to the number of judgments in main proceedings.

The procedure is quite simple. In general, the procedure is initiated by a writ, followed by oral pleadings and the decision of the President of the court. Usually, appeal and cassation are allowed.

In questions which fall within the absolute jurisdiction of the *kantonrechter* there is a comparable procedure for a provisional judgment (art. 116 Rv).

Other summary proceedings in the Netherlands occur much less and are also less adequate. They will not be discussed here. These proceedings include the accelerated final procedure discussed in section 8.4.2 which is similar to the French *bref délai* proceedings.

8.7.3. SMALL CLAIMS PROCEDURES

The Netherlands no longer has a separate small claims procedure. Until the introduction of the new rules of procedure for the *kantongerecht* on 30 December 1991 there used to be a procedure to obtain a legal order for payment which provided an accelerated procedure to collect claims up to Fl.

2,500 arising out of contract. The current procedure in the *kantongerecht* is still designed for relatively small claims, but is nevertheless not as appropriate for the collection of small amounts as the old procedure was. Increasingly, presidents of *arrondissementsrechtbanken* issue orders for payment by way of provisional judgments in *kort geding* (section 8.7.2). The *kantonrechters* are also allowed to issue provisional payment orders in cases which belong to their absolute jurisdiction (so normally only in small cases with an interest up to Fl. 5,000).

8.7.4. SECTOR PROCEDURES

Special rules of Netherlands civil procedure apply to certain subjects, in particular to family law (including divorce law), which is governed by the general rules applicable to the procedures commenced by petition (arts. 429a-t Rv).

Other subjects with different procedural rules are employment law, landlord and tenant law and the law of bankruptcy.

8.8. Protective Measures and Enforcement Measures

8.8.1. INTRODUCTION

The rules in respect of both protective measures and enforcement measures have been drastically amended by the introduction of Books 3, 5 and 6 BW, which came into force on 1 January 1992. The enforcement measures are provided for in Book II Rv and protective measures in Book III together with a number of special procedures.

Protective measures usually require leave from the court, but as a rule for enforcement measures an enforceable title is sufficient (this is most often a judicial decision, but it could also be another title such as an authentic, often notarial, deed or a judicial memorandum of an amicable settlement or an arbitral award). For the enforcement of arbitral awards and foreign enforceable titles in the Netherlands an exequatur (leave to enforce) from the President of the *arrondissementsrechtbank* is required.

In case the debtor goes bankrupt, both protective and enforcement measures by attachment are absorbed by the bankruptcy (art. 33 *Failissementswet* (Bankruptcy Act)). Bankruptcy is a comprehensive attachment of all the debtor's assets.

Protective and enforcement measures may be classified as follows: protective measures other than attachment (section 8.8.2), protective measures by attachment (section 8.8.3), enforcement measures by attachment (section 8.8.4) and enforcement measures other than attachment (section 8.8.5).

8.8.2. PROTECTIVE MEASURES OTHER THAN ATTACHMENT

Protective measures other than attachment are of minor importance in the Netherlands. Putting goods under seal is nowadays mainly of academic interest. Another protective measure other than attachment is the making of an inventory of an estate which does sometimes happen, in particular when a minor is involved as heir to an estate. The protective measures of keeping goods under lock and appointing a trustee over the goods are sometimes used, too.

8.8.3. PROTECTIVE MEASURES BY ATTACHMENT

Book III Rv lays down rules for protective measures by attachment. They are used very frequently in the Netherlands. Their function is dual: they traditionally offer protection to the creditor but also serve as a means of collecting a debt. In particular, the attachment of bank accounts and the embargo of ships and planes are very effective in practice.

Once an enforceable title has been obtained and served, the protective measure by attachment becomes enforcement measure by attachment. We refer to section 8.8.4 for the relationship between protective attachment and bankruptcy.

Special rules apply depending on the object to be attached, in particular in respect of the manner in which attachment is made.

8.8.4. ENFORCEMENT MEASURES BY ATTACHMENT

Enforcement measures by attachment have been provided for in Book II Rv. They also occur frequently in the Netherlands, either independently or following protective measures by attachment.

Yet in many cases enforcement by attachment is not effective: often, once this stage has been reached there is no further redress against the debtor (if the debtor had been capable of paying, he would have paid much sooner).

Depending on the object attached there are again special rules, also in respect of the selling of goods following attachment.

8.8.5. ENFORCEMENT MEASURES OTHER THAN ATTACHMENT

The main enforcement measure other than attachment is enforcement by the creditor himself pursuant to judicial authorisation. This is a type of specific performance. Enforcement with the assistance of the police - for instance, the eviction of squatters with the help of the riot police, now less prevalent than twenty years ago - also forms a direct and specific way of enforcement. The same applies to enforcement by delivery as provided for in art. 491 Rv and to the specific performance of arts. 3:300-301 BW. The latter constitutes an interesting *novum* in the new Netherlands Civil Code: when a debtor refuses to perform a legal act to which he is committed, the court may order that the effect of its judgment is identical to the effect of a legally drawn up deed from the debtor, or the court may appoint a *dwangvertegenwoordiger* (compulsory representative) to perform the legal act on behalf of the debtor. In case the defendant is under an obligation to draw up a deed together with the plaintiff, the court may determine that its judgment shall take the place of the deed or of a part of the deed. By recording the court's decision in the public registers it is also possible to effect delivery of registered goods (especially immovable property and larger aircraft and ships).

There are two indirect measures of enforcement other than attachment: the penalty and civil imprisonment. The penalty is governed by arts. 611a-i Rv. It is based on a Benelux treaty and is a tried and tested and highly effective way of enforcement. Civil imprisonment, on the other hand, is little used but may sometimes be an effective way of enforcement. The explanation for the difference in use of these two indirect ways of enforcement is obvious: civil imprisonment must only be used as an *ultimum remedium*. Both means of enforcement can only be taken with the court's permission. A court is easily prepared to impose a penalty, but for the reason stated above is not likely to impose civil imprisonment.

8.9. Duration and Costs

8.9.1. INTRODUCTION

There are no specific data available about the duration and costs of civil procedures in the Netherlands.

Although it may be difficult to make reliable statements in respect of the duration and costs of proceedings, we will below provide some general information.

8.9.2. DURATION

The *kort geding* procedure in general takes no more than a few weeks from the issue of the writ to judgment. Depending on the urgency, the President in *kort geding* tends to give judgment extremely quickly (sometimes even on the day of the oral pleadings). That is one of the reasons why the *kort geding* is so successful.

A normal procedure before the *kantongerecht* usually takes only several months.

A procedure before the *arrondissementsrechtbank* at first instance (in adversarial proceedings) may easily last one year.

The appeal procedure before the *arrondissementsrechtbank* and the *Gerechtshof* on average lasts six to twelve months, whilst the cassation procedure lasts one to two years.

A procedure in three instances will therefore normally last two to four years. Many procedures in three instances last longer, but only few shorter.

Compared to some other European countries, such as Italy up till now, the Netherlands cannot be unhappy with this result. Yet it must be possible to reduce the length of the proceedings even more. Leaving aside problems of overloading, the fact that the procedure at first instance is strongly decentralised plays a role also. That problem has not yet been solved, although enough has been written about it and in particular consideration has been given as to whether the German 'Stuttgarter Modell' (*see* section 9.4.2c) should be introduced into the Netherlands, albeit slightly amended.

8.9.3. COSTS

Another reason for the popularity of the *kort geding* is no doubt the fact that it is not very expensive because in general it is not very labour-intensive.

A procedure before the *kantongerecht* is also relatively inexpensive, in particular if no lawyer is instructed.

The procedure before the *arrondissementsrechtbank* at first instance in general costs many thousands of guilders, as is the case for the appeal procedure before the *arrondissementsrechtbank* and the *Gerechtshof* and for the cassation procedure.

A procedure in three instances may easily cost tens of thousands of guilders.

In particular, the fees charged by the lawyers are considerable. A lawyer's fee is usually based on an hourly rate which reflects the difficulty of the case and the amount involved. A lawyer will generally follow the tariff of fees used by the Netherlands Bar Association, a scheme which has been established under the auspices of this organisation and which is adjusted periodically to take into account any fluctuations in the price index.

Depending on the amount in dispute, the fixed court fees have recently been increased considerably: if the procedure continues in three instances the court fees could run to several tens of thousands of guilders, depending on the financial interest of the case.

In general, the fees payable by the winning party will not be covered by the costs awarded to him at the expense of the losing party (in particular the costs of legal representation of the winner and the fixed court fees paid by the winning party). This can be explained by the fact that costs for legal representation are awarded on the basis of fixed amounts which usually do not cover the real costs.

It must also be noted that the winning party himself is responsible for the enforcement of the costs award.

Legal aid and a reduction of the other costs of proceedings is available to persons of limited means. As of 1 January 1994 the rules governing legal aid have largely been laid down in the *Wet op de rechtsbijstand* (Legal Aid Act) and its implementing decrees. Any costs awarded against a legally aided person must always be borne by that person. Furthermore, a personal contribution towards the legal aid costs is often required.

8.10. Proceedings Outside the Courts

8.10.1. SURVEY

Two types of proceedings outside the courts have been provided in Netherlands private law: arbitration and binding advice. Mediation, minitrial and other types of alternative dispute resolution without a binding decision of a third person have not been provided for. In addition, there are forms of proceedings outside the courts which are based on public law initiated by the government, for example the procedure to obtain leave to dismiss an employee, which leave can be obtained from the regional director of labour relations, and the procedure before the rent tribunal as a prelude to a procedure before the cantonal court.

The phenomenon of proceedings outside the courts can explain that in the Netherlands the number of judges and lawyers per 100,000 inhabitants is considerably lower than in surrounding countries.

Here we shall consider only arbitration and binding advice.

8.10.2. ARBITRATION

Since 1 December 1986 a completely new Arbitration Act has been in force in the Netherlands, which Act forms the new Book IV of the Code of Civil Procedure. This Arbitration Act has been drafted in close collaboration with practical experts. It shows a marked influence of international (model) arbitration rules. The UNCITRAL Model Law in particular has influenced the substance of the new Act.

The Act contains a great number of provisions that bear witness to modern ideas in the field of arbitration: art. 1053 establishes the doctrine of separability (the validity of the arbitration agreement must be decided independent from the principal contract between the parties); art. 1020 contains the so-called quality arbitration (arbitration outside a dispute); there are ample guarantees for the hearing of both parties; arbitrators have the right to determine that arbitration will take place at another place than the place prescribed by law (in order to avoid unnecessary travel; art. 1037); it includes so-called summary arbitral proceedings if parties agree thereto (art. 1051); appeal to a second arbitral tribunal is possible if parties agree (art. 1051); rectification and supplementation of an arbitral award are possible without any need for appeal (arts. 1060-1061 Rv). The court has important functions of service and control, though it does not determine the arbitration. The court decides, for instance, on an application to challenge arbitrators, appoints arbitrators if necessary, grants leave for enforcement subject to exceptional reasons for disallowing leave (arts. 1062 and 1063 resp. 1075 and 1076) and sets aside arbitral awards on restricted grounds which are exhaustively listed (art. 1065).

The Netherlands Arbitration Act can be characterised generally by a considerably liberal tendency: as appears from many provisions in the Act, it depends on the parties how the arbitral procedure will be conducted.

See for an English treatment of this subject *Netherlands Arbitration Law* by A.J. van den Berg, R. van Delden and H.J. Snijders, Kluwer Law & Taxation Publishers, Deventer/Boston 1993.

8.10.3. BINDING ADVICE

Binding advice is a form of private dispute resolution which developed in practice (i.e. outside the law).

Binding advice has recently been given a statutory basis in the New Civil Code (i.e. as a species of the so-called '*vaststellingsovereenkomst*' ('determination agreement' in Book 7), but this basis remains very general. Binding advice is an extension of the agreement between the parties by a decision from a binding adviser. That decision indeed binds the parties subject to the criteria of reasonableness and fairness, but it can be set aside. These criteria concern both the way in which the advice was realised and material substantive reasons. In respect of the realisation of the advice, one may think in particular of the violation of fundamental principles such as hearing both parties.

Leave to enforce (an '*exequatur*') cannot be obtained in respect of binding advice. However, in various trades there are commissions (under the auspices of the Association of Commissions for the resolution of disputes in Consumer matters) which deal with disputes in those trades and give binding advice, the enforcement of which is guaranteed by the members of that trade.

9. German Civil Procedure*

Peter Smits and Marc Ynzonides**

9.1. Overview/Sources

9.1.1. INTRODUCTION

Present *Zivilprozessrecht*, as German civil procedure is called, has two historical roots, namely Roman law and Germanic law. It has therefore been influenced by the Roman procedures *per formulas*, whereby a dispute was decided by subsumption of the case under the conditions for allowing the claim as stated by the Roman magistrate in his proceedings form. Under Roman law disputes were decided on the basis of objectively formulated rules of law. Germanic law, on the other hand, which did not differentiate between civil and criminal law, was based on the concept of an injustice suffered by the plaintiff through an act of the defendant, which had to be put right by the defendant. The plaintiff sued and the defendant had to exonerate himself by adducing evidence to the contrary. The community (the people's tribunal) pronounced judgment, but assumed an extremely reticent position during the proceedings; the proceedings were led summarily by a chairman only. The proceedings were characterised in particular by publicity, party autonomy and strong formalism.

In the Middle Ages German rules of procedure were subject to the influence of rules of procedure which were developed in the Italian cities. The people's tribunal, derived from Germanic law, was replaced by judicial officials. Civil procedure in Germany was also strongly regulated.

In the nineteenth century the influence of the French *Code de procédure civile* led to a reform of German procedure. This resulted in the *Zivilprozessordnung* (ZPO), the German Code of Civil Procedure, which is in force today.

The area where German civil procedure applies has been expanded due to the *Einigungsvertrag* of 31 August 1990 between the Federal Republic of Germany and the former German Democratic Republic. Since 3 October 1990 the law of the Federal Republic of Germany has been in force in five

* This English edition of the original Dutch text was prepared by P. Smits alone.

** Thanks are due to Ms. Hildegard Weidinger (Rechtsanwältin at lawyers' office Boekel de Nerée, Amsterdam) and Dr. Paul Gotzen (Rechtsanwalt, Düsseldorf).

new federal states, the *Bundesländern* Brandenburg, Mecklenburg-Vorpommern, Saxony, Saxony-Anhalt and Thüringen. However, the rules of procedure of the old FRG fully apply only in East Berlin. In the five new federal states, there are important exceptions which relate to the special situation still existing in former East Germany.

A summary of the historical development of German rules of procedure can be found in Rosenberg/Schwab, *Zivilprozessrecht*, München, 15. Auflage, 1993, p. 16 ff.

9.1.2. ACT AND CONVENTION

The *Zivilprozessordnung* dates back to 1877 and is the major source of German rules of procedure. It contains rules relating to contentious proceedings (*streitige Gerichtsbarkeit*) before the *ordentliche Gerichte*, i.e. the courts judging civil and criminal disputes (§ 13 GVG).

The *Gesetz über die Angelegenheiten der freiwilligen Gerichtsbarkeit* (FGG) also forms part of the rules of civil procedure. Whereas the *streitige Gerichtsbarkeit* deals with the enforcement of rights which are in dispute, the *freiwillige* (*nichtstreitige*) *Gerichtsbarkeit* concerns the determination, amendment or abolition of rights and legal relationships, without there being a dispute; in other words, it is voluntary proceedings. Thus the *Gesetz über die Angelegenheiten der freiwilligen Gerichtsbarkeit* lays down rules of procedure e.g. for family and inheritance matters, for matters relating to the status of persons and for matters involving the land register and commercial register. Apart from the *Gesetz über die Angelegenheiten der freiwilligen Gerichtsbarkeit*, the *Gesetz über die Kosten in Angelegenheiten der freiwilligen Gerichtsbarkeit* is also of importance.

The following Acts are also relevant: the *Gerichtsverfassungsgesetz* (GVG) provides for the organisation and jurisdiction of the ordinary judiciary. The *Deutsche Richtergesetz* (DRiG) contains rules relating to the profession and the position of judges. The *Rechtspflegergesetz* (RPflG) provides for the transfer of judges' duties - to lighten their caseload - to the so-called *Rechtspfleger* (*see* section 9.3.1). The *Gerichtskostengesetz* (GKG) contains rules relating to the legal costs payable by the parties. The *Bundesrechtsanwaltsordnung* (BRAO) provides rules for lawyers practising their profession, whereas the *Bundesgebührenordnung für Rechtsanwälte* (BRAGO) regulates the lawyers' fees. The *Zwangsversteigerungsgesetz* (ZVG) deals with the sale of immovable property and ships as a measure of enforcement.

All these laws can be found in the law edition *Schönfelder Deutsche Gesetze*, München, 81. Auflage, 1994, publisher C.H. Beck. There is also a paperback edition of the *Zivilprozessordnung* containing most of the above-mentioned relevant laws in two different versions: the *Rote Reihe* (München, 47. Auflage, 1992) and the *Weiße Reihe* (München, 23. Auflage, 1993), both also published by C.H. Beck.

In addition to German laws a number of international conventions is relevant: in particular the European Convention for the Protection of Human Rights and Fundamental Freedoms (ECHRFF; entry into force 3 September 1953), the European Convention on Jurisdiction and the Enforcement of Judgments in Civil and Commercial Matters (Brussels Convention; *see* section 3.1.1), the Lugano Convention (entry into force 1 March 1995), the Hague Convention on the Service Abroad of Judicial and Extrajudicial Documents in Civil or Commercial Matters of 1965 (entry into force 26 June 1979) and the Hague Convention on the Taking of Evidence Abroad in Civil or Commercial Matters of 1970 (entry into force 26 June 1979). In Germany the European Convention on Information on Foreign Law of 1968 (entry into force 19 March 1975) also applies, as well as the Hague Convention on Civil Procedure of 1954 (entry into force 1 January 1960). For arbitration the New York Convention of 1958 (*see* section 9.10.2) and the European Convention on International Commercial Arbitration of 1961 (entry into force 25 October 1965) are relevant.

These conventions form part of Federal law pursuant to art. 25 Grundgesetz (GG); national laws may be tested against these conventions and every citizen can derive rights and obligations from these conventions and invoke them before the German courts.

9.1.3. LITERATURE AND CASE LAW

Extensive commentaries on the rules of civil procedure in Germany have been published. Handbooks or books containing article-by-article commentaries consisting of more than a thousand pages are not at all exceptional. The chief handbooks/commentaries on German litigation include: Rosenberg/Schwab, *Zivilprozeßrecht*, C.H. Beck'sche Verlagsbuchhandlung, München, 15. Auflage, 1993, Baumbach/Lauterbach/Albers/Hartmann, *Zivilprozeßordnung*, C.H. Beck'sche Verlagsbuchhandlung, München, 53. Auflage, 1995 and Stein/Jonas, *Kommentar zur Zivilprozeßordnung*, Tübingen, 20. Auflage 1977-1989, 21. Auflage/Buch 1 (§§ 1-90): 1993, Buch 2 (§§ 91-252); 1994, Buch 5/2 (§§ 92-703d):1993. Less voluminous and primarily introductory books are, for example, Baur/Grunsky, *Zivilprozeßordnung*, Frankfurt am

Main, 7. Auflage, 1991, Jauernig, *Zivilprozeßordnung*, München 24. Auflage, 1993 and Wieser, *Grundzüge des Zivilprozeßrechts*, Köln, 1986. In respect of 'freiwillige Gerichtsbarkeit' *see also* the commentary of the same title by Keidel/Kuntze/Winkler, München, 12. Auflage, 1986/1987.

Journals in which both articles and case law on *inter alia* civil procedure are published, include *Monatschrift für Deutsches Recht* (MDR), *Juristenzeitung* (JZ), *Neue Juristische Wochenschrift* (NJW), *Der Deutsche Rechtspfleger* (Rpfleger), *Juristische Rundschau* (JR) and *Zeitschrift für Zivilprozeß* (ZZP).

Case law is published in the *Entscheidungen des Bundesgerichtshofs in Zivilsachen* (BGHZ; edition Heyman-Verlag) and the *Entscheidungen der Oberlandesgerichte in Zivilsachen* (edition C.H. Beck'sche Verlagsbuchhandlung). There is also the *Nachschlagewerk des Bundesgerichtshofs* (München, from 1961) published by Lindenmaier/Möhring.

9.1.4. DATA BASES

In Germany, publisher C.H. Beck in Munich provides several data bases: by means of the CD-ROM edition NJW-Volltext it is possible to search in all articles and judgments which have appeared in the NJW since 1981. Schönfelder-Plus (another CD-ROM edition) gives a survey of all legislation that has appeared. These data bases are updated several times a year. Another important data base is LSK (Leitsatzkartei des Deutschen Rechts) in which literature and case law can be searched under a particular headword. Heymans Verlag in Cologne publishes BGH-DAT, which includes all judgments of the BGH since 1986. Finally, the data base Juris contains summaries of judicial decisions.

9.2. Fundamental Principles

9.2.1. INTRODUCTION

In Germany fundamental principles of civil procedure apply which correspond in a substantial way with and in some cases exceed the minimum limits set in a supranational connection (art. 6 ECHRFF and art. 14 CCPR). In Germany nearly every expert on civil litigation uses his own list of fundamental principles of civil procedure. The way these principles are named and described may also vary among the experts. However, by analysing the principles on the various lists and their common factors, one can arrive at a more or less generally applicable list of fundamental principles. The fundamental principles referred to below also supplement those laid down by art. 6 ECHRFF.

Administration of justice in two factual instances and supervision by one supreme court over the administration of justice are not regarded as fundamental principles. It is nevertheless true in German procedure that judgments are *grundsätzlich anfechtbar*, which means that they are subject to appeal (*see* Rosenberg/Schwab, *Zivilprozeßrecht*, p. 804). Decisions at first instance are in principle subject to appeal by way of *Berufung* and appeal judgments by way of *Revision*. *See* section 9.6 ff. for the means of recourse.

The *richterlichen Unabhängigkeit und Objektivität*, i.e. the independence and impartiality of the judiciary, are also not considered to be fundamental principles of civil procedure. However, similar to art. 6 ECHRFF, art. 97 GG and § 1 GVG state that the judiciary is independent of the legislature and executive authorities. In addition, the courts must be impartial, which is guaranteed by the possibility of *Ausschließung* (§ 41 ZPO), *Ablehnung* (§ 42 ZPO) and *Selbstablehnung* (§ 48 ZPO), which are rules providing for the challenge and exemption of judges.

Finally, the principle of motivating a decision does not as such form part of the list of fundamental principles. *See, however*, § 313 ZPO. The same applies to the mandatory legal representation (*see* section 9.3.3).

9.2.2. PRINCIPLE OF PARTY AUTONOMY (DISPOSITIONS- ODER PARTEIHERRSCHAFTSGRUNDSATZ)

It is the parties who decide whether proceedings will be commenced, what the subject of the proceedings will be and whether the proceedings will be continued to the very end.

This freedom of the parties is based on the idea that the main purpose of civil proceedings is to enforce private rights, whereby the parties need ample latitude to realise their rights. This principle would be violated if the rules of civil procedure denied these rights to parties.

This *Dispositions- oder Parteiherrschaftsgrundsatz* has been reflected at various places in the law: in their pleadings the parties determine the extent of the court's consideration of the case (§§ 308, 536 and 559 ZPO); the plaintiff can withdraw his claim (§ 269 ZPO); the appellant can withdraw or relinquish a means of recourse (§§ 514, 515 and 566 ZPO). The plaintiff may also determine the contents of the judgment by defaulting (§ 306 ZPO), the defendant may do so by an admission (§ 307 ZPO), and the parties can terminate the proceedings prematurely by concluding a settlement or by declaring the main dispute resolved.

An important exception to the *Dispositions- oder Parteiherrschaftsgrundsatz* is laid down in § 139 ZPO: the *richterliche Aufklärungspflicht*. This duty of the court will be discussed further in section 9.2.3.

Another restriction of the parties' procedural freedom lies in the fact that the court leads the proceedings (*see further* section 9.4.2c).

The opposite of *Dispositionsgrundsatz* is *Amtsverfahren*: the court takes the initiative to commence proceedings. This *Amtsverfahren* occurs in *freiwillige Gerichtsbarkeit*. The court may of its own motion commence proceedings, for example, if a minor is neglected.

9.2.3. PRINCIPLE OF THE PARTIES ADDUCING THE FACTS (VERHANDLUNGS- ODER BEIBRINGUNGSGRUNDSATZ)

Verhandlungs- oder Beibringungsgrundsatz determines that it is the parties who have to adduce the facts which, if having been proven, must lead to the judicial decision desired. The rationale underlying this principle is the same as the rationale underlying the *Dispositionsgrundsatz*.

When stating facts the parties must, however, observe the *Pflicht zur Vollständigkeit und Wahrhaftigkeit* (§ 138 ZPO) and the *Mitwirkungs- und Förderungspflicht*, which means that the parties must be complete and truthful in stating their facts and must cooperate in adducing the relevant facts as quickly as possible.

The court must in principle base its judgment on only those facts which have been presented by a party in the proceedings. It is, however, possible for the court to discover certain facts itself by means of the *richterliche Aufklärungspflicht* (§ 139 ZPO). The court must aim to obtain a complete presentation by the parties of the facts which are materially and procedurally relevant, in particular by requiring that insufficient statements and inconclusive evidence be supplemented. The court may also order the parties to appear in court to give information (§ 141 ZPO).

The opposite of the *Verhandlungs- oder Beibringungsgrundsatz* is the *Untersuchungsgrundsatz*. This implies that the court of its own motion and independently of the parties must find out the factual configuration. The *Untersuchungsgrundsatz* applies to the *freiwillige Gerichtsbarkeit* (*see* § 12 FGG) for reasons of public policy which often play a part in *freiwillige Gerichtsbarkeit*.

9.2.4. PRINCIPLES OF ORALITY, IMMEDIACY AND PUBLICITY (GRUNDSÄTZE DER MÜNDLICHKEIT, UNMITTELBARKEIT UND ÖFFENTLICHKEIT)

The principle of *Mündlichkeit* applies to the starting-point of the oral consideration of the case, when only that which has been presented orally may form the basis of the judicial decision (§ 128 ZPO). This does not alter the fact that sometimes a judgment may be given without oral consideration (*see* the *schriftliche Verfahren*, the proceedings on the documents, in § 128(1), (2) and (3) ZPO) and written documents may also be considered (*see* § 137(3) ZPO).

The principle of *Unmittelbarkeit* means that the entire proceedings must be conducted before the same court (*erkennende Gericht*) (*see* §§ 128 and 355 ZPO). It is, however, possible for the production of evidence to be delegated to another judge (*see* §§ 361 and 362 ZPO). Only those judges who took part in the oral consideration of the case may give judgment. The aim of *Unmittelbarkeit* is to accomplish that judgment is only passed by a court which has complete and, preferably, personal knowledge of the case.

The principle of *Öffentlichkeit* determines that - to strengthen confidence in the administration of justice - the hearings and the delivery of the judgment must be public (§ 169 GVG; *see also* art. 6 ECHRFF).

9.2.5. PRINCIPLE OF FREE EVALUATION OF EVIDENCE (GRUNDSATZ DER FREIEN RICHTERLICHEN BEWEISWÜRDIGUNG)

The *Grundsatz der freien richterlichen Beweiswürdigung* refers to the court's freedom in the evaluation of the evidence produced by the parties. Only in exceptional cases is the court bound by rules of evidence (§ 286 ZPO). In the grounds for the decision the court must indicate which points of view were conclusive in deciding the case.

9.2.6. PRINCIPLE OF PROCEDURAL EFFICIENCY (KONZENTRATIONSGRUNDSATZ - BESCHLEUNIGUNG DES PROZESSES)

In order to keep the proceedings as brief as possible, both the court (*see* § 273 ZPO) and the parties are under a *Prozeßförderungspflicht*, a duty to participate actively in the swift completion of proceedings. The court's duty forms part of the *Aufklärungspflicht* mentioned in section 9.2.3 (§ 139 ZPO), but can also be found in § 273 ZPO, pursuant to which the court may take measures to prepare the oral consideration of the case. These measures must render it possible to conclude the case at its oral consideration. The court must also choose between the *frühe erste Termin* (§ 275 ZPO) and the *schriftliches Vorverfahren* (§ 276 ZPO), an efficient way of dividing simple and complicated cases (*see further* section 9.4.2.c). Finally, the setting of time-limits allows the court to ensure the smooth running of the proceedings. Parties are under an obligation to submit or communicate all *Angriffs- und Verteidigungsmittel* in time, i.e. all grounds for their claim and possible grounds of defence (§ 282(1) and (2) ZPO). *Angriffs- und Verteidigungsmittel* which have been produced too late by the parties will not be considered (*Präklusion*). *See* for the sanctions on exceeding time-limits, for example, §§ 230 and 296 ZPO.

9.2.7. PRINCIPLE OF ACCESS TO THE COURT (ANSPRUCH AUF RICHTERLICHES GEHÖR)

The right of parties to be given the opportunity to be heard is based on art. 6 ECHRFF and art. 103 GG. It is further elaborated in various provisions in the ZPO (*see* §§ 278(3) and 335(1) third sentence ZPO)

9.3. Principal Characters

9.3.1. INTRODUCTION

The principal characters who will be discussed in this chapter are the judge (section 9.3.2), the lawyers (section 9.3.3) and the parties (section 9.3.4).

Before discussing each of these principal characters in detail, some other persons involved in civil litigation will be considered:

- Each court has a *Geschäftsstelle* (a registry), at which officials called *Urkundsbeamten* carry out administrative (i.e. non-judicial) duties (§ 153 GVG). The work of the *Urkundsbeamten* includes recording the proceedings and making the files.
- The *Rechtspfleger* is an independent figure whose work can be classified as lying between that of a judge and that of an *Urkundsbeamte*. His original task was to relieve the judge of routine cases. At present the scope of his work is much wider (*see* § 20 *Rechtspflegergesetz*): his work in particular includes the completion of the *Mahnverfahren* (*see* section 9.3.7), the determination of maintenance for children in simple actions

and taking measures in the *Prozeßkostenhilfeverfahren* (*see* section 9.9.3). He has considerable powers in the area of *Zwangsvollstreckung* (section 9.8.4).

– Finally, the main task of the *Gerichtsvollzieher* (bailiff) is in the *Zwangsvollstreckung*, the enforcement of judicial decisions. He also serves writs to appear before the court (§ 154 GVG).

9.3.2. THE JUDGE

a. Introduction

The *Gerichtsverfassungsgesetz* (GVG) provides rules for the organisation of the ordinary judiciary and the absolute and relative jurisdiction of the various courts.

To the ordinary judiciary (*Gerichte der ordentlichen Zivilgerichtsbarkeit*) belong the *Amtsgerichte* (AG), *Landgerichte* (LG), *Oberlandesgerichte* (OLG) and the *Bundesgerichtshof* (BGH). *See* § 12 GVG. The *Amtsgericht* and the *Landgericht* are courts of first instance (*Eingangsgerichte*). The *Landgericht* and the *Oberlandesgericht* are appeal courts (*Berufungsgerichte*). The *Bundesgerichtshof* is the supreme court (*Revisionsgericht*). Following an amendment, the Gerichtsverfassungsgesetz also applies to the new Länder (Mecklenburg-Vorpommern since 1 July 1992, Saxony-Anhalt since 1 October 1992, Saxony since 1 January 1993, Thüringen since 1 September 1993 and Brandenburg since 1 December 1993); *see also* Kissel Gerichtsverfassungsgesetz (commentary no. 2 Auflage 1994, no. 36 *ad* § 1 EGG).

The *Amtsgericht* consists of single professional judges (*Einzelrichtern*; §22(1) GVG). The *Familiengericht* (the court for family and adoption matters and the like) forms part of the *Amtsgericht* (§ 23b GVG). The *Landgericht* comprises one or more civil chambers consisting of one or three professional judge(s) (§§ 60 and 75 GVG and § 348 ZPO) and - not mandatory - chambers for commercial cases, consisting of one professional judge and two lay judges (§§ 93 and 105 GVG). The *Oberlandesgericht* consists of civil chambers (*Zivilsenate*) of three professional judges, or - if the parties agree - of one judge (§§ 116 and 122 GVG) and, finally, the *Bundesgerichtshof* consists of *Zivilsenate* of five professional judges (§§ 130 and 139 GVG).

It is noteworthy in respect of the court's jurisdiction that the court must of its own motion apply the rules concerning the *ausschließliche Zuständigkeit* (the imperative rules of jurisdiction). Throughout the proceedings parties can invoke the fact that the court lacks jurisdiction in this respect.

Literature concerning the judiciary and the independence of the judges includes: Schilken, *Gerichtsverfassungsrecht*, Köln/Berlin 1990 and Schmidt/Jortzig, *Richteramt und politische Betätigung*, NJW 84, 2057.

b. International jurisdiction

There are no universal rules of jurisdiction. To a significant extent the Brussels Convention provides rules of international jurisdiction for the German court. In case the Brussels Convention or another bilateral or multilateral convention does not apply, the ZPO has only a few provisions which explicitly determine the international jurisdiction of the German court (*see* §§38(2), 606a and 640a). In cases not covered by any act or convention, the prevailing opinion is that the rules concerning the *örtliche Zuständigkeit* (relative jurisdiction) also govern international jurisdiction (*see inter alia* BGH 26 January 1979, NJW 1979, 1104).

c. Sectoral jurisdiction

Whereas the demarcation of jurisdiction between the civil and the criminal courts does not pose any problems (the civil court tries civil matters, the criminal court criminal matters), the demarcation of jurisdiction between the civil court and other courts such as the social security court (*Sozialgericht*), the industrial court (*Arbeitsgericht*), the fiscal court (*Finanzgericht*) and the administrative court (*Verwaltungsgericht*) is more complicated.

With respect to these courts the so-called *Prioritätsprinzip* applies. This means that a civil court can independently and without the cooperation of the other (kind of) courts decide on its jurisdiction. If it declines jurisdiction, the case is transferred at the request of the plaintiff to the court which *is* deemed to have jurisdiction. This court is bound by the transfer, i.e. it cannot transfer the case back to the civil court. The *Prioritätsprinzip* also applies *vice versa* from the other court to the civil court (§ 17 GVG).

The majority of demarcation problems occur between the civil and the administrative court. This is due to the fact that a civil court will decline jurisdiction if an administrative procedure is available (§ 13 GVG), and that an administrative court will decline jurisdiction if any other court has jurisdiction (§ 40 *Verwaltungsgerichtsordnung*). Different theories are used (whereby a distinction is made whether the state acts as such or acts as a special person) to try and draw a demarcation line between the two courts. The wealth of case law on this issue shows that this is not always simple. *See* on this problem *inter alia* Krause, *Verfahrensrechtliche Probleme der Entscheidung über den Rechtsweg*, ZZP 83, 289 and Menger, *Zum Stand der Meinungen über die Entscheidung von öffentlichem und privatem Recht*, Festschrift für Hans J. Wolff, München 1973, p. 149 ff.

d. Absolute jurisdiction

The following system applies to the absolute jurisdiction (*sächliche Zuständigkeit*) of the various courts.

The *Amtsgericht* has absolute jurisdiction in disputes up to DM 10,000 (§ 23 No. 1 GVG as laid down by the Act of 11 January 1993 Bundesgesetzblatt I, p. 50), in disputes as defined by § 23 No. 2 GVG, and in matters of family, matrimonial, property and juvenile law set out in § 23 a GVG. In these last cases the *Amtsgericht* has jurisdiction also in respect of amounts higher than DM 10,000.

The *Landgericht* at first instance has absolute jurisdiction in civil matters in which the amount in dispute exceeds DM 10,000 and in all civil matters which do not come under the jurisdiction of the *Amtsgericht* (§ 71 GVG). In addition, the *Landgericht* is the appeal court (*Berufung*) from decisions of the *Amtsgericht*, with the exception of decisions of the *Amtsgericht* in matters concerning matrimonial and juvenile law from which appeal lies to the *Oberlandesgericht* (§ 72 GVG).

The *Oberlandesgericht* is the appeal court from decisions at first instance by the *Landgericht* and, as stated, from decisions at first instance by the *Amtsgericht* in matters concerning matrimonial and juvenile law (§ 119 GVG).

The *Bundesgerichtshof* (based in Karlsruhe) decides on appeals (*Revision)* against decisions of the *Oberlandesgericht* and exceptionally (*Sprungrevision*) against first instance decisions of the *Landgericht* (§ 133 GVG). In the case of *Sprungrevision* there is no *Berufung* which can only be done with permission of the opposing party (§ 566a ZPO).

To determine the value of the claim (*Streitwert*) § 2 *et seq*. ZPO provide a few guidelines. *See* for the (limited) possibilities to agree to deviate from the rules of absolute jurisdiction §§ 38-40 ZPO (*Gerichtsstandsvereinbarung*).

The diagram on p. 288 may serve to clarify the German civil court system and the possible ways to appeal.

e. Relative jurisdiction

The rules of relative jurisdiction (*örtliche Zuständigkeit*) are included in § 12 *et seq*. ZPO. The starting-point is the jurisdiction of the court of the place

DIAGRAM JUDICIAL ORGANISATION IN CIVIL CASES IN GERMANY

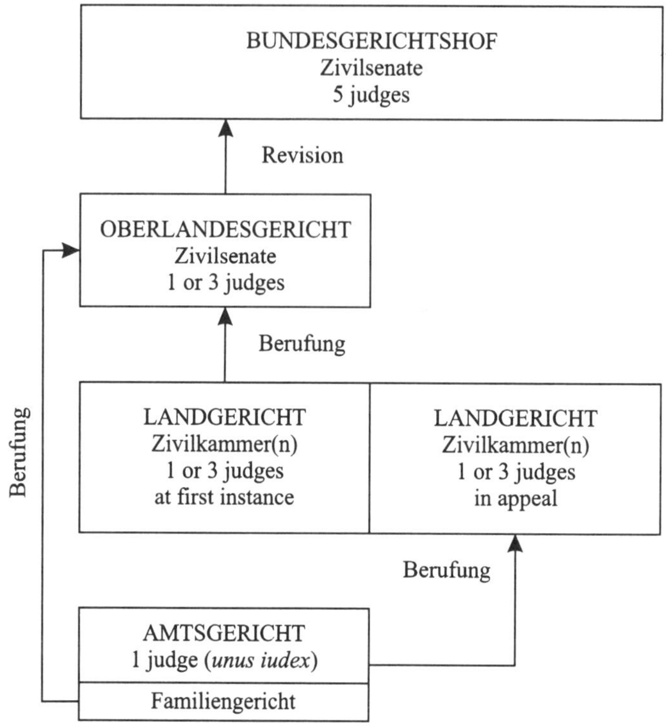

where the defendant is domiciled. In tenancy matters and matters concerning registered property, jurisdiction lies with the court of the place where the registered property is situated.

9.3.3. THE LAWYERS

In procedures before the *Landgericht*, the *Oberlandesgericht* and the *Bundesgerichtshof*, and in certain family matters before the *Familiengericht* (a division of the *Amtsgericht*), the parties must be represented by a lawyer who is admitted to the relevant court (*Anwaltsprozeß*; § 78 ZPO). Subject to certain exceptions (*see* e.g. §136(4) ZPO), the parties themselves cannot perform acts of procedure; they are not *postulationsfähig* (§ 78 ZPO).

§ 80 *et seq*. ZPO contain rules relating to the mandate to proceed. A lawyer only needs to show his mandate in case this is disputed by the opposing party (§ 88 ZPO).

Rules applying to the profession of *Rechtsanwalt* (lawyer) are laid down in the *Bundesrechtsanwaltsordnung* (BRAO). In the five new Bundesländer the *Rechtsanwaltsgesetz* of the GDR still applies (*see* appendix 1. Kapitel 3, Sachgebiet A, Abschnitt 1 Nr 5 Einigungsvertrag). The BRAO will be introduced in the new *Bundesländern* once it has been amended. If a lawyer fails to perform his duties the disciplinary rules (*Ehrengerichtsbarkeit*) can be applied, whereby the heaviest sanction is disbarring.

In Germany the *Grundsatz der freien Advokatur* and the principle of *Lokalisierung* apply, the latter meaning that a lawyer is admitted to a certain court only. It is not unusual for lawyers to form a partnership with tax consultants (*Steuerberater*) and/or accountants (*Wirtschaftsprüfer*), or to combine these functions in their own person.

9.3.4. THE PARTIES

§§ 50-90 ZPO concern the parties to the proceedings and provide rules *inter alia* concerning the capacity to act as parties in an action; the so-called *Streitgenossenschaft*; and the joinder of third parties in the proceedings.

In a formal sense there are two parties to the proceedings: the party who files the claim and the party against whom the claim is filed. Both natural persons and legal persons (e.g. a 'GmbH', the German equivalent of a company with limited liability) can be parties (they are *parteifähig*; *see* § 50 ZPO). Certain kinds of partnership without legal personality may also be parties, such as the *offene Handelsgesellschaft* (OHG) and the *Kommanditgesellschaft* (KG). An association without legal personality may be a defendant, but not a plaintiff (§50(2) ZPO).

Those who can independently enter into obligations by concluding contracts (§ 52 ZPO) are capable of conducting proceedings (*prozeßfähig*). The judge must of his own motion review the *Parteifähigkeit* and the *Prozeßfähigkeit* (*Prozeßvoraussetzung*; *see* § 56 ZPO). One can say that *Parteifähigkeit* is roughly equivalent to legal capacity and *Prozeßfähigkeit* to persons' power to dispose of a matter. The capacity to be parties and the capacity to conduct proceedings are conditions for the validity of acts in the proceedings (*Prozeßhandlungsvoraussetzung*). A person without the capacity to conduct proceedings, but who is a party (e.g. a bankrupt or a minor) must be represented in the proceedings by a legal representative (e.g. a receiver or parents).

We speak of a *Streitgenossenschaft* (Str.G.) where there are several persons (*subjektive Klagenhäufung*; subjective cumulation) either involved as plaintiffs (*aktive* Str.G.) or as defendants (*passive* Str.G.). There is mention of *einfache Streitgenossenschaft* if, for example, the court decides to consider several cases simultaneously (joinder; § 147 ZPO), so that there are several parties on the plaintiff's or on the defendant's side. If two procedures are pending which result from the same traffic accident (party A versus party B, respectively party C versus party B), then joinder results in parties A and C together opposing party B. The *einfache Streitgenossenschaft* does not detract from the independence of the various proceedings between the parties. Should it be necessary, on the other hand, to involve both parties in the proceedings together, then this is called a *notwendige Streitgenossenschaft* (§ 62 ZPO). In this case there is one dispute, which ends in a uniform judgment by which all parties are bound. Think of an application for nullification of a resolution of the general meeting of shareholders. If the court honours the application, its judgment which nullifies the resolution affects all shareholders (*see* § 248 Abs. 1 *Aktiengesetz*); this means that all shareholders must of necessity (*prozessual notwendig*) be involved in the proceedings.

It is unclear to what extent an association of persons - with or without legal personality - may take procedural steps to protect more general or group interests. In German litigation this is referred to as *Prozeßführungsbefugnis*. The possibility of a *Verbandsklage*, a representative action, has been included in a number of laws (e.g. in § 13 of the *Gesetz gegen den unlauteren Wettbewerb*; unfair competition Act). Apart from these provisions in various laws, some writers have supported the possibility of a collective action (*Popularklage*) - for example to protect environmental interests (*see* e.g. Koch, *Prozeßführung im öffentlichen Interesse*, Frankfurt am Main, 1983).

9.4. Basic Procedure for Contentious Jurisdiction at First Instance

9.4.1. INTRODUCTION

In Germany the basic procedure for contentious jurisdiction is called the *Entscheidungs-* or *Erkenntnisverfahren*, also referred to as *Urteils-* or *Klageverfahren*. Through the *Vereinfachungsnovelle* (a regulation to simplify civil procedure) which entered into force in 1977, the *Zivilprozeßordnung* was changed drastically. This *Novelle* influenced the entire construction and progress of civil procedure in the *Zivilprozeßordnung*. Thus measures were taken to accelerate the procedure. The courts were given more powers, in particular in respect of penalties. An attempt at deformalisation was made also: the old § 274 ZPO in which most *Prozeßvoraussetzungen* and *Prozeßhindernissen* (preconditions and impediments for proceedings) were listed, was abolished. Now the law merely mentions *Rügen* (objections) against the *Zulässigkeit* of the *Klage* (the admissibility of the claim). This abolition has, however, not resulted in any change; a distinction is still made between *Prozeßvoraussetzungen* and *Prozeßhindernissen*. *See* Rosenberg/ Schwab, *Zivilprozeßrecht*, p. 534 ff.

The literature regarding the German civil procedure is considerable. The handbooks and commentaries mentioned in section 9.1.3 all contain more or less extensive descriptions of the proceedings at first instance, both before the *Landgericht* and the *Amtsgericht*.

9.4.2. PROCEDURE BEFORE THE LANDGERICHT

a. Introduction

The procedure before the *Landgericht* is governed by §§ 253-494 ZPO and consists, broadly speaking, of the following main stages: *Klageerhebung* (lodging the claim), *mündliche Verhandlung* (oral consideration), *Beweisaufnahme* (evidence) and *Urteil* (judgment). The procedure may involve three kinds of claims (*Klagen*). The *Leistungsklage* (§§ 257-258 ZPO) leads to a judgment whereby the losing party is ordered to do something, the *Feststellungsklage* (§ 256 ZPO) to a declaratory judgment and the *Gestaltungsklage* to a judgment which creates a new legal relationship or amends or nullifies an existing legal relationship.

b. Commencement of proceedings

The proceedings are commenced by the *Kläger* or *Antragssteller* (plaintiff) filing a *Klageschrift* (the document which introduces the proceedings containing the claim) with the court which has absolute and relative jurisdiction (§ 253 ZPO). The proceedings begin when the claim is filed (§ 261 ZPO). The court sends the *Klageschrift* to the *Beklagte* or *Antragsgegner* (defendant) who is given a time-limit to react.

The contents of the *Klageschrift* must satisfy the requirements laid down in §253(2) and (3) ZPO: the parties, the court, the claim and the grounds upon which the claim is based must be stated. In order to be valid, the *Klage-*

schrift must also satisfy the requirements set for written legal documents in general (*Schriftsätze*; § 130 ZPO).

If the plaintiff files more than one claim, this is called *objektive Klagenhäufung* (§ 260 ZPO).

The *Streitgegenstand* (the dispute) must be *klagbar*, i.e. must not explicitly or implicitly be of no value legally. Other proceedings between the same parties in respect of the same case may not be pending elsewhere and the case may not already have been decided in other proceedings. Finally, the case must be *rechtsschutzfähig*, which means that there must be a sufficient interest in the case.

c. Proceedings

On the basis of the *Klageschrift* the court must decide how the proceedings shall continue. It is the legislator's intention (§272(1) ZPO) to concentrate the civil procedure in one single, extensively prepared for, hearing, the so-called *Haupttermin* (§ 278 ZPO). In order to deal with the procedure in one *Haupttermin* the law provides two ways: the court may at its discretion choose the *frühe erste Termin* (§ 275 ZPO), or the *schriftliches Vorverfahren* (§ 276 ZPO).

If the court chooses a *frühe erste Termin* (an early oral hearing), then the defendant is forthwith served with an authenticated copy of the *Klageschrift* by the court, along with a notice to appear before the court (§§ 274 and 271 ZPO). The *frühe erste Termin* is prepared by the court by taking appropriate measures: these may include ordering the parties to appear in person or hearing witnesses or experts (§ 273).

If, however, the matter cannot be decided at this first hearing (for example because of its complex nature), then the court must take all the necessary measures for the *Haupttermin*, so that the case may be dealt with there (§275(2) ZPO).

At the *schriftliches Vorverfahren* (documentary preparatory procedure) the defendant is served with the *Klageschrift* forthwith and is summoned to inform the court of his *Verteidigungsbereitschaft* (i.e. his intention to defend himself) within two weeks and, if so, to submit his *Klageerwiderung* (defence) within a further two weeks (minimum time-limits; *see* § 276 (1) and (2) ZPO). Subsequently the plaintiff may be given a time-limit to react in writing to the defence (§ 276 (3) ZPO). If the defendant fails to inform the court of his intention to defend himself, then the court decides the case at the plaintiff's request without a further hearing on the basis of the plaintiff's documents (§ 331 (1) ZPO). Otherwise the court, after sufficient written preparation, determines a date for the *Haupttermin* (§ 273 (3) ZPO). Leaving aside *Anerkenntnis* (when the defendant admits the claim), *Klageverzicht* (when the claim is abandoned by the plaintiff), and *Prozeßvergleich* (when a settlement is reached between the parties), the *Haupttermin* results in adversarial proceedings. On the basis of the extensive preparation it will be evident which of the facts alleged by the plaintiff will be decisive, what is and what is not in dispute between the parties, which evidence has been adduced or is available and which legal questions must be answered. When, finally, the dispute is ready to be decided, judgment is pronounced.

Overall, contentious litigation in Germany can be characterised as informal, oral and concentrated.

d. Judgment

Following deliberations in chambers (§§ 192-197 ZPO), the court pronounces judgment.

If the defendant does not defend the proceedings, they will end in a *Versäumnisurteil* (default judgment; § 331 ZPO). If the defendant does defend the proceedings, adversarial proceedings will follow which are determined in a *streitiges Urteil* (adversarial judgment).

Proceedings in which oral consideration by the court is obligatory are decided in an *Urteil* (§ 313 ZPO). Certain proceedings prescribed by law (e.g. § 281 ZPO) and proceedings in which oral consideration is optional are decided by *Beschluß*.

If the court pronounces judgment on the substance of the case, it is called a *Sachurteil*. If on account of procedural facts the court is unable to arrive at a judgment on the facts (e.g. if the court has no absolute jurisdiction), it is called a *Prozeßurteil*.

There is also a distinction between *Endurteil* and *Zwischenurteil*. An *Endurteil* is a final judgment on (a part of) the claim. It may be a full or partial final judgment (*Vollendurteil* or *Teilurteil*). *Zwischenurteile* (§ 303 ZPO) are decisions on essential points in the dispute between parties, without affecting the final judgment on (a part of) the claim. These decisions are binding on the court (§ 318 ZPO). The court may also give a *Vorbehaltsurteil*, which is a judgment deciding the dispute subject to the outcome of proceedings pending in respect of facts denied by the defendant.

Finally, *Verfügungen* are a type of minor decisions relating to the progression of the procedure which decisions are mostly not appealable (*see* § 329 ZPO).

The court may of its own motion pronounce its judgment provisionally enforceable with or without requiring security (*vorläufige Vollstreckbarer-*

klärung; § 708 *et seq.*). The judgment will also contain a decision on the costs of the proceedings (§ 91 ZPO).

The judgment is pronounced in public either immediately or at a later court hearing (§§ 310 and 311 ZPO) and must be motivated (§ 313 ZPO).

Finally, German rules of procedure allow for the possibility of *Berichtigung des Urteils oder Tatbestandes* (§§ 319 and 320 ZPO) and *Ergänzung des Urteils* (§ 321 ZPO), whereby apparent (factual) errors or defects in the original judgment can be corrected or supplemented.

e. Special aspects of procedure

1. Non-appearance

A party is *säumig* if, having been summoned, he either does not appear in the proceedings before the case is considered by the court or does not perform any procedural acts.

Säumnis (default) of the plaintiff results in the claim being dismissed as unfounded, at the defendant's request, in a *Versäumnisurteil* (default judgment; § 130 ZPO). The claim is dismissed as *unzulässig* (inadmissible) if the content of the *Klageschrift* is defective (*mangelhaft*) or if there is no *Prozeßvoraussetzung* (*see* section 9.3.4).

Säumnis of the defendant allows the plaintiff to request judgment in default against the defendant. This *Versäumnisurteil* will usually be given if the claim does not appear unfounded or unjust to the court, if there are no defects in the *Klageschrift* and all the other *Prozeßvoraussetzungen* have been complied with.

2. Third parties in the proceedings

Intervention by third parties in proceedings of their own initiative is possible on the basis of § 64 ZPO (*Hauptintervention*). Joinder either on the side of the plaintiff or on the side of the defendant (*Nebenintervention*) is also possible (§ 66 ZPO). Finally, either party may also involve a third party in the proceedings (*Streitverkündigung*; § 72 ZPO).

3. Amendment of claim

The plaintiff may amend his claim if the opposing party agrees or the court deems the amendment relevant (§ 263 ZPO). Certain changes are not regarded as amendments of the claim (*see* § 264 ZPO). The court's decision concerning an amendment of the claim is not subject to appeal (§ 268 ZPO).

4. Counterclaim

The defendant may file a counterclaim (*Widerklage*), whether conditional or not (*see* e.g. §§ 33, 145 (2) and 256 (2) ZPO). The *Widerklage* must be connected with the main claim or with the defence against the main claim (§ 33 (1) ZPO).

5. Production of evidence

The starting-point for the rules of evidence is that each party must prove those alleged facts which lead to the legal consequences sought by the relevant party. In certain cases (mostly pursuant to specific provisions of law in e.g. the *Bürgerliches Gesetzbuch* (BGB), but sometimes based on suspicions or if either party makes it impossible for the other party to produce evidence) the burden of proof will be reversed. Parties can and will usually adduce evidence of their own statements (§ 282 (1) ZPO). An offer by a party to adduce such evidence may not be disregarded, subject to certain exceptions (see for example § 296 ZPO). The court may also of its own motion order a party to adduce evidence, except evidence by witnesses (§ 273 ZPO). If facts are not admitted, only facts which are relevant must be proved. Facts of general knowledge, rules of experience with which the court is familiar and objective law require no proof. Foreign law occupies a special place in this respect: proof of (the content of) law applicable abroad must only be produced inasmuch as the court is not familiar with the relevant foreign law. The ZPO emphatically states that, in respect of this point, the court is not limited to what the parties adduce, but may also consult other sources (§ 293). From this provision, case law derives an official duty (instead of an authority) on the part of the judge to determine the content of the applicable foreign law. Pursuant to German law, the judge is also under an obligation to apply the conflict of laws rules which lead to the designation of the applicable foreign law.

Orders on evidence are made by *Beschluß* and evidence may be adduced prior to or following upon the oral consideration of the case (§ 358 and 358a ZPO). Production of evidence in accordance with the provisions of the *Zivilprozeßordnung* is also called *Strengbeweis*, which takes place before the court and as a rule follows immediately after the oral consideration of the matter. In specific cases production of evidence takes place before a specially appointed judge (*beauftragter Richter*; § 355 (1) ZPO). Parties are entitled to attend (§ 357 ZPO). An exhaustive list of the means of evidence is laid down in the ZPO: *Augenschein* (judicial inspection of the site; §§ 371 and 372a ZPO), *Zeugen* (witnesses; §§ 373-401 ZPO), *Sachverständige* (experts; §§ 402-414 ZPO), *Urkunden* (deeds; §§ 415-444 ZPO) and finally the *Parteivernehmung* (hearing of the parties by the court) as an alternative means of evidence (§§ 445-455 ZPO).

Appraisal of the evidence is left to the court (*freie Beweiswürdigung*; §§ 286 and 287 ZPO).

6. *Settlement*

The settlement out-of-court, if reached through lawyers, is provided for in § 1044b ZPO (added by Artikel 1 Z 68 *Rechtpflegevereinfachungsgesetz*). In general a settlement out-of-court has no direct effect on the proceedings pending. However, by amending the claim in the summons (*Klageänderung*) a judgment may be obtained in accordance with the settlement reached.

9.4.3. PROCEDURE BEFORE THE AMTSGERICHT

The procedure before the *Amtsgericht* is governed by §§ 495-510 ZPO. It is identical to the one before the *Landgericht* subject to certain specific exceptions (§ 495 ZPO). Thus certain procedural acts may also be done orally (§ 496 ZPO) and there is no mandatory legal representation. If the *Amtsgericht* has no absolute or relative jurisdiction then it must point at this lack of jurisdiction and the possible consequences thereof to the plaintiff (§ 504 ZPO). Increasing the claim may result in its transfer to the *Landgericht* (§ 506 ZPO).

9.5. Basic Procedure for Voluntary Jurisdiction at First Instance

9.5.1. INTRODUCTION

Only part of the rules of *freiwillige Gerichtsbarkeit* (voluntary jurisdiction) apply to the whole of the Federal Republic. The rest is left to the individual federal states and the relevant rules can be found in the *Landesgesetze* (legislation of the individual federal states).

The *Gesetz über die Angelegenheiten der freiwilligen Gerichtsbarkeit* (FGG) provides the framework for voluntary jurisdiction. The procedure as determined by this Act applies to different kinds of cases (*see also* section 9.1.2). The point of departure is that the procedure only applies if the legislator (whether federal or otherwise) has declared it to be applicable, as he has done, for instance, for guardianship and inheritance cases. If a case is brought before a *Gericht der streitigen Gerichtsbarkeit* although a *Gericht der freiwilligen Gerichtsbarkeit* has jurisdiction, or *vice versa*, then the case is transferred to the court which does have jurisdiction by analogy with § 17 GVG.

The general provisions of §§ 1-34 FGG apply to all cases of voluntary jurisdiction, unless the special provisions determine otherwise. In the following sections of the FGG additional provisions are laid down relating to *inter alia* guardianship cases (§§ 35-64k FGG), inheritance cases (§§ 72-99 FGG) and commercial cases (§§ 125-158 FGG).

Literature on voluntary jurisdiction includes Baur/Wolf, *Grundbegriffe des Rechts der Freiwilligen Gerichtsbarkeit*, Stuttgart, 2. Auflage 1980, Bumiller/Winkler, *Freiwillige Gerichtsbarkeit*, München, 5. Auflage 1992 and Habscheid, *Freiwillige Gerichtsbarkeit*, München, 7. Auflage 1983.

9.5.2. PROCEDURE

The procedure for voluntary jurisdiction will only be considered in brief. The courts of *freiwillige Gerichtsbarkeit* are the same as the courts of *ordentliche Gerichtsbarkeit*. As discussed in section 9.3.1, cases which must be tried by the *Amtsgericht* at first instance are usually dealt with by *Rechtspfleger*.

In comparison with the basic procedure for contentious jurisdiction the procedure of *freiwilligen Gerichtsbarkeit* is much more informal. Unlike the basic procedure for contentious jurisdiction, this procedure can in many cases also be commenced by the court itself (*Amtsverfahren*). The proceedings are commenced by a petition which in principle is an informal document (*Antrag*; *see also* § 11 FGG). Any opposing party may file a written defence (*Erwiderungsschrift*). The court has an active role during the proceedings, because pursuant to § 12 FGG it may examine the facts itself and may also order evidence itself. In respect of evidence, the so-called *Freibeweis* applies in principle. The court is not bound by particular means of evidence or special provisions concerning the production of evidence (*but see* § 15 FGG). Procedural acts may be performed by the parties both orally and in writing. The proceedings are not public. Decisions are in the form of a *Verfügung* (§ 16 FGG), from which lies the recourse of *Beschwerde* (*see* §§ 19-30 FGG). No *Urteile* are pronounced, which excludes the recourse of *Berufung* and *Revision*. The recourse of *weitere Beschwerde* lies from decisions by the *Beschwerdegericht* (§ 27 (1) FGG). *See* for the costs of the procedure the *Gesetz über die Kosten in Angelegenheiten der freiwilligen Gerichtsbarkeit*.

9.6. MEANS OF RECOURSE

9.6.1. INTRODUCTION

The following means of recourse are available in Germany: *Berufung*, *Revision* and *Beschwerde*. The first two means may be used against *Urteile* (i.e. judgments in contentious cases), the latter against *Beschlüsse* and *Verfügungen* (which decisions are given both in contentious proceedings and in voluntary proceedings). Applying these means of recourse suspends enforcement (*Suspensiveffekt*; § 705 ZPO), unless the decision was declared provisionally enforceable. The person who lodges the means must do so within a fixed time-limit stating his grounds for appeal and he must be affected by the decision against which he appeals, i.e. he must have an interest in the appeal. The appellate court may not give a judgment which would be more detrimental to the appellant than the judgment of which he appealed (prohibition of *reformatio in peius*; §§ 536 and 559 ZPO). The opposing party on appeal may also - even after the time-limit has expired - lodge a means of recourse, the *Anschlußrechtsmittel* (§§ 521 and 556 ZPO). It is possible to withdraw a means of recourse, as is the withdrawal of the claim at first instance (§§ 515 and 566 ZPO).

The *Einspruch* (against a judgment in default, *Versäumnisurteil*, § 338 ZPO), *Erinnerung* (against judgments of the Rechtspfleger, § 11 RPflG) and *Nichtigkeitsklage* (§ 579 ZPO) are not considered to be means of recourse.

One peculiarity of German law is worth mentioning here. It is the concept of the *Berichtigung*: clerical errors, computational errors and similar obvious incorrectnesses which occur in a judicial decision can at all times be *'berichtigt'* (remedied) by the court (§ 319 ZPO). The manifest advantage of this possibility is that unnecessary appeals are thus prevented.

Other judicial incorrectnesses, particularly in the representation of the facts in a judicial decision, can be exposed by either party within a period of two weeks (§ 320(1) ZPO). The court must decide this *Antrag zur Berichtigung* after oral proceedings - as if it were a kind of internal appeal.

Both in case of an official *Berichtigung* and in case of an *Antrag*, the *Berichtigung* is noted on the judgment and on the bailiff's copy (§§ 319(3) and 320(4) ZPO).

Literature: Gilles, *Rechtsmittel im Zivilprozeß*, Frankfurt am Main, 1972, Schumann, *Die Berufung in Zivilsachen*, München 4. Auflage 1990 and Schwinge, *Grundlagen des Revisionsrechts*, 2. Auflage 1960. *See also* Gilles, *Ziviljustiz und Rechtsmittelproblematik*, 1992.

9.6.2. EINSPRUCH

No ordinary appeal lies against a *Versäumnisurteil* (judgment in default). However, *Einspruch* may be lodged against *Versäumnisurteile* (§§ 338-346 ZPO). *Einspruch* is not considered to be a means of recourse. *Einspruch* has no devolutive effect which means that the case is not referred to a higher court (*see* Rosenberg/Schwab, *Zivilprozeßrecht*, p. 615). *Einspruch* does not need to be motivated, because there is no review of the *Versäumnisurteil*. The dispute is simply considered again at first instance. *See* on *Einspruch* Rosenberg/Schwab, *Zivilprozeßrecht*, p. 615 ff.

9.6.3. BERUFUNG

Berufung (§§ 511-544 ZPO) is only allowed if the value of the dispute exceeds the sum of DM 1,500 (§ 511a ZPO). *Berufung* is the means of recourse against final and certain interim judgments at first instance of the *Amtsgericht* and the *Landgericht* (§ 511 ZPO), whereby both questions of fact and of law may be considered again. *Berufung* introduces a second instance. This means of recourse must be instituted within one month after service of the judgment in a manner prescribed by law (§§ 516 and 518 ZPO). The notice of appeal must name the *Berufungskläger* and the *Berufungsbeklagte* (appellant and respondent) as well as the *Urteil* against which the appeal lies. The main requirement is that the *Berufung* must be motivated (§ 519 ZPO). In principle the dispute, i.e. as much of the original dispute as the parties have brought before the appeal court, is considered afresh by the appeal court (§ 525 ZPO). The procedure is identical to the procedure before the *Landgericht*, in so far as the appeal procedure does not determine otherwise (§ 523 ZPO). For instance, the parties are not allowed to produce unlimited new facts and means of evidence (§ 528 ZPO).

The appeal court may declare that the appeal is not admissible or reject the *Berufung*. If it allows the *Berufung*, the inferior court's judgment is quashed and the appeal court itself decides the case (*Abänderung*; § 536 ZPO). Referral to the court of first instance rarely takes place (*see* §§ 538-540 ZPO).

9.6.4. REVISION

Revision (§§ 545-566a ZPO) is a means of recourse against *Urteile* from the *Oberlandesgericht* on appeal (not from the *Landgericht*!; § 545 ZPO). The aim of *Revision* is to protect the law, to safeguard its uniformity and to promote its development. It is instituted with the *Bundesgerichtshof.*

Revision can always be instituted against *Urteile* from the *Oberlandesgericht* in which a *Berufung* was declared *unzulässig* (inadmissible; § 547 ZPO).

Leave from the *Oberlandesgericht* to institute *Revision* is required in respect of disputes involving an amount of less than DM 60,000 and for non-financial disputes (§ 546 ZPO; *Zulassungsrevision*). Such leave may be given if the case involves important legal principles or if the law applied in the judgment differs from the case law established by the *Bundesgerichtshof.*

In disputes exceeding DM 60,000 (*Streitwertrevision*) and in case of *Sprungrevision* (recourse from the first court directly up to the *Bundesgerichtshof*), no leave is required from the court which gave the decision. However, the *Bundesgerichtshof* may in these cases disallow the *Revision* if there are no fundamental questions of law involved (§ 554b ZPO).

In *Revision* the court only considers whether rules of law have been violated (*Nachprüfung in rechtlicher Hinsicht*), facts are no longer at issue. *See* § 551 ZPO for the grounds which give rise to *Revision* in any event. Restrictions on *rechtliche Nachprüfung* can be found in § 559 ZPO.

The rules for the procedure at first instance before the *Landgericht* apply accordingly to the procedure in *Revision* (§ 557 ZPO). Excluded, however, is judgment by a single judge (§ 557a ZPO). Certain provisions of the appeal procedure also apply (§ 566 ZPO).

The court may decide that *Revision* is inadmissible or that there are no grounds for *Revision*, but if the court considers the case founded, the previous decision will be quashed (*aufgehoben*) and the case will in principle be referred back to the *Berufungsgericht* (§ 565 ZPO). The court to which the case is referred is bound by the legal principles laid down by the judgment from the *Revisionsgericht* (§ 565 ZPO). In exceptional cases the *Bundesgerichtshof* itself decides the case (§ 565 (2) ZPO).

9.6.5. OTHER MEANS OF RECOURSE

a. Beschwerde and weitere Beschwerde

The rules of the *Beschwerde* and the *weitere Beschwerde* are included in §§ 567-577a ZPO.

Beschwerde (a means of recourse not known in any of the other countries discussed in this book) is a remedy which may be used only if explicitly allowed by law.

Beschwerde may be lodged against interim judgments, *Zwischenurteile* (*see* §§ 71, 135 and 387 ZPO), *Beschlüsse* and *Verfügungen*. Furthermore, Beschwerde may be lodged against the *Kostenentscheidung des Anerkenntnisurteils* (decision on the costs) (§ 99 (2) ZPO). It is also open against decisions which do not require oral consideration by the court, whereby a party's request concerning the procedure has been disallowed (§ 567 (1) ZPO). No *Beschwerde* lies, for instance, against a rejection of a separate consideration of the case (§ 145; *Prozeßtrennung*).

Beschwerde may be based on new facts, like *Berufung* (but not *Revision*) (§ 570 ZPO).

Erste Beschwerde refers to *Beschwerde* to a higher court (e.g. the *Landgericht*) against a *Beschluß* from the court of first instance (e.g. the *Amtsgericht*; *see* § 568 (1) ZPO). *Weitere Beschwerde* refers to *Beschwerde* against *Beschwerde* decisions at the second instance and is lodged with the next court up (in the above example the *Oberlandesgericht*).

In the *Beschwerde* procedure, oral consideration of the case is not required; the *Beschwerdegericht* usually decides by *Beschluß*. If the *Beschwerde* is upheld, the case is either referred or it is decided by the *Beschwerdegericht* itself (§ 575 ZPO).

b. Wiederaufnahme des Verfahrens

The *Wiederaufnahme des Verfahrens* (§§ 578-591 ZPO) is a procedure which may be followed after a decision has been made in a case by a judgment which has become *res iudicata*. The law allows for this in two cases: in case certain formal requirements have not been complied with and non-compliance must by law lead to invalidity of the decision a *Nichtigkeitsklage* (§ 579 ZPO) may be lodged, and if, for example, forged documents have been submitted or witnesses have committed perjury, a *Restitutionsklage* (§ 580 ZPO) may be lodged.

9.7. Special Procedures

9.7.1. INTRODUCTION

Zivilprozeßordnung provides for a number of special procedures, for instance: the *Aufgebotsverfahren* (§§ 946-1024 ZPO), which is a procedure to publicly summon people to present claims or rights, used in inheritance cases; and the *Urkunden- und Wechselprozeß* (§§ 592-605a ZPO; a procedure to accelerate payment in respect of claims to money, goods or securities based on documentary evidence produced in *Urkunden* (deeds)).

Below the summary procedure, the small claims procedure and sector procedures will be considered.

9.7.2. SUMMARY PROCEDURES

The *Sicherungsverfahren* (§§ 916-945 ZPO) is an accelerated procedure which leads to a provisional judgment. There are two kinds of Sicherungsverfahren recognised by law: the *einstweilige Verfügung* (literally: a 'provisional measure') and the *Arrest* (attachment). Both are summary procedures to safeguard the creditor's claim. The *einstweilige Verfügung* provides provisional security for non-monetary claims, and the *Arrest* provides provisional security for monetary claims. The same procedure applies in principle to both the *einstweilige Verfügung* and to the *Arrest*. The plaintiff applies for either remedy at his own risk, i.e. if at a later stage the case is decided against the plaintiff, he is liable for any damage suffered by his opponent (§ 945 ZPO). Although both remedies form part of enforcement (§ 916 *et seq*. ZPO), the procedure is a simplified and accelerated procedure, resulting in an enforceable decision. See for a further discussion section 9.8.3.

Literature: Altendorf, *Das vorläufige Verfahren*, Darmstadt, 2. Auflage, 1979 and Dunkel/Möller/Baur/Feldmeier/Wetekamp, *Handbuch des vorläufigen Rechtsschutzes*, München, 2. Auflage, 1991.

9.7.3. SMALL CLAIMS PROCEDURES

The *Verfahren nach billigem Ermessen* (literally: the 'procedure in fairness') before the *Amtsgericht* (§ 495a ZPO) can be classified as a small claims procedure. This provides for a simplified way to decide claims up to DM 1,000. The procedure is characterised by a large amount of freedom for the *Amtsgericht* in respect of the manner of proceeding. In addition, the judgment does not need to state the facts or contain the grounds for the decision. Because of the amount involved no means of recourse lies against the judgment.

There are also procedures whereby the plaintiff can easily obtain an enforceable decision merely by demonstrating his claim. In section 9.7.1 the *Urkunden- und Wechselprozeß* was already mentioned. In this connection the *Mahnverfahren* (§§ 688-703d ZPO) is also relevant. The *Mahnverfahren* cannot, however, be called a small claims procedure, since there is no restriction on the amount of the claim. The procedure may therefore also be used for larger monetary claims.

The *Mahnverfahren* is intended to provide a creditor (*Antragsteller*) with an enforceable decision without *Klage*, oral consideration and *Urteil*. Each independent monetary claim may be effected in a *Mahnverfahren* (§ 688 ZPO). The defendant is protected because he has two opportunities to convert the procedure into adversarial proceedings. The procedure begins by a petition to issue a *Mahnbescheid*. Irrespective of the amount of the claim the *Amtsgericht* always has absolute jurisdiction and the *Amtsgericht* for the plaintiff's domicile has relative jurisdiction (§ 689 ZPO). The *Rechtspfleger* (within the *Amtsgericht*) then issues a *Mahnbescheid*, in which the defendant is ordered either to pay within two weeks, or to produce a defence (§ 692 (1) S. 3 ZPO). If the defendant produces a defence, adversarial proceedings follow once the case has been transferred to the competent court. If the defendant does not produce a defence, a *Vollstreckungsbescheid* (VB) is issued in respect of the plaintiff's claim (§ 699 ZPO). This has the same effect as a *Versäumnisurteil* (judgment in default) and can therefore be enforced without security. The defendant may lodge *Einspruch* (§ 338 ZPO) against a *Vollstreckungsbescheid*.

Literature: Huber, *Das erfolgreiche Mahnverfahren*, Planegg/München, 4. Auflage, 1992; *see also* Hansens, *Zum Rechtspflegevereinfachungsgesetz*, in Rpfl 1991, p. 133.

9.7.4. SECTOR PROCEDURES

Procedures exclusively used for a certain area of the law are the procedures in family matters (*Familiensachen*) which consist of *Ehesachen* (matrimonial matters; § 606 (1) ZPO, § 23b GVG) and of other family matters (§ 621(1) ZPO, § 23b GVG). The general rules applicable to *Ehesachen* (§ 606 *et seq.* ZPO), including the divorce procedure, differ in many respects from the ordinary rules of civil procedure. The other *Familiensachen* (*inter alia* concerning the parental care for children of the marriage and the right of parental access) are partly covered by the rules applicable to *freiwillige Gerichtsbarkeit* and partly by the rules applicable to *streitige Gerichtsbarkeit*.

Literature: Bergerfurth, *Der Ehescheidungsprozeß und die anderen Eheverfahren*, Essen, 8. Auflage, 1992 and Walter, *Der Prozeß in Familiensachen*, Bielefeld, 1985.

Other sector procedures apart from the *Familiensachen* include guardianship and maintenance matters (*Kindschafts- und Unterhaltssachen*; §§ 640-644 PO).

Outside the *Zivilprozeßordnung* there are provisions for procedures in industrial cases (laid down in the *Arbeitsgerichtsgesetz*), procedures concerning the appointment of a trustee to administer the affairs of an individual (laid down in the *Betreuungsgesetz*) and bankruptcy procedures (laid down in the *Konkursordnung* and the *Vergleichsordnung*)

9.8. Protective Measures and Enforcement Measures

9.8.1. INTRODUCTION

Through the *Sicherungsverfahren*, briefly discussed in section 9.7.2, it is possible to obtain protective measures. Once a plaintiff has obtained an enforceable decision, German law provides rules for actual enforcement, e.g. by means of a *Vollstreckungsverfahren*.

9.8.2. PROTECTIVE MEASURES OTHER THAN ATTACHMENT

The *einstweilige Verfügung* proceeds according to the rules applicable to the *Arrest* (§ 936 ZPO), inasmuch as §§ 935 and 937-945 ZPO do not determine otherwise. In addition to the requirements set by § 920 ZPO (in particular *Arrestanspruch* and *Arrestgrund*; *see* §§ 916 and 917 ZPO), it follows from § 935 ZPO that an *einstweilige Verfügung* is only possible if there is reason to fear that due to a change of circumstances or the continuation of an existing situation in respect of the opposing party, the realisation of the plaintiff's rights could be frustrated or made considerably more difficult.

There are three kinds of *einstweilige Verfügung*, two of which are based on law:

- the *Sicherungsverfügung* (§ 935 ZPO) concerns provisional security for non-monetary claims (e.g. sequestration of certain goods to prevent illegal competition). Oral consideration of the case in this procedure can only be relinquished in urgent cases (§ 937 (2) ZPO).
- the *Regelungsverfügung* (§ 940 ZPO) provides for the possibility to obtain a provisional judgment within the framework of a disputed legal relationship (e.g. relating to absolute rights like trademark and patent rights).
- the *Befriedigungs- oder Leistungsverfügung* (which has no legal basis), leads to a performance being exacted (e.g. the supply of gas and electricity), the nature of which, however, remains provisional.

The making of an inventory as a protective measure is unknown in Germany. However, *Inventar* of an estate is possible (§ 77 FGG and § 1993 *et seq.* and in particular § 2003 BGB).

In Germany sealing (*Anlegung von Siegeln*) forms part of enforcement. If the goods to be attached are not taken away by the *Gerichtsvollzieher*, sealing is possible (*see* § 808 (2) ZPO).

9.8.3. PROTECTIVE MEASURES BY ATTACHMENT

Protective attachment (*Pfändung*) may take place pursuant to an *Arrestbefehl* (leave to attach). The *Arrest* has been provided for in §§ 916-934 ZPO.

Commencing proceedings to obtain an *Arrestbefehl* is separate from instituting proceedings in the main case. Decisions on attachment are characterised as provisional decisions, which implies that they do not affect the outcome of the main case. The outcome of the main case may therefore not be anticipated in the decision on attachment. The main procedure need not be commenced within a certain time-limit, unless the debtor files a petition to that effect (§ 926 ZPO). Jurisdiction lies with both the court which (if the main procedure has already commenced) has or (if the main procedure is not yet pending) would have jurisdiction in the main case and the *Amtsgericht* in the district where the property to be attached is situated (§ 919 ZPO). After a petition for attachment (*Arrestgesuch*) has been filed, the petitioner must show that both his actual claim and the grounds to obtain a protective measure are reasonable (§ 920 ZPO). *Arrest* is only allowed if there is reason to fear that without an *Arrest* enforcement of a judgment will be more difficult or even impossible; it is not intended to merely improve the position of the creditor. The precarious financial position of the debtor is in itself not a ground for an *Arrest.* The opposing party need not be informed of the petition. Only if a hearing before the court takes place will the opposing party be heard. If after oral consideration of the petition the court decides the case in an *Urteil* (§ 922(1) ZPO), *Berufung* lies from this *Urteil* (no *Revision*; § 545(2) ZPO). If the court decides without oral consideration and thus without hearing the defendant, it will give its decision in a *Beschluß*. The *Arrestbefehl* issued with the decision is immediately enforceable, unless the defendant provides sufficient security (*see* § 923 ZPO). The *Gerichtsvollzieher* will serve the *Arrestbefehl* and at the same time attach the various articles of the debtor's property. In order to be able to proceed with the sale of the goods, the plaintiff must possess an enforceable judgment. If the debtor files a Widerspruch against the *Beschluß* with the same court, oral consideration of the case follows (§ 924 ZPO) and the court will then decide in an

Urteil whether the *Arrestbefehl* is confirmed or lifted (§ 925 ZPO). From this *Urteil Berufung* lies. Finally, the debtor may request the attachment to be lifted (§ 927 ZPO).

9.8.4. ENFORCEMENT MEASURES BY ATTACHMENT

The rules of *Vollstreckungsverfahren* are contained in Title 8 of the *Zivilprozeßordnung*, where the various kinds of enforcement are preceded by general provisions (§§ 704-802 ZPO). It appears from these general provisions that Endurteile (*see* section 9.4.2d) which are *rechtskräftig* or *für vorläufig vollstreckbar erklärt* (i.e. have obtained the force of *res iudicata*, or have been pronounced provisionally enforceable) are enforceable. Except in a limited number of cases (§ 708 ZPO) the judgment creditor seeking attachment must provide security if he wants to obtain a judgment that is provisionally enforceable. Enforcement of a judgment which has not yet acquired the force of *res iudicata* is precarious: if the judgment given at first instance is quashed on appeal, the original judgment creditor must not only refund the value of any property already sold pursuant to the attachment, since he is no longer entitled to the proceeds of the sale, but he must also reimburse the original judgment debtor any damage which the latter may have suffered due to the attachment (§ 717 ZPO). The general provisions also include rules relating to the enforcement of foreign judgments, conditions of enforcement, powers and duties of the *Gerichtsvollzieher* and opposition against enforcement. Following the general provisions, the rules of enforcement in the ZPO are subdivided in (1) the enforcement of monetary claims (§§ 803-882 ZPO); and (2) enforcement to obtain the surrender of goods and enforcement of an obligation to perform or refrain from an act (§§ 883-898 ZPO).

When enforcing monetary claims it is possible to attach different articles of the debtor's property. Attachment of movable property which has not been registered (*das bewegliche Vermögen*; §§ 808-827 ZPO) and of claims and other property rights (§§ 828-863 ZPO) is done by taking possession of the goods and, if appropriate, by selling them at a public auction (*Pfändung* and *Versteigerung*). Attachment of the immovable property (the *unbewegliche Vermögen* which includes land and ships; §§ 864-871 ZPO) is done by means of a *Zwangshypothek* (compulsory mortgage) and by the *Zwangsversteigerung* (compulsory public auction) the rules of which are laid down in a separate law, the *Zwangsversteigerungsgesetz*. Finally the ZPO provides some rules relating to the *Verteilungsverfahren* (division among the creditors of the enforced goods) (§§ 872-882 ZPO).

9.8.5. ENFORCEMENT MEASURES OTHER THAN ATTACHMENT

Enforcement to obtain the surrender of goods takes place by compulsory *Herausgabe* (surrender) of those goods to the *Gerichtsvollzieher.*

An obligation to perform or to refrain from an act can be enforced by imposing an *Ordnungsgeld* or by applying *Ordnungshaft* (§ 890 ZPO; comparable to a penalty and to civil imprisonment). In Germany there is also a possibility to obtain a substituting judgment (*see* § 894 *et seq.* ZPO) as a means to enforce acts. If, for example, a party refuses to make a statement which is a constitutive requirement for the legally valid performance of a legal act (e.g. spouses have an obligation towards each other to have their marriage settlement registered in the matrimonial property register by mutual *Antrag*; § 1561 BGB), a judgment can be substituted for such a statement.

If all the above ways of enforcement do not achieve the desired result, it is possible to compel the debtor to submit an *eidesstattliche Versicherung* before the court (§ 900 ZPO), when the debtor declares on oath that the information which he provides the court about his financial position is complete and correct. The *eidesstattliche Versicherung* is a powerful tool in the judgment creditor's hands: not only may it lead to the debtor confessing that he possesses other property against which a judgment can be enforced, the *eidesstattliche Versicherung* is also recorded in a central and public register (to which banks and finance institutions also have access). Registration in this register often implies that the debtor loses future possibilities to obtain credit. The frightening prospect of being included in the register frequently induces the debtor at the last moment to find the means to (partly) satisfy his creditors. If even that fails, the only option left to the creditor is to apply for the debtor's bankruptcy.

Literature: Heussen/Fraulob, *Zwangsvollstreckung für Anfänger*, München, 4. Auflage, 1993, Jauernig, *Zwangsvollstreckungs- und Konkursrecht* (Kurzlehrbuch), München, 19. Auflage, 1990, and Riedel, *Zwangsvollstreckungsrecht*, 1990.

9.9. Duration and Costs

9.9.1. INTRODUCTION

Litigating in Germany has its attractions: as far as the duration and costs of proceedings are concerned, Germany compares favourably with countries such as Italy, where procedures take an extremely long time, or the United

Kingdom, where there is a very high percentage of out-of-court settlements due to the fact that proceedings are enormously expensive. How does Germany manage to do so well?

9.9.2. DURATION

The *Vereinfachungsnovelle* of 1977 has greatly influenced the structure and efficiency of civil procedures in Germany. The original aim of concentrating the proceedings by considering the case in one *Hapttermin* (*see* section 9.4.2c) has largely been achieved. Although the courts deal with a large volume of cases, 90 per cent of proceedings at first instance are concluded within 12 months. An ordinary appeal case will take one to two years. Voluminous statistics on the duration of procedures may be found in a 630-page government report which was published in 1986 in response to a parliamentary inquiry (Bundestagdrucksache 10/5317).

Literature: Walchshöfer, *Die Auswirkungen der Vereinfachungsnovelle in der gerichtlichen Praxis*, in ZZP, Band 94, p. 179; *Justizstatistik 1989* (Statistisches Bundesamt, Fachserie 10, Reihe 2);

Rottleuthner/Rottleuthner-Lutter, *Die Dauer von Gerichtsverfahren*, 1990.

9.9.3. COSTS

The costs involved in certain procedures can be predicted fairly well. The rules governing the costs of legal proceedings are laid down in the *Gerichtskostengesetz*. Court fees (*Gebühren*) are related to the amount involved in the case, the *Streitwert*. The Streitwert is easy to determine in case of a monetary claim. If the case does not concern a monetary claim, the amount involved in the case is determined on the basis of §§ 3-9 ZPO or alternatively the court must decide it as part of the proceedings.

Lawyers' fees are also related to the *Streitwert*. Statutory rules have been laid down in the *Bundesgebührenordnung für Rechtsanwälte* (BRAGO). The lawyer's fees are not at all related to how long he has been involved with a case and how many hours he has spent on the case. Hourly rates are only used in the non-litigation practice, if agreed in advance, although actually a *Gebühr* should also be charged.

Legal aid is provided for in the *Prozeßkostenhilfeverfahren*. §§ 114-127a ZPO provide rules for a (provisional) exemption from the costs of proceedings, so that persons who cannot, can only partly or cannot at once afford to pay these costs are still able to defend their legal rights. The criteria are the net income and capital of the party who wishes to qualify for *Prozeßkostenhilfe* (PKH). No contribution is required from persons with an income of less than DM 850 per month, while persons with an income of DM 2,400 pay the maximum contribution of DM 520 (in these figures the size of an applicant's family, which does affect the amount of the contribution payable, has not been taken into account). Applicants with incomes higher than DM 2,400 per month do not qualify for legal aid.

In order to be eligible for legal aid, the court proceedings must have a reasonable chance of success (§ 114 ZPO).

The awarding of costs is provided for in § 91 ZPO. The losing party will be ordered to pay the total costs of its opponent, including court fees and the lawyer's fees. In addition, the losing party must pay other costs which were reasonably incurred by the opposing party, such as telephone and postage costs. These costs can easily become an issue since they are not related to the Streitwert.

If only part of the claim is allowed, the costs are set off (§ 92 ZPO).

The judgment will only state which party must pay which proportion of the costs. The *Rechtspfleger* calculates the exact amount and the parties must submit their lists of costs to him. These lists are the basis on which the *Rechtspfleger* issues a *Kostenfestsetzungsbeschluß*.

In principle an award for the costs of proceedings may be enforced by the parties in the same way as any other judgment to pay a sum of money, i.e. via the *Vollstreckungsverfahren* (section 9.8.4). However, the *Gerichtskosten* and *inter alia* the costs of the *Gerichtsvollzieher* are recovered by the courts themselves on the basis of a *Justizbeitreibungsordnung*.

Literature: Hartmann, *Kostengesetze*, 24. Auflage, 1991; Lappe, *Justizkostenrecht*, München, 1982; Schneider, *Die Kostenentscheidung im Zivilurteil*, München, 2. Auflage 1976; Kalthoener/Büttner, *Prozeßkostenhilfe und Beratungshilfe*, 1988.

9.10. Proceedings Outside the Courts

9.10.1. INTRODUCTION

In Germany arbitration and binding advice are both used as forms of proceedings outside the courts. Binding advice occurs less frequently than arbitration. Especially in the large Hanseatic cities such as Hamburg and Bremen, many disputes are resolved by arbitration.

9.10.2. ARBITRATION

Book ten of the *Zivilprozeßordnung* is dedicated to the *Schiedsrichterliche Verfahren* i.e. arbitration (§§ 1025-1048 ZPO). Parties may, before or after a dispute has arisen, agree not to submit their dispute to a court but to one or more arbitrators (*Schiedsrichter*). By law the agreement has to comply with certain requirements (*see* §§ 1025-1027 ZPO). The agreement (*Schiedsvertrag*) must be concluded in writing, unless the parties belong to the so-called *Vollkaufleute* (commercial traders; § 1027(2) ZPO). An arbitration agreement is void if either party is at an advantage when appointing arbitrators (§ 1025(2) ZPO). If, despite the existence of a valid arbitration agreement, a dispute is submitted to a national court and the opposing party invokes the agreement, then the court must reject the claim (§ 1027a ZPO). Unless the parties have provided otherwise, arbitrators are appointed by the parties (§ 1028 ZPO). Failing such they are appointed by the court (§ 1029(2) ZPO). *See* for the challenge of arbitrators § 1032 ZPO. Unless provided otherwise by the parties, the arbitral tribunal determines the procedure (§ 1034(2) ZPO). The parties must be heard in any event (§ 1034(1) ZPO). Arbitrators decide by a majority of votes, unless otherwise agreed (§ 1038 ZPO). The award must comply with certain formal requirements (§ 1039 ZPO) and must usually state the reasons for the award (*see* § 1041(1) s. 5 and (2) ZPO). In their award arbitrators are bound by substantive law, unless the parties have agreed - within the limits of good morals and public policy - to a *Billigkeitsentscheidung*, a decision based on reasonableness and fairness (*see* Rosenberg/Schwab, *Zivilprozeßrecht*, p. 1102). An arbitral award must be declared enforceable by *Beschluß* of the national court (*Vollstreckbarerklärung*; § 1042 ZPO). *Widerspruch* lies from this *Beschluß* (§ 1042c(2) and 1042d ZPO). Only under certain conditions can the award - even after *Vollstreckbarerklärung* - be set aside (so-called (*nachträgliche*) *Aufhebungsklage*; §§ 1041 and 1043 ZPO).

The question which law applies to the arbitration is in principle determined by the intention of the parties. If they have failed to agree the applicable law, the law of the country where the arbitration takes place becomes applicable. *See* Rosenberg/Schwab, *Zivilprozeßrecht*, p. 1126.

For the recognition and enforcement of foreign arbitral awards the New York Convention of 1958 on the Recognition and Enforcement of Foreign Arbitral Awards (entry into force 28 September 1961) is important.

Literature on arbitration includes Maier, *Handbuch der Schiedsgerichtbarkeit*, 1979 and Baumbach/Lauterbach/Albers/Hartmann, *Zivilprozeßordnung*, 52. Auflage, 1994, p. 2110 ff.

9.10.3. BINDING ADVICE

The law does not explicitly provide rules for binding advice. A statutory basis may be found in § 317 BGB which relates to the *Bestimmung einer Leistung durch einen Dritten* (i.e. the determination of a performance by a third party). The rules for arbitration (§§ 1025-1048 ZPO) do not apply to binding advice (*Schiedsgutachten*).

The difference between binding advice and arbitration in Germany is *inter alia* that there are no specific formal requirements for an agreement to settle a matter by binding advice (which there are for an arbitration agreement) and that the court cannot be called on (§ 1029) to appoint the binding adviser (*Schiedsgutachter*) (as it can in case of arbitration). Furthermore, there is only one ground on which the court can set aside binding advice, namely if such advice is unreasonable. This implies that there is only a marginal checking of binding advice by the court; judicial influence is stronger in case of arbitration (§ 1041 ZPO).

10. Italian Civil Procedure*

Margreet B. de Boer
(with the assistance of Patrizia Marcucci**)

10.1. Overview/Sources

10.1.1. INTRODUCTION

Italy's complex history since the fall of the Roman Empire is also reflected in the history of its law of civil procedure. During the Middle Ages and the Renaissance the Romano-canonical system, based on Longobard and predominantly on late Roman law, was developed in the different States and Communes of the Italian peninsula. In the interpretation of Justinian's *Corpus Iuris Civilis* the glossators met the demands of the changing times. This system of law, which spread throughout the European continent and is known as the *ius commune*, was applied whenever local legislation or custom was not expressly prevalent. However, as proceedings under the *ius commune* were formal and complicated, more flexibility was needed to accommodate the flourishing of trade and commerce. New practices were therefore developed (e.g. summary procedures), instigated by Canonical decrees (e.g. *Saepe*, issued in 1306 by Pope Clement V), statutes of the city-states or German custom. Frequently these new practices were subsequently absorbed into the *ius commune*.

Later on in the history of continental Europe, when power became centralised, reforms were introduced by the central rulers - and, on a more restricted scale, also by the rulers of the many States on the Italian peninsula - which reforms were needed *inter alia* to cope with the variety and diversification of the sources of civil procedure. Of great importance was the *Ordonnance civile*, promulgated in 1667 by Louis XIV, the so-called *Code Louis*. The Napoleonic era brought the *Code de procédure civile* (1806),

* Thanks are due to Prof. Avv. Giuseppe Tarzia (Avvocato and Professor of civil procedural law at the Università degli Studi di Milano) for his valuable remarks and to Prof. T.A.W. Sterk (Professor of civil procedural law at Leiden University).

** Legal consultant (Breda and Milan).

based on the features of the *Code Louis* and elaborating thereupon: less cumbersome, more effective proceedings. During the restoration the *Code de procédure civile* served as a model for procedural legislation in various Italian States (resulting, for instance, in the Sardinian Codes of 1854 and 1859). The proclamation in 1861 of the Kingdom of Italy soon brought a unification of the rules of civil procedure: the *Codice di procedura civile* of 1865 for which inspiration was found from different sources (the Codes applicable in various Italian States, especially the Sardinian Codes, the French *Code de procédure civile* and its predecessor the *Code Louis*, and even the *ius commune*).

At the beginning of the 20th century procedural reform became a topic of discussion, instigated by scholars like Giuseppe Chiovenda and Francesco Carnelutti. In an attempt to eliminate the principal defects of the 1865 Code (e.g. procedures were in writing and could easily become fragmented by numerous interlocutory appeals), recent German and, particularly, Austrian legislation on civil procedure was the focus of attention. On 21 April 1942 a new *Codice di procedura civile* (Royal Decree of 28 October 1940, no. 1443) came into force. Due to the effects of the Second World War the reform was less extreme than originally intended, in order to protect individual liberty as much as possible against the defects of the totalitarian state, and even involved rigidity and inflexibility. Despite defects (for instance, the principle of orality only applied in part; *cf.* section 10.2.7 below), this new Code was an improvement upon the previous one (proceedings were relatively more efficient). In the following decades the 1942 Code was amended several times (*inter alia* in 1950, 1973 and 1978), sometimes implementing a radical reform (e.g. proceedings in employment disputes, in 1973). Meanwhile, strong consensus about the need for essential reforms was reached. This led to the Act of 26 November 1990, no. 353 (entitled *provvedimenti urgenti per il processo civile*, which became effective on 1 May 1995, having been postponed several times, and recently amended by *inter alia* the *decreto-legge* of 21 June 1995, no. 238 (entry into force 22 June 1995; *see* now the Act of 20 December 1995, no. 534, entry into force 21 December 1995)), intending *inter alia* to accelerate proceedings, while the Act of 21 November 1991, no. 374 (effective on 30 April 1995, having been postponed several times also) provides for the institution of the *giudice di pace*.

See for a more extensive overview of the history of civil procedure in Italy Mauro Cappelletti & Joseph M. Perillo, *Civil Procedure in Italy*, The Hague 1965, p. 25 ff., and more recently Enrico T. Liebman, *Manuale di diritto processuale civile. Principi*, 5th edition, Milan 1992, p. 37 ff. Crisanto Mandrioli, *Corso di diritto processuale civile* I, 10th edition, Turin

1995, p. 419 ff. deals especially with the reforms since the 1942 *Codice di procedura civile.*

In Italy the term *diritto processuale civile* is used for the rules of civil procedure, the term *procedura civile* for civil proceedings and the term *procedimento* for a special procedure.

10.1.2. ACT AND CONVENTION

In Italy there are different sources of civil procedure. First of all, there is the Constitution (*Costituzione della Repubblica Italiana*, which entered into force on 1 January 1948), in which a number of articles on (civil) procedure can be found.

The main source is the *Codice di procedura civile*, which consists of four books. Book 1, entitled *Disposizioni generali*, contains articles of a general nature, regarding the principal characters of civil procedure and the *atti processuali*, the deeds bearing on proceedings. Books 2 and 3 contain articles of a formal nature, regarding civil (contentious) proceedings in the different courts, on all levels, and proceedings in employment disputes (*Del processo di cognizione*) and enforcement proceedings (*Del processo di esecuzione*). In Book 4 (*Dei procedimenti speciali*) various special proceedings can be found, such as summary proceedings, proceedings for protective measures, proceedings involving non-contentious jurisdiction, the so-called *giurisdizione volontaria* (the greater part regarding family law), and arbitration. The *Disposizioni di attuazione del codice di procedura civile e disposizioni transitorie* (Royal Decree of 18 December 1991, no. 1368, which also entered into force on 21 April 1942, and has also been amended several times since 1942) provide transitional rules but also include a number of articles which supplement the *Codice di procedura civile.*

In addition, rules of procedure are found in other important sources, *inter alia* the *Codice civile* (including rules of evidence and enforcement of judgments) and the *Codice della navigazione*. The *Disciplina del fallimento, del concordato preventivo, dell'amministrazione controllata e della liquidazione coatta amministrativa* (Royal Decree of 16 March 1942, no. 267 and successive amendments), contains mostly rules of procedure in cases of bankruptcy.

The judicial organisation is governed by the *Ordinamento giudiziario* (Royal Decree of 30 January 1941, no. 12), which has been amended several times also, the most important reforms being those incorporated in the Act of 26 November 1990, no. 353, and in the Act of 21 November 1991, no. 374.

The editions of the *Codice di procedura civile* by the publishers Cedam (Padova) and Giuffrè (Milan), contain the *Disposizioni di attuazione del codice di procedura civile e disposizioni transitorie* as well as the *Ordinamento giudiziario* and other relevant legislation on procedure (e.g. the Acts dealing with the *Ordinamento delle professioni di avvocato e di procuratore*, the *Onorari di avvocato e di procuratore per prestazioni giudiziali in materia civile,* and the *Sospensione dei termini processuali nel periodo feriale*). A very handy edition of the *Codice di procedura civile* and other relevant legislation on procedure, with annotations and references to decisions of the *Corte di cassazione* is M. Battaglini - T. Novelli, *Codice di procedura civile e norme complementari con il commento della giurisprudenza della cassazione*, 8th edition, (Giuffrè) Milan 1990, updated by a supplement: *Aggiornamento al 30 giugno 1992*, (Giuffrè) Milan 1992. In the series *Breviaria Juris* by G. Cian and A. Trabucchi an article-by-article commentary has been published by Federico Carpi - Vittorio Colesanti - Michele Taruffo, *Commentario Breve al Codice di Procedura Civile*, 3rd edition, (Cedam) Padova 1994 (including the most important multilateral conventions).

Italy is a party to a number of (multilateral) conventions relating to civil proceedings, for instance the European Convention on Jurisdiction and the Enforcement of Judgments in Civil and Commercial Matters (entry into force 1 February 1973 (the Brussels Convention of 27 September 1968) respectively 1 May 1992 (the San Sebastian Convention of 26 May 1989)), and the parallel convention, the Lugano Convention of 16 September 1988 (entry into force 1 December 1992) (*see* sections 3.1.1 and 3.1.5), as well as the European Convention for the Protection of Human Rights and Fundamental Freedoms (ECHRFF; entry into force 26 October 1955) and the International Covenant on Civil and Political Rights (CCPR; entry into force 15 December 1978). As these conventions are self-executing, they are directly applicable in national courts of law.

Italy is also a party to *inter alia* the Hague Conventions on Civil Procedure of 17 July 1905 and of 1 March 1954 (entry into force respectively 27 April 1909 and 12 April 1957), the Hague Convention on the Service Abroad of Judicial and Extrajudicial Documents in Civil or Commercial Matters of 15 November 1965 (entry into force 24 January 1982), the European Convention on Information on Foreign Law of 7 June 1968 (entry into force 11 July 1972), the Hague Convention on the Taking of Evidence Abroad in Civil or Commercial Matters of 18 March 1970 (entry into force 21 August 1982) and the European Agreement on the Transmission of Applications for Legal Aid of 27 January 1977 (entry into force 7 July 1983). In respect of arbitration we refer to the New York Convention of 10

June 1958 on the Recognition and Enforcement of Foreign Arbitral Awards (entry into force 1 May 1969) and the European Convention on International Commercial Arbitration, Geneva, 21 April 1961 (entry into force 1 November 1970).

10.1.3. LITERATURE AND CASE LAW

Traditionally, a large number of studies on civil procedure are published in Italy. Very useful ones, taking into account the recent reforms, include: Salvatore Satta, *Diritto processuale civile*, 11th edition by Carmine Punzi, (Cedam) Padova 1992, and Crisanto Mandrioli, *Corso di diritto processuale civile* I-III, 10th edition, (G. Giappichelli, Editor) Turin 1995; Giuseppe Tarzia, *Lineamenti del nuovo processo di cognizione*, (Giuffrè) Milan 1991 (supplied with an *Appendice di aggiornamento* (1993)), deals in particular with the amended basic procedure for contentious litigation. A beautiful, lucid book, outlining the basic points of civil proceedings, is *Manuale di diritto processuale civile. Principi*, 5th edition, (Giuffrè) Milan 1992 by Enrico Tullio Liebman, which includes an overview (p. 46 ff.) of relevant handbooks and monographs. Recent reforms are discussed in *Provvedimenti urgenti per il processo civile*, edited by Giuseppe Tarzia and Franco Cipriani, (Cedam) Milan 1993 (reprint, with commentary by Achille Saletti on the Act of 4 December 1992, no. 477).

Important law reviews are *Rivista di diritto processuale*, edited by Cedam (Padova) and *Rivista trimestrale di diritto e procedura civile*, edited by Giuffrè (Milan); an influential encyclopedia is *Novissimo* (formerly: *Nuovo*) *digesto italiano*, edited by UTET (Turin).

Only decisions of the Constitutional Court (which jurisdiction includes final decisions on the constitutionality of laws; *cf.* art. 134 § 1 Cost.) are published officially in the *Gazzetta Ufficiale* and are subsequently collected in the *Raccolta ufficiale delle sentenze e ordinanze della Corte Costituzionale*, edited by the Istituto Poligrafico dello Stato (Rome). The *Giurisprudenza costituzionale* (Giuffrè, Milan), in which these decisions, often with annotations, are collected, is generally used by legal practitioners.

The decisions of the *Corte di cassazione* (like the decisions made by the lower courts) are summarised by its own office (the so-called *massimario*) into maxims or precepts (*massime*) and form non-binding precedents, although in practice their authority is persuasive, in view of the fact that judges generally do not dissent from these *massime*.

Decisions in civil proceedings at all court levels (except decisions as to mere facts) are published privately and are collected in reviews of case law, in which they appear either in official *massime* or in full. The most important reviews of *massime* are *Repertorio del Foro Italiano* (Foro Italiano, Rome), containing *massime* of all decisions from the magistrature; *Massimario della Giurisprudenza Italiana* (UTET, Turin), containing, in chronological order, *massime* of all decisions from the civil sections of the *Corte di cassazione*; and *Repertorio della Giustizia Civile* (Giuffrè, Milan). The most important decisions are published in full in *Il Foro Italiano* (Foro Italiano, Rome); *Giurisprudenza Italiana* (UTET, Turin); and *Giustizia Civile* (Giuffrè, Milan).

10.1.4. DATA BASES

The task of developing data bases is left entirely in the hands of private publishers (*inter alia* UTET, Giuffrè and Cedam).

The various reviews of case law mentioned in section 10.1.3 can also be found in data bases (CD Lex, CD ROM, Lex Iura).

10.2. Fundamental Principles

10.2.1. INTRODUCTION

The Italian Constitution contains a number of articles referring to fundamental principles of (civil) procedure. When Italy became a party to the ECHRFF and the CCPR, these principles were consolidated within an international context and bound the legislator even more in making rules on civil procedure accordingly (for instance, in respect of the principle of reasonable time-limits).

In addition to the fundamental principles based on the Constitution, there are also fundamental principles which are either deduced indirectly from the Constitution or which are not at all based on the Constitution; these principles are of a rather technical nature.

In sections 10.2.2 *et seq.* we shall briefly discuss the fundamental principles of Italian civil procedure according to Mandrioli (*Corso di diritto processuale civile* I, p. 425 ff.) and to Liebman (*Manuale di diritto processuale civile. Principi*, p. 9 ff.), who confines himself to constitutional and international principles.

The constitutional principles (*principi costituzionali*) are the principle of independence and impartiality (10.2.2), the principle of a judge appointed in accordance with the rules of law (10.2.3), the principle of right of access to the court (10.2.4), the principle of equality of the parties (10.2.5) and the principle of public hearings and judgments (10.2.6).

Other fundamental principles are *inter alia* the principle of orality (10.2.7) and the principle of two instances (10.2.8). The principle of form appropriate to the purpose or of servitude of the form (*principio della congruità delle forme allo scopo o della strumentalità delle forme*) will not be discussed here, nor will the principle that the nullity of a procedural act has no wider effect than is necessary (*principio della conservazione degli atti processuali*, based on the motto *utile per inutile non vitiatur* (the useful is not vitiated by the useless)); *cf.* also sections 10.4.2e (4) and (5) below.

10.2.2. PRINCIPLE OF INDEPENDENCE AND IMPARTIALITY (L'INDIPENDENZA DEL GIUDICE E LA SUA IMPARZIALITÀ)

The independence of the judge is ensured by art. 104 § 1 Cost.: the judicature forms an autonomous institution, independent of any other powers. The basis for this rule lies in art. 101 § 2 Cost., which states that judges are subject only to the law, and in art. 107 § 1 Cost., which states that judges are irremovable.

Independence is a precondition of impartiality, but impartiality implies that *nemo iudex idoneus in propria causa* (no one ought to be a judge in his own case). In accordance with this adage the Constitutional Court (12 July 1967, no. 110) ruled that 'one of the properties by which a body can be characterised as jurisdictional, is the absence of interest in the case which has to be decided'.

10.2.3. PRINCIPLE OF A JUDGE APPOINTED IN ACCORDANCE WITH THE RULES OF LAW (LA GARANZIA DEL GIUDICE NATURALE)

Following the principles of art. 6 ECHRFF and art. 14 CCPR the Constitutional Court (1 April 1958, no. 29, and 3-7 July 1962, no. 88) interpreted art. 25 § 1 Cost. (nobody can be kept from a judge appointed in accordance with the rules of law) as follows: *giudice precostituito per legge* in art. 25 § 1 Cost. is synonymous with *giudice naturale*, i.e. 'a judge appointed on the basis of previously determined general criteria' (i.e. not appointed in order to deal with particular controversies).

10.2.4. PRINCIPLE OF RIGHT OF ACCESS TO THE COURT (IL DIRITTO DI ACCESSO AI TRIBUNALI)

Article 24 § 1 Cost. states that everybody is entitled to proceed in law in order to protect his own rights and his legitimate interests, thereby endorsing the principle of a court being available for the protection of individuals' rights (*il principio della disponibilità della tutela giurisdizionale*) as well as the principle that a claim must be filed on a party's initiative and that there is an object of proceedings available (*il principio della domanda e il principio della disponibilità dell'oggetto del processo*). A manifestation of the *principio della domanda* is the principle that allegations determining the extent of the claim must be made by the parties (*principio dell'allegazione*), often expressed by means of *iudex secundum alligata partium iudicare debet. Cf.* also art. 2907 Cc as well as arts. 81, 99 and 112 Cpc.

10.2.5. PRINCIPLE OF EQUALITY OF THE PARTIES (L'UGUAGLIANZA DELLE PARTI)

Article 3 § 1 Cost. states that all citizens are equal in the eyes of the law. This implies more than a formal equality of the parties and means that the parties must be given the opportunity to play an active role in the case in order to be able to influence its outcome.

In addition, art. 24 § 2 Cost. lays down the supreme right to defend an action at every stage and level of proceedings (*audiatur et altera pars*). In respect of civil proceedings this fundamental principle of hearing both parties (*principio del contraddittorio*) has been elaborated in art. 101 Cpc.

10.2.6. PRINCIPLE OF PUBLIC HEARINGS AND JUDGMENTS (LA PUBBLICITÀ DEI GIUDIZI)

The Constitution does not provide for public hearings and judgments. Instead, the Constitutional Court ruled (14 April 1965, no. 25, and 2 February 1971, no. 12), referring to art. 101 § 2 Cost., that this requirement is 'also essential in respect of the principles to which, in a democratic society founded on the sovereignty of the people, the administration of justice, which has been founded on that very sovereignty, must conform itself'. Article 128 Cpc provides that oral pleadings are in principle heard in public (*see* section 10.4.2d) subject to certain exceptions; in order to make judgments public, art. 133 Cpc prescribes that decisions are deposited at the registrar's office.

Other aspects related to the principle of publicity are the requirement that all jurisdictional measures (*provvedimenti*) must be motivated (art. 111 § 1 Cost.) and must be in accordance with the law (art. 101 § 2 Cost. and art. 113 § 1 Cpc), and the possibility of a review by the *Corte di cassazione* in case of a violation of the law (art. 111 § 2 Cost.).

10.2.7. PRINCIPLE OF ORALITY (PRINCIPIO DELL'ORALITÀ)

The principle of orality - as well as the principles of concentration and immediacy connected with it - was originally introduced by the 1942 *Codice di procedura civile*. However, this principle was based on a compromise: the facts of the case were examined by an examining judge (*giudice istruttore*), whereas the judgment was delivered by a panel of judges which included the examining judge. The rigid 1950 reform, also known as *controriforma*, abolished oral hearings and restored procedures in writing; what remained of the old principle was that one of the judges in the panel deciding the case also acted as the examining judge (*giudice istruttore*). The principle of orality became more prominent as a result of the recent reform (*cf.* art. 183 Cpc; *see* section 10.4.2c), as has been the case since 1973 in employment disputes (*cf.* art. 420 Cpc); the 1990 reform also introduced the figure of the *giudice istruttore* who subsequently decides the case alone (*see* sections 10.4.2c and d).

10.2.8. PRINCIPLE OF TWO INSTANCES (PRINCIPIO DEL DOPPIO GRADO DI GIURISDIZIONE)

This principle bears on the number of instances of jurisdiction: a procedure at first instance (*primo grado*) may be followed by a procedure on appeal (*secondo grado* or *appello*), though not without restrictions (*see* sections 10.3.2d and 10.6.2).

10.3. Principal Characters

10.3.1. INTRODUCTION

The principal characters in civil proceedings in Italy have much in common with their colleagues in other continental EC countries, but naturally there are characteristic particularities and differences.

Not only the judge forms part of the courts (*organi giudiziari*) but also the court clerk (*cancelliere*) and the process-server or bailiff (*ufficiale giudiziario*). The court clerk assists the judge in several ways, particularly with documentation and recording the minutes of the proceedings (*cf.* arts. 57 and 58 Cpc). The activities of the bailiff include assisting the judge during the hearing, service of legal documents (e.g. the writ) and legal enforcement (*cf.* art. 59 Cpc). Other persons involved with the court on an *ad hoc* basis only are the so-called auxiliaries (*ausiliari*): the expert in technical matters (*consulente tecnico*; art. 61 Cpc) and the *custode*, who safeguards and administers attached goods (art. 65 Cpc).

The *Pubblico Ministero*, the public prosecutor (a judge forming part of the *magistratura requirente* (as opposed to the *magistratura giudicante*, i.e. the judges who decide cases)), represents public interest. Although in theory functioning under the supervision of the Minister of Grace and Justice (art. 69 Ord. giud.), he is in fact independent. In civil proceedings his function is limited. He commences actions in those cases provided by law (art. 69 Cpc) (e.g. art. 58 Cc: to obtain a declaration of presumptive death). He may intervene in any case which is of public interest (art. 70 § 3 Cpc) and is sometimes even obliged to do so in order to make the proceedings valid (art. 70 §§ 1 and 2 Cpc). An important function of the *Pubblico Ministero* is his mandatory intervention in all proceedings before the *Corte di cassazione* (arts. 70 § 2 and 72 Cpc); in practice this means that he must attend all hearings before the *Corte di cassazione* and give his oral opinions on all the cases which are brought before the *Corte di cassazione*. If neither party appeals (in due time) to the *Corte di cassazione*, the *Pubblico Ministero* may appeal himself, requesting that the judgment in dispute be reversed in the interest of the law, in which case the parties are not materially affected by a reversal of the judgment by the *Corte di cassazione* (art. 363 Cpc).

Below, special attention will be given to the judge (section 10.3.2), to the lawyers (section 10.3.3), and to the parties (section 10.3.4).

10.3.2. THE JUDGE

a. Introduction

Article 102 § 2 Cost. determines that the power to administer justice rests with ordinary judges, appointed in accordance with and subject to the *Ordinamento giudiziario*. Leaving aside criminal cases, ordinary judges (*giudici ordinari*) have civil jurisdiction in all cases in respect of any rights (*cf.* art. 2907 Cc: the judiciary power provides for the jurisdictional protection *dei diritti* ...), whether private or civil (*cf.* art. 2 Act of 20 March 1865, no. 2248 allegation E: *diritto civile o politico*), which are not explicitly excluded (*cf.* art. 1 Ord. giud.).

As stated in art. 1 Ord. giud., the ordinary courts (who have to exercise civil jurisdiction according to the rules of the *Codice di procedura civile* unless otherwise determined by law (art. 1 Cpc)), are comprised of (1) the *giudice di pace* (substituting the *giudice conciliatore* per 30 April 1995: court of first instance mainly for minor matters); (2) the *pretore* (court of first instance mainly for matters of more importance); (3) the *tribunale* (court of first instance mainly for major cases and appellate court for judgments at first instance by both the *giudice di pace* and the *pretore*); (4) the Court of appeal (*Corte d'appello*: appellate court for judgments given at first instance by the *tribunale*); and (5) the *Corte di cassazione* (reviewing appellate judgments and non-appealable judgments of courts of first instance).

Article 102 § 2 Cost. prohibits the appointment of extraordinary judges or special judges (however, *see below* under c). Still pursuant to art. 102 § 2 Cost., only special sections (*sezioni specializzate*) may be set up within the ordinary judicial bodies to deal with particular matters, in which panels capable citizens from outside the magistrature may also participate. Within the civil magistrature there are the following specialised panels of judges: the courts for minors (*tribunale per i minorenni*, as listed in art. 1 Ord. Giud., and at second instance the specialised sections of the Courts of appeal), which have jurisdiction *inter alia* in cases of parental authority and of legal declarations in respect of paternity (art. 38 *Disposizioni per l'attuazione del codice civile e disposizioni transitorie*), and the agricultural sections (*sezioni specializzate agrarie*, in the *tribunali* and the Courts of appeal; *cf.* art. 1 Act of 2 March 1963, no. 320), which have jurisdiction in cases relating to the determination of ground rent and the extension of agricultural agreements (*cf.* art. 47 Act of 3 May 1982, no. 203).

The review of the constitutionality of Acts is the exclusive province of the Constitutional Court (*Corte Costituzionale*), seated in Rome. If there is doubt as to the constitutionality of a legal rule to be applied (*dubbio di costituzionalità*), the judge may, at the request of the parties, or must, on his own motion, submit such a question to the Constitutional Court, suspending the relevant proceedings (art. 134 § 1 Cost.; art. 23 Act of 11 March 1953, no. 87).

b. International jurisdiction

Rules on jurisdiction in international cases have been laid down in Title II (arts. 3-12) of the Act of 31 May 1995, no. 218 (entitled *Riforma del sistema italiano di diritto internazionale privato*, effective on 1 September 1995). These rules only apply in so far as they do not detract from the application of international conventions which have entered into force for Italy (art. 1 § 2). Pursuant to art. 3 § 1 there is jurisdiction if the other party has his residence or domicile (*residenza* or *domicilio*) in Italy or has a representative there who is authorised to appear in court, as referred to in art. 77 Cpc, and in the other cases laid down by the law. Article 3 § 2 stipulates that there is also jurisdiction pursuant to the criteria determined by sections 2, 3 and 4 of Title II of the Brussels Convention as it applies in Italy, even if the other party is not domiciled in the territory of a Contracting State and it concerns a case which falls within the scope of the Brussels Convention; in respect of other cases there is also jurisdiction pursuant to the criteria which determine relative jurisdiction (*cf.* below under e).

c. Sectoral jurisdiction

Within the (ordinary) magistrature, jurisdiction in criminal cases is separate from jurisdiction in civil cases. In respect of jurisdiction in administrative cases, the Constitution provides for separate bodies deciding administrative disputes, which consist of special judges: a claim against the public authorities (*Pubblica Amministrazione)* in order to protect legitimate interests must be brought before the regional administrative court (*Tribunale regionale amministrativo* at first instance, with recourse to the *Consiglio di Stato*, as laid down by the Act of 6 December 1971, no. 1034), whereas a claim of a citizen against the public authorities in order to protect a right (*diritto soggettivo*) must in general be brought before the ordinary civil judges (art. 103 § 1 Cost. and art. 2 Act of 20 March 1865, no. 2248 allegation E). There are (still) also other, less important, types of special judges (*Consiglio di Stato, Tribunali superiori delle acque pubbliche, Commissari regionali liquidatori di usi civici*). Also worth mentioning are the special tax commissions: *Commissioni tributarie* (at first and second instance) and the *Commissione tributaria centrale* (in cassation) (instituted by Presidential Decree of 26 October 1972, no. 636).

Below we shall only discuss civil proceedings before ordinary judges.

d. Absolute jurisdiction (competenza per materia e valore)

Article 7 *et seq.* Cpc determine over which matters the various courts have jurisdiction. This depends on two criteria: the amount in dispute and the subject matter of the action (*competenza per materia e valore*), the subject matter taking precedence.

The *tribunale* has jurisdiction in all cases that do not fall under the jurisdiction of the *giudice di pace* and of the *pretore*; in addition, the *tribunale* has exclusive jurisdiction in all tax cases (if not falling under the jurisdiction of the *Commissioni tributarie*, *cf.* above under c), in all cases concerning the status and capacity of persons, honorary rights, forgery of documents, and generally in all cases of an indeterminate value (art. 9 Cpc). The *pretore* has jurisdiction in cases not exceeding a value of Lit. 50 million in respect of movable (from a value of Lit. 5 million upwards) and immovable property; in addition, the *pretore* has unlimited jurisdiction *inter alia* in repossession actions and in tenancy cases concerning immovable property in cities (art. 8 Cpc). The *giudice di pace* has jurisdiction over cases not exceeding a value of Lit. 5 million in respect of movable property; he also has jurisdiction *inter alia* over cases on compensation for road accidents not exceeding a value of Lit. 30 million (in case of a value of more than Lit. 30 million, the *tribunale* has jurisdiction), and unlimited jurisdiction in some specific cases (art. 7 Cpc).

Rules to determine the value of a claim are laid down in art. 10 *et seq.* Cpc.

In general, appeal is open against all judgments of courts of first instance, although there is an appealability limit for judgments of the *giudice di pace* of Lit. 2 million (art. 339 § 3 in conjunction with art. 113 § 2 Cpc). In addition, there are some other exceptions. Appeal from judgments of the *giudice di pace* and the *pretore* lies to the *tribunale* and from judgments of the *tribunale* to the *Corte d'appello* (*see* section 10.6.2).

Decisions in cassation are entrusted to the *Corte di cassazione* (*see* section 10.6.3); the *Corte di cassazione* also has jurisdiction directly to hear disputes concerning sectoral jurisdiction (*regolamento di giurisdizione*) (*see below* under f). *See* the diagram on p. 326.

e. Relative jurisdiction (competenza per territorio)

Article 18 *et seq.* Cpc lay down rules of relative jurisdiction (*competenza per territorio*).

The principal rule is *actor sequitur forum rei*: competent is the court of the place where the defendant has his residence or domicile (*residenza* or *domicilio*) or, if these are unknown, of the place where he abides (art. 18 § 1 Cpc). However, the court of the plaintiff's place of residence has jurisdiction if the defendant does not have a residence or a domicile or a place of abode in Italy or if his place of abode is unknown (art. 18 § 2 Cpc). For legal persons in general the court of the place of the registered office (*sede*) has jurisdiction or, under certain conditions, the court of the place where it has an

DIAGRAM JUDICIAL ORGANISATION IN CIVIL CASES IN ITALY

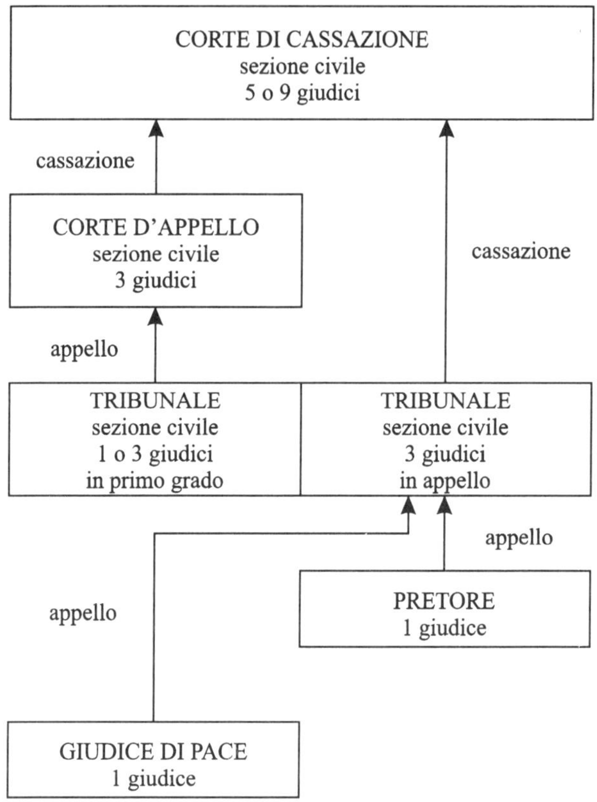

establishment (art. 19 Cpc). Residence, domicile and registered office are determined pursuant to Title III of Book 1 (art. 43 *et seq.*) of the *Codice civile*.

In cases involving contractual obligations, additional courts have jurisdiction (art. 20 Cpc) and in cases involving *inter alia* rights *in rem* on immovable property, inheritance matters and legal enforcement, exclusive courts (respectively *forum rei sitae, foro per le cause ereditarie, foro dell'esecuzione forzata*) have jurisdiction (art. 21 *et seq.* Cpc).

f. Additional remarks

At any stage or level of the proceedings, lack of international (art. 11 of the Act of 31 May 1995, no. 218; entry into force 1 September 1995) or sectoral jurisdiction (art. 37 Cpc) may be raised by a party or by the court of its own motion. It is also possible for either party to have the question of sectoral jurisdiction directly decided by the *Corte di cassazione* as long as the court at first instance has not given its decision (art. 41 Cpc, the so-called *regolamento di giurisdizione*).

Lack of binding jurisdiction (absolute jurisdiction as well as certain rules of relative jurisdiction as indicated in art. 28 Cpc; *cf.* also art. 6 Cpc) must be raised no later than the first hearing of the case (*cf.* section 10.4.2c) either by the parties or by the court of its own motion (art. 38 § 1 Cpc). The defendant may raise an objection of (non-binding) relative jurisdiction, at the latest in the *comparsa di risposta* (*see* section 10.4.2b), but he is obliged to designate a court which does have jurisdiction; if the plaintiff agrees with this designation, the proceedings may be continued, as in case of lack of binding jurisdiction, before the court so indicated (art. 38 § 2 and art. 50 Cpc).

The *giudice di pace* and the *pretore* decide cases sitting alone (*unus iudex*); the *tribunale* normally consists of one judge and only in special matters of three judges (including the examining judge); the *Corte d'appello* sits with three judges, the *Corte di cassazione* with five judges and with nine 'in united sections'.

Rules concerning abstention, challenge and (civil) liability of judges are laid down in arts. 51-56 Cpc.

10.3.3. THE LAWYERS

Although legal advice is also provided by notaries (*notai*) and accountants (*dottori commercialisti*), legal representation in proceedings has been reserved for lawyers in private practice (*difensori: procuratori* and *avvocati*). A *procuratore* may also act as *avvocato,* albeit only within the district of the *Corte d'appello* where he is registered as *procuratore legale*. An *avvocato* is entitled to act as such throughout the country.

The *difensore* represents a party in legal proceedings and his client must grant him an authenticated general or special power of attorney (*procura alle liti*; art. 83 Cpc). The *difensore* has to submit and receive all documents in the proceedings as far as this has not been explicitly reserved for his client by law (art. 84 Cpc). One or more *avvocati* may assist a party (art. 87 Cpc) and may formulate arguments, either orally or in writing, on behalf of their client; otherwise this is done by his *difensore.*

Legal representation by a *procuratore* is generally compulsory in proceedings before the *pretore*, the *tribunale* and the *Corte d'appello*; before the *Corte di cassazione* legal representation by a properly registered *avvocato* is required (art. 82 § 3 Cpc). An exception has been made for proceedings before the *giudice di pace* if the disputed amount does not exceed Lit. one million; otherwise the assistance of a *difensore* is usually mandatory (art. 82 §§ 1 and 2 Cpc).

10.3.4. THE PARTIES

Natural persons who possess the unfettered power to assert their rights, may act as parties in proceedings (art. 75 § 1 Cpc and art. 2 Cc). Other natural persons must be represented by their statutory representatives (art. 75 § 2 Cpc); this means that a minor must be represented by his parent, a mentally infirm person under legal custody by his guardian. Legal persons may also act as parties in proceedings and are represented in accordance with the rules of law or in accordance with their articles of association (art. 75 § 3 Cpc). Associations and committees (e.g. for charitable or social purposes) which do not possess legal capacity, are, however, entitled to act as parties in proceedings and are represented by those persons indicated in art. 36 *et seq.* Cc (art. 75 § 4 Cpc).

In order to bring an action against a person (or to defend an action) an interest in the matter is required (art. 100 Cpc): *difetto di interesse e, quindi, difetto di azione* (*point d'intérêt, point d'action*). Unless the law expressly provides otherwise (*see*, for instance, art. 2900 Cc), no party in an action can on his own behalf claim legal protection of a right belonging to somebody else (*cf.* art. 81 Cpc).

In the case of collective interests (*interessi collettivi*, whereby there is an organised structure to represent the collective interest) there is legislation allowing a representative action. Trade unions are allowed to assert the rights of their associates, including those rights which (may) concern their associates only indirectly (arts. 18 § 4 and 28 Act of 20 May 1970, no. 300, the so-called Statute of the rights of the workers). More recently, associations for the protection of the environment which satisfy certain requirements have been allowed to denounce facts causing environmental damage in order to induce the State or local authorities to bring an action of compensation; they may also intervene in the relevant proceedings before the (ordinary) judge and may act before the administrative judge as well (art. 18 §§ 4 and 5 Act of 8 July 1986, no. 349).

If the decision involves more parties, they must act jointly as plaintiffs (or defendants) in the relevant proceedings (*litisconsorzio necessario*; art. 102 § 1 Cpc). More persons may act jointly as parties, either plaintiffs or defendants, if there is connexity regarding the *causa petendi* or *petitum* or if the decision (totally or partly) depends on identical questions of (mostly) law to be resolved (*litisconsorzio facoltativo*; art. 103 § 1 Cpc).

10.4. Basic Procedure for Contentious Jurisdiction at First Instance

10.4.1. INTRODUCTION

The basic procedure for contentious jurisdiction (*processo di cognizione*) before the different courts of first instance is laid down in Titles I and II of Book 2 of the *Codice di procedura civile*. Until recently (*see* section 10.9.2) most procedures (at first instance) took place before the *tribunale*, which has the widest jurisdiction, and the *processo di cognizione* before the *tribunale*, set out in Title I (arts. 163-310 Cpc) and discussed in section 10.4.2, was therefore regarded by the legislator as a model for proceedings before the other courts. The first article of Title II, dealing with the *processo di cognizione* before the *giudice di pace* and the *pretore* (arts. 311-322 Cpc), therefore refers to Title I as much as possible unless otherwise provided by law (*see* section 10.4.3, where the main details are discussed).

It may be observed by the way that the legislator has drawn up Book 1 of the *Codice di procedura civile* with the *processo di cognizione* in mind in particular.

10.4.2. THE PROCEDURE BEFORE THE TRIBUNALE AT FIRST INSTANCE COMMENCED BY WRIT

a. Introduction

The procedure before the *tribunale* commenced by writ has been divided into three stages: the introductory stage (*fase introduttiva*), the examination stage (*fase di istruzione*) and the decision stage (*fase di decisione*).

In Italy, the plaintiff is called *attore*, the defendant *convenuto* and the claim *domanda*.

b. Commencement of proceedings (fase introduttiva)

The introductory stage starts with the service (*notificazione*) of the writ (*citazione*) by the bailiff, which must comply with art. 137 *et seq*. Cpc. The requirements as regards the contents of the writ are laid down in art. 163 Cpc and include the requirement that the date of the *udienza di comparizione* (the hearing of appearance), the *vocatio in ius* and any specific evidence on which the plaintiff intends to rely must be mentioned in the writ and in particular the documentary evidence which will be submitted by the plaintiff.

If the writ is invalid, the judge will order of his own motion that a new, amended writ be served within a fixed, strict time-limit. However, the appearance of the defendant will in general remedy any defect of the writ (*cf.* art. 164 Cpc).

Following service of the writ, which commences the proceedings, both parties must enter an appearance (*costituirsi in giudizio*). Within ten days after the service of the writ the plaintiff must enter an appearance through a *procuratore* who deposits a request to enter the case on the court's list (*nota d'iscrizione a ruolo*) at the registrar's office accompanied by a file (*fascicolo di parte*), containing the original of the writ, his power of attorney (*procura*), and any documentary evidence (art. 165 § 1 Cpc). At least twenty days before the day stated in the writ for the hearing of appearance, the defendant must enter an appearance through his *procuratore* who deposits his file at the registrar's office, containing his defence (*comparsa di risposta*), a copy of the writ served upon the defendant, his power of attorney, and any documentary evidence (art. 166 Cpc). In the *comparsa di risposta* the defendant must include all the arguments which he raises against the allegations by the plaintiff, the evidence on which he intends to rely as well as his conclusions (art. 167 § 1 Cpc; *see* for the formal requirements also art. 125 § 1 Cpc). The defence must also include any counterclaim, on penalty of forfeiting this counterclaim (art. 167 § 2 Cpc); *see* for the objections as to (absolute and relative) jurisdiction section 10.3.2f above.

When the case is registered on the court's list, the court clerk will at the same time open an official file (*fascicolo d'ufficio*), which will contain all records of the procedure including a copy of the operative part (*dispositivo*) of the judgments (*cf.* art. 168 Cpc). Once the *fascicolo d'ufficio* has been opened and forthwith submitted to the president of the court, an examining judge (*giudice istruttore*) must be appointed within two days following the appearance of one of the parties (art. 168-*bis* §§ 1 and 2 Cpc). Immediately following the appointment of the examining judge, the court clerk registers the case on the list of the relevant section (*sezione*) and on the list of the examining judge and gives him the *fascicolo d'ufficio* (art. 168-*bis* § 3 Cpc), thereby bringing the introductory stage of the proceedings to a close.

c. Examination (fase di istruzione)

The examining judge is the key figure in the *fase di istruzione*. It is his duty to prepare the case for judgment (which is given by himself or, exceptionally, by a panel of judges). However, this stage is not limited to the gathering of evidence, since the examining judge's duty also comprises the co-ordination of the proceedings, the issue of directives and the taking of initiatives: the case is considered by him in full (*trattazione*) (*cf.* art. 175 Cpc). He may give orders (*ordinanze*, which are briefly motivated pursuant to art. 134 § 1 Cpc), which may not prejudice the case (arts. 176 § 1 and 177 § 1 Cpc). These orders can always be amended or revoked by the examining judge, unless provided otherwise, and either party may conditionally object (*reclamo*) to the order by applying to a full panel of judges (*collegio*; *cf.* arts. 177 §§ 2 and 3 and 178 Cpc).

The examination of the case starts with the first hearing of the case (*prima udienza di trattazione*). At the hearing of appearance (*udienza di comparizione)* the *giudice istruttore* fixes the date of the *prima udienza di trattazione* and sets a time-limit for the defendant to raise objections which are not raised of the judge's own motion; at the hearing of appearance the examining judge can, if requested, also authorise written pleadings (*comunicazioni di comparse* or, more properly, *memorie*) (art. 180 § 2 Cpc).

Pursuant to art. 183 Cpc the examining judge interrogates the parties without restriction at the first hearing of the case and tries to reach a settlement if the nature of the case allows it (§ 1); thereupon, on the basis of the alleged facts, the examining judge orders the parties to explain the allegations if necessary and of his own motion determines the issues to be considered (§ 3); after this the parties may specify or amend their claims, the objections and the conclusions already formulated (§ 4; *see also* below under 10.4.2e(3)). At any stage of the examination the examining judge may make a fresh attempt to reach a settlement (art. 185 § 1 Cpc). There may be further hearings, after which the examining judge commences the proof-taking stage (*l'istruzione probatoria;* arts. 191-266 Cpc), unless he considers the case ripe for a decision (arts. 184 and 187 Cpc). In that case or once the evidence stage has been completed, the examining judge transfers the case to a panel of judges (art. 188 Cpc), unless he decides as *unus iudex* (*see also* below under d), and invites the parties to specify to him orally the conclusions they intend to submit to the adjudicating panel (*precisazione delle conclusioni*) (art. 189 Cpc). Finally, the parties must deposit their written pleadings (*comparse conclusionali* and subsequently *memorie di replica*) each within a specific time-limit and after referral of the case to the panel (art. 190 Cpc). Article 190-*bis* § 1 Cpc provides rules of procedure for the examining judge who decides the case sitting alone: after the parties have informed the judge which conclusions they intend to submit (*precisazione delle conclusioni*) (*see* art. 189 Cpc), the judge deals with the exchanges of the written pleadings (*see* art. 190 Cpc).

If requested, the examining judge may order any measures he thinks fit (art. 186 Cpc), in particular payment of sums which are not contested by the other party (who has appeared) in the proceedings (*ordinanza per il pagamento di somme non contestate*; art. 186-*bis* Cpc) or an order to pay or to deliver (*ordinanza di ingiunzione di pagamento o di consegna*; art. 186-*ter* Cpc). The examining judge may, once the case has been considered, by *ordinanza*, partly or fully award a monetary claim or a claim to deliver at the request of the party who has instituted the action, to the extent that sufficient evidence for this has been adduced (art. 186-*quater* § 1 Cpc).

d. Judgment (fase di decisione)

The possibility of the examining judge deciding the case as an *unus iudex* was introduced *inter alia* by the 1990 reform. However, in the cases listed in art. 48 § 2 Ord. giud., the *tribunale* still decides with three judges, one of whom is the examining judge (e.g. when making decisions on appeal; when the intervention of the *Pubblico Ministero* is required; when the case is reserved for special panels of judges; in case of an approval of an arrangement in case of bankruptcy).

The judgment must be made public (*pubblicazione*) by depositing it at the registrar's office (art. 133 § 1 Cpc) within sixty days after the time-limit for depositing the replies (*memorie di replica*) has expired (art. 190-*bis* § 1 *casu quo* art. 275 § 1 Cpc). Before making its decision the court may deliberate in chambers (art. 276 Cpc). However, at the request of either party the decision-making will be preceded by a public (art. 128 § 1 Cpc) hearing of oral pleadings (*udienza di discussione*) (art. 190-*bis* § 2 *casu quo* art. 275 §§ 2 and 3 Cpc).

Article 132 Cpc provides the contents of a judgment which must include the facts and legal grounds upon which the judgment is based (*cf.* also art. 111 § 1 Cost.) as well as the relief granted (*dispositivo*). Quoting legal authors is not allowed (art. 118 Disp. att. Cpc). In addition, the judgment must contain an order for costs (*see further* section 10.9.3). A judgment at first instance is provisionally enforceable (*esecuzione provvisoria*; art. 282 Cpc).

Article 279 § 1 Cpc sets out the forms in which the adjudicating panel must give its decisions, taking into account their content (*ordinanza* or *sentenza*) and art. 279 § 2 Cpc provides in which cases the panel will pronounce a final or an interim judgment. *Sentenze definitive* bring the proceedings to an end, in contrast to *sentenze non definitive*, which only resolve a prejudicial or preliminary question, e.g. an affirmative answer to the question of jurisdiction (*cf.* art. 187 § 3 Cpc). This distinction is of importance, because appeal and appeal in cassation against *sentenze non definitive* may be reserved (*see* arts. 340 and 361 Cpc). Questions which concern the examination stage of the proceedings are decided by order (*ordinanza*) (art. 279 §§ 1, 3, 4 and 5 Cpc), e.g. referring the case back to the examining judge for (additional) proof-taking, although, if necessary, the panel may decide that the evidence must be adduced before the panel (art. 281 Cpc).

Decisions may be corrected (*correzione delle sentenze e delle ordinanze*; *cf.* art. 287 *et seq.* Cpc).

e. Special aspects of procedure

1. Non-appearance (contumacia)

If a defendant does not enter a (formal) appearance and does not appear at the hearing of appearance either, the judge, having ascertained that the writ was duly served, by order enters default (*contumacia*) against the defendant (*cf.* art. 291 § 2 Cpc). The proceedings will now continue as a *processo contumaciale*, which is subject to the same rules as adversarial proceedings (*processo in contradditorio*), but which makes due allowance for the position of the party in default (*cf.* art. 292 Cpc). This party may as yet enter a formal appearance at any time until the hearing when the conclusions must be specified (*precisazione delle conclusioni*) as meant in art. 189 Cpc (art. 293 § 1 Cpc).

2. Intervention

Voluntary intervention (*intervento volontario*) is provided for in art. 105 Cpc: in proceedings that are pending a third party may pursuant to § 1 on his own behalf file a claim against both parties or against one of the parties and pursuant to § 2 he may support the plaintiff or the defendant. Besides, at the initiative of one of the parties (*su istanza di parte*; art. 106 Cpc) or by order of the judge (*per ordine del giudice*; art. 107 Cpc) the involuntary intervention (*intervento coatto*) of a third party may be effected.

3. *Amendment of claim*

Generally, an amendment of claim is not allowed. Only at the first hearing of the case (*prima udienza di trattazione*) may the plaintiff amend his claim and raise objections in response to any objections raised and any counterclaims filed by the defendant; furthermore, only at this first hearing may the claims filed, the objections raised and the conclusions already formulated be specified and amended by both parties (art. 183 § 4 Cpc). The conclusions are specified (*precisazione delle conclusioni*) definitely before the examining judge decides the case (art. 190-*bis* § 1 Cpc) or refers it to the panel (art. 189 § 1 Cpc).

4. *Counterclaim (domanda riconvenzionale)*

A counterclaim can only be made if it is connected with the facts underlying the plaintiff's claim or with facts which were already introduced into the case as objections (e.g. an application for compensation) (art. 36 Cpc). This is a consequence of the *principio dell'economia processuale*. To be valid, a counterclaim must be lodged by the defendant in his *comparsa di risposta* (art. 167 § 2 Cpc).

5. *Production of evidence*

In general, rules on the production of evidence can be found in the *Codice di procedura civile* (arts. 191-266) and rules on the admissibility and the effectiveness of a number of means of evidence in the *Codice civile*, Title II of Book 6 (arts. 2697-2739), which begins by determining the burden of proof: *onus probandi incumbit ei qui affirmat, non ei qui negat; actore non probante reus absolvitur*, and *reus in excipiendo fit actor* (i.e. the onus of proof rests with the plaintiff, not with the defendant; if the plaintiff fails to prove his case the defendant wins, and the defendant becomes plaintiff once he raises any objection) (art. 2697 Cc).

Evidence is produced under the direction of the examining judge, who admits the evidence proposed (*see above sub* b) if he considers it admissible and relevant; at the request of either party he may set a time-limit for the production of new documentary evidence and for the listing of new evidence which was not stated in the writ or the *comparsa di risposta* (art. 184 § 1 Cpc).

The means of evidence are limited by law (*tipicità dei mezzi di prova*) to: documents (*documenti*; arts. 2699-2720 Cc), the confession (*confessione*; arts. 2730-2735 Cc), formal questioning (*interrogatorio formale*; art. 230 Cpc), the statement under oath (*giuramento*; arts. 2736-2739 Cc), and testimony by witnesses (*testimonianza*; arts. 2721-2726 Cc); in addition, the judge is allowed to interrogate the parties freely (*interrogatorio libero* or *di chiarificazione*; art. 117 Cpc), to appoint experts (*consulente tecnico*; art. 191 Cpc), and to order the inspection of persons, sites and property (*ispezione*; art. 118 § 1 Cpc). Facts of common knowledge and experience do not have to be proven (*fatti notori*; art. 115 § 2 Cpc). Important are also presumptions (*presunzioni*; arts. 2927-2929 Cc), and evidence which may be deduced from indications (the *indizi*), particularly from the behaviour of the parties (*cf.* art. 116 § 2 Cpc).

The judge must form an opinion about the truth of the alleged facts only on the basis of evidence produced by the parties and the *Pubblico Ministero*. This principle (*principio della disponibilità delle prove*), also known as *iudex secundum probata partium iudicare debet*, is embodied in art. 115 § 1 Cpc, but subject to the phrase 'unless provided otherwise' (*see inter alia* arts. 117, 118 and 213 Cpc). Pursuant to art. 116 § 1 Cpc the court is free to interpret and evaluate evidence (*principio della libera valutazione delle prove*) unless otherwise provided. This principle is modified, however, by many exceptions (*see inter alia* arts. 2700, 2702, 2733 and 2738 Cc).

6. Settlement

A settlement reached at the initiative of the examining judge (*see above sub* c) must be laid down in an official report, which serves as a title for execution (*titolo esecutivo*) (art. 185 § 3 Cpc) and terminates the proceedings *ipso iure*. This does not apply to a settlement involving only the parties and not the examining judge (*transazione*) (*cf.* art. 1965 *et seq*. Cc).

10.4.3. THE PROCEDURE BEFORE THE GIUDICE DI PACE AND THE PRETORE COMMENCED BY WRIT

As far as possible, the rules of the *processo di cognizione* before the *tribunale* also apply before the *giudice di pace* and the *pretore* unless otherwise provided by law (art. 311 Cpc).

The main difference in the procedure before the *pretore* is the possibility provided in art. 315 Cpc to order oral pleadings (*discussione orale*) instead of written pleadings (art. 314 in conjunction with art. 190 Cpc). Once these oral pleadings have finished, judgment is pronounced immediately. Otherwise the judgment must be deposited with the registrar's office within thirty days after expiry of the time-limit for depositing replies (*memorie di replica*) (art. 314 Cpc).

The *giudice di pace* decides on the basis of fairness if the amount in dispute does not exceed Lit. 2 million (art. 113 § 2 Cpc), or if the parties request him to do so, even if he thereby exceeds his absolute jurisdiction (the so-called *non-contenziosa* function of the *giudice di pace*). The official report of a possible settlement serves as a title for execution (*titolo esecutivo*) as referred to in art. 185 § 2 Cpc, if the judge has not exceeded his jurisdiction (art. 322 § 2 Cpc); otherwise the official report has the status of a private document which is recognised by the law (art. 322 § 3 Cpc).

Other characteristics of the *processo di cognizione* before the *giudice di pace* mainly affect the speed of the proceedings: the contents of the writ (*cf.* art. 316 § 1 Cpc), entering an appearance (*cf.* art. 319 § 1 Cpc), the consideration of the case (*cf.* art. 320 Cpc), and the decision stage (pursuant to art. 321 § 1 Cpc, after the specification of the conclusions the case is pleaded orally, thus eliminating written pleadings) are all simpler than in proceedings before the *tribunale*. The *giudice di pace* must deposit his judgment with the registrar's office within fifteen days after the oral pleadings of the case (art. 321 § 2 Cpc).

10.5. Basic Procedure for Voluntary Jurisdiction at First Instance

10.5.1. INTRODUCTION

Proceedings of voluntary jurisdiction (*giurisdizione volontaria*) are a form of special proceedings.

Chapter VI (arts. 737-742-*bis*) of Title II of Book 4 of the *Codice di procedura civile* contains general provisions for proceedings in chambers (*disposizioni comuni ai procedimenti in camera di consiglio*). These provisions apply to all proceedings wherein a decision is pronounced in chambers, described in the chapters of Title II which precede chapter VI (*inter alia* divorce by mutual request (art. 711 Cpc) and proceedings concerning the estate of absent persons and of persons declared presumably dead (arts. 721 and 725 Cpc) and of minors and of persons without legal capacity (arts. 732-734 Cpc)).

The general provisions for proceedings in chambers also apply to proceedings in chambers as described in separate Acts (e.g. the rectification of deeds regarding the civil status of persons (Act of 9 July 1939, no. 1238)) as well as to the proceedings leading in general to a measure to be pronounced by a judge or a body consisting of one person, as described in Title III (issue of a copy from the public records and inspection of such copy (arts. 743-

746)), Title IV (proceedings as to a deceased's estate (arts. 747-783)), and Title VI (release from a mortgage (arts. 792-795)) of Book 4 of the *Codice di procedura civile* (*cf.* also art. 742-*bis* Cpc).

10.5.2. THE PROCEDURE COMMENCED BY PETITION

The procedure concerning voluntary jurisdiction is commenced with a petition (*ricorso*) filed with the registry of the competent court (*cf.* art. 737 Cpc): the president of the *tribunale* (*casu quo* the *tribunale per i minorenni*) or the *pretore* (who mostly acts as a judge supervising a guardianship (*giudice tutelare*; *see*, for instance, art. 374 Cc)). The specific article on which the proceeding is based usually indicates which judge has absolute jurisdiction. If not provided by law, relative jurisdiction is usually based on the place where the person, whose legal position is under discussion, is staying (*Cass.* 16 January 1975, no. 167, *Repertorio del Foro Italiano* 1975, I, 2043). The petition must be signed by a lawyer who has a power of attorney from his client (*difensore con procura*).

One of the judges of the *tribunale* is appointed as *relatore* by the president: before reporting in chambers the *relatore* (or, as the case may be, the *pretore*) will carry out a concise examination which may include a kind of proof-taking (art. 738 §1 and 3 Cpc). Other persons interested in the matter may be joined in the proceedings. If the *Pubblico Ministero* must be heard, the papers must be sent to it in time (*cf.* art. 738 § 2 Cpc).

The decision must be given by a decree (*decreto*), which is motivated unless the law stipulates otherwise (*cf.* art. 737 Cpc) and which may be declared immediately effective (*cf.* art. 741 § 2 Cpc).

10.6. Means of Recourse

10.6.1. INTRODUCTION

Title III of Book 1 of the *Codice di procedura civile*, entitled *Delle impugnazioni*, lists the various means of recourse against judgments given in proceedings commenced by writ (*processo di cognizione*). *Impugnazione* means either the whole proceedings or the procedural act whereby any attack on a judgment is instituted, whatever its form.

The first chapter of Title III (arts. 323-338 Cpc) contains provisions of a general nature, including legal time-limits (arts. 325-328), express or implied waiver (art. 329), and separate and cross-appeals (arts. 333-335).

The party instituting the means of recourse must naturally have an interest in contesting (*interesse ad impugnare*) (*see also* section 10.3.4 above).

Ordinary means of recourse against judgments are: appeal (*appello*), *regolamento di competenza*, cassation (*ricorso per cassazione*), and ordinary revocation (*revocazione ordinaria*); extraordinary means of recourse are: extraordinary revocation (*revocazione straordinaria*) and third-party opposition (*opposizione di terzo*) (*cf.* art. 323 Cpc). The importance of this distinction becomes clear when reading art. 324 Cpc: a judgment has the authority of *res iudicata* when all ordinary forms of recourse are exhausted or when the legal time-limit for lodging such means has expired (the so-called *cosa giudicata formale)*.

The *regolamento di competenza* (arts. 42-50 Cpc) is a form of recourse against judgments which only decide a question of absolute or relative jurisdiction (*see also* section 10.3.2f) falls outside the scope of this book. So does revocation (arts. 395-403 Cpc), which, pursuant to arts. 395 and 396 Cpc, applies on a limited number of grounds only (e.g. if a judgment is the result of fraud (extraordinary revocation) or if the judgment has been based on a factual error, manifest from records of the case (ordinary revocation)). Third-party opposition (arts. 404-408 Cpc), which is possible on two grounds only (*cf.* art. 404 Cpc)) will not be discussed either. Attention will be devoted to appeal (arts. 339-359 Cpc; *see* section 10.6.2) and cassation (arts. 360-394 Cpc; *see* section 10.6.3) against judgments.

In case of voluntary jurisdiction as referred to in arts. 737-742-*bis* Cpc (*cf.* section 10.5 above), complaint (*reclamo*) is generally the only means of recourse (*see* section 10.6.4).

10.6.2. APPEAL (APPELLO)

In the *processo di cognizione* all judgments at first instance are appealable, unless determined otherwise by law or by agreement between the parties pursuant to art. 360 § 2 Cpc (art. 339 § 1 Cpc). The law determines that judgments based on fairness which are given following a request by the parties pursuant to art. 114 Cpc (art. 339 § 2 Cpc) or by the *giudice di pace* (art. 339 § 3 Cpc; *see also* section 10.4.3) are not appealable.

Appeals will be heard by the full court next in the hierarchy: the *tribunale* for judgments of the *giudice di pace* and the *pretore*, and the *Corte d'appello* for judgments of the *tribunale* (*cf.* art. 48 § 1 and art. 53 § 1 Ord. giud. respectively, and art. 341 Cpc). The appellant (*appellante*) institutes his appeal by service of a writ upon the respondent (*appellato*) (*cf.* art. 342 § 1 Cpc), within 30 days (art. 325 § 1 Cpc) after the service of the judgment at first instance (*cf.* art. 326 § 1 Cpc; *see also* art. 285 Cpc). The party in default at first instance must also follow this procedure in case of an appeal against a judgment given in the *processo contumaciale* (*cf.* above, section 10.4.2e (1)).

Subject to the special provisions contained in arts. 342-358 Cpc, the proceedings before the *tribunale* sitting in appeal or the *Corte d'appello* are conducted as far as possible pursuant to the rules for the *processo di cognizione* before the *tribunale* at first instance (art. 359 Cpc). The appeal proceedings have a so-called devolutive effect within the limits of the demand of appeal: *tantum devolutum quantum appellatum* (*cf.* section 10.2.2 above (*principio della domanda*) and also art. 346 Cpc). As appeal is considered as *revisio prioris instantiae*, new claims or new objections are not allowed; in general, new evidence is not allowed either, although the production of new documentary evidence is considered to be possible (*cf.* art. 345 Cpc). The appeal is examined by a panel of judges (art. 350 §1 Cpc). When he institutes his (principal or incidental) appeal, a party may request (in the *citazione* or the *comparsa di risposta*) that at the first hearing the panel order the (whole or partial) suspension of the enforceability or of the enforcement of the disputed judgment; the panel can do so if there are pressing reasons to do so (art. 283 Cpc; *see also* art. 337 Cpc).

10.6.3. CASSATION (RICORSO PER CASSAZIONE)

Judgments given on appeal and judgments which are not appealable (at first instance) may be attacked by means of *ricorso per cassazione* (*see* art. 360 § 1 Cpc, which only refers to judgments (*sentenze*); *cf.* art. 362 Cpc for decisions or conflicts regarding sectoral jurisdiction). However, according to the Constitutional Court, art. 111 § 2 Cost. (which provides that appeal in cassation is always allowed on the ground of violation of the law) does not only apply to measures in the form of a judgment, but also to every other measure not capable of appeal, given by a judge and containing a decision on rights. It is *inter alia* the task of the *Corte di cassazione*, seated in Rome, to ensure the exact observance and uniform interpretation of the law, the unity of national law and to effect observance of the limits of the various jurisdictions (art. 65 Ord. giud.). The grounds for cassation, summarised in art. 111 § 2 Cost. as violation of the law, have been listed in art. 360 § 1 Cpc as *errores in procedendo* (nos. 1, 2, and 4) and *errores in iudicando* (no. 3: violation or wrong application of rules of law, and no. 5: omission of, insufficient or contradictory motivation regarding a decisive point in dispute).

The proceedings must be commenced within sixty days (art. 325 § 2 Cpc) following the service of the disputed judgment (*cf.* art. 285 Cpc). Cassation is instituted by petition (*ricorso*) directed to the *Corte di cassazione* (*cf.* art. 365 Cpc) and first must be served upon the opponent (*resistente*, the party instituting cassation being called *ricorrente*) (*cf.* art. 369 Cpc). The opponent may file a *controricorso* against the *ricorrente*'s *ricorso* which must first be served upon the *ricorrente*. If the opponent fails to serve his *controricorso* on the *ricorrente*, he may pursuant to art. 370 § 1 Cpc not produce any written pleadings (*memorie*) and may only participate in the oral pleadings (*discussione*) (*see below*). The requirements for the *ricorso* and the *controricorso* (*cf.* art. 370 § 2 Cpc) are laid down in arts. 365 and 366 Cpc. The deposit, with the *ricorso* or, as the case may be, the *controricorso*, of documents which were not produced during the proceedings at the lower instance(s) is generally not admitted (*cf.* arts. 369 *casu quo* 370 § 3, and 372 Cpc).

Cassation does not suspend enforcement of the disputed judgment. However, at the request of either party the judge who delivered this judgment, may order (by *ordinanza non impugnabile*) suspension of the enforcement or may order that sufficient security is provided, if there is a risk of grave and irreparable damage resulting from enforcement (art. 373 § 1 Cpc).

This introductory stage is followed by the decision-making stage. In cassation there is obviously no examination stage. The parties can deposit their pleadings (*memorie*) at the registrar's office at least five days before the hearing (*udienza*) (art. 378 Cpc), the date of which is determined by the (first) president. He also appoints the reporting judge (*consigliere relatore*) (art. 377 § 1 Cpc). At the hearing the reporting judge gives a concise report of the case, then the lawyers argue their case before the court, followed by the oral opinion of the *Pubblico Ministero*, after which brief written pleadings (*osservazioni*) may be presented by the lawyers (art. 379 Cpc). The Court (sometimes in 'united' sections; *see* art. 374 Cpc), immediately retires to deliberate about the decision in chambers (art. 380 § 1 Cpc). Sometimes the Court will dispense with the hearing and will decide in chambers directly, for instance if the Court recognises that the *ricorso* must be declared inadmissible because it is not based on the grounds described in art. 360 Cpc. In that case the decision must be given by order (*ordinanza*) (*cf.* art. 375 § 1 Cpc). The disputed judgment will then become *res iudicata*.

If the judgment is reversed by the Court, in general the case is either remitted (*rinvio*) to a lower court (*cf.* arts. 383 and 384 § 1 Cpc), or it is decided by the Court itself (art. 384 § 1 Cpc: if, in case of violation or an incorrect application of rules of law, no further establishment of the facts is necessary).

10.6.4. COMPLAINT (RECLAMO)

In petition procedures as referred to in arts. 737-742-*bis* Cpc appeal from a *decreto* must be made to the next court in the hierarchy by means of complaint (*reclamo*) (art. 739 § 1 Cpc). The time-limit for this type of appeal is ten days, either after the communication of the *decreto* if one party is involved, or after its service if more parties are involved (art. 739 § 2 Cpc). The *Pubblico Ministero* may appeal from a *decreto* of the *giudice tutelare* and of the *tribunale*, if its opinion was required; *reclamo* must be lodged within ten days after the communication of the *decreto* (art. 740 Cpc).

In these petition procedures appeal (*reclamo*) against a *decreto* at second instance by the *Corte d'appello* or the *tribunale* is not allowed in principle (*cf.* art. 739 § 3 Cpc); it is concluded from this that appeal in cassation is not allowed. However, within this context it must be taken into account that a *decreto* may at any time be amended or revoked, albeit without prejudice to rights acquired in good faith by third persons (art. 742 Cpc). Yet there are cases in which the *Corte di cassazione* has deemed appeal in cassation admissible; *see* for a survey Battaglini-Novelli, *Codice di procedura civile*, note 6 to art. 739 and Carpi-Taruffo, *Commentario Breve Cpc*, note 22 *et seq.* to art. 739.

10.7. Special Procedures

10.7.1. INTRODUCTION

In section 10.7.2 summary procedures will be discussed. In section 10.8.2 attention will be given to proceedings for protective measures other than attachment (*procedimenti cautelari* and *procedimenti possessori*), which are also characterised by a summary nature (*see also* section 10.8.1).

Section 10.7.3 deals with sector procedures, which are also governed by rules outside Book 4 of the *Codice di procedura civile*.

In Italy there is no special procedure for small claims.

10.7.2. SUMMARY PROCEDURES (PROCEDIMENTI SOMMARI)

The injunction procedure (*procedimento d'ingiunzione*; arts. 633-656 Cpc) leads to a condemnatory decision (judicial order) whose function is mainly aimed at enforcement. It has a summary character and postpones the right of defence (the so-called *contradditorio differito*). The injunction procedure belongs to the category of *processi speciali di cognizione.*

The injunction procedure, commenced by petition (*ricorso*) (*cf.* art. 638 § 1 Cpc), is available to a creditor of a claimable debt, consisting of a sum of money or a specific amount of fungibles or a specific chattel (*cf.* art. 633 § 1 Cpc). The judge who would have jurisdiction in normal proceedings also has jurisdiction in summary proceedings: the *giudice di pace*, the *pretore* or the president of the *tribunale* (art. 637 § 1 Cpc). The judge grants an injunction pursuant to art. 633 Cpc, if (in general) the applicant produces documentary evidence of the alleged debt (§ 1); if the applicant alleges facts from which his fulfilment of possible obligations or conditions can be presumed (§ 2); and if the service of the injunction upon the other party does not take place outside the Italian Republic (§ 3) (*see also* section 3.3.3 *sub* a). In that case the judge orders the other party in a motivated decree (*decreto*) to pay the debt (or to fulfil his obligations) in general within forty days after the service of the decree, warning the other party that, if he does not pay (or fulfil his obligations) or raise an objection against the injunction (*opposizione*) within that period, the order can be enforced (art. 641 § 1 Cpc). If the claim is based on *inter alia* a bill of exchange, a cheque, or a notarial instrument, the judge may upon request declare the decree provisionally enforceable; in that case the other party must pay (or fulfil his obligations) immediately (*cf.* art. 642 Cpc).

Opposizione against the injunction is lodged by writ, the procedure continuing as an ordinary procedure (*processo di cognizione*) with everything that entails, except that the opposing party may halve the time-limits for entering an appearance and the hearing of appearance (*cf.* art. 645 Cpc).

No appeal lies from a rejection of the petition. In this case the petitioner can commence fresh proceedings in a *procedimento d'ingiunzione* or in ordinary proceedings on the merits of the case (*processo di cognizione*) (art. 640 § 3 Cpc).

Another type of procedure belonging to the *processi speciali di cognizione* is the eviction procedure (*procedimento per convalida di sfratto*; arts. 657-669 Cpc) in case of an expired lease or arrears of rent. This summary procedure serves the same purpose as the injunction procedure, but is instead adversarial. It remains in force in spite of the recent introduction of the *rito locatizio* (*see below*, section 10.7.3).

10.7.3. SECTOR PROCEDURES

There are some special procedures which by their nature differ from the *processo di cognizione,* while preserving the characteristics of the latter. These *procedimenti speciali di cognizione* include: proceedings in employment disputes (*controversie in materia di lavoro*, laid down in Title IV of Book 2: arts. 409-447 Cpc, and the Statute of the rights of workers (*Statuto dei diritti dei lavoratori*, Act of 20 May 1970, no. 300)), upon which the so-called *rito locatizio* has been modelled for all cases listed in art. 8 § 2 no. 2 Cpc, *inter alia* concerning the tenancy of immovable property in cities (*cf.* art. 447-*bis* Cpc, introduced by the 1990 reform), and proceedings on family law and the status of persons: divorce (arts. 706-710 Cpc), incapacity (arts. 712-720 Cpc), absence and declaration of presumed death (arts. 722-731 Cpc), and proceedings on the dissolution of a community of property (arts. 784-791 Cpc).

Further sector proceedings which must be mentioned are bankruptcy proceedings, set out in the *Disciplina del fallimento* (Bankruptcy Act) (*see also* section 10.1.2 above).

10.8. Protective Measures and Enforcement Measures

10.8.1. INTRODUCTION

The proceedings to obtain protective measures (*procedimenti cautelari*; arts. 669-*bis*-702 Cpc) and the repossession proceedings (*procedimenti possessori*; arts. 703-705 Cpc) together form a group of special proceedings. These proceedings are typically intended to safeguard rights (*attività cautelare*) and are of a summary nature. They are completely different from the *processo di cognizione* (*see* sections 10.8.2 and 10.8.3). The requirements for the granting of these measures are *periculum in mora* and *fumus boni iuris*.

Book 3 of the *Codice di procedura civile* (arts. 474-632) deals with enforcement proceedings, the *processo di esecuzione,* whereby judgments may be enforced. It is distinct from the *processo di cognizione,* which is intended to determine rights only.

Before enforcement proceedings (*see* sections 10.8.4 and 10.8.5) can be commenced, the judgment to be enforced (or another *titolo esecutivo*; *cf.* art. 474 Cpc) and the so-called *precetto* must be served, unless otherwise provided (*cf.* art. 479 Cpc). The *precetto* is a formal order by the creditor to his debtor to fulfil his obligation within a time-limit of not less than ten days, together with a notice that enforcement proceedings will be commenced if he fails to comply (art. 480 § 1 Cpc). The judgment to be enforced must be enforceable, i.e. must be provided with the *formula esecutiva* (*cf.* art. 475 Cpc).

Opposition to the enforcement (*opposizione all'esecuzione*) must be brought in separate proceedings (*processo di cognizione*), provided for in arts. 615-622 Cpc as well.

10.8.2. PROTECTIVE MEASURES OTHER THAN ATTACHMENT

Proceedings for protective measures (*procedimenti cautelari*) other than attachment include:

- proceedings concerning the reporting of construction works and of feared damage (*procedimenti di denuncia di nuova opera e di danno temuto*; arts. 688-691 Cpc and arts. 1171-1172 Cc) to adjoining property (which may be) caused by work in progress or by an existing situation (e.g. a dilapidated wall); and
- proceedings concerning urgent measures (*provvedimenti d'urgenza*; arts. 700-702 Cpc), which may be applied for (by *ricorso*) in other cases than those provided in arts. 688-691 and 692-699 Cpc (the latter referring to provisional testimony etc.) when imminent and irreparable damage is threatening.

General rules for these proceedings are laid down in arts. 669-*bis*-669-*quaterdecies* Cpc (*see* section 10.8.3).

Another protective measure other than attachment may be obtained in repossession proceedings (*procedimenti possessori*; arts. 703-705 Cpc and arts. 1168-1170 Cc). Once this protective measure has been obtained, it remains in force, even if no final proceedings to ascertain the property rights of the parties (*procedimento petitorio*) are brought (within a specific time-limit).

10.8.3. PROTECTIVE MEASURES BY ATTACHMENT

The most important protective measure is *sequestro* (arts. 670-687 Cpc), a kind of attachment, which appears in two main forms:

- the judge may authorise *sequestro giudiziario* of movable or immovable goods, firms or other entities, if property or possession thereof is disputed and their temporary safeguarding or administration is opportune (art. 670 § 1 Cpc) and the judge may authorise *sequestro giudiziario* of documentary or tangible evidence (books, ledgers, records, registers etc.), if the right to exhibit or submit such evidence is disputed and its temporary safeguarding is opportune (*cf.* art. 670 § 2 Cpc); and

– *sequestro conservativo* of movable or immovable goods or of debts, authorised by a judge at the request of a creditor, who fears on good grounds that he may lose the guarantee that he will be paid a sum of money by his debtor (art. 671 Cpc).

The *sequestro conservativo* is converted into enforcement by attachment (*pignoramento*) the moment the creditor obtains an enforceable condemnatory judgment (art. 686 § 1 Cpc).

The 1990 reform also introduced art. 669-*bis*-669-*quaterdecies* Cpc (*procedimenti cautelari in generale*), containing general provisions applicable to all proceedings for protective measures (including the form of the petition (*ricorso*), jurisdiction, proceedings, security, appeal (*reclamo*)). Of particular importance is art. 669-*octies* §§ 1 and 2 Cpc, pursuant to which, if a protective measure is granted, final proceedings must be instituted within a fixed, strictly applied time-limit, if such proceedings are not already pending. Otherwise the protective remedy will lose its effect by operation of law (*cf.* art. 669-*nonies* § 1 Cpc). *See also Il nuovo processo cautelare*, edited by Giuseppe Tarzia, (Cedam) Padova 1993.

10.8.4. ENFORCEMENT MEASURES BY ATTACHMENT AND BANKRUPTCY

Judgments ordering the payment of a sum of money can be enforced by expropriation (*esecuzione per espropriazione*), based on art. 2910 § 1 Cc: in order to obtain what is owed him, the creditor may have property of the debtor expropriated in accordance with the rules of the *Codice di procedura civile.*

General rules concerning expropriation are found in arts. 483-512 Cpc. Expropriation is commenced by attachment of the debtor's property, ordered by the *ufficiale giudiziario* at the request of the creditor (*cf.* art. 492 Cpc). Following the depositing at the registrar's office of a report of the attachment by the bailiff, sometimes together with the *titolo esecutivo* and the *precetto* (*cf.* arts. 518, 543 and 557 Cpc), a file (*fascicolo dell'esecuzione*) is opened by the court clerk (*cf.* art. 488 § 1 Cpc). Thereupon a judge (*giudice dell'esecuzione*) is appointed under whose direction expropriation will take place (*cf.* art. 484 Cpc). Other creditors may intervene (art. 499 § 1 Cpc), but not later than the first hearing determined for the authorisation of the sale (*cf.* art. 525 § 2 and art. 563 § 2 Cpc; however, *see also* art. 525 § 3 Cpc), or the first hearing of appearance (art. 551 § 2 Cpc). In general the attached property will be sold (*vendita forzata*), although an assignment to the creditor(s) (*assegnazione*) is also possible (*cf.* art. 505 Cpc). The sale is followed by payment of the money due to the creditor (or distribution of the proceeds among the creditors) (*cf.* art. 510 Cpc). Specific provisions regarding expropriation of movable property in the debtor's possession are laid down in arts. 513-542 Cpc; specific provisions regarding (money) claims of the debtor against third parties or movable property of the debtor in the possession of third parties can be found in arts. 543-554 Cpc, and specific rules regarding immovable property in arts. 555-598 Cpc.

In case of bankruptcy, which by operation of law deprives the debtor of the unfettered management and disposal of his property (*cf.* art. 42 § 1 *Disciplina del fallimento*), a (possible) liquidation is not preceded by measures of attachment. Instead, the debtor's goods and chattels are immediately sealed pursuant to art. 752 *et seq.* Cpc (*apposizione dei sigilli*) (*cf.* art. 84 §§ 1 and 2 *Disciplina del fallimento*).

10.8.5. ENFORCEMENT MEASURES OTHER THAN ATTACHMENT

In the *Codice di procedura civile*, two types of enforcement proceedings not involving attachment are described.

The first one concerns the compulsory assignment of specific, movable or immovable property, if the debtor does not fulfil his obligation (*esecuzione forzata per consegna di cose mobili o rilascio di immobili*; arts. 605-611 Cpc), and is based on art. 2930 Cc. In addition to the requirements laid down by art. 480 Cpc, the relevant property must be described in the *precetto* (art. 605 § 1 Cpc). Upon request of the creditor, the *ufficiale giudiziario* effects the enforcement (*cf.* arts. 606-608 Cpc). In case of problems which admit no delay, each party may ask the *pretore* to order the necessary, temporary measures (art. 610 Cpc).

The other type of enforcement proceedings concerns enforcement of judgments by which the defendant is ordered either to do something specific or to refrain from something specific (*esecuzione forzata degli obblighi di fare e di non fare*; arts. 612-614 Cpc), based on arts. 2931 and 2933 Cc. In this type of proceedings the *pretore* gives an order (*ordinanza*), determining the conditions for enforcement at the request (*ricorso*) of the creditor, having heard the other party. By the same order the *pretore* appoints an *ufficiale giudiziario* who must proceed to enforcement, and the persons who must carry out the act which the defendant was ordered to do or undo what the defendant did (art. 612 Cpc).

In Italy a penalty for delay in the compliance with and performance of a mandatory or refraining order is extremely rare and civil imprisonment is unknown.

10.9. Duration and Costs

10.9.1. INTRODUCTION

As far as possible, this chapter will give some general outlines of duration and costs of civil proceedings in Italy.

10.9.2. DURATION

Traditionally, proceedings in Italy take a long time. Neither the 1865 *Codice di procedura civile* nor the Code of 1943 succeeded in changing this. *See also* ECHR 25 June 1985, *Publ. ECHR*, Series A, vol. 119 (*Capuano* v. *Italy*). Since the 1970s attempts to reform civil procedures have been made which culminated in the 1990 reform. This reform was introduced in 1995 at long last. This reform is *inter alia* intended to accelerate proceedings by means of a more or less strict and stringent system. The immediate enforceability of a judgment will no doubt also be instrumental in this purpose. However, the practical effects of this reform are still unknown.

Before the recent reform the average duration of a procedure at first instance was more than five years, and seven years in the big cities; the standard length of a procedure including appeal and cassation before the reform was ten years. Hence many people are sceptical of a 'quick' recovery of civil justice. On the other hand, hopes are high that the recent modifications will result in judgments being given in a period of two years.

There is pessimism about the chance of success of the recent reform. Much will also depend on the way in which the newly introduced rules of absolute jurisdiction will be assimilated in practice. As a result of these new rules, an estimated 50 per cent of all cases must be brought before a different judge: the *giudice di pace* instead of the *pretore* or the *tribunale*; and a great many of the remaining cases must actually be brought before the *pretore*. This big influx of cases, in particular before the *giudice di pace*, is due to the fact that the *giudice di pace* now has absolute jurisdiction in cases dealing with compensation for road accidents (40 per cent of all cases) not exceeding a value of Lit. 30 million, cases concerning joint ownership of homes (15-20 per cent of all cases), and the other types of cases, in particular in respect of movable goods with a value not exceeding Lit. 5 million (*cf.* art. 7 Cpc).

10.9.3. COSTS

Proceedings entail expenses: legal dues, lawyers' fees, costs of producing evidence (witnesses etc.), costs connected with the activities of the registrar's office (court office fees, fees in respect of actions by the bailiff, etc.). Initially, each party has to bear his own expenses (*onere dell'anticipazione*), unless legal aid has been granted (*cf.* art. 90 Cpc). In his final judgment the judge must order the losing party to reimburse the winning party for these expenses and must determine their amount (*cf.* art. 91 § 1 Cpc; *see* for the *procedimento d'ingiunzione* art. 641 § 3 Cpc). The costs of the enforcement proceedings are borne by the person against whom the measure of enforcement has been taken (*cf.* art. 95 Cpc for expropriation, arts. 611 and 614 Cpc).

The judge determines the amount of the lawyers' fees to be borne by the losing party within the limits he considers appropriate to be paid by the losing party, thereby eliminating any excessive and superfluous costs (*cf.* art. 92 § 1 Cpc). The professional tariff system is in accordance with this (*Tariffa forense in materia civile, penale e stragiudiziale* (Ministerial Decree of 5 October 1994, no. 585)).

In addition, the judge may wholly or partly set off the costs between the parties if both parties have lost parts of the case (*soccombenza reciproca*) or in case of justified grounds (*giusti motivi*) (art. 92 § 2 Cpc), e.g. the difficulty of the case, or a change in case law occurring in the course of the proceedings.

Legal aid (*gratuito patrocinio*) (*cf.* also art. 24 § 3 Cost.) is still, though partly, governed by the Royal Decree of 30 December 1923, no. 3282, which is generally considered to be anachronistic and inadequate. Article 14 of this Decree states that any person of limited means (*stato di povertà*), i.e. unable to bear the expenses of litigation, is allowed the benefit of legal aid. A committee consisting of judges and lawyers has been attached to each *tribunale*, *Corte d'appello* and the *Corte di cassazione*. This committee grants legal aid, if there is an issue at stake which may result in a judgment in favour of the applicant. Together with the decision to grant legal aid, a *difensore* is assigned.

This system was amended in part by art. 11 of the Act of 11 August 1973, no. 533 (introducing the new proceedings in employment disputes (*see* Title

IV of Book 1 of the *Codice di procedura civile*)) and also by the Act of 30 July 1990, no. 217 (referring mainly to proceedings in criminal cases and only marginally to civil cases).

This Decree and these Acts will remain in force until the introduction of general rules in respect of legal aid (*disciplina generale del patrocinio dei non abbienti*).

10.10. Proceedings Outside the Courts

10.10.1. INTRODUCTION

In Italy arbitration (*arbitrato rituale*) and binding advice (*arbitrato irrituale* or *libero*) are available to resolve disputes without the intervention of a national court. Distinct from *arbitrato* is the so-called *arbitraggio*, based on art. 1349 Cc (an agreement between the parties that the performance to be delivered by one of them shall be determined by a third person).

10.10.2. ARBITRATION (ARBITRATO RITUALE)

Arbitration (*arbitrato rituale*) is described in Title VIII of Book 4 of the *Codice di procedura civile*: arts. 806-840 (recently amended, together with related articles of the *Codice civile*, by the Act of 5 January 1994, no. 25, effective on 17 April 1994). An article-by-article commentary has been published by Briguglio-Fazzalari-Marengo, *La nuova disciplina dell'arbitrato*, (Giuffrè) Milan 1994.

Pursuant to art. 806 Cpc, parties may submit almost all their disputes to arbitration. The parties determine the place of the arbitration, which must be in the territory of the Italian Republic; otherwise this is done by the arbitrators during their first meeting (art. 816 § 1 Cpc). Furthermore, the parties may decide the rules according to which the arbitrators are to proceed; otherwise, the arbitrators are to proceed in the manner they consider opportune (*cf.* art. 816 §§ 2 and 3 Cpc). In any event, in accordance with the main principles of civil procedure, in particular the adversarial principle, the arbitrators must set the parties certain time-limits to produce documents, and to present pleadings (*memorie*) and replies (*repliche*) (art. 816 § 4 Cpc). Arbitrators are not allowed to order *sequestro* or any other protective measures (art. 818 Cpc). These measures belong to the jurisdiction of the ordinary judge (*cf.* art. 669-*quinquies* Cpc; *see also* art. 669-*octies* § 4 Cpc (*see* section 10.8.3 above)), and so do injunctions resulting from the *procedimento d'ingiunzione*.

Unless otherwise agreed by the parties, the arbitrators must generally give their award (*lodo arbitrale*) within one hundred and eighty days from the acceptance by all arbitrators of their appointment (*cf.* art. 820 Cpc). The arbitrators must decide in accordance with the rules of law, unless the parties, in whatever manner (e.g. the arbitrators must decide as *amichevoli compositori*) have authorised them to decide as good men in equity (art. 822 Cpc).

Enforcement of the arbitral award on the territory of the Italian Republic is possible only after it has been declared enforceable by the *pretore* of the place of arbitration. Having ascertained that the award satisfies all formal requirements, the *pretore* declares the award enforceable in a decree (*decreto*) (*cf.* art. 825 §§ 2 and 3 Cpc). Only a decree refusing enforceability of an award may be attacked (*reclamo*) by petition (*ricorso*) before the *tribunale*. Having heard the parties, the *tribunale* decides in chambers in an order (*ordinanza*), from which no appeal lies (*cf.* art. 825 § 5 Cpc).

Pursuant to art. 827 Cpc an arbitral award may be attacked by three means: (1) an objection on the ground of nullity (arts. 828-830 Cpc, art. 829 listing the cases of nullity which can be summarised in general as *errores in procedendo* and *errores in iudicando*); (2) (extraordinary) revocation; and (3) third-party opposition (art. 831 Cpc). It is possible to request correction of an arbitral award (art. 826 Cpc).

The 1994 Arbitration Act introduced two new chapters to Title VIII (*Del l'arbitrato*) of Book 4 of the *Codice di procedura civile*: chapter VI, dealing with international arbitration (*arbitrato internazionale*; arts. 832-838), and chapter VII, dealing with foreign awards (*lodi stranieri*; arts. 839-840).

Article 832 § 1 Cpc, the first article of chapter VI, states that, if one of the parties is resident abroad or has his actual seat (*sede effettiva*) abroad, or if an important part of the obligation resulting from the legal relationship at issue in the dispute is to be performed abroad, the provisions of chapters I-V (arts. 806-831) are applicable, unless chapter VI determines otherwise. Pursuant to art. 832 § 2 Cpc, the provisions agreed upon in international conventions (in particular the European Convention of Geneva of 1961) remain fully applicable in any case. Chapter VI furthermore contains provisions regarding the form of the arbitration clause (*clausola compromissoria)* (art. 833), the applicable law (art. 834), the language in which the arbitration takes place (art. 835), the challenge of arbitrators (art. 836), the deliberations about the award (art. 837, also allowing deliberations by means of a videoconference) and means of recourse (art. 838).

Recognition and enforceability of foreign arbitral awards in the Italian Republic is governed by art. 839 Cpc, determining in § 1 that a petition (*ricorso*) must be brought before the president of the *Corte d'appello* of the place of residence of the other party or, if this party is not resident in Italy, of the *Corte d'appello* in Rome. After the president has ascertained that a foreign award satisfies all formal requirements, he declares the foreign award effective in the Italian Republic in a decree (*decreto*), unless pursuant to Italian law the dispute could not be the subject of an arbitration agreement or the contents of the award are contrary to public policy (art. 839 § 4 Cpc). The decree which allows or denies effect to the foreign award may be attacked by means of opposition (*opposizione*), to be raised by writ before the *Corte d'appello* (*cf.* art. 840 § 1 Cpc); the judgment (*sentenza*) of the *Corte d'appello* may be attacked by means of cassation (*cf.* art. 840 § 2 Cpc). Pursuant to § 6 of art. 840 Cpc, the provisions agreed upon in international conventions (in particular the New York Convention of 1958) remain fully applicable in any case.

10.10.3. BINDING ADVICE (ARBITRATO IRRITUALE)

The use of the *arbitrato irrituale* is widespread and is based on the mandate to reach a settlement (*mandato a transigere*). The parties will usually sign a blank sheet of paper (the *bianco-segno*), which is subsequently completed by the arbitrators and contains the text of their advice. This advice, usually based on fairness but sometimes on law and realised in an adversarial manner, has the form of a settlement (*transazione*). The advice may be disputed but only on general contractual principles concerning annulment (if the advice is the result of a false perception or representation of reality).

Subject Index

(B) = Belgian law
(E) = English law
(F) = French law
(G) = German law
(I) = Italian law
(L) = Luxembourg law
(N) = Netherlands law

A

B

D

E

F

G

H

I

J

K

L

M

N

O

P

S

T

U

V

W

Z